Psychological Treatment Approaches for Young Children and their Families

An Overview of Therapeutic Interventions for Children Aged 3–5 years

Edited by

Ingeborg Stiefel, Matthew Brand and Tanya Hanstock

AUSTRALIANACADEMIC**PRESS**

First published 2024 by Australian Academic Press Group Pty. Ltd.
Samford Valley, Australia www.australianacademicpress.com.au

A catalogue record for this book is available from the National Library of Australia

Psychological Treatment Approaches for Young Children and Their Families
ISBN   978-1-925644-66-1

DISCLAIMER: Parenting programs, dyadic parent-child interventions, individual and system's models of therapy undergo changes and updates, some more then others and some at a faster rate. The editors and authors therefore recommend that readers refer to the relevant websites of the programs for further information.

Publisher & Editor: Stephen May
Cover design: Australian Academic Press
Typesetting: Australian Academic Press
Printing: Lightning Source

To our families: Past, present
and those we have worked with.

This wonderful book does exactly what it says it will do on the cover, and never disappoints. It offers a concise authoritative guide to psychological approaches for treating young children and their families. The editors and contributors are expert clinicians with a wealth of experience working in this field. They present a strong argument highlighting the value of early intervention. Relatively brief and inexpensive interventions, can resolve psychological difficulties in under 5s. Were these problems left untreated, they would develop into chronic conditions requiring more intensive long-term intervention, at considerably greater economic and psychological cost. Their book describes a number of well-established clinical models for early intervention. It opens with a practical, well-informed guide to assessment, with information on psychological tests, parent interviews and checklists designed specifically for children under 5. The first section of the book gives guidance on evaluating children's problems within the context of the child's development and their family context. The way assessment provides a basis for treatment selection and planning is also considered.

Therapeutic models associated with four treatment formats are presented in the following four sections of the book. These formats are working with the individual child, with parents, with parent-child dyads, and whole families. There are chapters on Play Therapy and Cognitive Behaviour Therapy (CBT) in the section on child-focused approaches. There are chapters on Circle of Security (COS) and the Triple P parent training program in the section on parent-focused approaches. The section on dyadic approaches contains chapters on Parent Child Interaction Therapy (PICT), Child Parent Psychotherapy (CPP), Integrated Family Therapy (IFI), Dyadic Developmental Psychotherapy (DDP), and Watch, Wait, and Wonder (WWW). Narrative, Strategic, Structural, and Psychodynamic approaches to family therapy are each covered in separate chapters in the section on systemic therapy. This is a lot of ground to cover in one book. However, it has been done remarkably well. This excellent book provides the reader with an overview of the contemporary early intervention landscape with sufficient detail to allow readers to feel familiar with the key aspects of each approach, without overwhelming them with too much new information.

The structure of all chapters describing specific models follows a template developed by the editors. Chapters open with an introduction to the model and the historical background of its development. This is followed by sections on contemporary practices. These include subsections, as required, on key concepts, stages of therapy, session-by-session plans for highly structured programmes, and descriptions of therapeutic interventions, strategies and processes. An illustrative case study is then presented, followed by a summary of the evidence base. Most chapters conclude with useful information on how clinicians can train to use the model, and include exercises that may be used in classroom settings to promote theory-practice links. This chapter structure makes the book an excellent training resource for both trainers and professionals in training. The models are described with great clarity. Collectively the case studies are written in a way that leave readers in no doubt that chapter authors are expert therapists. They give readers an insight into how the model works at its best.

The three editors, Ingeborg Stiefel, Matthew Brand, Tanya Hanstock, and the contributors to the volume have done a remarkable job in making all of this material on early intervention accessible to professionals training in clinical psychology and related fields. This is vitally important because comprehensive books on working therapeutically with preschoolers are scarce, compared with treatment approaches suitable for older children and adolescents.

This book is a treasure-trove and delight to read. I hope you enjoy it as much as I did and find it as useful.

Alan Carr, PhD, FPSsl, FBPsS
Professor of Clinical Psychology, UCD, Ireland
Founding Director of the Doctoral Programme on Clinical Psychology
Family Therapist, Clanwilliam Institute, Dublin Ireland

Acknowledgements

We would like to thank Gayle Symons, Davida Hinchcliffe, Dr Neil Boris, Waverney Innes, Jessica Warren, Prof. Julie Larrieu and Prof. Mark Dadds for your help and encouragement.

This book is the result of many roads travelled. The inspiration to write a textbook that outlines a wide range of treatment models for young children developed in several contexts. First and foremost, in our therapeutic work with young children and their families, but also in the university environment of teaching and clinical training, in our own application of various treatment modalities and in our professional development as senior clinicians. However, this book is also an aspiration. We established that there is a treatment gap for this important cohort of young children. While the perinatal period (pregnancy to age 2) has received a strong focus, and interventions for school-aged children are growing, approaches for children within the age range of 3–6 years are not well established, despite the fact that mental health problems in preschoolers are common and if untreated, remain relatively stable over time or increase with age. This developmental stage is the second most important period in a child's life due to the relative plasticity of the child's brain, with rapid developmental progress and significant potential for change with the help of a stimulating, rewarding and safe environment. We believe it is imperative that treatment opportunities are realised as early as possible to ameliorate emerging mental health concerns. By outlining common and popular treatment options, we hope that this book breaches the gap in the existing literature.

Despite this important age, clinical training and placement opportunities for skills development of working therapeutically with preschoolers are scarce, and the general knowledge of treatment options is limited compared with treatment approaches suitable for older children and adolescents. Therefore, we hope this textbook will also be a solid source for all those undergoing training in disciplines related to child development, clinical child psychology and related fields.

We believe there is a need for a textbook that captures the most common approaches of available treatments for this age group, as systematic reviews are often limited to parent training as the predominant evidence-based treatment for this population. We combed through the available literature and learned via colleagues, through training and experience, what works and what does not work well for this age group. Based on the target of the intervention, the individual child, the parent, the child–parent dyad, or the complete family, we have divided the book accordingly into four sections. Each section describes a range of diverse models in a condensed yet comprehensive summary, offering information on treatment effects and adding our critical reflection. This textbook allows readers to get a snapshot of each model and may encourage further reading or training in specific models. We are also hoping that this book will help clinicians decide what treatments can be used for what presenting problem and under what conditions.

The three editors are experienced clinical psychologists with a special interest in paediatric clinical psychology. We have worked together clinically over many years, trained and supervised psychologists, clinical psychologists, and clinicians across disciplines both in the university context and in clinic settings.

Ingeborg Stiefel (RN, Soz. Paed. Grad., Diplom Psychologe, M. Psych. [Clin.]) is a Senior Clinical Psychologist, semi-retired, with over 40 years of clinical experience. She trained in nursing and social work before venturing into psychology. She completed her first psychology degree during the cold war years at the Freie Universitaet Berlin and completed her M Clin Psych at Macquarie University, Sydney, in 1990. The political conflict in the 1970s was also reflected in the field of psychology. Behaviourism and traditional empirical research clashed with a strong psychodynamic tradition in Germany, and critical psychology, anti-psychiatry and East European psychology started to develop a new voice that questioned the theories and clinical approaches of both sides. These formative years are still present in her questioning approach to clinical practice. Ingeborg trained in humanistic, psychodynamic, narrative and systemic therapies, and she has worked with children and families with a wide variety of clinical presentations in many settings, including at the Childrens' Hospital Westmead. She appreciates client-centred values as a base for all therapeutic endeavours, appreciates the depth of psychodynamic thinking, and enjoys the freedom and creativity both narrative and systemic approaches can offer to therapy, especially when working with young children. She has published widely in the field of family therapy.

Matthew Brand (B. Psyc. [Hons.], M. Psyc. [Clin.]) completed his Master of Clinical Psychology degree at the University of New England. He is a Clinical Psychologist specialising in the field of paediatric psychology. He has gained substantial expertise in both assessment and treatment of preschoolers and their families and has trained in a wide range of models tailored specifically to the age range of preschoolers, including several models of family therapy, cognitive behaviour therapy (CBT), Trauma-Focussed Cognitive Behavioural Therapy (TF-CBT), Parent–Child Interaction Therapy (PCIT), emotion coaching, Circle of Security (COS) and Child–Parent Psychotherapy (CPP), among others. Matthew believes diagnostic assessments for common neurodevelopmental problems emerging in the preschool years, such as Autism Spectrum Disorder (ASD), Attention Deficit Hyperactivity Disorder (ADHD) and global developmental delay, need to be comprehensive and consider a range of factors that influence a child's development. Over the past 10 years, Matthew has worked in several public health settings, for non-governmental organisations and in private practice in both assessment and treatment roles. Matthew has always been interested in prevention and early intervention to address mental health difficulties, advocating for the earliest treatment possible before emotional and behavioural difficulties become entrenched. He enjoys working with energy, enthusiasm, creativity and playfulness to meet the therapeutic needs of both children and their carers.

Dr Tanya Hanstock (BA. [Hons], D Clin and Health Psyc) completed her Doctor of Clinical and Health Psychology degree at the University of New England in 2003. She then worked in the public health system (in community settings as well as inpatient units), assessing and treating children and adolescents with developmental and/or mental health issues. Tanya has also worked at Riverina *headspace*. She has worked across, rural, regional and metropolitan areas. Tanya is a Senior Lecturer and the Convenor of the Clinical Psychology Programs in the School of Psychological Sciences, University of Newcastle. She has participated in academic teaching for undergraduate and postgraduate courses at the University of Newcastle (UON), The University of New England (UNE) and Charles Sturt University (CSU) for over 21 years. She has previously been the Director of The Clinical Psychology Programs at the University of New England. She teaches in all areas of Clinical Psychology, supervises the research projects of master of clinical psychology, honours and PhD students and supervises students on Clinical Psychology placements. Her particular interest is in teaching students about child development and the assessment and treatment of developmental and mental health issues in children and adolescents. Tanya's research is focused on the understanding, assessment and treatment of mental health disorders across the lifespan. Her special clinical interest is in bipolar disorder (BD), particularly its onset in young people. Tanya is in the process of completing her PhD in the field of BD.

We have also invited colleagues from Australia, New Zealand and Canada to contribute to this book with their special expertise.

Dr Fiona Perrett (B Psych [Hons], D Psych [Clin], [James Cook University]) is a Clinical Psychologist working in private practice. Prior to private practice, she worked across settings in non-government organisations, hospitals (NSW Health) and universities (University of Canberra and Australian National University). From the beginning of her career more than two decades ago, she was drawn to working with children, young people and families. She trained in family therapy (narrative, solution-focused and systemic family therapy) and Triple P Positive Parenting programs before developing a strong interest in attachment theory and its practical applications for helping children and families. She trained in Circle of Security (COS) interventions and enjoyed providing COS Intensive and COS P programs to families. This evolved to the provision of COS supervision for therapists, particularly supervision for COS Intensive programs. The research and measurement of attachment relationships is of particular interest to Fiona. This led to training and experience in conducting and classifying/assessing attachment relationships via the Strange Situation Procedure. Fiona also has an interest in developmental, educational and cognitive assessments. Her interest in attachment relationships extends to adult attachments. Fiona has extensive experience in the provision of Dialectical Behaviour Therapy (DBT) programs for adults who experience significant, treatment-resistant emotional and mental health concerns. Fiona continues to work across settings, working in clinical and organisational settings, including the provision of telehealth. She has a strong commitment to evidence-based treatments, including treatment for Post-traumatic Stress Disorder (PTSD), anxiety disorders and depression. She particularly enjoys her supervisory work, assisting Provisionally Registered Psychologists in their early career journeys.

Dr Denise Guy (MBChB, FRANZCP, Cert. Child Psychiatry) is a consultant Child Psychiatrist working in infant and early childhood mental health and coordinates training in Watch, Wait and Wonder (WWW) in Australasia. She trained in Dunedin and Sydney and established the 0–5 years — Early Intervention Unit (1987) as Director of Redbank House, Westmead. In Dunedin she was involved with the pilot study of WWW with E. Muir and A. Stupples, continuing its use clinically, and from 2005 developing the training program. She is a founding member of the Australian (1987) and New Zealand (2006) Affiliates of the World Association for Infant Mental Health (WAIMH). As Vice President and President in New Zealand, she developed two key initiatives, Facilitating Attuned Interactions (FAN) and Two Homes/Ngā Kainga e Rua. Denise provides supervision to practitioners across services working with families with young children and across disciplines. The mind that holds the child, the parent and the practitioner is of enduring interest. In 2021 she was recognised with an Order of New Zealand Merit (ONZM) for her services to IMH.

Marion Doherty is a Clinical Psychologist who has been working with children and their families at an ICAMHS (infant, child and adolescent mental health) service in Auckland for the past seventeen years. For the last 8 years, she has specialised in clinical work with children from 0–4yrs and their parents. Marion is the coordinator of the infant team at the service — Koanga Tupu, and is an executive member of IMHAANZ (Infant Mental Health Association Aotearoa New Zealand). She is accredited as an independent Watch, Wait, and Wonder practitioner. Marion also provides consult liaison for a paediatric service for children with restricted eating issues and supervises other infant mental health clinicians. Marion is particularly interested in infant mental health interventions, including WWW, which support parents to 'hold their child's mind in their mind' and promote a shift from rigid representations to a curious stance of reflection and wonder.

Dr Sian Phillips (PhD, C. Psych) is a Psychologist who lives in Ontario, Canada. She specialises in the assessment and treatment of developmental trauma and is a certified Dyadic Developmental Psychotherapy (DDP) therapist, consultant and trainer. She has a particular interest in helping educators become both trauma-informed and trauma-responsive and helping schools create the safety and sense of belonging that children need to learn. Sian has co-authored two books outlining how DDP principles can provide a map for educators and other professionals in this endeavour. Sian has the privilege of working with many creative and dedicated professionals in the pursuit of creating strong and safe relationships for some of our most vulnerable children and families.

Psychological Treatment Approaches for Young Children and Their Families

Ingeborg Stiefel, Matthew Brand and Tanya Hanstock

Early childhood is the most critical phase in human development. The first five years of life are characterised by rapid neurological and psychological development. Neurological changes include neuronal migration, synapse formation, dendrite sprouting, axonal pruning and elaboration of the myelin shape (Douglas et al., 2015). Neuro-anatomical changes and developments constitute the architecture for learning, behaviour and cognitive development and are the building blocks for later development. What is learned during early childhood becomes the foundation for subsequent learning (LeDoux, 2002). Experience plays a major part during this period, especially during critical phases, which act as windows for neural development (Knudson, 2004). Infancy, the preschool and early primary school years are phases of rapid physical and psychological growth; they offer the greatest opportunity for positive human development but also constitute periods where children are most at risk, and negative influences can contribute to irreversible life-long compromised outcomes.

During the preschool years, significant advances occur in all aspects of development. Language development is a hallmark of this period. During the preoperational stage (Piaget, 1932), between the ages of 2–7 years, there are major shifts in cognitive skills. Children learn to think symbolically, as evident in the emergence of pretend and symbolic play, and they begin to reason, wanting to know why things are the way they are, and act out imagined scenarios and fantasies. Increasingly, they apply cognitive ability to solve and master problems. Both gross and fine motor development assist the preschooler in gaining control over physical functions and achieving greater personal-social independence. Their play and interactions with others become more social, and friendships are formed with peers. Expectations on behaviour, academic learning and social integration increase. It is important to remember, however, that children in this age range can vary enormously in their development and their expression of personality (Postert et al., 2009), and gender differences become more pronounced.

The effects of experience are particularly strong and play a major part in the formation of neural circuits in the brain (Knudsen, 2004; Njoroge & Yang, 2012). Due to the relative plasticity of the brain, early childhood is also a developmental phase where interventions can have the greatest impact. Therefore, prevention, early intervention and treatment of problem presentations in young children are investments for the future, with long-term cost-saving benefits (Cavanagh, 2017; Charach et al., 2020). Well-planned, comprehensive interventions that take into consideration all aspects of the child and its environment, including health, education, nutrition, parenting and ecological factors, work best (Open Society Foundation, 2019).

Mental Health and developmental problems in children are common. Australian data for the period 2013 to 2014 reports that 13.9% of children between the ages of 4 and 11 years have psychological health issues, with Attention Deficit Hyperactivity Disorder (ADHD) and Anxiety Disorders being the most common presentations and boys outnumbering girls, with 17% males and 11% females respectively (Lawrence et al., 2015). More recent data from Australia suggests that 1 in 5 children present with high levels of emotional and social problems when they start school (Commonwealth of Australia, 2020). North American data in regard to prevalence figures specifically for preschoolers indicate an incident rate of 8–10% (Gleason et al., 2016), whereas others give higher prevalence estimates between 14 and 26.4% (Postert et al., 2009). Furniss and colleagues (Furniss et al., 2013) report prevalence figures for preschoolers with clinical range internalising and externalising behaviour of 12–18%, and they suggest that the rate is comparable to prevalence figures for school-age children. Reported mental health issues in young children include emotional difficulties, behavioural issues and relationship stress, in addition to the large number of children diagnosed with Autism Spectrum Disorder (ASD) and ADHD. In a large number of cases, symptom presentations are not transient but will have long-lasting effects if not addressed in a timely manner (Gleason et al., 2016). Children who meet diagnostic criteria at age 3 are five times as likely to meet criteria for a diagnosis at the age of 6, and there is continuity for the diagnoses of anxiety disorder, ADHD and Oppositional Defiant Disorder (ODD) (Bufferd et al., 2012). A recent Australian Government report suggests that there are substantial barriers for young children and their families to access required services and suggests early identification with the universal screening of both children and parents for mental health issues, investing in workforce training to equip professionals and para-professionals to work effectively with young children and carers, developing an overarching national framework that articulates the roles of both health and education, supporting early education settings and monitoring of effects of intervention programs (Commonwealth of Australia, 2020). The report states a clear case for investing in the early years from a policy and pro-ductivity point of view.

Psychological and relationship difficulties of young children overall are less entrenched and offer a wide range of options for remediation. The child's physical size may offer treatment options that are no longer available to an older child (such as using time out). Yet, while various interventions are available, the evidence base for psychological interventions with preschoolers is still emerging (Njoroge & Yang, 2012). Further, only 1 child out of 5 will receive the needed treatment. Gleason et al. (2016) give various reasons for this fact, including mental health funding restrictions, limited training experiences for interns and a lack of trained specialists. Mental health problems in young children are often underdiagnosed due to a number of factors, including inadequate diagnostic categories and insufficient knowledge regarding the symptoms in this young age group (Furniss et al., 2013).

In Australia, we see relative neglect in funding for specific interventions for preschoolers (Cavanagh, 2017). Further, training of staff presents its own challenge (Njoroge & Yang, 2012). Good quality specialist training is costly and time-consuming, and certain interventions require specific clinic setups that are not readily available to most clinicians. Therapy funding policies are also a barrier with a non-contextual focus on the child and the need to offer diagnostic labels to qualify for intervention support. The assessment of preschoolers presents its own challenge. Good diagnostic assessments require information from multiple sources, which is time-consuming. Standard diagnostic criteria appropriate for older children may not be relevant, valid, reliable or useful for this age group (Postert et al., 2009). Child neuropsychology has remained an understudied and poorly funded area, with the absence of standardised and normed neuropsychological tests and a lack of expertise and skills in assessing young children (Baron & Anderson, 2012). Session numbers are restricted, and gap fees present their own financial issues for many families with young children, who often have expenses that families with older children do not have, such as absences from work during parental leave and fees associated with daycare and preschool. Working with preschoolers and their families requires that the therapist adjusts to the developmental level of the child in regard to both cognitive and language levels. Standard training in many therapy professions often does not specifically focus on this age group and the needed skills to conduct effective assessment or therapy. In Australia, there have been recent funding initiatives, particularly for children with developmental delays or neurodevelopmental diagnoses (e.g., ASD). However, our experience suggests that this has not translated into significant increases in access to psychological interventions, and there is difficulty in accessing clinicians with experience in this area.

Once the child moves from the toddler stage into the preschool years and beyond, external systems and people outside the immediate family increasingly impact the child's life. Evidence for successful treatment for this age range supports the consideration of the child's context and the involvement of carers, families, extended family and professionals in care settings, such as daycare centres, preschools and schools (Njoroge & Yang, 2012; Open Society Foundation, 2019). Treatment decisions are influenced by several factors. First, treatment should follow assessment with an informed decision as to the most appropriate intervention for a given presentation. This decision should take into consideration the focus of therapy, which can be the child, the family, the parent-child dyad or the parent only. There is a wide range of empirically supported interventions for young children, their carers and families, but there are also treatment options that have clinical utility but with an evidence base only starting to emerge. However, treatment decisions may be simply based on what is and what is not available for a child and family, especially in rural and remote areas. Further, clinicians may have developed their preferred way of working therapeutically with children and families, and their training background and level of expertise can vary widely.

What This Book Offers

Psychological Treatment Approaches for Young Children and Their Families offers windows into a wide range of treatment approaches for children aged 3–5 years and their families, representing relevant and available psychological treatment models. In the book, we may refer to preschoolers. However, most of the treatments presented are also suitable for younger children, especially if they are developmentally advanced and for slightly older children up to 6 or 7 years old. We use the term parent and sometimes caregiver, referring to the primary person or persons caring for a child in all aspects of care, usually on a daily basis.

We present well-established therapeutic models and programs with a good evidence base, models and programs that are specifically developed for preschoolers, but also those that are less established but have clinical evidence and suitability for this age group or are adapted from treatment approaches for older children. The models are based on different philosophical backgrounds and theories of change, although some of the foundational theories form the basis of many models, and there is considerable overlap. The specific models in each section were chosen based on clinical utility for this age group, our training background, expertise in the models, and preferred ways of working with young children and their families. Where available to us, we utilised the latest training manuals. Since some of our training dates back some years and sources of all therapy programs are not freely available, the latest changes and updates of some of the programs may not have been included. In condensed ways, we provide the history and underlying theory, describe the treatment process and treatment techniques, the current clinical evidence for each model, discuss strengths and weakness, and training requirements and describe clinical application with 'created' cases that reflect our clinical work with this age group. Each chapter offers a reader's activity that will assist with active engagement, reflection and absorption of the text, and we conclude with a list of relevant references.

We hope this book will serve several purposes. Firstly, to help clinicians and students understand what each model offers so that it helps determine referral pathways for this clinical population. This book can also guide clinicians at different stages in their professional development with decisions regarding ongoing professional development and training in models that match their values as a therapist, their client's needs and their own preferred way of working therapeutically with this client group. However, the summarised version of each model cannot replace the training required to become proficient in each model. We encourage all clinicians interested in a particular model to attend the accredited training pathway that the developers of the program established. In Australia, dissemination and access to training have increased significantly over time, with face-to-face and online training being offered by a number of providers all over Australia. By presenting the spectrum of treatment options, we hope that the clinical needs of preschoolers and their carers will come more strongly into focus and that these children receive the required treatments at the earliest age to prevent the long-term sequelae of adverse outcomes due to untreated emotional and behavioural problems and relationship stress.

We have divided the book into four sections based on the intervention's delivery mode and main focus, though some models can be delivered in different ways. The four sections are individual child treatments; parent-focused approaches, often offered in a group format; dyadic carer-child interventions; and family-systems models. This book does not address the specific therapy needs of diagnostic cohorts of children, although the clinical excerpts will give the reader an impression of the typical problem presentations for the different treatment modalities. We do not focus specifically on interventions provided exclusively in preschool settings or by early childhood teachers, although some models extend to early educational settings. We have not included models which are classified as generic prevention, standard population-based procedures that address transient issues of early childhood, or medical interventions, such as drug treatment for specific disorders. Further, this book does not include adult therapy models which focus exclusively on the psychological needs of parents, carers or other adult family members, although adult-only therapies can be highly relevant and indicated in the context of preschool symptom presentations.

By presenting major models and treatment options in one textbook, we hope this textbook will reach therapists, students, trainers and supervisors, referrers, researchers, funding bodies and parents. The book offers an overview of treatment options that may be appropriate for a given clinical presentation or for clinical settings that receive groups of young clients with specific presentations. Finally, this textbook has been developed primarily within the Australian context and, as such, represents contemporary thinking and clinical practice in Australia. Yet we believe that it has relevance for clinicians working with young children in different cultures and, depending on the model, will offer both applicability and adaptability to the clinician's context of work.

The Outline of the Book

Chapter 1: Developmental Milestones, Assessment and Treatment Options for Young Children and their Families provides an overview of typical developmental milestones, and the developmental issues and challenges encountered during the early years. It addresses the need for good assessment by suggesting assessment strategies and procedures and compares treatment options for young children and their families.

Section 1: Child-Focused Approaches

Chapter 2: Play Therapy explores the internal world of the child through play and action. Play therapy aims to help the child understand challenging current or past life events. Play therapy encourages the expression of thoughts and feelings through play and through verbal exchanges with the therapist, helping the child to solve problems and modify unhelpful behaviour within the realms of a positive therapeutic relationship. Play Therapy capitalises on children's natural ability to express thoughts and feelings through play. The child's context is relevant insofar as the caregiver needs to support the child as the child progresses through different stages of therapy, even when regression occurs.

Chapter 3: Cognitive Behaviour Therapy (CBT) focuses on the link between thoughts, emotions and behaviours, specifically how unhelpful thoughts and behaviours can lead to problem development. CBT aims to replace maladaptive cognitions, emotions and behaviours with more adaptive forms. CBT for preschoolers requires adjustment of strategies to the developmental level of the young child, and compared with CBT with older children, stronger caregiver involvement is required, assisting with assimilation of material and with homework tasks. CBT materials are presented in concrete, visual and playful format, including actions and practice tasks.

Section 2: Parent-Focused Approaches

Chapter 4: Circle of Security (COS) is a reflective parenting program based on attachment theory. The program helps parents to understand the principles of secure attachment, which allows the child to venture out and also return to the secure base provided within the realm of the parent–child relationship. The program encourages the parent to reflect upon their own upbringing and attachment style and their relationships with important others, past and present. The aim of the program is to strengthen the relationship between parent and child, to develop a secure base that will act as a protective factor for life, but which will also help ameliorate current concerns, such as relationship stress, and behavioural or emotional difficulties experienced by the child.

Chapter 5: Tuning Into Kids (TIK) is part of a suite of parenting programs based on the principles of emotional intelligence. TIK introduces the concept of emotion coaching and combines skills training with an understanding of the child's needs for attuned and empathic parenting. The program also focuses on the emotional connection between parent and child and utilises situations of stress as opportunities for coaching. Empathy, perspective-taking, genuineness, warmth, and mutual and effective problem-solving are cornerstones of this program, though limit setting is also required if emotions are expressed in highly socially inappropriate or dangerous ways.

Chapter 6: Positive Parenting Program (Triple P) is a behavioural parenting program based on social learning theory and principles of behaviour modification. Triple P offers a range of programs with increasing levels of intensity, length and therapist support. The program is a toolbox of parenting strategies for different levels of parent-child relationship challenges. The program has a strong skills-training component, though it does allow time for reflection. It teaches parents to reinforce desirable child behaviour, thus strengthening the connection between parent and child while also dealing more effectively with problem behaviour. The program aims to help parents to become more confident and effective in their parenting.

Chapter 7: Integrated Family Intervention for Child Conduct Problems (IFI) is a family-based manualised parenting intervention with a semi-structured format. IFI is an evidence-based treatment based on behavioural and attachment theories, suitable for parents of young children presenting with conduct problems and for parent-child relationship stresses with coercive cycles of interaction. The therapy is commonly delivered individually with the parent/s and their child. However, the therapy can also be delivered in a group format as a preventative intervention. Parents are encouraged to increase positive and effective behavioural parenting strategies, those which reinforce desirable behaviour. IFI also introduces attachment-rich techniques that foster closeness and security in the relationship between parent and child.

Section 3: Dyadic Therapies

Chapter 8: Parent-Child Interaction Therapy (PCIT) is based on social learning and behaviour theory, play therapy and attachment theory and focuses on changes in the interactional patterns between parent and child. The uniqueness of PCIT is that it provides intensive, direct, in-session didactic instructions and coaching by the therapist, guiding the parent's behaviour and reinforcing effective parenting strategies based on observations in session. Ideally, the parent-child interaction is observed behind a one-way mirror, and therapist instructions are given through audio technology, of which the child is usually unaware. PCIT aims to increase parental attention to desired child behaviour, disrupt negative cycles of interaction early with the help of specific parenting strategies, to improve compliance with caregiver commands and increase parental consistency.

Chapter 9: Child-Parent Psychotherapy (CPP) is based on attachment theory and integrates psychodynamic, developmental, trauma, social learning theories and cognitive behavioural therapy, with a special focus on the inter-generational transmission of relationship patterns. The aim of this model is to strengthen the attachment relationship between the child and caregiver as the primary method of improving children's mental health. The experiences of both the child and caregiver are the focus of the intervention. The model is highly reflective but also allows gentle guidance by the therapist to address challenging behaviour in the session and to encourage alternative responses in the caregiver. The model's uniqueness is that it increases parental awareness of triggers that lead to unhelpful parental responses. Initially developed as a treatment of trauma to help both caregiver and child to process their trauma experience by developing a joint trauma narrative, CPP now has a wider application as an appropriate treatment for a range of childhood presentations.

Chapter 10: Watch, Wait, and Wonder (WWW) is an evidence-based dyadic psychotherapeutic intervention for parents and young children based on attachment research and relational theories derived from the field of psychoanalysis. In child play, the parent is encouraged to observe and follow the child's lead without directing the child's play, action and interaction. This is followed by a discussion where the therapist supports the parent to recall what they saw and think about their child's communications with them. Here, the therapist maintains the same stance of watching, waiting and wondering asked of the parent, not offering their observations or wonderings, not criticising, and allowing the parent to discover their child. WWW is offered as a clinical intervention and is useful where there are significant parent-child relationship concerns and/or the child presents with social and emotional difficulties.

Chapter 11: Dyadic Developmental Psychotherapy (DDP) is a relationship-focused therapy based on attachment theory, interpersonal neurobiology and the concept of intersubjectivity. DDP grew out of clinical experiences that showed that mainstream contemporary psychotherapies were not helpful for children who learned to mistrust their primary caregivers (or caregiver) given experiences of abuse, neglect, lack of attunement or multiple separations early in life. Nor were they helpful in supporting the adults who tried to care for this group of children. DDP, whether in its original psychotherapy form or in practice form, focuses on creating the safety in relationships that children need to move from mistrust to trust. They then can make use of relationships in ways that strengthen their resilience and help them integrate past traumatic experiences.

Section 4: Systemic Models

Chapter 12: Narrative Therapy is a conversational form of therapy broadly defined as a postmodern form of psychotherapy. The model considers and questions the life stories people develop about themselves and about others and helps clients to challenge thoughts, behaviours and interactions that maintain problematic narratives. In the paediatric context, this therapy offers a playful and, at times, creative approach to families, unravelling the development and current influence of the problematic narrative, and with the help of reframes in the form of externalisations and playful practise strategies, assisting child and family in developing a plan that will help in overcoming problems commonly experienced during the preschool years.

Chapter 13: Strategic Family Therapy (SFT) is based on family systems theory. The model is present, problem and solution focused and a fairly short-term form of family therapy. SFT aims to disrupt family interaction patterns that lead to problems and stress between family members. SFT considers the interactional sequences between family members as the focus for assessment and intervention and can also consider the wider context of the family if relevant. SFT allows the therapist a degree of creativity in developing treatment ideas for change based on a systemic formulation of the symptom presentation.

Chapter 14: Structural Family Therapy (SRFT), as the name implies, considers the structural components of family systems, including hierarchies, boundaries, alliances, rules and subsystems. SRFT is primarily present-focused and is also a time-limited model of therapy. The aim of SRFT is to disrupt dysfunctional interactional patterns by generating a more functional family structure with clear boundaries, subsystems, hierarchies and rules for each member of the family. The therapist's role as a skilled conductor is pivotal in the process of change. SRFTconcepts and techniques are particularly helpful when working with families with a poor parental hierarchy and confusing roles.

Chapter 15: Psychodynamic Therapy (PDT) is based on psycho-analytic and psychodynamic theory, attachment theory, developmental psychology, neurobiology and family systems theory. A central tenet of the model is that unconscious processes occur within a person, are played out within relationships, and can lead to relationship stress and symptom development in the child.

Further, PDT is built on the assumption that early experiences in people's life, including the quality of the attachment relationship between parent and child, have powerful effects on the child's development. The chapter describes a contextual approach to psychodynamic work with children and their families. The relationship between family members and therapist is central, both as a secure base for a child's unconscious interactions that can be explored but also as a vehicle for the developing transference relationship, which acts as a tool for understanding unconscious processes.

References

Baron, I. S., & Anderson, P. J. (2012). Assessment of preschoolers. *Neuropsychology Review, 22*, 311–312. https://doi10.1007/s11065-012-9221-2

Bufferd, S. J., Dougherty, L. R., Carlson, G. A., Rose, S., & Klein, D. N. (2012). Psychiatric disorders in preschoolers: Continuity from ages 3 to 6. *American Journal of Psychiatry, 169*(11), 1157-1164. https://-doi.org.10.1176/appi.ajp.2012.12020268

Cavanagh, S. (2017). Early childhood matters most. *InPsych, 39*(6), 8–10. https://psychology.org.au/inpsych/2017

Charach, A., Mohammadzadeh, F., Belanger, S. A., Easson, A., Lipman, E. L., McLennan, J. D., Parkin, P., & Szatmari, P. (2020). Identification of preschool children with mental health problems in primary care: Systematic review and meta-analysis. *Journal of the Canadian Academy of Child and Adolescent Psychiatry, 29*, 76-105. https://www.ncbi.nlm.nih.gov/pmc/issues/357460/

Commonwealth of Australia (2020). *Productivity Commission Inquiry Report. Mental Health*. Australian Government Productivity Commission Inquiry Report, No 95. Canberra Australia. https://www.pc.gov.au/inquiries/completed/mental-health/report

Douglas, C. D., O'Muircheartaigh, J., Dirks, H., Waskiewicz, N., Walter, L., Doernberg, E., Priyatinsky, I., & Deoni, S. C. L. (2015). Characterising longitudinal white matter development during early childhood. *Brain Structure and Function, 220*, 1921–1933. https://doi:10/1007/s00429-014-0763-3

Furniss, T., Müller, J. M., Achtergarde, S., Wessing, I., Averbeck-Holocher M., & Postert, C. (2013). Implementing psychiatric day treatment for infants, toddlers, preschoolers and their families: A study from a clinical and organisational perspective. *International Journal of Mental Health Systems, 7*(12). http://www.ijmhs.com/content/7/1/12

Gleason, M. M., Goldson, E., & Yogman, M.W. (2016). *Addressing early childhood emotional and behavioural problems*. Council on Early Childhood. https://doi.org/10.1542/peds.2016.3025

Knudsen, E. I. (2004). Sensitive periods in the development of the brain and behaviour. *Journal of Cognitive Neuroscience, 16*(8), 1412–25. https://doi10.1162/ 0898929042304796

Lawrence, D., Johnson, S., Hafekost, J., Boterhoven de Haan, K., Sawyer, M., Ainley, J., & Zubrick, S. R. (2015). *The Mental Health of Children and Adolescents. Report on the second Australian Child and Adolescent Survey of Mental Health and Wellbeing.* Department of Health, Canberra, ACT.

LeDoux, J. (2002). *Synaptic self. How our brains become who we are.* Penguin Books.

Njoroge, W. F. M., & Yang, D. (2012). Evidence-based psychotherapies for preschool children with psychiatric disorders. *Current Psychiatry Reports, 14,* 121–128. https://doi10.1007/s11920-012-0253-3

Open Society Foundation (2019). *Why investing in early childhood matters.* https://www.opensocietyfoundations.org/explainers/why-investing-early-childhood-matters

Piaget, J. (1932). *The moral judgement of the child.* Free Press.

Postert, C., Auerbeck-Holocher, M., Beyer, T., Mueller, J., & Furniss, T. (2009). Five systems of psychiatric classification for preschool children: Do differences in validity, usefulness and reliability make for competitive or complimentary constellations? *Child Psychiatry and Human Development, 40*(1), 25–4. https://doi:10/1007/s10578-008-0113-x

Developmental Milestones, Assessment and Treatment Options for Young Children and Their Families

Ingeborg Stiefel and Matthew Brand

During the preschool years major changes occur in all aspects of development, including social-emotional, physical, cognitive, language and behaviour. For many children, this period sees an integration into an early childhood setting or Kindergarten, with longer periods of separation from the family. New relationships form outside the family, with teachers and peers, and behavioural expectations increase. The new setting requires the child to understand and respect new rules, routines and interactions with others and learn to regulate behaviour and emotions in age-appropriate ways. New social skills include sharing, waiting, taking turns, playing with others and making friends. Preschoolers may show a preference for particular peers, and they generally like to help others. They enjoy praise and recognition from their teachers. Young children of normal development show affection and express empathy and understanding when someone is hurt. Joint attention and mutual enjoyment are expressed in play with others, but also assertiveness, likes and dislikes, without displaying overt aggression or anger. Preschoolers like to sing, dance and act, and they become aware of gender differences.

Fine- and gross-motor development changes includes the increasing ability to control movement. Preschoolers can hop, skip, run, jump, climb, play with equipment, catch a ball and overall enjoy movement. Fine motor development is displayed in increasing control of hand movements, learning to draw, paint, use scissors, hold a pencil, and draw basic shapes and people. Physical independence is expressed in learning to dress self, independent eating, brushing teeth and mastering toilet training during the day. Cognitive milestones include the ability to name and recognise shapes, colours, and many common objects, understanding opposites and positions, and the child's attention span increases. Preschoolers start learning to count, copy objects and letters of the alphabet, manipulate blocks and puzzles constructively and create their own play using sand, water, paper, glue and other materials. They can recall events, and they understand stories appropriate for their developmental level. Their language development shows an increasing number and use of words, length of sentences and clarity of speech. Preschoolers can recall experiences, anticipate future events and tell stories. They understand simple instructions, enjoy jokes, and ask many questions wanting to know why things are the way they are.

Despite these incredible leaps forward, clinicians should be mindful of the developmental limitations that children at this age still have. Preschoolers tend to be egocentric and instead may think that other people think, see and feel as they do. They may believe that they are the cause of events that occur in their world, both good and bad. Children at this age may think that their parents are always right, know everything and can do whatever they want, and events that occur in the world are because their parent 'felt like it'. They may feel responsible when a parent is angry or upset. Young children want to please their parents and fear their disapproval. They are afraid of getting hurt and losing part of their body, which corresponds to increased phobias, such as fear of monsters and the dark. They have trouble focusing on more than one characteristic of an object. Children may not be able to express their feelings with words and instead act or play them out. They tend to have short emotional spans, with brief periods of intense emotional expression, which reflects their limited ability to tolerate sustained intense emotions.

Many preschoolers also need to learn to cope and adjust to life events and stressors. These may include the birth of a sibling or disruption of the family due to separation and divorce. Parent vulnerabilities and family stress can affect the child in direct or indirect ways. Risk factors include adult mental health issues, substance misuse or disabilities, relationship conflicts within the home or with significant others, social isolation, poverty, parental unemployment or employment with long hours of work, financial stress and changes due to family breakup, which may include moving house, having to adapt to a blended family, or witnessing ongoing conflicts between the biological parents. More challenging situations may include neglect, abuse, family violence, or separation from the family. These stressors may stretch the young child's coping ability, leading to problems in one or several aspects of development, particularly behaviour, emotion regulation or interactions with others.

Premature birth, illness early in life or chronic, specific or global developmental delays, sensitive temperament, and impairments in hearing or vision may present vulnerabilities that can increase stress in both child and family. The absence of sufficient protective factors may lead to developmental concerns and symptom development. Unusual patterns of development, developmental delay, concerning behaviour or emotions may be observed by the parents or grandparents, the early childhood educator, the General Practitioner (GP) or paediatrician, or an early childhood nurse screening the child's development, leading to the referral for either assessment or intervention or for both.

Assessment of Young Children

There are a wide range of reasons why a child may be referred for assessment or treatment, and depending on the purpose, request, needs, and clinical presentation, assessment methods, procedures and techniques can vary considerably. A parent, a relative, or a professional may be concerned about the child's development, an observed lack in gaining age-appropriate skills in specific areas, slow overall development or an atypical developmental profile. Speech and language, cognition, and fine- and gross-motor skills may be behind age expectations. There may be concern about the child's social development, emotional immaturity or functional ability, such as achieving toilet training milestones. There may even be regression in development with an apparent loss of skills. The child's behaviour may be the primary reason for concern. Symptoms may include hyperactivity, dysregulation of behaviour, oppositional behaviour, or poor anger control. A child may display extreme shyness, fears and anxiety, hindering their social integration when entering a preschool setting. A stressed caregiver-child interaction or family separation may be another reason for concern, leading to the referral. With greater awareness of the effects of trauma on children, the emotional, behavioural or developmental concerns may be a response to a traumatic experience the child has experienced, for example, an accident or illness or one that has affected the whole family, such as in cases of family violence, storms, floods or bush fire, severe adult relationship stress and caregiver mental health or substance use. The effects of neglect or abuse may be the reason for referral or grief and loss experienced by the child. Attachment-based problems may be present, or stress may arise in the context of the preschool setting, with peer conflicts being evident. The impetus for assessment may occur in the legal context, with a family law court-ordered assessment of the child, parent, and/or family with the purpose of developing a functional parenting plan. The child protection context constitutes another specialised area of assessment in cases of substantiated or expected abuse or neglect of a child. Finally, concerning symptoms may develop as a result of a medical condition or a diagnosed developmental disability.

The clinician will need to consider a number of questions when approaching the assessment. Is the referral for diagnostic purposes, for example, in the context of funding, for treatment, or for both? What does the referrer request and expect? What needs to be assessed, who will need to be involved in the assessment, and at what stage? Is information from multiple sources needed, such as a report from the preschool? Is an observation of the child in a natural setting warranted to better understand the child's behaviour? How important is it to understand the developmental history and the family's history for assessment and treatment planning? How much formal assessment in the form of questionnaires or standardised assessment tools (such as an IQ assessment) is required to complete the assessment? Does the clinician have the time, training, skills and resources to complete the needed assessment? Who pays for the assessment? What is the way forward if the carer cannot pay but waiting lists for public clinics are long, for example, 12 or 24 months? What happens if there is a mismatch between the clinician and the carer regarding the needs of the child? What is the best assessment format? Are there gold standards or clinical practice guidelines? Is it acceptable to take shortcuts in some cases?

Assessments are multi-faceted tasks that integrate formal and informal information. Good assessments should have a clear purpose and offer a good understanding of the presenting problems from the report and ideally also from observation of the child in a natural environment or from observation by a third person, such as a preschool teacher. Formal and informal assessment tools may be required. Price-Robertson (2018) proposes a biopsychosocial model for diagnosis based on the fact that children are sensitive to and dependent on their social context. In similar ways, Achenbach and Rescorla (2001a; 2001b) recommend an assessment of the young child in different contexts, such as home and school. Aspects of a psychosocial assessment can also be approached from a trauma or attachment perspective and can include consideration of the child's whole life experience.

The assessment format and sequence can vary. Some clinicians prefer gathering information from relevant caregivers first before seeing the child and keeping information that is highly charged away from the child. Others propose that the first assessment should ideally be a family assessment session so the clinician can engage with all but also obtain a first-hand view of the family constellation and interaction. Jenkins (1994) suggests that conjoint family appointments are probably superior in detecting important family issues that may be relevant for case conceptualisation and therapy planning, and hence, at least a brief family appointment should form part of a diagnostic assessment. Where trauma, abuse, neglect or severe stress has occurred, the assessment of context variables becomes even more relevant. It might be important to understand how the caregiver dealt with a significant life event such as a natural disaster, parental conflict, or other traumatic event. Furniss et al. (2013) suggest that the purpose of the assessment is to disentangle child symptoms in the context of other factors, such as parental risk factors, adult couple relationship issues, and attachment issues, and to base treatment decisions on a good understanding of all components.

However, the assessment of preschoolers presents many challenges (Postert et al., 2009). Development in young children occurs rapidly with great individual differentiation, depending on the child's genetics, level of maturity and environmental factors. Therefore, deciding conclusively whether the child's presentation falls outside the normal range and expectations may be hard. Second, we currently lack a widely used, reliable, valid and useful diagnostic classification system that captures presentations during the preschool years (Postert et al., 2009). Many categories in both the International Classification of Diseases, Eleventh Revision (ICD-11; World Health Organization, 2019) and the Diagnostic and Statistical Manual of Mental Disorders, Fifth Edition, Text Revision (DSM-5-TR; American Psychiatric Association, 2022) derive from adult psychopathology and are not sensitive to age and developmental specificity in preschool-age children. The Diagnostic Classification of Mental Health and Developmental Disorders of Infancy and Early Childhood (DC:0-5) (ZERO TO FIVE, 2016) has been developed specifically to diagnose mental disorders in infants and toddlers. The DC:0-5 aims to provide a developmentally informed, relationship-based, contextually, and culturally grounded classification system. However, our experience is that the DC:0-5 is not yet recognised by governmental organisations that require a confirmed diagnosis, nor is it yet widely available in many early childhood contexts with which we work.

Compiling the assessment information comprehensively will help the clinician to make informed treatment decisions. At what level does the treatment need to be offered, the level of the individual child, the parent, the child-parent dyad, the couple or family system, the adult only, or does treatment even need to leave the boundaries of the family and include other systems, such as a childcare setting? Multi-model therapy may also be indicated to address the different needs of the child, adult or family. Treatment decisions will also need to take into consideration what is known empirically about the treatment for specific disorders in preschoolers. Treatment availability, training, experience and preference of treating clinician will be factors determining what can be offered to a particular child in a particular setting, as are caregiver commitment and available time. An assessment of the parent's current parenting style may also be a consideration for treatment decisions. For example, a warm yet poorly structured parent may benefit from an intervention that focuses more strongly on supporting routines, rules, consistency and structure in the home, whereas a highly organised, rigid and structured parent may benefit from an intervention that aims to increase attuned and sensitive parenting. Finally, the frequency, intensity and duration of intervention may need to be considered in the context of families with high-stress risk situations that involve child protection agencies. These questions, and more, will help the clinician decide what therapy, for whom, and under what conditions will be most helpful for the young child.

There are a wide range of assessment tools available to complete or supplement the clinical assessment, though some tests require specific qualifications and training, and test equipment can be costly to purchase and hard to access. The assessment tool may assess the broad-based functioning of the child or a specific area of concern, such as behavioural problems or anxiety. Psychometric testing has an important role when there are developmental concerns, such as a delay in a specific area or globally, or when there are neurodevelopmental concerns indicative of Autism Spectrum Disorder (ASD), Attention-Deficit Hyperactivity Disorder (ADHD), chromosomal disorders or Fetal Alcohol Spectrum Disorders (FASD). The input of other health professionals may also be required, including paediatricians, occupational therapists and/or speech pathologists. Questionnaires also offer an opportunity to obtain an impression of the child completed by a second source (e.g., teacher) and can verify parental reports or contradict it. Scales that assess the parent's level of functioning or parenting skills may be helpful in situations where the clinician has a concern with parental functioning.

We have listed examples of tests and questionnaires which we have found useful in our clinical practice in a therapeutic setting. While formal, good-quality diagnostic assessments are not always needed, are hard to obtain, expensive and time-consuming, the assessment of the child and family should at least offer a formulation that explains what the presenting issues are, how the presentation is conceptualised by the clinician, and giving the reason why a particular form of treatment is indicated based on the initial assessment.

Examples of Commonly Used Assessments in the Early Years

- **Ages and Stages Questionnaire — Third Edition:** This instrument is a parent-reported developmental screen in five areas of development to determine whether further assessment with a professional may be required, and includes the domains of Communication, Gross Motor, Fine Motor, Problem Solving and Personal-Social skills (Squires & Bricker, 2009).

- **Griffiths Scales of Child Development — 3rd Edition:** The Griffiths is a formal and standardised face-to-face assessment of the child with an overall measure of the child's development in five different developmental domains, including cognition, language and communication, fine motor skills, personal-social skills and gross motor skills (Stroud et al., 2016).

- **Wechsler Preschool and Primary Scale of Intelligence — Fourth Edition (WPPSI-IV):** This is an IQ test based on a formal and standardised face-to-face assessment of the child. The test can be helpful in determining the child's cognitive ability, especially when there are cognitive and language concerns (Wechsler, 2012).

- **Adaptive Behaviour Assessment System — Third Edition (ABAS-3):** This scale consists of an interview with the caregiver and offers a complete assessment of adaptive skills and behaviour of the young child in domains such as communication, home and community skills and self-care. The scale assists in the diagnosis of intellectual disability (Harrison & Oakland, 2015).

- **Vineland Adaptive Behaviour Scale — Third Edition:** This instrument is similar to the ABAS and is often utilised in the assessment of children with a suspected developmental disability (Sparrow et al., 2016).

- **Diagnostic Infant and Preschool Assessment (DIPA):** This instrument is helpful in the diagnostic assessment of young children, administered in interview form with the caregiver, assessing DSM-IV symptoms in young children (Scheeringa & Haslett, 2010).

- **Conners-Early Childhood:** The Conners offers a multi-informant assessment of the child's behaviour and development as reported by parents and other carers and is suitable for preschool-age children (Conners, 2009).

- **Achenbach System of Empirically Based Assessment (ASEBA):** The ASEBA method of assessment includes a parent-based scale called the Child Behaviour Checklist (CBCL) with a version for 1.5–5 years and 6–18 years and a teacher version called the Caregiver-Teacher Report Form (C-TRF) for 1.5–5 years and the Teacher Reporting Form (TRF) for 6–18 years (Achenbach & Rescorla, 2001a; Achenbach & Rescorla, 2001b). The CBCL and C-TRF/TRF are comprehensive questionnaires providing quantitative and descriptive data on childhood problems covering a wide range of emotional and behavioural problems in children and allowing multi-informant comparison of ratings between different carers. The teacher rating form also offers information about the child's academic performance and adaptive function.

- **Parenting Sense of Competence Scale:** This self-report measure is freely available and assesses parental self-efficacy and can be helpful in the context of parenting intervention (Gibaud-Wallston & Wandersman, 1978, as cited in Johnston & Mash, 1989).

- **Strength and Difficulties Questionnaire (SDQ).** This instrument is freely available and offers a parent rating of emotional, behavioural, attention/hyperactivity problems, peer relationship and social concerns in the child (Goodman, 1997).

- **Preschool Anxiety Scale:** This scale offers an assessment of parent-reported presence and frequency of anxiety symptoms in young children and helps in identifying the specific category of anxiety disorder (Edwards et al., 2010).

- **Eyberg Child Behaviour Inventory:** The Eyberg is a parent report assessing the intensity and frequency of behaviour problems in the child and can be helpful in the context of diagnosis or assessment of the progress of treatment (Eyberg & Pincus, 1999; Eyberg & Ross, 1978).

- **Trauma Symptom Checklist for Young Children**: This measure assesses trauma symptoms and post-traumatic presentation in young children based on caregiver reports (Briere, 2005).

Treatment Options for Young Children and Their Families

Treatment decisions are based on a variety of factors, including the therapeutic setting, therapist factors such as expertise and training, caregiver and referrer expectations, child presentation, and the child's diagnosis. Research evidence is another important component, considering what is known about the treatments of children with specific disorders. Other factors that influence treatment decisions are funding issues, financial resources, and available session numbers in a given context. Clinician preference also plays a part. Some therapists clearly favour an evidence-based clinical approach, utilising models with a strong research base, which may include manualised treatments with a semi-structured format. In contrast, others enjoy a degree of freedom in developing their own treatment techniques or strategies within a specific model or within a more integrative approach. Treatment decisions are also based on the agent for change. Which part of the family unit would benefit most from the intervention, and what is the most effective and efficient way to achieve the desired outcome?

Individual child therapy may be indicated if the assessment and clinical evidence suggest that direct input to the child will most likely facilitate change in the presenting problems. Individual therapy can be cathartic, reflective or based on new learning and skills development, or it can include all. The most common individual therapy options include play therapy (which can include sand tray therapy and art therapy), cognitive behaviour therapy and psychodynamic therapies. Though usually offered as an individual treatment, some of these approaches can also be successfully applied within a group setting. Individual child therapy is usually undertaken as a multi-modal therapy with at least some involvement of the child's carer or family in the form of parallel work or intermittent sessions offered to the carer. Some approaches even require parent involvement, such as assisting the child in completing homework tasks. Individual approaches can be strongly child-directed, in which the therapist takes a reflective stance; they can be insight-oriented or more structured by the therapist, assisting the child in working through issues of trauma, loss, relationship conflict, social stress or emotional issues. Some approaches have a strong skills training component. The therapy helps process experience, understand links between feelings, thoughts and behaviour and prepare the child to deal more effectively with challenging situations and social relationships. However, even the most structured format will be presented in a playful and developmentally appropriate format. Individual child therapy is based on the belief that direct input to the child will be of the most benefit or the most successful way of engaging the child and family to achieve a positive change in the presenting problem.

Parent interventions, often offered in a group format, focus on the parent as the main agent for change and often require the attendance of the parent only. The underlying assumption is by addressing parenting behaviour, knowledge, skills and/or cognition, this change will have a rippling effect on the parent-child relationship and the symptom presentation of the child. A wide range of group program options are available for parents in Australia and worldwide. Like child-focused interventions, parent interventions vary in their theoretical models and formats. However, most programs are semi-structured, allowing time for new content absorption but also discussion, reflection or skills training. The underlying theories vary widely and include attachment and psychodynamic theories, theories of social learning, behaviour modification, cognitive theory and the concept of emotional intelligence. Group programs have a distinct advantage, allowing participants to benefit from group learning, including sharing of ideas, normalisation of experience, peer support from each other, skills training in the form of role plays and forming of social connections. Group programs can also be a cost-effective way of facilitating therapeutic change.

Dyadic therapies involve both the child and the main caregiver and perceive the dyadic unit as a positive focus for change. There are a wide range of dyadic therapy options for this group of children, representing different theories of change, including behaviour and social learning theory, psychodynamic, humanistic and attachment theories, play therapy models and trauma theory. Many models represent an integration of underlying theories. Some models address the quality of the parent-child relationship with a more reflective format, while others are highly structured or strongly skills focused. Though each model has a different target and employs different treatment processes, the aim of all dyadic therapy is to enhance the parent-child relationship as the primary means of improving mental health, improving parenting skills and addressing presenting problems in the child. Dyadic therapies focus on the relational realm but also on parenting behaviour and perceive anchoring points for change by involving more than one family member. Indications for dyadic therapy may be a stressed parent-child relationship, challenging child behaviour, parenting deficits or parental struggles due to mental health issues. Dyadic therapy is also an option for parents and children dealing with trauma, including the effects of intergenerational trauma.

Family and contextual approaches to therapy focus on the family system as an important leverage for change. Whole family attendance can offer valuable observation of family interaction and an understanding of the dynamics that may contribute to the symptom development in the referred child. As such, systems models help the therapist formulate hypotheses about the presenting problem, which guide the development of interventions. Depending on the model, family therapy can focus on overt behaviour and interaction, on cognitions such as beliefs, assumptions and presuppositions, and can be highly problem/solutions focused or more reflective in format. Contextual models can also consider the child's wider environment. Family therapy models are based on different epistemology, including cybernetics, systems theory, psychodynamic ideas and postmodernism. Family therapy models can extend the relational realm from the nuclear family to other parts of the family, as found in divorced and blended families. The therapist's focus can include intergenerational systems, preschools, schools, child protection agencies and other legal systems, or even the larger societal context in its conceptualisation of child presentations.

The place of treatment is usually the clinic or the child's home, but it may also include the child's educational environment, the daycare centre, preschool or school, or a medical or residential setting. This can occur for various reasons. First, the educational or medical setting may be the only place where problems occur. A child may have a medical condition or disability that requires prolonged hospital admission, stretching the child's coping ability. Hence, the hospital may be the optimal place to address the stress response in the child. A child may be functioning well at home but struggles with the transition to the preschool or may display deficits in social-emotional development such as extreme shyness and poor social integration, or with inappropriate behaviour towards peers, which can include behaviours such as physical aggression, problematic sexualised behaviour, taking of food or belonging of others. Hence, the best place for intervention may be preschool, where the behaviour can be observed and directly addressed with appropriate intervention. Sadly for some children, clinical and psychosocial assessment indicates that the educational setting is the only or the most powerful place where behavioural change can occur. These children's homes may offer little stimulation and constitute neglectful or abusive environments, yet to the degree that does not lead to the child's removal. In these situations, the alternative environment may be the place where investment into intervention will have the strongest impact. Several treatment models designed for parents, dyads or families can be applied in or adapted to alternative settings. Internet options for treatment are increasing, stimulated by the COVID-19 epidemic, but may also be the only viable option for clients living in remote parts of the world.

The discussion as to what works best for which child, dyad, parent or family cannot be concluded without consideration of the debate on common factors in therapy. We now know that psychotherapy works in general, regardless of therapeutic modality (Moldovan & Pintea, 2015). Further, there is now strong evidence that the quality of the therapeutic relationship is a major factor for change, and specific factors include the bond between client and therapist, goal consensus and agreement about therapy tasks (Laska et al., 2014; Sprenkle, 2009). However, the mechanisms for change are not well understood. Brown (2015) argues that there may be similar principles and procedures across different therapy models. Yet based on the different theoretical bases underlying each model, similar procedures have been given different names. Understanding the important mechanisms for therapeutic change in the therapies of young children may be a topic left for future researchers to explore.

A good assessment that offers an understanding of the child and family's therapeutic needs, the selection of the best model of treatment in a given situation, goal consensus, a respectful client-therapist relationship, seeking the consultation of other professionals if needed, engaging in good supervision and adopting an openness to assess if the treatment offered meets the needs of the clients are solid starting points in the treatment of young children and their families.

References

Achenbach, T. M., & Rescorla, L. A. (2001a). *Manual for the ASEBA Preschool Age Forms and Profiles.* University of Vermont, Research Center for Children, Youth and Families.

Achenbach, T. M., & Rescorla, L. A. (2001b). *Manual for the ASEBA School-Age Forms and Profiles.* University of Vermont, Research Center for Children, Youth and Families.

American Psychiatric Association (2022). *Diagnostic and Statistical Manual of Mental Disorders: Diagnostic and Statistical Manual of Mental Disorders*, Fifth Edition, Text Revision. American Psychiatric Association.

Briere, J. (2005). *Trauma Symptom Checklist for Young Children (TSCYC): Professional Manual.* Psychological Assessment Inc.

Brown, J. (2015). Specific techniques vs common factors. Psychotherapy integration and its role in ethical practice. *American Journal of Psychotherapy*, 69(3) 301–316, https://10.1176/appi.psychotherapy.2015.69.3.301

Conners, K. (2009). *Conners Early Childhood Manual.* MHS Assessments.

Edwards, S. L., Rapee, R. M., Kennedy, S. J., & Spence, S. H. (2010). The assessment of anxiety symptoms in preschool-aged children: The revised Preschool Anxiety Scale. *Journal of Clinical Child and Adolescent Psychology*, 39(3), 400–409. https://doi.org/10.1080/15374411003691701.

Eyberg, S.M., & Pincus, D. (1999). *Eyberg child behaviour inventory and Sutter-Eyberg student behaviour inventory-Revised. Professional manual.* Psychological Assessment Resources.

Eyberg, S.M., & Ross, A.W. (1978). Assessment of child behaviour problems: The validation of a new inventory. *Journal of Clinical Child Psychology*, 7, 113–116.

Furniss, T., Muller, J.M., Achtergarde, S., Wessing, I., Averbeck-Holocher, M., & Postert, C. (2013). Implementing psychiatric day treatment for infants, toddlers, preschoolers and their families: A study from a clinical and organisational perspective. *International Journal of Mental Health Systems*, 7, 12. https://doi.org/10.1186/1752-4458-7-12

Goodman, R., 1997. The Strengths and Difficulties Questionnaire. *Journal of Child Psychology and Psychiatry*, 38, 581–586. http://dx.doi.org/10.1111/j.1469-7610.1997.tb01545.x

Harrison, P., & Oakland, T. (2015). *Adaptive Behavior Assessment System (3rd Ed.).* Western Psychological Services.

Jenkins, H. (1994). Family interviewing: Issues of theory and practice. In: M Rutter, E. Taylor & L Hersov. *Child and Adolescent Psychiatry.* Blackwell.

Johnston, C., & Mash, E. J. (1989). A measure of parenting satisfaction and efficacy. *Journal of Clinical Child Psychology, 18,* 167–175. https://doi.org/10.1207/s15374424jccp1802_8

Laska, K. M., Gurman, A. S., & Wampold, B. E. (2014). Expanding the lens of evidence-based practice in psychotherapy: A common factors perspective. *Psychotherapy, 51*(4), 467–481. https://doi.org/10.1037/a0034332

Moldovan, R., & Pintea, S. (2015). Mechanisms of change in psychotherapy: Methodological and statistical considerations. *Cognition, Brain, Behavior: An Interdisciplinary Journal, 19*(4), 299–311.

Price-Robertson, R. (2018). *Diagnosis in child mental health. Exploring the benefits, risks and alternatives.* Child Family Community Australia, Paper 48. Australian Institute of Family Studies, Commonwealth of Australia, Southbank Vic.

Postert, C., Averbeck-Holocher, M., Beyer T., Mueller, J., & Furniss, T. (2009). Five systems of psychiatric classification for preschool children: Do differences in validity, usefulness and reliability make for competitive or complimentary constellations? *Child Psychiatry and Human Development, 40,* 25–41. https://doi10.1007/s10578-008-0113-x

Scheeringa, M. S., & Haslett, N. (2010). The reliability and criterion validity of the Diagnostic Infant and Preschool Assessment: A new diagnostic instrument for young children. *Child Psychiatry and Human Development, 41,* 299–312. https://doi10.1007/s10578-009-0169-2

Sparrow, S. S., Cicchetti, D. V., & Saulnier, C. A. (2016). *Vineland Adaptive Behaviour Scales: Third Edition (Vineland-3).* NCS Pearson.

Sprenkle, D. H. (2009). *Common factors in couple and family therapy: The overlooked foundation.* Guilford Press.

Squires, J., & Bricker, D. (2009). *Ages & Stages Questionnaires,* Third Edition (ASQ®-3): A Parent-Completed Child Monitoring System. Paul H. Brookes Publishing Co., Inc.

Stroud, L., Foxcroft, C., Green, E. M., Bloomfield, S., Cronje, J., Hurter, L., et al. (2016). *Griffiths Scales of Child Development 3rd Edition; Part 1: Overview Development and Psychometric Properties.* Hogrefe.

Wechsler, D. (2012). *Wechsler Preschool and Primary Scales of Intelligence (4th ed.) (WPPSI-IV).* Psychological Corporation.

World Health Organization (2019). *International Classification of Diseases* (11th Revision). World Health Organization.

ZERO TO FIVE. (2016). DC: 0-5™. *Diagnostic classification of mental health and developmental disorders of infancy and early childhood. Revised Edition.* Zero To Three Press.

Section I:

Child-Focused Approaches

Chapter 2

Play Therapy

Ingeborg Stiefel

Play Therapy (PT) is a therapeutic modality that provides a planned and purposeful intervention, based on a systematic application of theories of play and child development, guided by experienced mental health professionals or formally trained play therapists (Peterson & Boswell, 2015). The primary premise of PT is that therapeutic play helps alleviate stress and conditions that cause social, emotional and behavioural problems, those that can compromise the child's long-term adjustment and developmental outcome. Trained clinicians offer a therapeutic environment that is safe and engaging and encourages free expression of self through a variety of play-related activities. PT is a developmentally appropriate model of working with young children presenting with a wide range of social, developmental and psychological concerns. Through play, games, creative visualisation, role play and words, children can express their thoughts and feelings, reveal their inner struggles and conflicts, re-enact challenging experiences, achieve growth and development, and process difficult experiences (Guzzi DelPo & Frick, 1988).

Play is a natural form of communication for children as it is their universal and preferred language. Play is also a medium for exchanges with others and fosters self-healing (Landreth, 2012). Play facilitates communication between child and therapist. In spontaneous or semi-structured play, children communicate through action, choice of activities and toys, as well as through engagement or non-engagement of the therapist. Repeated themes, actions or patterns reveal internal struggles, past or current conflicts with the external world, stressful life experiences and the child's emotions about these, including fears, hopes, wishes, frustrations, longing and anger, although some children may hold back their feelings. Furthermore, children may have distorted cognitions about events in their lives, leading to a feeling of responsibility or guilt. Play as symbolic communication conveys what cannot or cannot yet be expressed in words. Language may accompany play, and words used may confirm or contradict what is communicated through play. Through play, children re-enact, re-construct and re-invent significant life experiences (both pleasant and unpleasant) and reality. Play can assist in de-intensifying, resolving and integrating stressful life events (Guzzi et al., 1988), and play helps the child to develop a sense of self. Children often use play to practice roles and routines they observe in their environment. Play is motivating, and most children enjoy playing and spend the majority of their time engaging in it (Landreth, 2012). PT models which utilise the parent as facilitator, such as Filial Therapy, also foster a stronger parent-child relationship and more secure attachment between child and caregiver.

Historical Development

Play therapy originally dates to the beginning of the last century with approaches developed by Anna Freud in the 1920s and Melanie Klein in the 1930s (Landreth, 2012). The early models were based on psychodynamic and psychoanalytic theory. Play was perceived as the substitute for free association in adult psychoanalysis. Klein's model proposed that play provides access to the child's unconscious, and the aim of therapy was to resolve past and current unresolved conflicts, especially those stemming from the earliest relationship experiences of the child. The therapeutic purpose was to uncover the past, make urges, fantasies, wishes and defensive behaviour conscious with the help of interpretation to achieve ego strength and integration. Compared with Klein's approach, Anna Freud's model focused more strongly on the therapeutic relationship and the attachment between therapist and child. Anna Freud also utilised interpretations to help the child understand and integrate unconscious motivation and needs. Both models considered the transference relationship and the therapist's countertransference responses as a tool to understand the child's projection into the play and into the therapeutic relationship. Kleinian playrooms offered fewer symbolic and representational (real) life play materials compared with contemporary models. Children received their own box with play items, and the box also contained the child's own creations from the sessions. The box symbolised the safety and containment of therapy. Klein recommended that toys should be simple, small and varied, non-mechanical, with basic human figures representing different sizes and gender (Meshiany & Krontal, 1998).

The non-specificity of the material, such as glue, paper, string, pencils, match sticks, and small wooden figures of people and animals without clear facial expression, allows the child to project inner struggle and conflict into the play, including the projection of thoughts and feelings into the therapist via transference. The aim of both models was to make the unconscious conscious with gradual interpretation of the meaning of play and an increasing understanding on the part of the child as to the significance of the play. Further, therapist interpretations also allowed the child to understand the meaning of the interactions between child and therapist. Psychodynamic models of PT are still offered in countries with a strong psychoanalytic therapy tradition, but probably to a somewhat lesser degree in Australia.

A more structured approach to PT, Release Play Therapy, was developed by David Levy in the 1930s (Landreth, 2012). Release PT has some parallels with modern exposure therapy. Abreaction of affect, re-enactment of trauma, and release of pain and tension are played out and allow the child to develop control of the feelings associated with past stressful experiences, integrating the experience and developing a new sense of self. Hambidge's combined model utilised directive play after an initial non-directive phase (Leggett & Boswell, 2017).

The 1930s saw the emergence of Relationship PT (Landreth, 2012) with a stronger focus on present issues and also on the therapist-child relationship. Arguably the most influential stream of development in PT stems from the humanistic movement in the 1940s. Axline, a student of Carl Rogers, developed client-centred play therapy based on humanistic principles of Rogerian theory. This non-directive movement is strongly relationship-focused and based on the assumption that children can resolve their problems through play given a facilitating environment. Today, client-centred play therapy is widely practised, and this model has the strongest research base.

An important development in the field of non-directive PT occurred with the introduction of Filial Therapy by Bernard and Louise Guerney and their colleagues in the 1960s. Filial therapy engages the caregiver as an active partner in therapy by training caregivers (or paraprofessionals) in the principles of non-directive play therapy (VanFleet, Ryan, & Smith, 2005). The caregiver becomes the agent for change by providing an environment characterised by empathy, sensitivity to the child's need, reflective/non-intrusive responses, encouragement and calm limit setting. Filial therapy enhances the parent-child relationship, empowers the parent, and teaches parents how to play effectively using both structural and attuned parenting components.

Current Mainstream Play Therapy Approaches in Australia: Directive, Non-Directive and Integrated Models

There are broadly three approaches to PT currently practised in Australia, non-directive models, directive (structured, focused and prescriptive) models and combined models (Leggett & Boswell, 2017; Rasmussen & Cunningham, 1995), which integrate non-directive with directive techniques. Training advertised in Australia suggests that some integrated models also utilise psychodynamic and attachment-based concepts, including consideration of unconscious processes in PT.

Non-Directive Play Therapy

Theoretical Underpinning of Non-Directive Play Therapy

Non-Directive Play Therapy, also referred to as child-centred, client-centred, or humanistic PT, was initially developed by Virginia Axline in the 1940s, and was further developed, refined and described by Landreth (Landreth, 2012). Landreth refers to non-directive PT as Child-Centred Play Therapy (CCPT) and stresses that CCPT is not an application of technique but an intentional commitment to a specific therapist attitude, a belief in the capacity and resilience of children and a belief that children are constructively self-directing. By this he means that children have the innate ability to grow, develop and move forward, and they have self-healing capacity, a term referred to as self-actualisation. CCPT offers a relationship that facilitates this process. Landreth's model strongly represents the premises of humanistic/client-centred therapy applied to the paediatric setting. The therapist's position is central to the process. Play reflects growth symbolically, but it also represents the drive towards growth through engagement with the human and non-human environment in the form of activities, play, and playful interactions with others. Within the parameters of specific safety rules and boundaries, non-directive play therapy gives the child a choice in selecting activities, play materials and themes. The child decides whether to engage the therapist in this process. The therapist's role is to be present, tuned in and focused in a non-leading yet consistent and confident way so the child can develop trust and a therapeutic relationship is formed.

According to Landreth (2012), three key concepts are at the basis of child-centred PT. First, the powerful belief on the part of the therapist that humans have the innate capacity to strive towards growth, maturity and self-realisation. Second, maladjustment results from incongruence between the actual experience and the developing concept of self as a result of an environment that is non-attuned, evaluative, or restricts the child's emotional expression. Third, CCPT offers a facilitating relationship with attunement, genuineness, warmth, acceptance and empathy which releases the child's inner resources for self-growth. Based on these assumptions, non-directive PT utilises a number of highly specific therapist variables.

Therapist Variables and Key Therapy Techniques of Non-Directive Play Therapy

1. Genuineness and Congruence. Genuineness and Congruence are pivotal to CCPT. Jayne (2013) describes this variable as an awareness, an openness to one's moment-to-moment experience, thoughts and feelings in a real and natural way. Openness and presence are expressed in non-verbal therapist behaviour, such as open body posture, relaxed tone of voice and joint focus on the child's activity. Congruence is an integration within the therapist between internal awareness and external expression and between verbal and non-verbal communication. Genuineness refers to a therapist's stance that is real without pretence and is felt by both child and therapist at a personal and interpersonal level. Lack of congruence may be experienced by a therapist during a play therapy session that consists of extremely repetitive play (a child burrowing a toy figure in the sand tray over and over), with the therapist making tracking comments on the play, such as 'Oh it is underneath the sand again' or 'Burrowed deeply in the sand' but feeling disengaged. Becoming aware of this and her own sense of boredom, she may self-reflect, 'What is the child telling me?', and responds with different comments, which include the question she is asking herself, such as 'You are burrowing the doll, again and again', 'Now the same is happening again', 'Like it will never end' or 'The doll seems to get lost in the sand again after being found', and the child may then give the therapist a verbal response such as 'She hasn't been found!' or 'She needs to be found', 'Somebody has to find her' to which the therapist may respond " Ah, somebody needs to find her or she will be burrowed in the sand again and again'.

2. Unconditional positive regard/ Unqualified Acceptance. Unconditional positive regard is conceptualised as the complete acceptance of every aspect of the child's experience and the belief that the child can grow. The therapist refrains from any value statement, positive or negative, approval or disapproval, instead conveying to the child that whatever is expressed in play is accepted by the therapist within the safety boundaries stated at the beginning of therapy. Unconditional positive regard communicates to the child that anything the child does or says matters. This therapist attitude allows the child to be herself without the fear of restriction of external evaluation or judgement. The therapist for example would avoid statements such as 'Oh, I am glad you told me that the doll needs to be found; that is really helpful; you are a clever girl'. Or if the child asked, 'Are you happy I told you?', the therapist would refrain from saying, 'Yes, you made me happy' and instead may respond with 'I am wondering, …(pauses) … what do you think, is it helpful that we both know that she needs to be found?'.

3. Tracking/Descriptions of Play and Activities. Descriptions are verbal statements that neutrally describe the child's action. At the beginning of therapy, these may be more factual and concrete, describing what the therapist sees, such as 'You are trying to place the yellow blocks on the fence', and 'You gave the doll a bottle and now she is getting an apple'. In the middle phase, the descriptions may refer to more challenging issues the child is working through, such as 'This seems to be a hard choice. You are not sure if this is the right doll' or 'You want me to help to decide, you are hesitating', addressing the child's conflict or dissonance. Verbal descriptions of child behaviour are brief and succinct and appropriate to the young child's language and developmental level. They are running commentaries on the child's play, yet these are also selectively chosen depending on the stage of therapy, the phases in therapy and the significance and meaning of the child's play in the context of the referral. Descriptions are verbal tracking statements and indicate to the child that the therapist is following the child's action and experience. Descriptions facilitate a growing understanding and processing of the meaning of play for the child.

4. Reflections. Reflections are verbal responses to verbal communication and can be expressed in the form of brief statements, repeating words in a child's sentence, 'Oh five doggies', or they can reflect longer verbal statements in the form of paraphrases or reframes such as 'Oh, you said teddy is crying. He is so sad, he lost his mum!', or 'Teddy is heartbroken, he is not sure when he will see her again'. Or, in case of the doll being burrowed in the sand tray, the child may say, 'Gone again', and the therapist may repeat, 'Gone again' or 'Underneath the sand'.

5. Empathy. Empathy helps the therapist to take the child's perspective and understand the child's internal frame of reference. Empathic responses capture the child's emotional state as experienced by the therapist in the session or as imagined/assumed by the therapist when the therapist puts herself into the child's shoes. Empathy is a felt response to the child's play and is expressed through verbal statements (putting into words what the feeling state might be). However, empathy can also be experienced by the therapist without necessarily reflecting it back to the child if the timing may not be appropriate. Empathy serves several purposes. Through empathy, children feel understood and acknowledged in their emotional experience. Empathy helps the child to develop trust that his experience can be understood and shared with an adult. The child learns that there is a range of emotional experiences and words to describe them and eventually finds ways of integrating these with the help of a reliable and sensitive adult. Empathy is both a cognitive and an affective understanding of the child's experience, with sensitivity to the child's internal world and attunement to the child's experience from moment to moment (Jayne, 2013).

6. Boundaries. CCPT stresses the need to establish rules that provide safety for both therapist and child, that create respect for play materials and establishes boundaries that anchor children in reality (Landreth, 2012). Boundary statements may refer to child aggression, with a therapist response such as 'Toys are not for breaking' or 'Play is not for hurting others'. Sessions should also have a clear start and finish and adhere to the arranged session time.

The Therapy Process of Non-Directive Play Therapy

In contrast to other models, CCPT does not clearly describe stages of therapy. The model suggests initial separate sessions with the caregiver to understand the caregiver's concern and to assess the suitability for PT. PT is explained, including the expected process and caregiver requirements (Landreth, 2012). Showing the caregiver the playroom can be helpful. Instead of phases, CCPT describes therapeutic tasks which include the establishment of a therapeutic relationship between child and therapist. The client-centred therapist variables facilitate both engagement and the working-through process. Landreth describes the therapeutic stance as a communication to the child that conveys the message that the therapist is present, listens to the child and tries to understand what the child is expressing in play (Landreth, 2012). Boundaries are clearly stated in the beginning, and the child is prepared for each ending of the session. Clean-up tasks remain with the therapist, not the child. Limits are set, if needed, such as how much water can be used, how much glue can be spread, where glue and wet paints can be used etc. Change can occur gradually, and indicators of movement are changes in child behaviour, emotions and relationships both inside and outside the therapy room.

CCPT creates an atmosphere of safety and acceptance, which encourages the child to explore her inner world in an uncensored way with the help of play and the focused and attuned attention of the therapist. CCPT is considered to be a culturally sensitive approach that allows the child to express herself in culturally appropriate ways, verbally or non-verbally. Depending on the referral issue, CCPT can be applied as a short-term intervention of 10-12 weekly sessions. However, for highly stressed, traumatised, abused children or children with significant emotional problems, more intensive formats may be required with a higher weekly frequency of sessions, at least in the initial phase of treatment (Landreth, 2012). CCPT also allows the flexibility to be provided in group format or to sibling groups.

Directive Play Therapy (DPT)

Directive Play Therapy (DPT) differs from non-directive models in that the therapy process is focused and the therapist's role is active in structuring and directing the therapy process by suggesting activities and play themes and selecting a focus for the session. DPT is based on a diversity of theoretical approaches, including trauma-focused exposure and processing, Solution-Focused theory, Cognitive Behaviour Therapy (CBT), Post-Jungian models and can be practised in a format that integrates different directive models and techniques (Leggett & Boswell, 2017). The purpose of DPT is to accelerate the therapy process and steer the session in a direction that is believed to be of benefit in addressing the child's issues. As such, DPT is goal oriented and there is a rationale for the selection of the focus for the sessions. The focus, activity or theme must be such that it addresses and eventually confronts the issue that led to the referral, yet without causing undue anxiety or increased unhelpful defensive responses in the child. In DPT, the therapist is both a director and a facilitator (Jones et al., 2003).

DPT has been utilised in the context of trauma (Schauer et al., 2004) and childhood abuse (Rasmussen & Cunningham, 1995). Directive play therapy is a suitable approach for fears, anxiety and stress in the context of medical procedures where there is a specific focus for the session. Activities are chosen for a special purpose with a specific aim in mind (Jones et al., 2003), for example, medical equipment, needles and stethoscope if the child has experienced a stressful medical life event. The model has also been utilised in a group format to foster social competence in preschoolers (Stone & Stark, 2013). The selection of themes should consider the following: 'What are the needs of the child? What are the issues the child is dealing with? What will be the purpose of the activity, and what is the goal to be achieved? How will the play help the child to integrate the play experience and achieve this hoped-for outcome? How will it foster a positive relationship between child and therapist that will serve as a base for the therapeutic work to take place?

DPT offers an unlimited number of therapy techniques (Schaefer & Cangelosi, 2016). Therapists may develop their own repertoire, utilise existing ones or adapt those to the needs of the child. Hall, Kaduson and Schaefer (2002) suggest that the selection should be based on the goal of the therapy, such as reduction in fear and anxiety following a frightening event, reducing symptoms of depression after a loss, increasing awareness of feeling states, anger management and problem-solving, improved self-regulation and empowerment. Therapy with an emotionally restricted child may include feeling games and activities that increase the child's understanding of emotions in self and others. Structured activities which aim at increasing self-esteem and agency in an abused child may introduce puppets or toy characters which portray power and strength with the hope that the child will identify with these strong characteristics. Nightmares and sleeping problems may respond to changes in the ending of a dream which the child reports and which can be drawn in the session.

Jones et al. (2003) differentiate between three phases in directive play therapy. The first phase has a fairly low level of intensity. The aim is to facilitate engagement and reduce anxiety. The middle phase consists of working through issues of importance, with can evoke high intensity of feelings, such as fear, anger and frustration, a phase in which traumatic or threatening issues are explored with the help of play. The last phase is the termination phase, which again moves to a lower intensity level in preparation for the ending of therapy. The authors point to the need for the therapist to both assess the intensity of feelings of anxiety and stress in an ongoing way and to adjust therapy activities accordingly. Topics of less intensity may be introduced at the beginning of therapy and during the termination stage, whereas those that address the core of the child's issue form part of the middle phase. Sequences in which topics are introduced also require careful consideration by the therapist. Flexibility is required, and deviation from a planned session may be needed if the child has experienced an unexpected stressful event during the working-through phase. The therapeutic goal is achieved if the issues of concern have been adequately addressed and processed both at an emotional and cognitive level.

Low-intensity techniques at the beginning of therapy may include feeling cards, books and therapy aides, which allow manipulation of facial features, helping the child to increase awareness of emotional states without specific reference to the child's experience. Progressing to the second phase, emotions are linked to the child. During the middle phase, structured activities may represent stressful situations with reference to expected feelings, followed by activities that increase agency and control, self-esteem, assertiveness and safety. Puppets may be chosen to represent a role the child may have carried, allowing the child to gradually work through the tumult of feelings from a position of distance via the puppet.

Jones et al. (2003) propose five steps to DPT. The first step is brainstorming topics and activities that are appropriate for the issues to be addressed and resolved. Activities and themes can come from a wide variety of resources, including books, therapy aides such as St Luke's (https://innovativeresources. org), free drawings produced by the child or theme drawings depending on the referral problem, but usually topics and activities that are not strongly linked to the reason for referral. The therapist then assesses the level of intensity the activity is likely to evoke. The therapist now chooses an appropriate activity for each stage of therapy (beginning, middle and end). Step four consists of a selection of activities that fit directly with the overall goal of therapy and will be introduced during the working-through phase. These include those that evoke strong feelings and may weaken the coping strategy the child has developed as a result of a highly stressful event. Toys and themes selected may lead to exposure to a traumatic event. For example, the therapist may select an ambulance, fire engine and police car if the child has been involved in an accident. The toys or activities represent aspects of the lived experience. Finally, the therapist selects activities for the ending stage of therapy, which include preparation for the termination of therapy. From the brainstorming list, activities are again chosen that are less intense in nature but may also include future coping and future situations of challenge. Depending on the theoretical orientation of the therapist, directive play therapy may close with a ritual, a letter or picture the child leaves for the therapist, a photo taken, a milkshake at a local coffee shop after the session with the parent or the permission given by the therapist for the child to take one important toy of the play therapy session home if the child chooses to.

Combined Models

Directive and client-centred models can be combined. Non-directive techniques may be suitable during the beginning of directive play therapy. Alternatively, a therapist may start with a directive model but finds that this approach increases the child's anxiety and decides instead to move to a child-centred approach, which allows the child to approach significant themes at the child's own pace. This especially applies to children with an experience of significant trauma. Lanktree and Priere (2017), in their PT approach to trauma, suggest that play allows for the symbolic representation, the re-enactment and eventually verbal processing of trauma, including the assumptions the child may have developed as a result of the trauma. In highly traumatised children, affect regulation may be required during sessions with the help of more structured intervention. Play therapy is perceived as therapeutic exposure which helps the child to process traumatic experiences without triggering over-whelming distress within the safety of the therapeutic relationship. Finally, there may be cases where a client-centred approach does not lead to changes, and more directive play therapy techniques are needed, assisting the child in addressing the traumatic experiences the child is trying to avoid.

Integrated models may also utilise techniques based on psychodynamic models, such as interpretations, to address the struggle a child is expressing in play. Interpretations may be phrased in question form to give the child an opportunity to opt-out if the interpretation is felt to be too confrontational. Interpretations are the link between processes that the child is not yet aware of (unconscious) and behaviour that expresses the presence of the conflict or a stressful issue. A play therapist may comment on repeated play with three dolls, father/mother/child and wonders if the 'child-doll' and its activity represent the child's experience in a conflict situation past or present in the context of parental separation. Interpretations can also refer directly to the therapist-child relationship. The therapist may say to a child with a neglect experience, 'It is hard for you to ask for help from me?' (when the child is struggling with a task and never asks for help). At a later stage in therapy, the therapist may point to a link between the child's behaviour and the child's experience in a natural setting 'Your mum left you. You had to do everything on your own'. 'It is still hard for you to ask for help, even here?', or 'You are not sure if I can really help you'.

When to utilise directive, non-directive or integrated methods is not well studied (Andrews, 2010), and there is limited research in understanding the benefits of integrated approaches. Further, the agents for change are not well understood in each of the play therapy models (Kenney-Noziska et al., 2012). Non-directive techniques however, may be more appropriate for the beginning phase of any play therapy, and the limited research suggests that many therapists prefer flexibility in method. However, treatment decisions are also based on the personality of the therapist, the therapist's training background, the expertise of the therapist in utilising different models and the comfort level of the therapist with different models and techniques (Andrews, 2010). Kenney-Noziska et al. (2012) suggest that it is time to move beyond 'which model is best', instead to understand which approach is best for what problem and for therapists to integrate principles and strategies of both approaches into their repertoire.

Regardless of the model, all play therapies require self-monitoring and tracking by the therapist. Self-tracking involves a reflection and an awareness of the therapist's own experience in the form of self-questions such as: 'What is the child communicating in play?', 'Is it best if I reflect or describe the child's play in fairly factual ways?', 'Which part of play expresses special challenges? Should I point these out now, or will this increase stress and a closing off?', 'How should I respond to the play? Do I need to set limits and reinforce the rule?', 'What is my countertransference experience telling me about the child and our relationship? What is the child saying with the repeated play?', 'Which part of the play is relevant? Should I point it out? Will this make an impact? What is it going to achieve?' or 'Is the therapeutic alliance strong enough yet?'. Self-tracking also includes an awareness of body sensations such as, 'When he played with these toys, I suddenly had this creepy feeling', 'It felt like my stomach was getting into a knot', or 'I had this warm feeling flooding my whole body, not sure what to make of it yet'. These sensations can indicate communication about the child's experiences that are not yet understood or revealed, early childhood experiences (at a pre-verbal level), or these may signify that important moments are occurring in therapy. Self-tracking involves pacing and timing and a reflection as to what type of response will fit best and will not unduly increase the child's level of stress, anxiety or anger to a high arousal level but will lead to an integration of the therapist's response in the child's internal world. Needless to say, supervision and peer consultation should be part of any play therapy practice and needs to be utilised, especially when impasses occur or when the therapist has difficulties processing aspects of the therapy.

Filial Therapy (Child Parent Relationship Therapy)

Filial Therapy (FT), renamed by Landreth as Child Parent Relationship Therapy (Bratton & Landreth, 2006), views the caregiver as an important agent for change. FT assists the caregiver in developing child-centred parenting play skills within a structured setting. FT is a suitable model for children of both pre- and primary-school age. The model can be applied in its original group format, as a shorter 10-session group intervention or in the context of individual family therapy (Topham & VanFleet, 2011). Initially, four parenting skills are introduced. These include structuring, empathic listening, child-centred imaginary play, and limit setting. Structuring refers to specific 1:1 play times with the child, with clearly defined boundaries, a beginning and an end. Empathic listening involves attunement and the ability of the parent to attend fully, reflecting verbally on the child's behaviour and feelings. Child-centred play involves an engaged parent who follows the child's invitation in play, allows the child to lead, and stays emotionally involved with appropriate facial expression, intonation and emotional involvement. Limit setting is required to maintain the safety and boundaries of the session and to help the child to understand acceptable behaviour (e.g., non-aggression towards the caregiver and non-destruction of toys). FT consists of 4 training phases, beginning with the caregiver observing the therapist utilising non-directive play therapy skills with the caregiver's child, followed by a theoretical introduction and reflection on the session. The second phase focuses on skills development, where the therapist acts in the role of the child and the caregiver is encouraged to apply the new sets of skills. In phase three, parent and child are present, with the therapist observing and later shaping the caregiver's behaviour, and finally, unsupervised 1:1 special parent-child play at home, with separate sessions for the parent to reflect and refine their skills. Once the parent is competent in all stages, the model allows for a reflection on the child's play, assisting the caregiver in understanding the meaning of the child's communication via play.

The therapist is an educator and coach but also a clinician who needs to be attuned, empathic and accepting of the parent, thus displaying a client-centred attitude towards the parent. FT focuses on the parent-child relationship, fosters attachment and closeness, but also helps address parenting skills deficits and child behaviour problems. FT has a good research base and has been applied to a wide range of referral problems (Baggerly et al., 2010; Topham & VanFleet, 2011), including relationship difficulties between parent and child, parenting deficits, and the host of childhood presentations, including externalising, internalising, social, developmental and trauma related problems. FT has been shown to reduce problem behaviour in young children, it is a suitable model for at-risk populations (Draper et al., 2009), and it is considered to be a culturally sensitive model of therapy (Alivandi-Vafa & Ismail, 2010). Filial therapy can be applied to a parent-child dyad or introduced in groups. Session length varies, with earlier models proposing treatment phases of 6-9 months, compared with more recent applications of 10-12 weekly sessions (Vigrass, 2011).

The Play Environment

Play therapy can be offered in different settings. The ideal setting is a playroom or a specially designed area with a table and chairs and a wide range of toys appropriate to the developmental level of young children in treatment. Play therapy rooms and environments should be predictable and consistent, with toys stored in the same containers easily accessible by the child (Lanktree & Priere, 2017). Sameness of presentation is important, and session materials from sessions with other children should not be left in the room. The play environment must offer an undisturbed space, free from distractions. Ideally, play sessions should be offered at the same time and on the same day of the week. However, this may not always be an option. Play therapy rooms may not be available or family commitments may interfere with this plan. Some children may not be able to attend a session in an office building or clinic. Portable play material may be needed for a sick child in hospital, for a child in a residential facility, or for play therapy in the family home. Peterson and Boswell (2015) suggest that even natural environments can be appropriate play therapy settings. The selection of play materials and environments also depends on the theoretical orientation of the therapist, the play therapy model applied, the purpose of play, the space available, the budget, the therapist's skills and the therapist's unique ideas for the therapy.

Play Materials

Play therapy materials depend on the purpose of the play therapy. For a child with a needle phobia following traumatic hospital experiences, the play materials may be very specific and include medical toys, small dolls, beds and bedding, a house representing a hospital, ambulance, doctor and nurses dolls if available, or a soft toy which can act as the 'patients'. Play may be highly structured, giving the child an opportunity to understand relevant aspects of the medical setting, allowing experimentation with medical equipment, understanding a medical procedure and performing a procedure on a soft toy animal, playing out the emotional experience for the patient 'teddy'. However, playrooms that meet the needs of a wide range of children with different issues usually provide a wide set of toys and play materials. These can be used for both directive and non-directive play therapy.

The literature suggests that toys must be appropriate for the purpose of therapy. These include toys that engage the child and allow for the expression of feelings and creativity without the need to use words. Toys should assist in exploring relationships and lead to a better understanding of self and mastery without the need to involve the therapist (Landreth, 2012). Toys must be sturdy, easy to manipulate, non-electronic and should not encourage competitiveness between child and therapist in the form of games.

Toy categories are:

1. Representation of real life and nature. The first set of toys represents the child's daily experience with the social and natural environment. These might include small doll figures, a doll house, domestic animals, possibly farm animals, doll house furniture, cars, trucks, trains, buses, aeroplanes, boats, trees, kitchen and food items, a cash register and phones. Engagement with these items will represent the child's social situation and life experiences within the child's ecology.

2. Craft materials/stationary. The second set of play materials encourages spontaneous creative expression and includes materials such as paper, cardboard and coloured pencils, scissors, glue, string, paper clips, play dough, sticky tape, whiteboard markers if there is a whiteboard and small blocks. These objects allow the child to create symbolically what is important to him, projecting his thoughts and feelings into the creation without the given cue from a 'real life' toy. These non-specific materials help create what is relevant to the child.

3. Toys that assist with emotional relief. These toys allow the child to act out, releasing pent-up feelings of aggression, frustration or fear, or express high control needs represented in the use of play weapons, wild/dangerous animals (e.g., snakes, crocodiles and tigers), toy soldiers, or scary figures/symbols representing 'Baddies'. Dress-up outfits can further signify the theme, helping the child to act out what is experienced emotionally.

4. Sand and water. A sand tray and (restricted) use of water may be available and allow the child to create 3D scenes in the space of the tray. The use of the sand tray allows the therapist to gain clues during assessment or treatment, for example, by assessing the distance at which certain symbols are placed within the tray, how the sand tray is used (e.g., as a battlefield with soldiers or a meadow with pretty flowers), or by generating meaning of the different activities that may be occurring in the tray in different corners.

5. Cultural identity. In the multi-cultural context, toys should also be available that represent parts of the child's cultural tradition or identification (Landreth, 2012). Within the Australian context, these may include boomerangs, digging sticks, toy spears, and small rocks appropriate for children in the outback or from remote areas.

Caregiver Involvement

As with all child therapies, PT requires an involved and committed caregiver who can support the therapeutic process by having an understanding of the therapeutic task, information about the expected process, the likely responses of the child during different phases of treatment, the expected length of therapy and the aim of the therapy. In trauma work, the caregiver themselves may need to work through their own traumatic issues and may initially not be able to support the therapy of the child. Timing factors will need to be considered with a possible delay in PT to increase the caregiver's emotional stability. Negative parental perceptions of the child and a need to place the relationship problems into the child by searching for a diagnosis that 'will explain' the child's presentation can be a challenge. Unless these issues are worked through, PT may not be the therapy of choice. Caregiver involvement can be achieved in several ways.

Ideally, parent sessions are offered separately with the help of another therapist (Landreth, 2012). However, financial or time constraints may not make this a viable option. Some therapists offer separate sessions for the parents at specified intervals (such as once per month). Others split the session and meet the parent before the child session starts, with the child being fully prepared for this change in session. In some cases, the caregiver takes part in all sessions, mostly as an observer, but if invited, also as a facilitator. PT may also be integrated with family therapy. Depending on model and therapist orientation and preference, initial referral information may be taken with the caregiver only being present at the beginning of therapy or in the form of a complete family session.

Termination of Therapy

Landreth (2012) lists reference points that help gauge if therapy is progressing. These are applicable to all models of PT but especially to CCPT. Indicators include changes in the child's emotions or behaviour, including changes in the parent-child interaction. Landreth (2012) suggests therapists should be aware of 'change for the first time', which may include a change in repetitive play theme, utilisation of the therapist in a different way, exploration in a previously restricted child, or limited testing for the first time. Indicators for progress in therapy are an increased sense of self, greater self-acceptance, increased verbal interaction, flexibility and tolerance, self-confidence, reduced aggression or regression, acceptance of limits, less dependence on the therapist, less concern about other children using the room and an ability to integrate good and bad experience, as for example evidenced in the child's ability to see the good and bad in others (Landreth, 2012). With more focused approaches, the aim of therapy is achieved when problematic behaviour or emotions decrease or diminish, and the child's ability to cope with a stressful situation is increased.

The Case of Angelica

The following is a hypothetical therapy excerpt, which nevertheless integrates real client scenarios from the therapist's clinical work. The first part of therapy aims at helping the child to understand why separation from her biological mother had occurred, exploring feelings and helping the child to see that she is not responsible for the separation. The therapist had met the child in two previous sessions, a first session with her complete foster family and a second session jointly with her aunt.

Angelica (6 years old) was taken into the care of child protection at the age of 18 months. Her mother had serious substance use issues, and Angelica had been exposed to severe neglect. Her mother went into a substance use rehabilitation centre and Angelica was restored back into her mother's care at 2 years of age. However, the placement was short-lived because the mother started reusing substances and also partnered with a man who also had serious substance use issues. At the age of 2.5 years, Angelica was placed into short-term foster care with one couple and several months later into the care of her aunt Ruth, who was substantially older than Angelica's mother and was able to provide a stable environment for the child. Ruth had good parenting capacity but struggled with Angelica's 'erratic behaviour', which had become more pronounced since Angelica started school. Ruth described behaviours such as suddenly crossing the road without thinking, leaving the playground and wandering the streets, and running away from busy shopping centres as she was unable to cope with the noise and busyness of the place. Food hoarding was also an issue, as were some oppositional behaviours, such as disregarding caregiver rules. However, Ruth's main concern was unpredictable behaviours in dangerous situations, with Angelica putting herself at risk of injury or abuse. Ruth felt Angelica had not worked through the loss of her mother who she would see 12 times per year, in addition to monthly phone calls. Contact visits were unpredictable, and when Angelica's mother did not call or did not turn up for a visit, Angelica went into severe meltdowns. These would last for up to seven days, with an increase in risk-taking behaviour. Ruth and the therapist decided that a focused form of play therapy may be helpful in exploring Angelica's feelings of loss, the perception of her mother and her understanding of the contact visits. The aim of the semi-structured directive play therapy was to help Angelica work through her early life experience with her biological mother, to help her understand why separation had occurred and to help her deal better with the contact visits. Directive play therapy was offered over 8 sessions with initially weekly sessions, then moving to fortnightly and then monthly sessions. We all felt it would be of most benefit if Ruth also attended sessions so therapeutic ideas could be followed up within the home environment, if appropriate.

In the first session, the therapist asked Angelica to draw her home with Ruth and the family. The therapist assumed that this topic was a safe start and would not lead to a high level of anxiety, as the relationship with Ruth appeared to be solid. Angelica produced a rich picture depicting the house and the family members in approximate size and order (e.g., the adults standing next to each other, biological children next, with Angelica standing slightly apart from the other children). Colour was used and the family dog was added. The family members had clear facial expressions, and the dress of Ruth and Angelica matched in colour. Looking at the overall picture, the therapist relied on an assessment tool utilised in previous research which assesses the quality of attachment represented in children's drawings (Clarke et al., 2002). One of the assessment tools is a rating of the overall impression of the child's drawings and the feeling the drawing evokes in the therapist. In Angelica's case, the drawing conveyed a feeling of containment and calmness with good balance and order.

The therapist then arrived at an important decision point. Should she progress by moving to the more central task of therapy or wait until the next session? She wanted to explore Angelica's understanding of her family of origin and her perception of her relationship with her biological mother. The therapist utilised her own subjective scale of a score of 50 and above (out of 100). The tool rapidly integrates the therapist's subjective experience, taking into account the child's state in therapy and can be conceptualised as a countertransference response. It assesses whether or not it is appropriate to move forward or if it is wiser to hold back. The therapist's task is to assess: Is it a good time to approach the subject, or is it better to wait for the next session? Does it feel right now, or is something holding me back? If the score is well over 50, the therapist decides to carefully approach the challenging topic. In this session, the score was above the 50 mark, and the therapist decided to introduce the topic of Angelica's mother.

The therapist explained that she had not met Angelica's biological mum and asked if Angelia could produce a picture of her. The therapist left it up to the child how she wanted to draw mum, also in which context. If the child had asked, the therapist would have responded, 'It is up to you', but if this had increased the stress level in the child, the therapist might have helped by suggesting, 'You could draw her at the place where you see her, or at some other place'. Angelica decided to draw a contact visit. In contrast to Angelica's rich first drawing, her representation of self and mother was very small, squeezed into the upper corner of the paper. The facial features were unclear, very little colour was used, and other environmental details were lacking. The therapist commented that it must be hard to draw her mum since she did not see her very often. Angelica revealed that her mum would sometimes not turn up, and at other times she would bring many sweets, toys and cakes. The therapist explored Angelica's feelings when visits were cancelled or not attended.

In the following session, the therapist helped Angelica explore why Mum was so small. This was done with the therapist adding information pictorially. The therapist first drew a picture of Angelica's mum, an approximation of Angelica's drawing. When asked about the size, Angelica responded 'not seeing mum often'. The therapist added a picture of Angelica, also very small and at a far distance, commenting that it was hard to see each other when there was such a big distance. Angelica then added spontaneously that her mum had done 'bad stuff' but could not elaborate further. The therapist suggested that they use the doll house and encouraged Angelica to show the therapist all activities that happen in her busy household with her aunt Ruth. Angelica freely engaged, showing how to cook meals in the kitchen, with her aunt doing most of the cooking. She also explained other daily routines the children had, such as making beds, brushing teeth, reading a story, going to bed, watching TV, feeding and taking the dog for a walk. The therapist asked specifically what jobs her aunt had to do, probing for many tasks, indicating that it must be a very big job to do it all every day. The session continued with the therapist introducing the idea that the 'bad stuff' Angelica had referred to was Mum taking drugs, which 'would make Mum's brain spin'. The therapist demonstrated this with one of the female adult dolls (the doll in spinning movement flitting from one activity to the next and not getting much done), indicating that with so much head spinning, a mum could not possibly do all the different jobs.

The following session focused on the feeling of loss but also on different feelings a child may experience in the context of separation from a biological parent. The therapist introduced the theme of separation by asking Angelica to draw the rainbow, the connection between herself and her mum. She suggested that Angelica place the mum on one end of the rainbow and herself on the other side. Angelica was then encouraged to send messages to her mum. Possible choices of transportation were suggested, such as shooting stars to the other side, using small letters which could be delivered by the sky postman, or sending symbols from one end of the rainbow to the other with different feelings. Any type of message and transportation was to be accepted. Angelica liked the idea of the sky postman. The therapist talked with her about the different feelings she may have, feelings of anger for being left, sadness and missing mum, frustration when mum does not show up or call and when these feelings may be strongest. The first feeling Angelica selected was one of sadness. She decided to send a letter with a teardrop to her mum, and with help of the therapist, she created a small envelope to post the message. Following this Angelica was encouraged to guess her mum's feelings when receiving the messages. This required a little help provided by the therapist, suggesting that 'Mum may also feel sad'. The therapist then added, 'Mum may also feel really bad for taking the drugs. I think she may say, 'I miss you. I should not have taken it. It makes my head spin'. The therapist's intent was to help the child release any feelings of guilt or responsibility she may carry for the separation.

Ruth, being a resourceful carer, decided to continue with the conversation at times when Angelica was most approachable to discussing her feelings. Bedtime was best, and Ruth would gently probe for more responses from Angelica at these times but then continue with the normal bedtime routine of reading a story to her. Contact visits and especially failed visits gradually became less stressful for Angelica. Angelica became increasingly able to express her feelings to both her aunt and the therapist. Toward the end of therapy, it was decided that a feeling box might be helpful as any bothersome feeling could go into the box. We gave Angelica the choice of drawing the feeling or 'catching it in the air' (demonstrated in the session) and putting it in the box so it would not bother her at the given times. Angelica liked the idea of catching them. However, the therapist suggested that Angelica and Ruth may like to open the box at other times to see if the feelings were still there. In this case, talk about them and discuss what they could do to make the feeling of sadness, anger or frustration shrink or disappear.

Training in Play Therapy

PT training is required to become an effective and skilled play therapist. There are a wide range of training options for beginning and experienced therapists, including short courses and more intensive and costly training programs with certification. Participation in ongoing supervision is strongly recommended as an opportunity to discuss complex referrals and assessment issues, reflect on challenging client situations, including stagnation in therapy, or specific therapist's issues in responses to young children in therapy or to their carers.

The Evidence Base for PT

A large meta-analysis of 93 studies concluded that PT is an effective therapeutic intervention, with a mean effect size of .80 (Bratton et al., 2005). Both directive and non-directive play therapy are effective treatments. However, non-directive PT is showing stronger treatment effects. Bratton et al. (2005) suggest that this finding should be treated with caution. Non-directive

PT has been studied most extensively, with a significant number of studies completed (Landreth, 2012). There is a large disparity of studies coded as non-directive versus directive, but also a lack of specificity of intervention in many research projects and a lack of consistency in treatment protocol even within the same treatment modality (directive and non-directive). These variables may account for the difference in outcome. According to Bratton et al. (2005), research evidence further suggests that an optimal number of sessions is 30-35. However, depending on childhood presentation, positive treatment effects for CCPT can be achieved with much shorter treatment protocols (Landreth, 2012). Neither age nor gender is a predictor of outcome; however there is some indication that older youth benefit to a lesser degree (Bratton et al., 2005). Overall, when standard PT is compared with FT, FT shows even stronger effect sizes, indicating that carer-conducted therapy is the most effective form of PT. Landreth, in summarising available research data, claims that the results unequivocal demonstrate that CCPT and FT are effective interventions for a wide range of childhood problems, utilising both time-limited and intensive treatment protocols (Bratton et al., 2005; Landreth, 2012). Further, cross-cultural application of CCPT is an effective intervention for a wide range of culturally diverse groups of children (Landreth, 2012).

Discussion

Directive, non-directive and combined models of PT have been applied to many presentations of childhood, including internal conflicts (Guzzi DelPo & Frick, 1988) and externalising problems (Landreth, 2012). PT can be applied in standard and non-standard settings. These include schools (Montemayor, 2014), residential facilities (Bratton et al., 2005), integrated with family therapy (Hirschfeld & Wittenborn, 2016), offered in medical settings (Guzzi DelPo & Frick, 1988), applied in the context of trauma (Schauer et al., 2004) and childhood abuse (Rasmussen & Cunningham, 1995). PT has been applied in standard format, in modified versions, adapted and extended to include the parent/caregiver as the facilitator of the therapy in the form of Filial Therapy (Topham & VanFleet, 2011).

PT is a suitable model for preschoolers but not necessarily the best form of treatment for all childhood presentations. Comprehensive parent, child and family assessment is needed to decide on the most optimal intervention for a given clinical presentation (Short, 2015). Further, the caregiver needs to be able to support the therapy when the child works through difficult issues, which may lead to regressive behaviour, increased arousal level, behavioural escalation or high expression of feelings. In some cases, active and regular involvement of the parent is needed, including a separate treatment of the parent whilst the child receives play therapy.

Further research is needed utilising well-designed research methodology to gain a better understanding of the treatment components of PT, the optimal length of treatment for various childhood disorders, and the best models for specific childhood presentations, with consideration of age, gender and cultural background of the child. Nevertheless, PT has taken an important place on the map of therapy options for young children, including as a stand-alone treatment modality, as an integrated model combining play therapy techniques with other treatment modalities, and finally, as an assessment tool that helps the therapist in the direction of treatment decisions. PT offers a rich choice of directive and child-centred techniques, and with this, is able to address effectively and in age-appropriate ways many of the clinical presentations of this young population of children referred for therapy. The recommended treatment length of 30 to 35 sessions for more complex presentations is a funding challenge in the current climate of mental health service delivery, with increasing pressure to reduce the overall number of sessions per client per year. Unless PT is provided within the protective realm of early intervention services with specially funded or public health services, play therapy interventions carry the risk of premature termination before an optimal level of change has occurred. PT also needs to continue to prove that it is efficient and that it can deliver superior and long-lasting outcomes compared with other competing treatment modalities for this age range, and this challenge will be the task of future play therapists and researchers.

Reader's Exercises

The following is an excerpt of a play therapy session with Tim (aged 4 years). The reader is encouraged to reflect on the therapy session, review the non-directive therapy variables and consider therapist responses.

> Tim and his mother Norma (age 31) were seen in parallel therapy sessions by two different therapists. Reasons for referral were longstanding conflicts between Norma and Tim, with Tim's demanding and non-compliant behaviour, tantrums and angry outbursts occurring frequently and daily. Norma shared with her own therapist that Tim was an unplanned pregnancy. She was living with Tim's father at the time. She described Tim's father as having extreme control needs, increasingly taking charge of her finances, cutting out her contact with her old friends and her relationship with her mum, a relationship which Norma described as having been fragile for all of her life. She described domestic violence in her parents' relationship during her growing up years, and she said she had lost contact with her father following the divorce of her parents when she was 13 years old. Norma said she had no memories of the pregnancy with Tim, was in a state of mental fog, and when Tim was born, could not find enjoyment in looking after the baby.

She developed postnatal depression (PND) and is still struggling with ongoing low moods. Seeking counselling following a crisis, she had just found out that she was pregnant again, and the pregnancy was the result of a casual relationship. She was contemplating an abortion but said she had had a Catholic upbringing, and an abortion was against the Church's beliefs. Norma also mentioned that her mother had moved interstate and that her mother had been providing regular childcare for Tim.

Tim initially presented as an anxious and shy boy. In the first 2 sessions, he did not talk much and asked a few questions, such as 'Will mum come back? When will we finish, is mum next door, what is the woman's name' (referring to the mother's therapist). He predominantly played with a toy train engine, trying to link up a carriage with great difficulty, which he then pushed towards the door of the playroom and then back to a spot near the therapist. The play theme was repeated over and over for another 2 sessions.

In session 4 there was a distinct change. He now appeared to feel free and started exploring various items in the play boxes. His utterances also increased. He gave the therapist jobs to do, such as holding paper and assisting him with a gluing task or opening the felt pens. He also wanted to know if other children would play in this room. He discovered the thumbnails, string and some wooden blocks in the play boxes. He asked for help pressing thumbnails into several wooden blocks and commented, 'When the other kids come, they will prick their fingers'. He then pulled a long string across the room, from the legs of the table to the legs of the chair, developing a spider web pattern and saying that these were booby traps. When the other kids came into the room they would fall and get trapped.

- What would be a safe way to reflect on the initial play with the toy train? What is Tim trying to convey? What is the possible meaning?

- In subsequent sessions, what do you think are his feelings about other children using the playroom or seeing the therapist? What are possible hypotheses? What responses might be helpful for this stage in therapy? What is the best timing for the responses?

References

Alivandi-Vafa, M., & Ismail, K. H. (2010). Parents as agents for change: What Filial Therapy has to offer. *Procedia- Social and Behavioral Sciences, 5*, 2165–2173. https://doi:10.1016/j.sbspro.2010.07.431

Andrews, C. (2010). *Who directs the play and why? An exploratory study of directive versus nondirective play therapy*. Theses, Dissertation, and Projects. 1169 Smith College School of Social Work: Northampton, Massachusetts. https://scholar-works.smith.edu.theses/1169

Baggerly, J. N., Ray, D. C., & Bratton, S. C. (2010). *Child-centred play therapy research: The evidence base for effective practice.* Wiley & Sons.

Bratton, S. C., & Landreth, G. L. (2006). *Child Parent Relationship Therapy (CPRT): Treatment manual.* Routledge. https://doi.org/10.4324/9780203956793

Bratton, S. C., Ray, D., Rhine, T., & Jones, L. (2005). The efficacy of Play Therapy with children: A meta-analytic review of treatment outcomes. *Professional Psychology: Research and Practice, 36*(4), 376–390.

Clarke, L., Ungerer, J., Chahoud, K., Johnson, S., & Stiefel, I. (2002). Attention Deficit Hyperactivity Disorder and attachment. *Clinical Child Psychology and Psychiatry, 7*(2), 179–198. https://doi.org/10.1177/1359104502007002006

Draper, K., Siegel C., White, J., Solis, C., & Mishna, F. (2009). Preschooler, Parent and Teacher (PPT): A preventive intervention with an at risk population. *International Journal of Group Psychotherapy, 59*(2), 221-242. https://doi.org/10.1521/ijgp.2009.59.2.221

Guzzi DelPo, E., & Frick, S. B. (1988). Directed and nondirected play as therapeutic modalities. *Children's Health Care, 16*(4), 261-267. https://doi.org/10.1207/s15326888chc1604_3

Hall, T.M., Kaduson, H. G., & Schaefer, C. E. (2002). Fifteen effective play therapy techniques. *Professional Psychology: Research and Practice, 33*(6), 515–522. https://doi.org/10.1037/0735-7028.33.6.515

Hirschfeld, M. R., & Wittenborn, A. K. (2016). Emotionally focused family therapy and play therapy for young children whose parents are divorced. *Journal of Divorce and Remarriage, 57*(2), 133–150. https://doi.org/10.1080/10502556.2015.1127878

Jayne, K. M. (2013). *Congruence, unconditional positive regard, and empathic understanding in child-centred play therapy.* Dissertation prepared for the degree of Doctor of Philosophy, University of North Texas. August 2013. Corpus ID: 141939018

Jones, K. D., Casado M., & Robinson, E. H. (2003). Structured play therapy: A model for choosing topics and activities. *International Journal of Play Therapy, 12*(1), 31–47. https://doi.org/10.1037/h0088870

Kenney-Noziska, S. G., Schaefer, C. E., & Homeyer, L. E. (2012). Beyond directive and nondirective: Moving the conversation forward. *International Journal of Play Therapy, 21*(4), 244–252. https://doi.org/10.1037/a0028910

Landreth, G. L. (2012). *Play therapy: The art of the relationship.* Routledge.

Lanktree, C. B., & Priere, J. N. (2017). *Treating complex trauma in children and families.* Sage.

Leggett, E. S., & Boswell, J. N. (2017). *Directive Play Therapy. Theories and techniques.* Springer.

Meschiany, A., & Krontal, S. (1998). Toys and games in play therapy. *The Israel Journal of Psychiatry and Related Sciences, 35*(1), 31–7.

Montemayor, L. (2014). *Exploring the effectiveness of child-centred play therapy in young children: A quantitative single case research design.* Texas A & M University, Corpus Christi.

Petersen, D., & Boswell, J. N. (2015). Play therapy in a natural setting: A case example. *Journal of Creativity in Mental Health, 10*, 62–76. https://doi:10.1080/15401383.2014.935545

Rassmussen, L. A., & Cunningham, C. (1995). Focused play therapy and non-directive play therapy: Can they be integrated. *Journal of Child Sexual Abuse, 4*(1), 1–20. https://doi.org/10.1300/JO70V04n01_01

Schaefer, C. E., & Cangelosi, D. M. (2016). *Essential play therapy techniques. Time-tested approaches.* Guilford Press.

Schauer, E., Neuner, F., Elbert, T., Ertl, V., Onyut, L., Odenwald M., & Schauer, M. (2004). Narrative exposure therapy in children: A case study. *Intervention 2*(1), 18–32. https://nbn-resolving.de/urn:nbn:de:bsz:352-opus-42151

Short, J. (2015). Play therapy: Working creatively with children. *InPsych 37 June* (3), Highlights. www.psychology.org.au

Stone, S., & Stark, M. (2013). Structured play therapy groups for preschoolers: Facilitating the emergence of social competence. *International Journal of Group Psychotherapy, 63*(1), 25-50. https://doi:10.1521/ijgp.2013.63.1.25

Topham, G., & VanFleet, R. (2011). Filial Therapy: A structured and straightforward approach to including young children in family therapy. *The Australian and New Zealand Journal of Family Therapy, 32*(2), 144–158. https://doi.org/10.1375/anft.32.2.144

VanFleet, R, Ryan, S. D., & Smith, S. K. (2005). Filial Therapy: A critical review. In L.A. Reddy, T.M. Files-Hall, & C.E. Schaefer (Eds.). *Empirically-based play interventions for children* (pp. 241–264). American Psychological Association. https://doi.org/10.1037/11086-012

Vigrass, A. (2011). *Connecting parents and children through Filial Therapy: Eight family therapy group session plan.* A project submitted to the school of graduate studies of the University of Lethbridge in partial fulfilment of the requirements for the degree Master of Education. February 2011. Faculty of Education, Lethbridge, Alberta. Retrieved from https://hdl.handle.net/10133/3403

Chapter 3

Cognitive Behaviour Therapy (CBT)

Matthew Brand, Ingeborg Stiefel and Tanya Hanstock

Cognitive Behaviour Therapy (CBT) is an umbrella term describing a group of treatment approaches that seek to understand and change unhelpful ways of thinking and learned patterns of behaviour with the help of a wide range of therapeutic strategies (Beck et al., 1979; Beck, 2020). CBT explores how thoughts (cognitions) impact emotions which then, in turn, influence one's behaviour. The main premise of CBT is that psychological problems are mostly based on learned, unhelpful ways of thinking and behaving and that people can learn more adaptive and effective ways of dealing with challenges. CBT helps clients to replace dysfunctional, unhelpful, irrational or negative thoughts with more helpful, balanced and rational thoughts. In the context of the therapeutic work with young children and their families, CBT can include the teaching of new skills, assertiveness training, problem-solving and anger management, and the behavioural components of the model are often more emphasised. CBT is a goal-oriented, structured, directive, and time-limited therapy. It is focused on current life challenges and encourages a collaborative working relationship between the client and the therapist. Being goal and action-focused, CBT focuses on what is perpetuating a problem rather than what originally caused it. However, it does also consider precipitating and presenting factors in the case formulation of a problem or symptoms. Since its inception in the 1960s, CBT has been one of the most widely used therapeutic models applied to psychological problems for people across the lifespan. CBT is a popular treatment modality for children as young as 3 years of age, addressing the spectrum of issues children may encounter, such as posttraumatic stress disorder (PTSD), anxiety, specific phobia, selective mutism, encopresis, anger and social issues. CBT is a well-researched model of psychotherapy with a strong evidence base for its effectiveness. CBT for young children can be offered in a range of therapy formats such as individual therapy, group therapy, a parent-only therapy for their child, as a family systems approach, and can be delivered both in person and online.

Historical Development of CBT

Miller (2003) states that CBT is the result of two revolutions in psychology, the behavioural and the cognitive. Blackwell and Heidenreich (2021) describe CBT as a family of approaches that have developed over four stages; the behavioural stage, the cognitive stage, the CBT stage and what has been described as the 'Third Wave of CBT'.

1. The Behavioural Stage

The behaviourist movement of the 20th century developed as a result of several important influences on the field of psychology. There was dissatisfaction with the then-popular Freudian psychoanalytic therapy with its focus on intra-psychic processes and lack of scientific evidence exploring treatment effects (Westbrook, 2007). Further, experimental psychology started to show that behaviour can change, can be observed, and new learning can occur with procedures involving both classical and operant conditioning. Pavlov, a Russian physiologist, showed in animal studies that learning occurs by associating a stimulus with a response. Pavlov's theory of classical conditioning was later confirmed in an experiment with an eleven-month-old infant called 'Little Albert' by the U.S. psychologist John Watson in the 1920s, where a phobia was created by pairing a white rat with a loud noise, creating a fear response in Albert. After conditioning (repeated exposure of Albert to the white rat and noise), Albert displayed the fear response to the white rat only (Watson & Raynor, 1920). Wolpe, in 1948, introduced systematic de-sensitisation as a treatment for anxiety, a treatment approach placed on neurophysiology and on the theory of classical conditioning (Blackwell & Heidenreich, 2021).

Also within the behavioural tradition, B. F. Skinner, a North American Psychologist, developed a different model for new learning and behavioural change called operant conditioning (Staddon & Cerutti, 2003). Operant conditioning focuses on the consequences that follow a behaviour, which can either increase or decrease the likelihood for that behaviour to re-occur. Behavioural Therapy became popular in the 1960s (Benjamin et al., 2011) and was able to show positive treatment gains with a relatively low number of treatment sessions (Westbrook, 2007).

2. The Cognitive Stage: The Development of Cognitive Theory

The second stage in the evolution of CBT is termed by Miller (2003) the 'cognitive counter-revolution to Behaviour Therapy'. This occurred with the development of cognitive theory, the realisation that internal processes can also shape people's behaviour, and dissatisfaction with the limitations of a purely behavioural approach, which did not give credit to thoughts, beliefs, interpretations and internal images, and neglected the process where people give meaning to events and that these different meanings can lead to vastly different behavioural outcomes (Westbrook, 2007). Cognitive therapy developed in the U.S. in the 1950s and 1960s (Westbrook) and is associated with Albert Ellis (Clinical Psychologist) and Aaron Beck (Psychiatrist), both trained in psychodynamic therapy. Ellis's approach, termed Rational Emotive Therapy (RET), focused on internal events, such as irrational beliefs, attitudes, thoughts, and conditioned assumptions, whereas Beck, 'the father of CBT', focused on conditional reflexes and control of behaviour (Blackwell & Heidenreich, 2021).

3. The Third Stage: The Development of CBT

The third stage of CBT integrated Behaviour Theory and Cognitive Theory (Kazantzis, 2021). All models of CBT attempt to change clients' relationships with their thoughts, but CBT also focuses on interpersonal effects and behaviour (Kazantzis, 2021). CBT brings cognitive phenomena into applied psychology but maintains an empirical approach which was so strongly emphasised in Behaviour Therapy. The principles of both behaviour theory and cognitive theory grew together into a formulated theory and practice of CBT to address major psychological issues (Benjamin et al., 2011). CBT developed in the 1980s, and this model is now well-established worldwide. The behavioural emphasis on empirical evidence is maintained in CBT with rigorous research designs, proving the model's effectiveness and efficacy. The first applications focused on the treatment of anxiety disorders (Blackwell & Heidenreich, 2021). The third stage of CBT is the main model still used with children, adolescents and adults.

4. The Fourth Stage: 'Third Wave CBT'

The final stage emerged in the late 1990s and early 21st century and is based on clinical experience, which revealed that standard CBT does not fit all client presentations. Kazantzis (2021) refers to a third, evolving wave of CBT. 'Third-wave CBT' is an umbrella term for CBT approaches that integrate new thinking and therapy practices, including holism, context, personal values, mindfulness, acceptance, spirituality and interconnectedness (Blackwell & Heidenreich, 2021). Whereas CBT challenges the client's unhelpful thinking and behaviour, 'Third Wave CBT' focuses on how clients relate to their experience. Blackwell and Heidenreich categorise several models as 'third wave' CBT models, such as Schema Therapy, Dialectic Behaviour Therapy (DBT), Acceptance and Commitment Therapy (ACT) and Mindfulness Based Cognitive Therapy.

The chapter in this book describes a CBT approach primarily based on the third stage of CBT. However, clinicians working with young children may also include therapy techniques from the behavioural stage and/or the 'Third Wave CBT' into a therapy plan.

Theoretical Underpinning and Assumptions

Beck's cognitive theory (1976), based on treating depression in adults, resulted in the development of several key concepts, including dysfunctional attitudes, cognitive errors, negative automatic thoughts, and the negative cognitive triad, which are negative thoughts about the self (e.g., 'I am hopeless'), the future (e.g., 'The future will be bad') and the world (e.g., 'The world is a horrible place').

A CBT case formulation is based on the diathesis–stress model proposed by Beck and colleagues (Beck, 1976). The diathesis–stress model explains the emergence of an emotional disorder in terms of a developmental and emotional vulnerability precipitated by stressful triggers, maintained by negative and self-defeating cognitive schemas, which include both emotional vulnerabilities represented in terms of verbalisable self-related cognitions called core self-beliefs, and rigid dysfunctional behaviours called coping strategies (Beck, 2011).

Dysfunctional attitudes are persistent attitudes that affect how information is processed by an individual. When an attitude is activated by an external stressor, cognitive errors occur, which distort thinking in an unrealistic way. Thoughts about the self, future and world are expressed via automatic negative thoughts, which influence how we feel and the symptoms of depression (Beck, 2020).

Kaplan et al. (1995) define CBT as a group of therapy approaches that aim to alter cognitive processes as a way of reducing problematic behaviours and distress. Inherent to all CBT models is the assumption that feelings and behaviours are primarily related to cognition, how we think, and includes people's beliefs, assumptions, presuppositions and interpretations of events in their lives. Consequently, CBT aims to change how we think, how we feel and how we behave. CBT assumes that distress or mental health problems are often the result of cognitive processing, in particular cognition distortions or deficits. Hopkins (2021), in his outline of Beck's theoretical model, summarises that cognitions strongly influence how people experience and deal with life's challenges. Cognitive vulnerability can be laid down early in life, especially from negative life experiences during critical developmental phases in the child's life and can invite cognitive distortion of reality.

There are different levels of cognition, each varying in their level of importance:

- **Core beliefs:** Core beliefs refer to deeply held beliefs that are central to a person's understanding of themselves, others, and/or the world. These core beliefs tend to act like a lens through which life experiences are interpreted. Negative core beliefs are often thought to have developed from negative early childhood experiences. Examples include 'There is something wrong with me', 'I am a bad person' and 'I am unlovable'.

- **Dysfunctional assumptions**: Assumptions are rigid beliefs or rules that people develop about themselves, other people or the world. Their rigidity means they are often unrealistic and maladaptive. Examples of assumptions include 'If I do everything perfectly, I will be good enough', 'I must never show my emotions to others', 'My dad loves my sister more' and 'If I behave, my parents will get back together'.

- **Automatic negative thoughts**: Automatic negative thoughts are negative thoughts that arise quickly and often come into the mind involuntarily, usually out of awareness, in response to an event or situation. Automatic negative thoughts might be produced after an event, such as someone not waving back or a child not being picked for a game, 'They don't like me', or when facing a difficult test, 'I can't do it', or when encountering an anxiety provoking situation such as going on a flying fox 'I will fall off it and hurt myself'.

Westbrook (2007) summarises six core principles of CBT. The first is the **Cognitive Principle** which postulates that peoples' emotional reactions and behaviours are strongly influenced by cognition. Different cognition can give rise to different emotions. The second core idea is based on the **Behaviour Principle**, which posits that behaviour, our action, and what we do, is crucial in both the maintenance and the change of cognitive states. The third principle, the **Continuum Principle**, perceives problems as being on a spectrum from normal to exaggerated or extreme versions of normalcy. This view contrasts with classification systems such as diagnostic categories, which categorise mental conditions as distinct disorders. The fourth principle refers to CBT as a present-focused model, interested in the **Here and Now** and focused mostly on current processes that maintain the problem. The fifth principle called the **Interacting Systems Principle**, proposes that problems develop as a result of interaction between cognitions, affects/emotions, behaviour and physiological states, including the person's environment. The final principle, the **Empirical Principle**, refers to the commitment of CBT to rigorous research exploring both theory and therapy endeavours of this treatment modality.

Core Therapy Techniques in CBT

Case Formulation: Prior to developing an intervention, the clinician should complete an assessment and develop a case formulation. A formulation is a way of organising relevant assessment information, and there are several case conceptualisation models available. The 5Ps model describes the main **P**resenting, **P**recipitating, **P**erpetuating, **P**redisposing, and **P**rotective aspects that have an impact on the presenting problem (Mcneil et al., 2012). Presenting the case formulation to the client may be the first part of psychoeducation for the client.

Psychoeducation: Psychoeducation is usually presented at the start of CBT, where the therapist typically explains the link between thoughts, feelings and behaviours. This forms the basis for providing an understanding of the central role unhelpful cognition and behaviours can have in the development and maintenance of the problem the client is seeking to address.

Goal Setting: Goals of therapy are explored, agreed upon, and reviewed on an ongoing basis. Goals should be clearly defined and measurable so that treatment progress can be clearly identified.

Positive Reinforcement: Positive reinforcement of appropriate behaviour can be utilised in a number of different ways, including self-reinforcement (e.g., positive self-talk statements), rewards (e.g., tangible objects) or enjoyable activities (e.g., walking on the beach). Social reinforcement from others (e.g., family) may also be used and can be especially powerful in encouraging clients to undertake new steps towards their goals.

Affect Education: Affect education assists the client in identifying and understanding core emotions such as anger, anxiety or sadness. Clients are taught the names of different feelings to help them understand the difference between a thought and a feeling. Physiological responses may also be part of this exploration (e.g., identifying bodily sensations or locating feelings in the body).

Affect Monitoring: The monitoring of emotions can help to identify when and where particular emotions occur and in which context (e.g., place, time, people present, activity the person was engaged in), which may include an exploration of accompanying cognitions.

Affect Management: Affect management approaches include formal relaxation strategies such as breathing, progressive muscle relaxation (PMR) or visual guided imagery to address strong feelings or physiological sensations in the client.

Thought Monitoring: Thought monitoring involves the recording of a person's thoughts and emotions in specific situations. The aim of this technique is to identify unhelpful, distorted and negative thoughts, core beliefs, automatic negative thoughts and assumptions, helping the client to become more aware of their presence and their negative effects.

Identifying Cognitive Distortions: This technique helps to identify specific cognitions and the effect these have on emotions and behaviours. Common cognitive distortions include 'all or nothing thinking' (either something is 100% right or 100% wrong) such as 'I am either a bad kid or a good kid', 'overgeneralisation' (because something bad happened once, it means it will happen over and over again) such as 'I could not ride my bike without the trainer wheels and I will never be able to ride a bike without trainer wheels', 'minimisation' (when something important happened it is not really a big deal) such as 'I only got that reward as the teacher felt sorry for me', or 'catastrophising' (a small incident is inflated to being very significant) for example 'I have ripped that part of the sticker when I peeled it off so it is all ruined now' to name a few.

Challenging Thoughts: Once identified, unhelpful cognitions can be evaluated and challenged, as well as being replaced by new cognitions. Balanced thinking or cognitive restructuring are terms used to describe this process. This may involve looking for new information about a particular cognition, looking from another person's perspective, exploring the evidence for and against a cognition, reflecting on the implications of holding a certain belief, possible reasons for the belief, and other approaches, to determine whether these cognitions are still relevant, or whether they can be altered or replaced with new cognitions that are more balanced or realistic. This technique is also called guided discovery or Socratic questioning (Padesky, 1993).

New Cognitive Skills: The range of new cognitive skills that can be taught is varied, but may include distraction, thought blocking, self-affirming statements (such as 'I can do it'), positive or helpful thoughts, and problem-solving skills.

Activity Scheduling: Activity scheduling can include planned activities between sessions that result in positive emotions or alternatively reduce activities that result in negative ones. This technique may also help clients create new routines or re-establish previous ones. Therapists can help clients break down a large number of items or seemingly large tasks into smaller and more manageable sections, as well as plan when these tasks will be completed. This may also reduce procrastinating and repeated decision-making. Behavioural monitoring with the help of charts can be helpful in assessing progress.

Behavioural Experiments: Clients are encouraged to take risks and experiment with particular tasks. Sometimes, thoughts about 'what will occur' versus 'what did occur' after the experiment are contrasted and help clients re-evaluate some of their beliefs and thoughts.

Exposure: Exposure in vivo (real life) or imagined is commonly used in the treatment of anxiety or trauma and involves the client confronting the feared object, situation or activity in a safe way, with gradual mastery of the steps from the least to the most anxiety arousing tasks.

Role Play, Modelling and Practice: Role plays allow clients to practice and experiment with new skills in the safe environment of the therapy session first. Different responses can be tested out and practised, and the client can explore which response may work best before implementing the strategy in a real-life situation.

CBT with Young Children

CBT with young children within the age range of 3–6 years needs adaptation of the typical CBT techniques for older children, adolescents and adults due to the child's language and cognitive capacity and the child's dependency on relevant caregivers. CBT involves identifying and challenging unhelpful cognitions and replacing them with more adaptive thoughts, which requires some level of cognitive processing, abstract thinking, and sometimes perspective-taking of others. Some authors may argue that CBT may be more suitable for middle childhood or older children (Kaplan et al., 1995). However, we agree with MacGregor and Herger (2011) that CBT can be used with young children when concepts have been simplified and play and narrative components are integrated to suit the developmental abilities of the child. We also recommend the utilisation of concrete visual aids and more focus on behaviour. The term Cognitive Behavioural Play Therapy, for example, integrates play therapy with CBT concepts that are developmentally appropriate for young children (Knell, 1998). For very young children, the cognitive component of the intervention may be limited, and cognitive strategies may be provided to the child (e.g., positive self-talk) rather than developed in a collaborative approach. CBT interventions for young children can have significant behavioural components, and some may question whether these approaches can really be called CBT.

Clinicians should also be mindful that many thoughts that children have may be realistic, depending on the level of family functioning. The cognition 'I am not safe' may be a realistic appraisal of a dangerous domestic violence situation and, therefore not an irrational belief that can be challenged in CBT. CBT is also contraindicated if a child's cognitions reflect a parent's maladaptive view of capacity (Kaplan et al., 1995). Therefore, a thorough initial assessment of the child and the child's context is paramount.

Assessment

Assessment in CBT is generally conducted through the biopsychosocial model (Engel, 1977). Increasingly, for young children, it is also being conducted through a family systems lens (Mash, 2006). It may include one assessment session with the whole family or two sessions with the parents at one appointment and the child at another, depending on how much sensitive information needs to be discussed and the requirements of the service the clinician is working in.

In our practice with very young children, we initially spend a considerable amount of time discussing the current problems, asking questions about what the problem looks like in the child's behaviour, how the family responds, what behaviours occur, cognitions (or what is said by the child, usually at the time the problem occurs), what increases or reduces the intensity or frequency of the problem, what the family have tried, and how much the problem affects the child and the family. This generally occurs for each primary problem. We then obtain a family genogram, going back at least three generations (child, parent, grandparents) and sometimes four (if relevant), highlighting those that are particularly important and who provide additional care for the child. We then obtain a general history to understand the biopsychosocial factors that influence the problem, including pregnancy, exposure to medications or substances, how the parent felt about the pregnancy, the post-natal period, early temperament of the child, the parent–child relationship, general development (speech/language, motor, cognitive/learning, social, emotional, independence, sensory concerns), previous involvement from other health professionals, vision and hearing, bodily functioning (sleeping, toileting, weight, feeding), medical history, medications, family history of mental health and neurodevelopmental concerns, parent occupation and functioning, other people who help out with the family, court orders, apprehended violence orders, access arrangements (if applicable), social functioning, traumatic/stressful events for the whole family (not just the child) since the child was conceived and sometimes earlier, domestic violence, parental mental health and substance use, culture, and what the family think and feel about coming here.

Further assessment may be conducted focusing on a specific problem or disorder, often with multiple comorbidities. For example, if the primary concern is anxiety, a clinician may also ask specific questions such as physiological sensations, somatic complains, avoidance behaviour, past stressful experiences, parental anxiety, cognitions, the strength of these cognitions (on a rating scale), and any statements the child has made about their fear (e.g., they have said they are afraid a robber will break in the house). If the primary concern was trauma, questions might be asked about the traumatic event, how sudden the event was, how family members reacted, changes to the family since the trauma, trauma symptoms (e.g., re-experiencing, avoidance) and what the child was told about the event, among others.

A summary is provided to the parent about the clinician's understanding of the main concerns. The clinician may feel that additional assessments (e.g., meeting with grandparents, preschool observation), psychometric testing through the use of questionnaires or more formal measures (e.g., a cognitive assessment) or involvement of other professionals is needed at this stage (e.g., psychiatrist, occupational therapist). Part of the assessment process may result in consultation with a diagnostic manual and a diagnosis being made. We prefer to view assessment as an ongoing process, and our case conceptualisation and treatment may change as we know the child and family better and in response to the treatment.

Establishing Rapport With both Child and Caregiver

As with any therapy, establishing a therapeutic relationship and good rapport is highly important for both the child and the parent/caregiver. In the context of therapy with very young children, rapport building often involves play, as it is generally considered the language of children (Landreth, 2012). Depending on the child and the stage of therapy, this may range from unstructured child-led play to structured play with a particular therapeutic goal in mind. A child who is unwilling to communicate their thoughts and feelings or engage in therapy is unlikely to benefit from CBT, and an alternative treatment may be needed. Parent rapport is also vital, as parents will be bringing children to treatment, helping children to understand concepts, providing support and encouragement to develop new skills, completing homework, and providing rewards for participation in therapeutic tasks. The collaborative relationship between the therapist and the client has often been found to be the main factor in treatment success (Dattilio & Hanna, 2012).

Goal Setting: Developing a Therapy Plan

Goal setting in child CBT is often problem-specific or disorder specific. Similar to adult CBT, goal setting follows the SMART formula: **S**imple, **M**easurable, **A**chievable, **R**ealistic and **T**ime Limited. Parents are active participants in goal setting, but children are also asked to make a contribution towards their goal. The reason for seeking treatment is explained to the child in developmentally appropriate ways, avoiding blaming or stigmatising language, asking for a commitment from the child, and building the child's motivation as a joint partnership with the clinician in addressing this goal. This might include discussing how the problem gets in the way of life, an activity the child wants to do (e.g., sleepover) or simply so the child will feel better or differently. At times, the child may be ambivalent about treatment, but the parent is highly motivated for the child to engage. In these situations, a discussion about potential rewards may help to increase motivation to change.

Parents as Active Participants in Treatment

One of the challenges in CBT with young children is their ability to reliably report their feelings and behaviours. This often means that parents are providing information about their child based on their observations. Parents play a vital part in their treatment to ensure that skills are practised and homework tasks are completed. For children who are oppositional or non-compliant, general behavioural strategies may be needed. In Trauma Focused-CBT (TF-CBT), for example, parents may be taught how to use traditional parent-training techniques, such as active ignoring, labelled praise, how to give commands and strategies for non-compliance such as time out (Cohen et al., 2017).

Core Techniques Used in CBT With Young Children

The following are core techniques in CBT that have been adapted for young children. Some of these are highly consistent with adult-based CBT concepts, such as using relaxation as a competing response to anxiety-provoking stimuli; others have been clearly adapted for a younger audience, and some adult CBT techniques may not be considered appropriate for very young children, whereas other techniques are unique to CBT for very young children and would not be suitable for adolescents or adults. Get Lost Mr Scary, an early intervention program for children with anxiety aged 5–7 years, is a prototypical Australian program for adapting CBT concepts to young children and is referenced throughout. Other programs will also be referenced where applicable in explaining a technique.

Psychoeducation

Psychoeducation in CBT with young children can take many forms and may include education about what a particular problem is (e.g., what is anxiety, what is encopresis), or it can involve an exploration of a particular event the child has witnessed or experienced. This is often completed in a format appropriate for children and sometimes a separate parent education session. This in itself may correct some assumptions or maladaptive beliefs that children and parents may have (e.g., 'It was my fault that daddy hit mummy because I did not eat my dinner'). Parents are often taught the relationship between thoughts, feelings and behaviours and the cognitive triangle. In our experience, some young children can differentiate between a 'thought', a 'feeling' and a 'behaviour' and role-play this in a scenario but do require adult assistance to make a causative link between them. Depending on the referral problem, it can be helpful to provide education about different feeling states in developmentally appropriate ways, utilising visual charts depicting faces with basic emotions.

In Get Lost Mr Scary (GLMS), psychoeducation is taught in several playful ways, including the use of songs (the Get Lost Mr Scary song), identifying feelings that occur in the body by using a life-sized paper and tracing the child's body, stories, and by using of a rating thermometer (MacGregor & Herger,

2011). Psychoeducation about feelings may also involve children looking at somebody's face or body posture and guessing what the feeling might be. Minde et al. (2010) use the String Test (adapted by Vollmar, 2004), where a child is shown a picture of a child with a small weight attached to the end of a string. Therapists demonstrate how this weight can move by 'thinking about it moving' instead of trying to actively do so. The child is then given an opportunity to practice the same task and is often amazed when they are able to make the weight move just by thinking about it. Therapists then reinforce the concept of 'mind power' and that 'we can use our brain to talk back to scary thoughts'.

Affect Regulation/Relaxation

Many CBT programs for young children focus on methods to manage strong emotions, including coping strategies and relaxation. In terms of relaxation, children can be taught a range of slow breathing techniques, using characters, animals, or props to help facilitate learning. For example, children might be taught 'candle and rose breathing'. In this technique, a child uses their index finger as a prop. First, children are asked to pretend that their finger is a rose and to take a deep breath in to see how the flower smells. Children then pretend their finger is a candle on a birthday cake, and they practice taking a deep breath out to blow out the candle. Other techniques and metaphors can be used, including bubble breathing (breathing in and pretending to blow a bubble), balloon breathing (inflating the stomach with air, like a balloon) and dragon breathing (deep breathing in and breathing out fire like a dragon).

Children can also be taught to use PMR. This can be popular with young children who enjoy pretending to do various poses, such as giving themselves a big bear hug, flexing their muscles like a superhero, or scrunching up their face like they are eating a sour lolly. Other metaphors may be to tense up like uncooked spaghetti and then relax like cooked spaghetti or walk around like a stiff robot and then pretend to be a floppy jellyfish. There are a number of apps, video recordings, scripts and audio recordings available that are designed to appeal to young children.

Positive Reinforcement

Rewards are often used in CBT to reinforce positive behaviours such as completing homework, practising a particular skill or attempts at exposure exercises. Rewards can be in the form of verbal praise or tangible rewards (such as stickers), as we have found young children are less likely to find 'self-reward' motivating. Rewards may be small, medium or large, and usually, a system for how a child earns a reward, such as a sticker chart or collection of tokens, is discussed and agreed to with the parent and the child.

Role-play, Modelling, Practice and Stories

Therapists often model skills or concepts taught in session using puppets, props or characters that represent the problem. For example, therapists model the 'Butch the Watchdog' story in GLMS, where children are read a story of a dog who is scared of noises at night, which turn out to be a possum looking for food (MacGregor & Herger, 2011). However, the possum is also scared of dogs during the day. When they eventually meet, they realise they are afraid of each other. During the story, we use a dog, possum, bin and doghouse props and ask children to participate in the story's actions. The goal of this activity is to help children understand whether Butch's fear was silly (irrational) or sensible (rational), which many pre-schoolers can understand.

Role plays with miniatures (small toys) may also be used in situations that are more relevant to a particular child, for example, fear of cockroaches crawling onto a child, fear of being embarrassed, separating at preschool, or climbing up a really tall slide and sliding down. Therapists can role-play these situations using small figurines, and then children are invited to take a turn to role-play the situation. Therapists may encourage the child to try out new techniques such as slow breathing before going up the slide or using coping thoughts such as 'slides are made for kids to have fun'. Children can then role-play this situation and often gain some sense of mastery and understanding of what techniques they might try when they next face that situation.

Role plays are also particularly useful in social skills development. In our practice, we often role-play a social skill (e.g., body distance and eye contact) or how to manage a problem social situation, such as what the child should do when someone says something mean, is physically aggressive or takes something from them. Role plays often include modelling of the 'wrong way' and the 'right way' by the clinician, with children being asked what they noticed in each situation (e.g., 'Did I use good eye contact or did I look at the ground?', 'Did I use a clear voice, or did I mumble?'). Children are then invited to 'act out' only the right way. Labelled praise is given to the child for what they did well and suggestions for what they can try next time. For small problems (e.g., a child sticking their tongue out at them), we teach children to say 'stop it' and give three chances, and if the problem has not been solved, to walk away. For big problems (e.g., the child is getting hurt), we teach preschool children to tell an adult straight away. In our practice, we use props, including a Hollywood clacker board and pretend we are directing a movie, saying 'Lights, Camera, Action!' before each role play. For those with a video camera, children particularly enjoy recording and watching back themselves. We generally role-play the same situation until a child engages in 'good enough' assertive communication to solve the problem. Children are often given homework to practice this skill in real-life situations should it occur again.

Parents are also important role models for their children, and parents are especially helpful in modelling the skills for children to use at home or in challenging moments. This may include parent modelling of relaxation tasks and the use of cognitive strategies. It is generally recommended that when a parent models, they show the steps in problem-solving rather than mastery of the task (Rapee et al., 2008). For example, if a parent is modelling an exposure task for fear of heights, the parent may need to demonstrate fear ('Oh, it's very high, I am shaking!'), a coping statement ('It's ok, I am safe'), and a behavioural technique (e.g., breathing) before demonstrating the exposure task (walking to the edge of a building). This is in contrast to a parent who shows mastery, for example, a parent who goes to the edge of a building and says, 'See, it is not scary'.

The concept of practice is also important to highlight, as children will not be expected to master particular techniques and strategies immediately but will be required to practice them in session or at home as part of their homework. In GLMS, a section of the program focuses on how children get better when practising a particular skill (e.g., riding a bike) (MacGregor & Herger, 2011). They do this by role-playing a situation with a small child toy and a miniature bike. The child on the toy bike falls off initially, but by continuing to practice, they progressively get better and better with the skill until they can master it, doing backflips and tricks by the fifth attempt. Children are then provided with a range of miniature toys, and they have an opportunity to demonstrate a skill that they themselves have practised with the miniatures, showing the progression from learning a new skill to mastery. Common tasks that children practice include kicking a ball into soccer goals, learning to swim, writing their name, or learning the rules of a new game. Children respond well to this technique, particularly to exaggerated fails and silly scenarios. Practice as a concept is also applied to techniques learned in treatment, such as slow breathing or sensible thinking.

Rating Scales

Rating scales are integrated into many CBT programs. They can be used to measure the severity of a particular behaviour or feeling (e.g., 'Were you nervous, worried, scared or terrified?') and provide a marker of improvement, such as measuring the level of fear between sessions or after a certain technique is completed. For example, measuring a child's fear of spiders (6/10), completing an exposure exercise (watching a 10-second video of spiders), and then measuring the child's fear of spiders again (4/10).

In GLMS, a life-sized ruler is developed with three faces of varying levels of anxiety and numbers from 0 to 10, and children can walk between each rating (MacGregor & Herger, 2011). In Minde et al. (2010), children are asked to rate the intensity of their fear using a 'fear thermometer' and are asked to re-rate their fears on a weekly basis. We find that there can be considerable variability in these ratings from week to week. We also found that some fears can reduce dramatically following one or two exposure exercises.

Rating scales can be too cognitively demanding for some children, and instead of a scale from 0–10, this may be reduced to a scale from 1 to 5, a scale from 1 to 3 using symbols (e.g., a small star for 1, a medium star for 2, a big star for 3), or a two-point scale, such as a picture of a happy or sad face, or simply a child giving a thumbs up or down.

Behavioural Experiments

Behavioural experiments are often completed in the context of a homework assignment. Experiments are usually integrated into exposure exercises or in the development of new skills. For example, a child may be asked to experiment and see whether 'telling the teacher when a child hits you' resolved a situation or made it worse. Other experiments might be to practice a newly learned skill, such as walking away from a situation or telling an adult when something happens.

Identifying Thoughts, Challenging Thoughts and New Coping Skills

Cognitive interventions focus on thoughts that children may have in response to various scenarios. GLMS uses the concept of 'Silly' and 'Sensible' fears. This is discussed in several scenarios, such as children running away from tigers hiding behind a bush (sensible fear), children running away from bears that are chasing after them (sensible fear), and children running away from small puppy dogs that are wagging their tail (silly fear). These scenarios are brought to life with the use of small miniature toys, and clinicians can integrate puppets and other props to role-play the concepts. A very engaging example is a role-play of a scuba diver swimming with a puppet shark, where the scuba diver has the thought, 'Sharks are nice and won't bite me', followed by the scuba diver getting eaten. This 'sensible fear' is later contrasted to 'silly fears' such as being afraid of a cockroach which realistically can do no harm to a child.

The concept of 'Silly' and 'Sensible' thoughts is also introduced to explain how people can have polarising thoughts about the same exact situation. An example of a situation might be a young child and their mother walking down the street when they see a police officer. The clinician may role-play this with small dolls that represent the girl, one representing the mother, and one representing the police officer. As the girl gets closer to the police officer, she screams hysterically and says to herself, 'Ahhhhhhh! It's a police officer! They are going to arrest me and send me to jail!' and the clinician pretends the girl is running away home. Most children between 4–6 years of age can understand that this is a silly thought and response to the situation. The clinician then role plays a sensible thought situation, where the girl walks nearby the police office and says to herself, 'The police are here to protect me. I feel safe', and then continues to walk with her mother. Again, most young children can understand that this is a sensible thought and sensible response. Later in the program, children are encouraged to identify silly and sensible thoughts and practice enough so that they may eventually think of their own sensible thoughts.

GLMS also utilises stories and characters as a core component of their program. There are two characters, 'Mr Scary' and 'Mrs. Worry' who appear throughout the program and laugh at others and are the 'baddies' in the group. They get upset when the children start to show brave behaviours or practice some of the tasks. In several sessions, children throw paper balls at these characters and tell them firmly to 'Get Lost!' In other stories, 'Worried Wally' is afraid of moving to a new school, and children are asked to find 'silly' and 'sensible' thoughts that Wally may have. Children are then shown green balloons representing sensible thoughts and white balloons which represent silly thoughts. Children are asked to give an example of a silly thought, and clinicians write silly thoughts on the white balloons and practice letting them go. Children are also asked to give an example of a sensible thought, and the clinician writes them on the green balloons and ties them up so they can keep them. Children who cannot generate a silly or sensible thought themselves might be asked if a particular given thought is silly or sensible. Children can then take these balloons home with them to help them remember the concept of sensible thoughts.

Detective Dave is also a character introduced into the program to introduce the concept of 'Detective Thinking' and look for evidence of whether a particular thought is true or not. Detective Dave is one of the group facilitators dressed up in costume (which the children very much enjoy guessing is the real facilitator). After introducing himself and with his magnifying glass, Detective Dave talks about the girl who ran away from the police officer in the previous role play. He asks the children if the police really do put children in jail and what a police officer's job really is. Many children, even if they struggle to think of evidence themselves, can usually answer questions with a 'yes' or 'no' to these silly and sensible statements.

Children with limited cognitive or language abilities can often role-play scenarios they have experienced using small props and characters to represent people. By having a 'baddy' character and a 'goody' character that represents the child (usually held by the child), the baddy can pretend to talk to the child's character, verbalising the negative or unhelpful thoughts the child may have or that they may have said to the parent in difficult moments. The child often naturally talks back to the baddy, verbalising self-help statements. For example, with one child, the baddy (talking three-headed dragons) was breathing fire and laughing that there were robbers outside the house, and they would break in. The goody (the child, represented by a chicken puppet) challenged this unhelpful thought by saying, 'No, they won't; the windows are locked'. The dragon continued to provide lots of what-if statements, such as 'What if they weren't checked', 'What if the window just opened by itself', and 'What if mum was asleep and didn't hear', to which the child provided sensible and realistic answers for.

In our experience, we have found that young children are often unable to generate their own silly and sensible thoughts when asked to think about their own experiences. For example, if the clinician asks, 'What was a silly thought you had last night when you were scared?' or 'What could be a sensible thought for nighttime?'. Role play with props offers multi-sensory cues (visual, auditory, action), which appear to help with cognitive processing and self-assessment and represent a common learning format appropriate for children in the preschool age.

Developing New Skills

Young children often have difficulty generating alternative coping thoughts, and instead, children may be provided with very short coping statements, also known as 'mantras' or 'personal affirmations', which can be repeated when needed. Examples of short mantras include 'I am safe', 'I am ok' or 'slow breath'. We often write these mantras down or use visuals (e.g., a picture of someone breathing) to help children remember to use these skills.

Problem-solving skills may also be taught to a child. One technique that can be developed for a younger audience is the 'Turtle Technique' (Schneider & Robin, 1974). This technique asks children to withdraw into their imaginary shell (like a turtle), where their hands, legs and head come in close to their body and say to themselves, 'Turtle'. Older children may come up with or may be provided with a coping statement (e.g., 'I am ok'). Children are encouraged and rewarded for practising this technique at home as well as using this technique in real-life settings.

Homework

Homework ensures that concepts taught are reinforced in real life, and many children who have started school are used to some form of homework exercises. Homework is often checked at the start of each session, and new homework is provided at the end. In anxiety treatment, children are encouraged to practice a particular skill initially in a safe environment when their stress levels are low, progressing towards using the same technique in real life during a mildly to moderately stressful situation. Eventually, the goal is to use the same technique in the feared real-life situation. In anger management, children may be taught to use a skill initially when calm, then when they start to feel that anger is building up, and later in real-life situations where the child often reacts in an angry way (e.g., when their brother goes into their room). Often very young children have difficulty using practised strategies in high-stress situations due to their emerging ability to self-control, and instead, the CBT therapist may set a behavioural monitoring assignment for the parent to identify and prevent high-risk situations from occurring in the first place (e.g., 'Your brother will go to time out if he goes into your room', or 'Tell me if he goes in your room and I will deal with it').

Exposure

Exposure is one of the primary techniques in the treatment of anxiety-based disorders and posttraumatic disorder (Chorpita & Delaiden, 2007). Exposure means that children progressively face their fears, from mild fears to increasingly more intense fears. For example, a child may start out facing a fear that is rated a 3 out of 10 (mild fear). Once the child starts to master these small fears, children are encouraged to focus on more medium fears (e.g., 5 out of 10) and then on to high fears (8 out of 10). The pacing of exposure is an art, as moving too quickly through the exposure hierarchy can be too overwhelming for some children and as a result, they may be very reluctant to participate in any future exposure tasks, with some children even resisting coming back to treatment at all.

In GLMS, MacGregor and Herger (2011) address exposure by using miniature toys and figures as a means of vicarious exposure but do not directly require the child to do this in real life. In TF-CBT, a trauma narrative is developed midway through treatment, where the child is asked to recall the traumatic event that occurred in detail (Cohen et al., 2017). A trauma narrative is thought to be an exposure technique where a child recalls and elaborates on the trauma, which is intended to desensitise a child to trauma reminders and decrease avoidance and hyperarousal. In TF-CBT, children are asked to share this with the therapist first and eventually their parent. The trauma narrative also aims to identify and then later correct any maladaptive cognitions. Children may also complete in-vivo exposure tasks, where children are exposed to situations that may be trauma reminders and use strategies they have previously learned to manage their arousal level.

Activity Scheduling

Activity scheduling may be chosen to increase a child's experience of positive emotions or to complete daily tasks. This usually involves looking at a weekly schedule and scheduling a pleasurable activity or task. For a depressed child, an activity might be to go to the park and play on the equipment for 30 minutes three times a week. Quality time with a parent can be a special form of activity scheduling and is often the most sought-after experience, such as playing a favourite game or going to the park. This technique may also be known as 'attending'.

Children may also have activities broken down into manageable sequences that they struggle to complete, usually in visual form. A common schedule for pre-schoolers is to get ready in the morning, which might include waking up, eating breakfast, getting dressed and then brushing their teeth. Visuals can be used to demonstrate each step in various rooms of the house, and visuals can sometimes be moved from the 'unfinished' to 'finished' column to represent when each of these tasks has been completed.

Relapse Prevention

Relapse prevention is a technique that identifies antecedents to problems re-emerging or how to manage situations if things start to unravel. In GLMS, the characters of Mr Scary and Mrs Worry are eventually arrested by Detective Dave and either sent to jail or a deserted island where they cannot bother the children. However, they might find a way to come back and cause more problems in the future (MacGregor & Herger, 2011). At the last session, children are provided with coping cards (cards with pictures of the strategies that the children learned) to help them remember the skills they used during the program for a future time.

The Therapy Environment and Materials for CBT with Young Children

CBT with young children requires the use of resources, including toys, props, stories, exercise booklets, and printouts of homework exercises. Children are typically given homework that does not require any writing or reading, such as asking children to colour in a picture from a story they have listened to, draw a particular situation or event, to colour in the 'coping statement' from a choice of either a 'non-coping' and 'coping' statements, practice a technique (e.g., breathing) or to complete an exposure task. Parents are generally expected to help the child complete homework, write down any relevant details in the child's homework and provide rewards and encouragement for completion of tasks.

Evidence Base of CBT with Young Children

There have been several outcome studies on the effectiveness of CBT in pre-schoolers, mostly focusing on anxiety disorders. Minde et al. (2010) studied the effectiveness of CBT in 37 young children with anxiety, with parents attending part of each treatment session. Results of this study suggested that there was significant improvement from pre–post-treatment assessments, with an average of 8.3 treatment sessions. In their program, Hirshfield-Becker et al. (2010) completed a randomised controlled trial comparing 34 children with anxiety disorders who received a parent–child CBT intervention compared to 30 children in a 6-month waitlist control. Results suggested a significant decrease in anxiety disorders and an increase in parent-rated coping to controls, with treatment gains maintained at 1-year follow-up. They also reported that treatment response was unrelated to age or parental anxiety but negatively predicted by behavioural inhibition. Monga et al. (2015) compared a parent–child and parent-only CBT intervention with 77 children aged 5–7 years with an anxiety disorder. They found both treatments showed significant improvements post-intervention at follow-up, with significantly greater improvement noted in the child–parent intervention compared to the parent-only intervention. Bergman et al. (2013), in their pilot randomised controlled trial of 21 children with selective mutism aged 4–8 years of age, found a significant increase in speech after treatment compared to waitlist controls, with gains maintained at 3-month follow-up.

TF-CBT has been trialled with 64 3–6-year-old children randomly assigned to TF-CBT or a 12-week waitlist (Scheeringa et al., 2011). Results of this study suggested that the intervention group improved in symptoms of posttraumatic stress disorder compared to the control (but not other scales), and after the intervention group was completed for all children, effect sizes were large for improvements in posttraumatic stress disorder symptoms, depression, anxiety and oppositional defiant disorders. The majority of participants in the study were reported to be of a minority race without a biological father in the home, which the authors noted as a point of difference to other efficacy studies. A recent systematic review of TF-CBT with children aged 3–6 years (McGuire et al., 2021) concluded that TF-CBT appears to be a 'level two' or 'probably efficacious' intervention based on available evidence but note that TF-CBT does suggest considering the child's cognitive and language abilities, family context and culture.

In Australia, the four main CBT programs for pre-schoolers are the GLMS program, Fun FRIENDS, Cool Little Kids and the Take Action Program.

The GLMS program was compared in a non-randomised controlled trial to a waitlist for 134 children with anxiety aged 5–7 years in schools (Ruocco et al.,

2016). Results of this study suggested that children who attended the program showed significant reductions in anxiety and behaviour symptoms compared to children in the control group who showed no change. Once receiving the program, the control group also showed a similar improvement.

In their trial with 31 children (5–7 years) diagnosed with an anxiety disorder, the *Fun FRIENDS program* resulted in a significant decrease in measures of anxiety and behaviour inhibition and improvements in a measure of resiliency post-intervention and at 12-month follow-up; however, no control group was available for comparison (Barrett et al., 2015). Some evidence of the effectiveness of Fun FRIENDS has also been demonstrated in Brazil (Rinaldin Garcia et al., 2019).

Cool Little Kids (Rapee et al., 2010) is a preventative program for anxiety that was developed by researchers at Macquarie University. It is a six-session parent-only program for parents with children aged between 3 and 6 years to help improve confidence in children and to reduce the likelihood of the child developing an anxiety disorder. A randomised control trial of 146 inhibited preschool-aged children in Cool Little Kids was compared with a monitoring-only condition. The children who received the treatment had less frequency and severity of anxiety disorders and lower levels of anxiety symptoms on maternal, paternal and child reports.

The Take Action Program (Waters et al., 2008) is an engaging Australian-developed CBT program for children aged 4–7 years. There are books that clinicians use for the program (The Take Action Practitioner Guidebook) that details the assessment and treatment of child anxiety. This is used with the companion workbooks: Take Action Child Handout Workbook and Take Action Parent Handout Workbook. The program involves psychoeducation, somatic management, cognitive restructuring, exposure therapy, problem-solving, social skills development, assertiveness training and relapse prevention and maintenance using cartoon pictures of animals. The Take Action program has over 10 years of research and has been shown to be effective in reducing anxiety symptoms in children (Waters et al., 2009).

Training in CBT

Therapists using CBT must first have experience working with young children and their caregivers. They also require a good understanding of CBT theory and its application to young children. Therapists need to be creative and enthusiastic. They must be able to develop rapport with children and their parents, and other important people relevant to the treatment. They must be willing to be silly, creative, use humour, occasionally sing songs, complete puppet shows, act out scenarios, and make silly voices in a way that is appealing to young children. Clinicians who know good magic tricks, jokes, and puppeting techniques and have a range of resources will help to engage children more readily.

CBT is often the primary model in clinical psychology programs, meaning that many psychologists already have a good understanding of the theory, practice and evidence base of CBT. Developing psychologists may need additional practice and supervision in the application of these techniques in developmentally appropriate ways and integrating play into treatment. For those without CBT training at university level, there are numerous short courses, certificates and diplomas focussing specifically on developing skills in CBT techniques.

Clinicians may also be interested in training for CBT with a particular model or disorder. For example, the GLMS training component. TF-CBT has a newly developed training model in Australia and several textbooks, including the second edition treatment manual (Cohen et al., 2017), and TF-CBT treatment applications, including play adaptations for younger children and those with developmental disabilities. TF-CBT requires participants to complete an online course, attendance at a 2-day course, 12 months of ongoing supervision, and a knowledge test before being accredited. A manualised CBT intervention has also been developed for selective mutism (Bergman, 2013).

Case Example

Daniel is a 5-year-old boy referred by his mother due to extreme clinginess. Every time she tried to drop Daniel off at school, Daniel would resist and cry. When his mother left, he would continue to be upset for up to 30 minutes. Additional fears included fear of monsters and the dark, and Daniel would follow his mother around the house 'Like a little shadow'.

After the initial assessment with both Daniel and his mother, standardised assessments utilising questionnaires revealed that Daniel had significant anxiety and met the diagnostic criteria for a Separation Anxiety Disorder. Some obsessive and repetitive behaviours were also noted. Psychoeducation on anxiety was provided to his mother, which included information about common types of anxiety disorders in young children and their prevalence. An outline of the treatment plan was also provided.

In the first treatment session, the clinician introduced puppets and asked Daniel to choose a puppet he liked. He initially chose a monkey puppet, and when asked what their name was, he said 'Cheeky'. The clinician also chose a puppet, named them and modelled talking to the puppet and the puppet whispering back to him. The clinician then explained the fear thermometer and asked Daniel to rate how scary particular scenarios would be out of 10, such as going to a lolly shop, going to his friend's house, being in an earthquake, and being at school. He was able to rate these fears appropriately using the fear scale and appeared to understand the concept.

The clinician then asked Daniel how intense his fear was of 'Being away from mum' using the fear thermometer. Daniel was silent. The clinician suggested that Daniel whisper into Cheeky's ears what he would like to say, which he was able to do. The clinician then asked if Daniel could whisper to his mum, which he was also able to do. With Daniel's permission, his mother stated his fear thermometer number was '10'. Through this process of whispering either to his puppet or his mother, Daniel rated a number of big fears, including getting hurt, getting in trouble, fear of the dark, heights, ghosts, monsters, his parents going out, asking questions in class, being bullied, being away from home, dogs, loud noises, being late, germs, school and feeling sick. He rated most of these fears between 8–10 intensity out of a maximum of 10 on the fear thermometer, with few medium fears endorsed.

The clinician then demonstrated the concept of 'practice' and 'brain power' with an example of a boy who was learning to skateboard, falling off several times before riding the skateboard without falling off, and eventually, with more practice doing flips and tricks. The clinician asked Daniel to choose from a selection of toys, something that he had not been very good at initially but then got better at with practice. Daniel chose a small bike toy and demonstrated riding his bike. His mother commented that Daniel fell off his bike the first time he tried, but with practice, he is now really good at riding.

The clinician then demonstrated the 'string test' technique from Minde et al. (2010), which asks children to move a weight attached to the string by only thinking about it. Daniel was impressed with this trick and attempted to complete it without success in the session. Homework was set for Daniel to a) draw his puppet and b) practice using the 'brain power' technique at home to see if he could move the string only by thinking about it.

In the second session, Daniel had completed his homework of drawing his puppet. He had also mastered the brain power trick and had demonstrated it to his siblings and extended family. A review of the fears suggested no change in his ratings, and he was able to now verbalise these to the clinician. Daniel, in discussion with his mother, was then asked to choose one fear for the first intervention, which was his separation anxiety at home. His mother explained that Daniel was 'A little shadow' who followed her everywhere and did not like to be in a separate room from her, even in the middle of the day, let alone being upstairs alone at night. Daniel and the clinician role-played the situation and re-enacted his mother and Daniel at night time. Daniel thoroughly enjoyed this activity and liked to act out what he typically says when he is afraid and his mother's response. The clinician then introduced the concept of 'flower and candle' breathing to reduce feelings of anxiety. The clinician taught the concept of taking a deep breath in (to smell the flower) and a deep breath out (to blow out the candle). Daniel was asked to give ratings of anxiety in the session before breathing (4/10) and after breathing (0/10).

The clinician then chose a 'baddy' puppet, a figure of a three-headed dragon that flew down to see what was happening in the role play. Daniel chose another puppet, which he decided today would be the tiger puppet. The dragon laughed and said 'ha ha ha, we have a little scaredy cat here! He can't even leave his mum to go to the toilet by himself!' 'Hey!' Daniel's puppet replied. 'Go away, how dare you laugh at me'. The dragon replied, 'What! You can't even leave your mum alone for 30 seconds to go into another room. 'Yes, I can!' was the reply. 'No, you can't. 'Yes, I can'. 'What are you going to do?' 'uhhhh....' Daniel replied, and could not think of what he could do. At this point, Daniel's mother interjected. 'What about flower and candle breathing?'. 'Oh yeah...' and then looked at the dragon. 'I can do my breathing!' The dragon puppet then started to cry, 'No... don't do it! I don't want you to! I want you to be a scaredy cat. 'Yes, I will!' Daniel said. Daniel's puppet then bit one of the dragon's heads, and the dragon flew away crying. Homework for the next week was assigned for Daniel to a) practice flower and candle breathing and b) complete exposure exercises of spending 30 seconds away from his mother in the next room while playing his favourite activity (cars) during the middle of the day.

Therapy continued with a review of homework and ratings of his fears. The clinician then role-played more gradual exposure exercises (spending 1 minute away from his mother, 2 minutes away, 5 minutes away, and eventually downstairs at night), which were also practised in session: Daniel's mother and the clinician would leave the room for 1 minute, and Daniel would be in the room by himself, which he was able to do easily. Daniel appeared more and more confident, and the baddy dragon became more and more desperate and sad.

When Daniel rated fear of separation down to 0/10, we then moved to the fear of monsters. Interestingly, Daniel was adamant that he had actually seen a monster in real life and no amount of sensible or detective thinking convinced him otherwise. No homework was set for the week. Instead, the clinician, reflecting on the magical and fantasy thinking of this age range, wondered if he should challenge this belief or work with it.

In the next session, the clinician suggested we watch the 'Monsters Inc.' movie preview as part of in-vivo exposure to fear of monsters. In this 90-second clip, monsters practice scaring humans to get power to run their city. However, when a small child is trapped in the monster world, the whole city needs to go into lockdown as monsters are actually more afraid of humans than humans are of monsters. We watched this video in session, with Daniel completing slow breathing. His initial fear rating was 8/10 for the first exposure, followed by 5/10 fear on the second exposure, down to 3/10 and then 0/10 by the fourth exposure. Watching the preview at home was set as homework.

In the following session, Daniel said he was no longer scared of monsters. He had watched the entire movie (instead of the preview) and said that laughter makes more electricity for the monsters than tears do. He said that monsters are more afraid of humans than humans are of monsters and that there are also nice monsters that exist. The clinician congratulated Daniel for his clever thinking. Thought challenging was not required.

Sessions continued for approximately 6 weeks before re-administering the same questionnaires to Daniel's mother as at the start of treatment. Anxiety, as predicted, had dropped significantly and was now in the normal range. Daniel's mother noted that Daniel was much more confident, could be by himself and was no longer afraid of the dark. The clinician congratulated them on their success, briefly talked about what strategies he could do if worries came back, and invited them to recontact if there were any issues in the future.

Conclusion

CBT is a therapy model that focuses on the primary reason for referral and offers a range of strategies suitable for addressing the issues young children face during the early years, particularly anxiety-based disorders, social skills difficulties and regulation of emotions. It is components based and adaptable, meaning that some components can be selected and emphasised depending on the symptom presentation, the goals of therapy and the required interventions in achieving the goal, while other components may not be relevant in a specific case. It is respectful of the family's presenting issues and invites parents and children to become actively engaged in the therapy and homework component. It is a short-term intervention that encourages children to develop skills and a feeling of mastery when achieving their goals and to celebrate attempts and successes. It is an active therapy that requires the therapist to be creative in presenting the therapeutic strategy in such a way that it captures the child's interest but also achieves the desired outcomes for change. CBT is a widely used and predominant model in training clinical psychologists and other therapists. The evidence base for CBT with young children is developing, and based on the strong link between CBT and academic research, we will likely see further research which will indicate for which presentation this model is most suited for this young age range of children.

Reader's Exercises

Jason, a 4-year-old boy, is brought into treatment due to his intense fear of dogs. He had a negative experience when a large and overly excited dog jumped up on him and made him fall over. After the event, he said that he was scared that the dog was 'Going to bite or hurt' him. Since then, Jason does not tolerate seeing dogs in yards, dogs walking in public or puppies at friends' and family's houses. He avoids going to parks in case a dog might be there. His mother and father are engaged in treatment and demonstrated a commitment to completing exposure homework assignments out of session. Before coming to the clinic, he asked his parents if there would be dogs there. During the assessment, you hear Jason say three words to you in total, and instead of playing with any toys, he sits on his parent's lap for the entire appointment.

- What might be your first goal in treatment for Jason?
- What types of resources do you think might help engage Jason in the session?
- What might be a good first homework assignment for Jason and his parents to complete?
- If you wanted to start constructing a graded hierarchy with Jason and his family. What is the first step you might start with?

References

Barrett, P., Fisak, B., & Cooper, M. (2015). The treatment of anxiety in young children: Results of an open trial of the Fun FRIENDS program. *Behaviour Change, 32*, 231–242. https://doi.org/10.1017/bec.2015.12

Beck, A. T. (1976). *Cognitive therapy and the emotional disorders.* International University Press.

Beck, A.T., Rush, A.J., Shaw, B., & Emery, G. (1979). *Cognitive therapy for depression.* Guilford Press.

Beck, J. S. (2011). *Cognitive Behavior Therapy: Basics and beyond* (2nd Edition). Guilford Press.

Beck, J. (2020). *Cognitive Behavior Therapy: Basics and beyond (3rd Edition).* Guilford Press.

Benjamin, C. L., Puleo, C. M., Settipani, C. A., Brodman, D. M., Edmunds, J. M., Cummings, C. M., & Kendall, P. C. (2011). History of cognitive-behavioural therapy in youth. *Child and Adolescent Psychiatric Clinics of North America, 20*, 179–189. https://doi.org/10.1016/j.chc.2011.01.011

Bergman, R. L. (2013). *Treatment for children with selective mutism: An integrative behavioral approach.* Oxford University Press.

Bergman, L., Gonzalez, A., Piacentini, J., & Keller, M. L. (2013). Integrated behaviour therapy for selective mutism: A randomised controlled pilot study. *Behaviour Research and Therapy, 51*, 680–689. https://doi.org/ 10.1016/j.brat.2013.07.003

Blackwell, S. E., & Heidenreich, T. (2021). Cognitive behaviour therapy at the crossroads. *International Journal of Cognitive Therapy, 14*, 1–22. https://doi.org/10.1007/s41811-021-00104-y

Chorpita, B. F., & Delaiden, E. L. (2007). *2007 Biennial report: Effective psychosocial interventions for youth with behavioral and emotional needs.* Hawaii Department of Health.

Cohen, J. A., Mannarino, A. P., & Deblinger, E. (2017). *Treating trauma and traumatic grief in children and adolescents* (2nd Ed.). The Guilford Press.

Dattilio, F.M., & Hanna, M.A. (2012). Collaboration in cognitive behavioural therapy. *Journal of Clinical Psychology, 68(2)*, 146–158. https://doi.org/10.1002/jclp.21832

Engel, G. (1997). The need for a new medical model: A challenge for biomedicine. *Science, 196*, 129–136. https://doi.org/10.1126/science.847460

Hirshfeld-Becker, D. R., Masek, B., Henin, A., Blakely, L. R., Pollock-Wurman, R. A., McQuade, J., DePetrillo, L., Briesch, J., Ollendick, T. H., Rosenbaum, J. F., & Biederman, J. (2010). Cognitive behavioural therapy for 4- to 7-year-old children with anxiety disorders: A randomised clinical trial. *Journal of Consulting and Clinical Psychology, 78(4)*, 498–510. https://doi.org/10.1037/a0019055

Hopkins, L. (2021, Dec 7) *Beck's Cognitive Theory. Our blue sky minds.* https://www.ourblueskyminds.org/articles/7/12/2021

Kaplan, C. A., Thompson, A. E., & Searson, S. M. (1995). Cognitive behaviour therapy in children and adolescents. *Archives of Disease in Childhood, 73*, 472–475. http://dx.doi.org/10.1136/adc.73.5.472

Kazantzis, N. (2021). The evolution of CBT: Introducing a family of cognitive behavioural therapies. *InPsych, 43.*

Knell, S. M., (1998). Cognitive-behavioural play therapy. *Journal of Clinical Child Psychology, 27*, 28–33. https://doi.org/10.1207/s15374424jccp2701_3

Landreth, G. L. (2012). *Play therapy. The art of the relationship.* Routledge.

MacGregor, C., & Herger, K. (2011). *Get Lost, Mr. Scary. Facilitator's manual. An early intervention program for anxious children aged 5–7 Years.* NSW Department of Education and Training.

Macneil, C. A., Hasty, M. K., Conus, P., & Berk, M. (2012). Is diagnosis enough to guide interventions in mental health? Using case formulation in clinical practice. *BMC Medicine, 10*, 1–3. https://doi.org/10.1186/1741-7015-10-111

Mash, E. J. (2006). Treatment of child and family disturbance: A cognitive-behavioral systems perspective. In E. J. Mash & R. A. Barkley (Eds.), *Treatment of childhood disorders* (pp. 3–62). The Guilford Press.

McGuire, A., Steele, R. G., & Singh, M. N. (2021). A systematic review of the application of Trauma-Focussed Cognitive Behaviour Therapy (TF-CBT) for preschool-aged children. *Clinical Child and Family Psychology Review, 24*, 30–37. https://doi.org/10.1007/s10567-020-00334-0

Miller, G. A. (2003). The cognitive revolution: A historical perspective. *Trends in Cognitive Sciences, 7*(3), 141–144. https://doi.org/10.1016/S1364-6613(03)00029-9

Minde, K., Roy, J., Bezonsky, R., & Hashemi, A. (2010). The effectiveness of CBT in 3–7-year-old anxious children: Preliminary data. *Journal of the Canadian Academy of Child and Adolescent Psychiatry, 19*, 109–115.

Monga, S., Rosenbloom, B. N., Tanha, A., Owens, M., & Young, A. (2015). Comparison of child-parent and parent-only cognitive-behavioural therapy programs for anxious children aged 5 to 7 years: short- and long-term outcomes. *Journal of the American Academy of Child and Adolescent Psychiatry, 54*, 138–146. https://doi.org/10.1016/j.jaac.2014.10.008

Padesky, C. (1993, September). *Socratic questioning: Changing minds or guiding discovery?* [Conference presentation]. European Congress of Behaviour and Cognitive Therapies, London.

Rapee, R.M., Kennedy, S.J., Ingram, M., Edwards, S.L., & Sweeney, L. (2010). Altering the trajectory of anxiety in at-risk young children. *American Journal of Psychiatry, 167*, 1518–1525. https://doi.10.1176/appi.ajp.2010.09111619

Rapee, R. M., Wignall, A., Spence, S. H., Cobham, V., & Lyneham, H. (2008). *Helping your anxious child (2nd Ed.).* New Harbinger Publications, Inc.

Rinaldin Garcia, L., Salvo Toni, C., Batista, A., & Zeggio, L. (2019). Evaluation of the effectiveness of the Fun FRIENDS program. *Trends in Psychology, 27*, 925–941. https://doi.org/10.9788/TP2019.4-08

Ruocco, S., Gordon, J., & McLean, L. (2016). Effectiveness of a school-based early intervention CBT group programme for children with anxiety aged 5–7 years. *Advances in School Mental Health Promotion, 9*, 29–49. https://doi.org/10.1080/1754730X.2015.1110495

Scheeringa, M., Weems, C., Cohen, J., Amaya-Jackson, L., & Guthrie, D. (2011). Trauma-focussed cognitive-behavioural therapy for posttraumatic stress disorder in three through six-year-old children: A randomised clinical trial. *The Journal of Child Psychology and Psychiatry, 52*, 853–860. https://doi.org/10.1111/j.1469-7610.2010.02354.x

Schneider, M. & Robin, A. (1974). *Turtle Manual.* U.S. Department of Health, Education and Welfare, National Institute of Education.

Staddon, J. E. R., & Cerutti, D. T. (2003). Operant conditioning. *Annual Review of Psychology, 54*, 115–144. https://doi.org/10.1146/annurev.psych.54.101601.145124

Vollmar, K. (1994). *Autogenes Training mit Kindern: Grundstufe für Schulkinder; Gesundheit stärken, Konzentration steigern, Ängste abbauen*. Gräfe und Unzer.

Waters, A.M., Wharton, T.A., Zimmer-Gembeck, M.J., & Craske, M.G. (2008). Threat-based cognitive biases in anxious children: Comparison with non-anxious children before and after cognitive-behavioral treatment. *Behaviour Research & Therapy, 46*, 358–374. https://doi.org/10.1016/j.brat.2008.01.002

Waters, A.M., Ford, L.A., Wharton, T.A., & Cobham, V. (2009). Cognitive behavioural therapy for young children with anxiety disorders: Comparison of group-based child + parent versus parent only focused treatment. *Behaviour Research and Therapy, 47*, 654–662. https://doi.org/10.1016/j.brat.2009.04.008

Watson, J. B., & Rayner, R. (1920). Conditioned emotional reactions. *Journal of Experimental Psychology, 3*, 1–14. https://doi.org/10.1037/h0069608

Westbrook, D. (2007). Basic theory, development and current status of CBT. In, D. Westbrook, H. Kennerley, & J. Kirk (Eds.), *An Introduction to Cognitive Behaviour Therapy: Skills and Applications*. Sage Publications.

Section II:

Parent-Focused Approaches

Chapter 4

Circle of Security (COS)

Fiona Perrett and Tanya Hanstock

Circle of Security (COS; Powell et al., 2014) is a suite of reflective parenting/caregiver programs based on attachment theory that are designed to enhance the parent/carer-child or teacher relationship dyad. Caregivers can be anyone with a primary caregiving attachment relationship with a child, typically parents or people in a parenting role, such as foster parents or kinship carers. The main premise underlying COS is that secure attachment between the caregiver and child dyad fosters healthy social and emotional development in the child and is a powerful protective factor against current and future adverse events. A child's optimal learning occurs within a secure relationship between caregiver and child (Bowlby, 1955). The COS program is based on clinical practice and research which has shown that non-secure attachment styles can change with the help of appropriate intervention. While the COS programs were primarily designed for caregivers and children with an insecure attachment style, caregivers and children with a secure attachment style are not excluded from the intervention. It is the philosophical position of COS that all children and caregivers can benefit from COS intervention if they have the motivation to increase the security of their attachment relationship. It is assumed that all relationships, even secure relationships, can benefit from the intervention. COS invites parents to reflect upon their own attachments, particularly their relationship with their child and how they were parented themselves. COS is an evidence-based program originally developed for caregivers of children aged between 12 months and 5 years and is most commonly delivered in a group format (Powell et al., 2014). However, COS is currently recommended for parents with children up to 6 years of age (COS International, 2022). COS is a popular parenting program internationally, with the main COS graphic translated into 14 languages (COS International, 2022). The more intensive and individualised COS program named Circle of Security Intensive (COSI) was first developed in 1998, followed by the shorter version Circle of Security Parenting (COSP), developed in 2007. The Circle of Security

Classroom approach (COSC) was developed in 2016. This chapter focuses mostly on COSI and COSP for clinicians working with children and parents via the COS model in clinical practice.

Historical and Theoretical Context

History

COS was established in America in 1998 by Glen Cooper, Kent Hoffman, and Bert Powell, who were child and family clinicians working together in private practice for over 30 years. They were later joined by Bob Marvin who agreed to be a research investigator for their initial studies (COS International, 2022). They collaborated to create the COS graphic designed to translate the findings of attachment research into a visual representation to capture the essential aspects of attachment research and help parents absorb the program's main aspects. The COS graphic offers research findings in a condensed form that guides parents and caregivers in their interactions with their young children (see Figure 1). Head Start Federal Government research funding enabled the assessment of the first transition of the COS graphic into a 20-session early intervention group program. This involved parents meeting weekly to review edited videos of themselves and their child. This study found a decrease in both disorganised and insecure attachment styles from pre to post-treatment (Hoffman et al., 2006). This research program is described by Powell et al. (2014), and it formed the basis of the COSI program. COSP was developed from the original COSI program however was condensed to an eight-session parent reflection program in 2007. The main difference being instead of using individualised video reviews, parents watch video clips played by the COSP Facilitators in the sessions that display the specific goals of introducing attachment theory in an accessible way.

Theoretical Models

COS was particularly influenced by the work of John Bowlby and Mary Ainsworth, who studied parent and child attachment and the significance of attachment for an individual's lifelong adjustment and personal and social functioning (Ainsworth et al., 1978). Studies such as the longitudinal study of child attachment bonds and lifelong development conducted by the Institute of Child Development at the University of Minnesota also contributed significantly to the understanding of children's attachment and the importance of stable and secure parent–child attachment to a child's healthy emotional, social and intellectual development (Sroufe et al., 2009).

Attachment theory was originally developed by Bowlby, a British psychiatrist and psychoanalyst (1955). Bowlby described attachment as an enduring emotional bond between people. He believed the quality of the early attachment relationship between a child and their caregiver has an enduring effect on a person across their lifespan. He saw attachment as having an evolutionary benefit of promoting children to stay close to their parent (often their mother) as their primary caregiver to improve the child's safety. Bowlby believed children are born with an innate drive to seek attachment to caregivers. Behaviour theorists thought it was feeding that primarily motivated attachment, whereas Bowlby believed that nurturance and responsiveness were the primary determinants of attachment. The main premise of attachment theory is that when a child has a primary caregiver who is responsive and nurturing, the child feels safe. The child then learns that their caregiver is dependable, and this creates a secure base for them to develop self-confidence, explore their environment and learn new information (Powell et al., 2014).

Mary Ainsworth (a Developmental Psychologist in the 1970s) developed a clinical experiment called The Strange Situation Procedure (SSP) to assess attachment styles in children. The experiment involved observing how children (aged 12 to 18 months) respond when briefly left alone and then reunited with their primary caregiving parent. During the Strange Situation (SSP) assessment, a stranger enters the room, and the child is briefly left in the room with the stranger whilst the observer/coder and the child's caregiver are watching on the other side of a one-way screen. The main focus of the experiment is how the child reacts when reunited with their primary caregiving parent in terms of being upset and rejecting their parent or stressed and seeking comfort. From the outcomes of The Strange Situation, Mary Ainsworth suggested there were three types of attachment styles; secure attachment, anxious ambivalent-insecure attachment and anxious avoidant-insecure attachment. Later, Main and Solomon added a fourth attachment style, disorganised attachment, as a result of their research findings (1986). Disorganised attachment is different from the previously studied styles — disorganised attachment came about as Main and Soloman could not classify a small number of children according to the Ainsworth classifications, and these infants showed unusual behaviour (such as freezing their movements for no apparent reason). Securely attached young children often show distress when separated from their primary caregiving parent but can quickly be calmed on reunion and then re-engage with play. Children with insecure attachment can show a variety of response patterns which can include rejection, ignoring, or expressing ambivalence towards the caregiver on reunion. Children with avoidant attachment usually show little overt distress on separation and reunion.

COS Concepts and Strategies

There are a number of COS strategies that parents/caregivers are taught across all three COS programs (COSI, COSP and COSC).

The COS Graphic

The COS graphic (Figure 1) is the foundation of all COS programs. It is the first concept and strategy taught to parents/caregivers in the COS programs. The graphic offers a visual and condensed presentation of the core concept of COS, the secure base (the top side of the circle) and the safe haven (the bottom side of the circle) and what the child needs on these two different parts of the circle. It also helps caregivers to learn to pinpoint where the child's needs are on the circle and therefore helps them to understand what their child emotionally needs. The graphic often seems simple to understand compared to being able to follow it consistently in real life with one's own child. It can be especially difficult to follow it when the parent/caregiver and or the child is distressed.

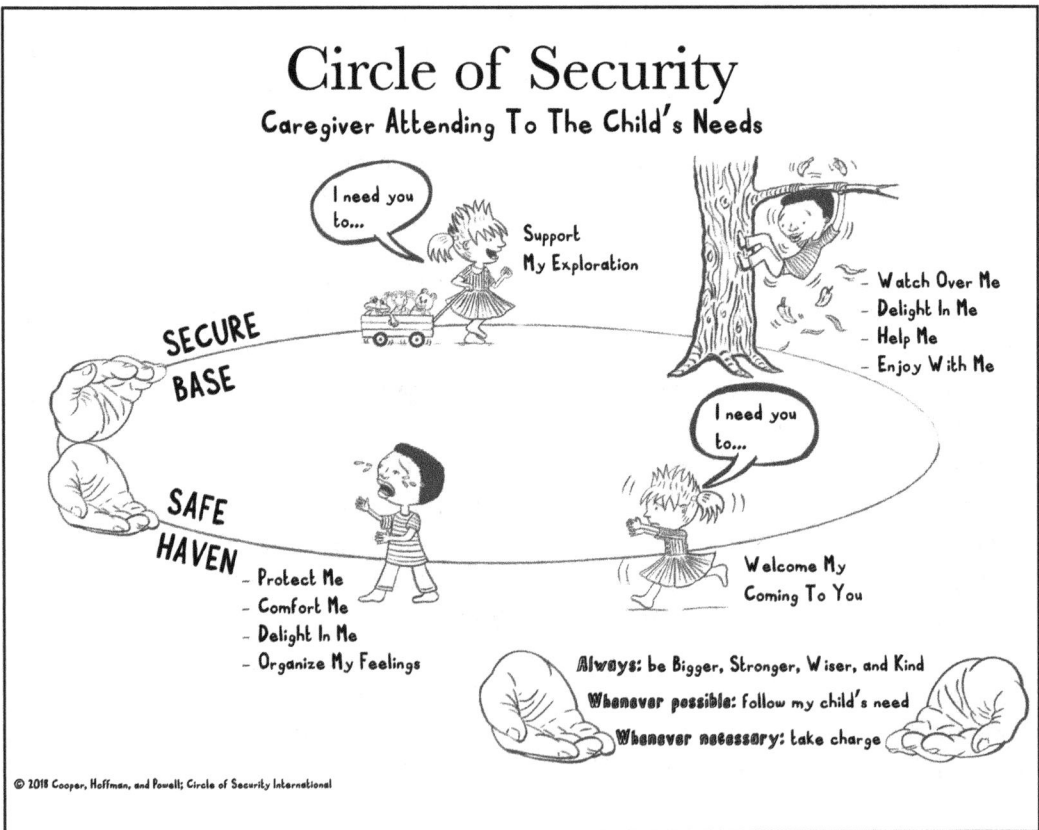

Figure 1. The Circle of Security Graphic

The graphic also includes the hands on the circle representing the caregiver and their responsiveness to the child. Children need to feel safe and secure in their primary attachment relationship with their caregiver, and the relationship must help the child to feel confident that their caregiver is both a secure base (to go and explore from) and a safe haven (to return to when needing comfort). A secure base refers to a steady, predictable, consistently available caregiver. When a caregiver provides this to a child, the child develops confidence in their ability to be able to shift their attention away from their caregiver in order to explore their environment. For children to explore their environment positively and confidently, they need their caregiver's support. They also need their caregiver to be close enough (yet not too physically close, even just observing rather than being physically sitting next to the child), supporting their efforts to explore. Children are learning, and they make mistakes; they need their caregiver to watch over them so that they can intervene to help when the child needs assistance. Children need their caregivers to be interested and delighted in their efforts to explore the world, as this helps them to feel good about themselves and confident in their accomplishments. Children need their caregivers to enjoy their exploration with them so that they learn how to enjoy sharing such times with others (Powell et al., 2014). Children alternate to the top and bottom of the circle many times. Parents can have 'mind-blindness', which refers to parents being unable to see where their child is on the circle. For example, the child may be indicating the bottom of the circle needs for comfort, but the parent responds to the child as if they are on the top of the circle and wanting to explore their environment. This mind-blindness is often due to the parent's own experience of being parented, their experience of trauma and their uncomfortable feelings when their child is part of the circle (Powell et al., 2014). Table 1 represents the child's need from the caregiver, a description and an example of this need. Table 2 represents the caregiver responses required, a description and an example of this response.

Cues and Miscues

In COS language, a cue is the child's behaviour that indicates an emotional need. The caregiver then interprets what the cue means and decides how to best respond. For example, a child running towards the parent with their arms out crying is a cue, and the parent can interpret this as the child needing comfort from the parent because they are upset. If this is what the child is communicating, then this is a clear cue of what they want their parent/caregiver to do (which is to comfort them by giving them a cuddle).

When a child hides or masks their needs from their caregiver, this is called a miscue. A miscue means that the child behaves in a way that is sometimes contrary or confusing as to what they want from the caregiver to meet their

Table 1. Position of the Circle and Caregiver Responses Required.

Position on Circle	Emotional Need	Description	Example
Top	Supporting My Exploration	Watching and encouraging (physically and verbally) the child to start and continue to explore their environment.	Watching and encouraging a child explore their toys or play at a park.
	Watch Over Me	Watching the child and not being distracted by other things, people, a mobile phone etc.	Attentively watching the child playing and exploring at home or when out.
	Delight in Me	Demonstrate enjoyment and interest in the child.	Smiling and laughing and talking positively to the child.
	Help Me	Assist the child through encouragement or activity to help them in doing something.	Helping a child make a toy work that they have tried to work on their own without success.
	Enjoy With Me	Demonstrating joy for a shared exploration.	Playing a game with a child and smiling, having good eye contact, positive verbal phrases and laughter to show how much you are enjoying this activity with them.
Bottom	Welcome My Coming to You	Being approachable in body language and voice to welcome the child to come to you for comfort.	Holding your arms out, having a comforting tone of voice and showing a welcoming face when a child approaches.
	Protect Me	Being able to take charge and help protect the child from danger.	Moving and helping the child out of danger or to help them manage a conflict with another child.
	Comfort Me	Providing verbal and physical comfort when the child is distressed.	Cuddling the child, patting them on the back, making soothing noises and matching facial expressions.
	Delight In Me	Demonstrate enjoyment and interest in the child.	Smiling, laughing, complimenting the child and cuddling.
	Organise My Feelings	Help the child to label and manage a big emotion by helping sooth, validate and comfort them and role modelling emotional regulation yourself.	For example, when a child falls over and gets upset, saying 'I would be upset too if I fell over. Let me help you and see if you are okay'.

Table 2. Consistent Caregiver Responses Required

When needed	Response	Description	Example
Always	Be Bigger, Stronger, Wiser and Kind	Demonstrating a balance of kindness and firmness when interacting with your child.	Be ready to take charge when needed but also stay guided by the child's needs and always be calm, helpful and respectful in your behaviour and language towards them. Being aware of where they are at developmentally and not expecting them to be small adults.
Whenever Possible	Follow My Child's Lead	Notice the child's communication and which need they are showing you on the Circle of Security. Meet the need the child is showing that they have.	Standing back and letting the child play if they are acting confident and curious and it is safe. Cuddle the child and comfort them if they are crying and reaching for you.
Whenever Necessary	Take Charge	Be the adult in the situation, act differently to the child's desires if necessary for their safety or well-being.	Picking the child up to protect them from running onto a road, towards an unfamiliar dog or any situation that is most likely unsafe.

emotional needs. For example, if a child is upset and wants comfort from the parent, they may run away from the parent instead of towards them.

A miscue often occurs due to the child being aware that the parent is uncomfortable with providing what they need. For example, a parent who is anxious about their child seeking comfort might respond angrily to an injured child and say, 'What have you done to yourself now!' or 'I told you not to jump off that rock!' in a harsh tone with an unwelcoming facial expression. Such a parental response may stem from many factors, for example, the parent being traumatised by a child's past accident and/or having had a similar response from their own parent when they had an accident and sought comfort from their parent.

Limited Circles

If a caregiver consistently does not respond to the specific needs of the top, bottom or hands of the circle, the circle is said to be limited. This is described as if an arc of the circle has been cut out of the circle, leaving a gap resulting in an attachment that is not secure (Powell et al., 2014). It is impossible for a parent to always meet their child's needs on both parts of the circle at all times. However, limited circles describe when the parent is consistently not meeting the child's needs on one or more parts of the circle. Children who are not feeling they are able to turn to their parents when on the bottom part of the circle are more likely to have an avoidant attachment, and those not able to have their parents watch over them while they are at the top of the circle are more likely to have an ambivalent attachment (Powell et al., 2014).

Shark Music

Shark Music is a COS term to describe when a parent/caregiver feels anxious or afraid of their children's needs (that are actually safe). It is safe for parents to meet their children's emotional needs, but because of a parent's own history, they may feel uncomfortable (scared or angry) when their children have particular needs on the COS Circle. Hearing shark music is often manifested in a physical anxiety response such as feeling hypervigilant, feeling anxious/scared, starting to feel hot, increased heart rate etc. It is called 'Shark Music' to help the parent/carer think about the frightening music in the Jaws movie, which indicates that something bad is about to occur (that the shark/danger is coming). An example of such a situation may be a toddler who is angry and screaming at their parent when they are told they cannot have a chocolate that they desperately want. The toddler needs their parent to help them calm down from their angry feelings and accept that they can move on with their day without the chocolate. On the COS, this is the bottom of the circle, take charge, and organise my feelings and emotional needs for the child. However, a parent may hear Shark Music at such a moment. If they have a history of people's angry feelings leading to punitive or violent behaviour, they may start to feel their heart beating fast, and they feel as though they have to get out of the situation immediately. It does not feel safe. If the parent reacts to their Shark Music without recognising that the situation is actually safe, they may miss their child's emotional needs. They might react by giving the toddler the chocolate or by yelling at the toddler and punishing them. In a different example, a parent may 'hear Shark Music' when their child runs off to explore their environment, as the parent feels worried the child may have an accident and fears that they will hurt themselves. The parent may have a history of their own parent feeling anxious and keeping them close when they were a child. As a consequence, the parent may not encourage the child to go out and explore their environment. Parents/caregivers often have Shark Music occur without realising it. The COS assessments and intervention help the parent to recognise when their Shark Music is playing and work on ways of responding differently, in line with the child's needs emotionally on the COS circle.

Being With

'Being with' a child means being able to sit with the child and be fully present and calm. Being with a child is harder when the child is distressed. It is also hard if the parent is distressed, and it is most difficult when the child and parent are both distressed (Stern, 2018).

Repairing Relationships with a Time In

It is not possible for any parent to recognise and meet all of their child's emotional needs at all times. Many times, these are minor moments, and the child quickly recovers. At times, however, these moments may be of importance to the child. If their parent is not tuned into their needs and able to help them, the child may be significantly upset and distressed. A rupture is when the parent steps off the circle (such as being unavailable to the child). When the child becomes distressed, it is an organise my feelings moment or a take charge of my feelings moment, which is different to a parent having no hands in the circle. The aim is not for parents to learn to avoid all relationship ruptures at all costs, as such an aim is not realistic. Rather, the aim is for parents to recognise when there has been a rupture in the relationship and to take the lead to repair their relationship with their child. This can be challenging, especially if the parent is also upset. The parent may find they need a time-out for themselves to look after their own emotions. Once they are calm, they are able to help their child with a time-in. They can find a neutral place with their child and sit calmly with them. It can be helpful to do something like read a book together or do a chore together and let the child know that their feelings can be acknowledged. The parent can then help by talking to the child about things they could do in the future if a similar situation occurs again (Powell et al., 2014).

Good Enough

Good enough parenting is a term that lets parents know that they do not have to get things right (meeting the child's needs) all the time (Winnicott, 1991). No parent is perfect, and perfection is not necessary to help children feel loved and secure in their relationship with their parents.

The COS Interventions

The three different types of COS interventions are COSI, COSP, and COSC. In practice, caregivers are given a choice of which program they want to take part in, depending on the availability of these groups. The suitability of a particular COS program also depends on whether they are a parent / primary caregiver or a paid professional caregiver such as a childcare or family daycare educator or a Child Health Nurse.

COSI (Circle of Security Intensive)

COSI was the original COS program developed and is the one with the most evidence base. Its unique structure is that it includes videotaping of the child and caregiver dyad before and after the program. COSI is the longest (with a 20-week duration if 6 parents are in the group) and the more focused group program. Families wanting to participate in the COSI first undertake the COS interactional assessment process. The licenced providers/COSI facilitators first invite the primary caregiver and the child to participate in a modified SSP which has been adapted adding a 'pack-up the toys' and 'reading together' section to the procedure. Following participation in the modified SSP, the parent participates in an individual semi-structured interview of approximately an hour in duration using the Circle of Security Interview (COSI; Powell et al., 2014). The COSI explores with the parent their experience of the SSP, their experiences of caregiving with the child and their experiences of their parents' caregiving when they were growing up as a child.

Following the assessment, the COSI facilitators and the caregiver make their decision about whether to proceed with the program. The parent is asked if they can attend the weekly 20-session group. It is also necessary that they are willing and able to view and reflect on their personal video clips of themselves and their child in a group setting. If these prerequisites are not met, a caregiver is generally recommended not to proceed with the program.

When the caregiver and facilitators mutually agree to proceed with COSI, the facilitators (typically two facilitators per group) jointly review and analyse the modified SSP and the COSI interview. They then create the individualised treatment plan for each caregiver who will participate in the group. In the video review, an attachment classification (such as disorganised or anxious-ambivalent) is not made. Instead, the linchpin struggle (the area the parent most struggles to meet their child's needs) is identified, and video clips are chosen to show back to the parent the linchpin struggle. The goal of the COSI assessment is to identify the strengths and weaknesses of this caregiver–child dyad on the top of the circle, bottom of the circle and the hands of the circle. A linchpin struggle is also identified, which represents the core problem that is maintaining problematic parent-child interactions and clarifies what needs to change to establish a secure attachment. Parents are also classified based on the Core Sensitivities, which is defined as an internal defensive process manifested in caregiver behaviour, an internal working model and a way of splitting that has become a moment-to-moment strategy in relationships. Understanding a parent's core sensitivity helps the clinician create a narrative in such a way that the parent is less likely to defend against the struggles identified. Becoming trained and reliable in coding and classifying strange situation procedures (into classifications such as secure, anxious-avoidant or anxious-ambivalent) is a specialist skill that requires training and examination separately from the COSI training. Licenced COSI facilitators may (or may not) be trained and reliable in classifying attachment relationships (Powell et al., 2014).

Segments of the videotaped parent-child interaction become the focus of the core part of the COSI. The parent-child interactions are utilised to exemplify where the child is on the circle and what needs they may have. The facilitators review the modified SSP, looking for brief segments of the procedure that will be helpful to review in the COSI group. They particularly search for moments that enhance and foster security in the relationship between the caregiver and child surrounding the linchpin struggle. As the facilitators review the COSI interview, they consider how the caregivers' core sensitivity and experience of parenting the child (and their experience of being parented as a child) has impacted the development of the caregiver's relationship patterns. They then plan how to review the caregiver and child video segments in the group setting in a way that best suits the caregiver's ways of relating to others and minimises the likelihood of defensive responses.

Each group typically includes six caregivers or fewer. The number of caregivers is critical, as each caregiver reviews the videotape of their relationship with their child in three separate sessions throughout the intervention. Fifteen of the twenty weeks of the group are devoted to watching and reflecting on the caregiver-child videos. Therefore, if more than six caregivers participate in a group, more than twenty sessions of the group would be required. Whilst it is possible to successfully make minor modifications to the group program (for example, if a caregiver is unable to complete a group, the entire group does not need to be cancelled), it is recommended that each group consists of six caregivers or less. It is recommended that childcare is available free of charge to the children of the caregivers whilst the caregivers attend the group to support the caregivers' attendance.

The first two weeks of the COSI group are educational in nature. The facilitators teach the caregivers about the importance of the attachment relationship and invite the caregivers to join the group in a supportive, open, non-judgemental environment. The caregivers learn about the circle of security graphic and have the opportunity to see examples of their own children experiencing the COS in their relationship (via the recorded strange situation procedures).

After the first two weeks of educational material, the next (approximately) six weeks of the group consist of each caregiver, in turn, reviewing the selected parts of their caregiver-child interactions on video. The facilitators thoughtfully choose the order in which the parents will review their videos so that caregivers can learn from each other as the group proceeds each week. Each caregiver is allocated to a facilitator, who takes responsibility for supporting the parent through the process of reflecting on their video and using the Circle of Security graphic to better understand their child's emotional needs and the aspects of their relationship that could be enhanced. The caregivers who are not watching their video are encouraged by the facilitators to support the parent in their reflections on their child's emotional needs and their parenting responses viewed on the videotape.

Midway through the group is another educational week. The caregivers are introduced to new concepts with respect to the attachment relationship. In particular, parents are introduced to the idea that their parenting and their responses to their children's emotional needs are, at times, based on their own experiences of being parented as children, rather than being based on their child's actual emotional needs in a given moment. Parents learn how to be aware of their own emotional responses to different needs of their children using the concept of Shark music. They learn how to reflect on the way that they might inadvertently communicate to their children that they are not comfortable with some of their children's emotional needs. They learn how this dynamic can impact the attachment relationship, increasing feelings of insecurity in the children. The parents learn about the concept of Shark Music at this stage.

The next (approximately) six weeks of the group build upon the educational weeks, helping parents put into practice the theory they have learned as they take turns to watch and reflect on additional parts of their caregiver-child videos. Parents are supported to consider which of their children's emotional needs are the most difficult for them and how they might change their ways of relating to their child to better meet their emotional needs in the future.

After the group has completed the second videotape review, the group does not meet for a week. Rather than the regular meeting, the caregivers and children each participate in another strange situation video assessment. The facilitators again review the videos and select segments of the new videos that highlight for the caregivers the positive changes they have made in their relationships with their children, along with any areas of continued difficulty. The next (approximately) three weeks involve another opportunity to review and reflect on the (new) videos of the relationships. The new videos are viewed, and the caregivers reflect on the changes they have made in their relationships with their children and the difficulties that they continue to encounter.

The final week of the group is a time of reflection on the things that have been learned. It is also a time for the celebration of positive changes that have been made and acknowledgement of the positive efforts that have brought about the changes. A final videotaping of the strange situation is recommended following the final week of the group. Whilst the final videotaping is not used directly in COSI (as the program is now complete), it is used by the facilitators to reflect on the outcome of the program for the children. It can also be used (along with the initial video) for coding by a trained attachment coder/classifier to independently ascertain whether the attachment relationship classification has changed and improved over the course of the intervention (Powell et al., 2014).

Recently, a manual for working with individual caregivers or couples has been developed, given that many private practitioners primarily do individual work. The individual and couples versions of COSI use the same assessment protocol and follow the same basic structure as the group model.

COSP (Circle of Security Parenting)

The shorter (8-10 weeks), structured and educational version of COSI is called COSP (Coyne et al., 2019). It is for parents/carers of children aged from 4 months to 6 years (COS International, 2022). It differs from COSI as it is of shorter duration, and the facilitators have different training requirements. It is more structured than the COSI program, and it does not allow observation of the parent/carer and child interventions via recording videos and reflective review by the parent of the recordings. Nor does it require an assessment of the parent-child relationship via a strange situation assessment. Rather, it relies on the parents' reports of their interactions with their child. It still requires the parents/caregivers to reflect on their and their child's interactions during the previous week. In addition, it encourages the parents/caregivers to reflect on their and their child's interactions after watching different segments of the training video and learning more about the COS concepts and strategies.

The course material of COSP includes video material of parents/carers and children's interactions and individual behaviours that teach concepts of COS. These concepts assist the parent to better understand and meet their child's emotional needs. It also includes video material of parents and children interacting together and parents' testimony of the COS intervention. The standard video material is used to structure the weekly COSP group sessions. The COSP group typically is of eight weeks duration (one video chapter per week). The size of the group is more flexible than the COSI group, as there is not an individualised program developed for each participant. A group of approximately six caregivers works well, although smaller or larger groups are also possible (Powell et al., 2014).

The COSP groups teach caregivers about the caregiver–child attachment relationship and the benefits to the child of increasing the security of the relationship. Specific ways of helping a child to feel more secure in the relationship are taught. For instance, caregivers learn the COS graphic (Figure 1), how to tune in to a child's emotional state and to be with them in their emotional experience, and how children may (at different times) show or hide their emotional needs. Caregivers also learn about the link between their parenting style and the way that they were raised as children by their own parents. They are invited to reflect on how they may misinterpret their children's needs at times, leading to children feeling insecure and uncomfortable showing some of their emotional needs to their caregivers. Caregivers have the opportunity to learn to recognise times when they do not sensitively tune in to their child's needs and how to repair these relationship ruptures with their children. This repair process helps children to feel more secure and confident in their relationship with their parents. Caregivers are supported to take a kind and non-judgmental approach to themselves as they recognise and repair ruptures in relationships with their children.

The COSP group is often the most commonly used and the most popular one due to the shorter duration and availability of trained facilitators. COSP is also less expensive compared to COSI to run in terms of supervision of the facilitators.

COSC (Circle of Security Classroom)

COSC exists for professional child carers (such as daycare and preschool child carers/educators). The aim is to help professional childcarers understand and meet the children's emotional needs through education and reflection on the child–caregiver relationship. Many children spend considerable time with their childcare and preschool professionals, and they develop important attachment relationships with them. If their classroom caregivers can understand this attachment relationship and gain knowledge of how to help the children feel increasingly secure in the relationship, it can help the children's development (Powell et al., 2014).

Training Required to be a COSI and COSP Facilitator

COS programs can only be provided by trained facilitators. COS International provides training programs for facilitators. The full COSI training is available to professionals who hold a licence to practice as a clinician. A licence may include, for example, holding full registration with the Psychology Board of Australia or being registered as a Social Worker and psychotherapist. Completion of the COSP training is a prerequisite for enrolment in the COSI training. Initially, the COSI training was delivered in the format of a 10-day in-person course. This training process has evolved and now involves a number of steps, with much use of online technology to aid the accessibility of the training.

To become a provider of the COSI intervention, it is necessary to complete a series of training courses delivered in person and online. It is necessary to successfully complete at least 4 cases (whether individual, couples or group protocol) under video supervision before COSI can be delivered independently. If trainee providers are successful in these endeavours, they can apply to become endorsed providers of COSI.

The training to become a COSP provider can be completed online or via a course delivered in person. The training is open to professionals of various professional backgrounds; for example, Psychologists, Social Workers, Nurses, Counsellors and Educators. The training is approximately 30 hours in duration, some of which is self-paced. Whether the training is conducted in-person or online, it includes live group reflection, guided by a certified trainer. The COSP manual and video chapters are provided to trainees with the appropriate level of training. The COSI website (https://www.circleofsecurityinternational.com/) has the most up-to-date details of the training involved in the COS programs.

Additional Training

Additional training and supervision/coaching is available. The 'Theory to Practice' COS course offers facilitators the opportunity to update their knowledge and their COSP resources. There are two courses which together provide in-depth focus on the 'Core Sensitivities': the first is called "Shark Music and the Core Sensitivities" and focuses on helping COSP Facilitators learn the basics of how psychological defenses about relationships might come up as one facilitates a program like COSP. The second course is called "The Human Condition" and is an experiential course in which clinicians learn about their own defenses and how to recognize patterns of defense in others. People engage in different patterns of defensiveness in their relationships in order to manage emotional pain. In depth understanding of the core sensitivities assists COS facilitators to more effectively support the caregivers in the COS programs. It also assists the COS facilitators to be more equipped to help the COS participants better understand themselves and their caregiving strengths and struggles. Fidelity Coaching is also available through COSI. Fidelity Coaching is specific coaching that assists COS trained facilitators to refine their knowledge and skills in practice, through reflection with a Certified Fidelity Coach.

COS Modifications and Emerging Practice

COS is a structured program. It is encouraged that facilitators follow the structure of the program (as they are trained to do) in order to ensure that the program participants have the opportunity to experience the positive outcomes that are expected from the program. However, COS International has overseen a number of additions and modifications to the program that emerging evidence suggests are beneficial.

One modification of the program is to use selected parts of the COSP video material to add to the COSI program. The COSP video explains some concepts (such as being with a child whilst they struggle emotionally) that are of benefit to caregivers who participate in the COSI program. Circle of Security International view this practice as a natural evolution of the COSI program.

Research on COS

Based on the strong link between insecure attachment and an increase in developmental risk, in particular social and emotional development, it is the aim of the COS program to enhance the security of the attachment relationships between children and their primary caregivers. There are three different COS interventions; COSI, COSP and COSC. Circle of Security Intensive (COSI) is the longest-established intervention and has the clearest evidence that it successfully helps children and their caregivers to enhance the security of their relationships. COSP and COSC research has indicated that these interventions provide positive results for children and their caregivers; however, whether or not they improve the security of the attachment relationship is not yet conclusively known and further research is required in this area.

COSP has preliminary evidence of improving a child's outcome. Reliable evaluation of the program has been a priority for the program founders from the early days of the program's conception (Hoffman et al., 2006). The program has a Level 2+ evidence rating meaning that the program has evidence for improving a child's outcome from a study involving at least 20 participants and representing 60% of the sample using validated questionnaires/measures. When considering the best evidence for the program's impact, it can achieve a positive outcome for children by enhancing their school achievement. The program also has some evidence of supporting outcomes for couples, parents and families (COS International, 2022).

Yaholkoski et al. (2016) conducted a meta-analysis that examined the efficacy of the COSI intervention in relation to child attachment patterns, quality of caregiving, caregiver self-efficacy, and caregiver depression. Ten studies were determined eligible for the meta-analysis. Results indicated a medium effect size for the efficacy of the intervention for child attachment security, quality of caregiving and reduction of caregiver depression. There was a significant large effect on improved caregiver self-efficacy. The COS Intensive program has also been researched in Australia with positive outcomes (Huber et al., 2015).

Clinical Vignettes

The Case of Jenny and Jack

Jenny (31) was struggling to let her son Jack (4) leave her side, for example, to play at the park or climb heights. Jack had a fall at home at age 2, where he hit his head, and since then started to experience seizures. Jenny was fearful that another accident would worsen his medical condition or it could be fatal. She was 7 months pregnant with her second child and was worried about how Jack would manage the new baby arriving and how she would manage both children as her husband worked away a lot. Jenny had joined a 20-week COSI group program. She was aware that she would get anxious when Jack moved away from her, and she did not know how she would manage when the new baby would need her attention as well. She worried about how she would be able to supervise Jack once her new baby also needed her attention. She joined the group to try and manage her anxiety around Jack's exploration.

In the COSI group, Jenny watched the video clips of herself and Jack which had been recorded earlier with the COSI facilitators. Jenny saw Jack's excitement when a new person came into the room and offered to play with Jack, sharing a different and interesting toy. She noticed that Jack's face fell with disappointment when she called to him to come back to sit with her on the couch. She was able to talk with the facilitators and the other parents in the group about her mixed feelings of anxiety and guilt when things like that happen to her and Jack. The facilitators and Jenny spoke about how important it was for Jack to have the chance to learn new things, play with new people and explore the world away from Jenny's side. Jenny wanted Jack to enjoy playtime; she felt guilty that she prevented him from going off to play. She also talked about how scared she was when he ran off; she felt like he would fall and hit his head again.

The COSI group supported Jenny to better understand that her anxiety was not just about Jack's physical safety. She had childhood memories of her favourite uncle coming to live with her when he was sick. He loved to spend time with her, and she felt guilty if she went to play and he was alone in his bedroom. She came to think that going to play was bad and dangerous, as her uncle might get even sicker if she left him. She stayed with her uncle, keeping him company, even when she would rather be outside playing with her siblings. As an adult, she realised that her uncle would not have wanted her to miss out on her playtime when she was a child. He would not have wanted her to be anxious and scared about Jack going out to play now, either. And it was not what she wanted, either, as Jack's Mum. She learned, from the COSI group, that she could label this misplaced anxiety as 'shark music'. Even though she felt scared when the suspenseful music played in a movie (like the shark movie named Jaws), she was actually safe sitting at home in front of the

TV. And even though she felt scared about Jack running off to play, she realised that these small risks are important and they help Jack develop the skills that he needs for life.

With the support of the COSI group, she explored the top of the COS circle. This helped her to better understand Jack's need to explore whilst she watched over him from a distance. When she did this, she saw that he could enjoy developing his self-confidence and independence. At home, in between the weekly COSI group sessions, she experimented with paying attention to her feelings when she was with Jack. When he moved away from her, and she felt anxious, instead of automatically calling him back to her, she reminded herself that Jack was safe and that he loved to play games like Lego and playdough on his own for a little while. When they went to the park together, she felt anxious about him going on the swings. She reminded herself that Jack was very confident on the swings and that he enjoyed being with the other children. She tried chatting with the other parents from the sidelines instead of insisting on swinging Jack herself. Although it didn't feel comfortable at first, and she felt some anxiety, she noticed herself feeling better about her relationship with Jack. She also noticed Jack was happier, and his friendships with the other children in their social circle were improving.

After Jenny and Jack did their second videotaping with the COSI facilitators, she watched the second videotape in the COSI group. She was pleased to see that Jack seemed much more confident to go to the toys and to play with the new person when she came in. She noticed that she smiled at him and helped him say hello to the new person instead of calling him back to the couch with her. The group facilitators and the other parents in the group were happy for Jenny and Jack and congratulated Jenny on the positive changes she had made. The childcare workers who cared for Jack whilst Jenny was attending the COSI group let Jenny know that they had noticed positive changes too. Jack was now happier when Jenny left him at childcare. He didn't cry for as long when she left, and he joined in the play with the other children more quickly. Jack showed that he was feeling more confident about spending time on his own and with his friends. Jenny was pleased that she had participated in the COSI group and was feeling more at ease with the upcoming birth of her second child.

The Case of Mark and Kelly

Mark (38) was enrolled in a COSP program. He was concerned about his daughter Kelly's meltdowns and her getting upset. Mark and his ex-partner had separated about six months ago. Kelly (three years of age) spends the majority of the time with her mother and spends every second weekend with her father. When Kelly came home from spending time with her Mum, she would often refuse to go to daycare the following morning. On daycare mornings, she often did not want to get dressed and would try to delay the process. She would not listen to her Dad or do as she was asked. In the car, Kelly would say she did not like the clothes she was wearing and she wanted her Dad to go home and get her a new outfit. Mark did not know what to do. Sometimes he would take Kelly home to change her clothes, hoping that would help her to feel better. But still, Kelly would scream and cry in the car on the way to daycare and cling to her Dad, refusing to let him get her out of the car at drop-off. Sometimes Mark would give up and take Kelly home. He would be very frustrated because he would have to telephone his workplace and make an excuse to his boss about not coming to work that day.

Mark found the educational videos at the COSP group very interesting. He learned about some new concepts, like 'being with' Kelly when she had strong upset feelings. He learned about 'miscues' and recognised that sometimes Kelly might ask for things that did not really reflect what she emotionally needed. When Kelly cried about having the wrong clothes on, he realised that she really needed comfort and help to understand her confused feelings about transitioning from her Mum's home to her Dad's home. And when Kelly clung to him and said she couldn't go to daycare, she was miscuing because what she really needed was for her Dad to take charge of the situation. Kelly needed Mark to be bigger, stronger wise and kind to help her transition from leaving him to settling in with her daycarers and friends. Mark learned from COSP that he is 'the hands on the circle'. Mark practised saying to himself what he learned at COSP; 'Always be bigger, stronger, wise and kind. Whenever possible, follow my child's needs. Whenever necessary, take charge.'

Mark learned from talking with the facilitators and the other parents that taking charge of the situation when his daughter was upset was difficult for him. He remembered that when he was a teenager, his mother was very stressed because they had financial troubles. She insisted that he get a part-time job and pay board to help with the family finances. When he complained, she became angry. It scared him. He stopped complaining and tried to do whatever his Mum asked so she would stop yelling at him. He learned from COSP about Shark Music. Even though he felt anxious when the suspenseful music played in a movie (like the shark movie of Jaws), he was actually safe sitting at home in front of the TV. And even though he felt anxious when Kelly had a meltdown, and he felt like he had to give her what she wanted to make her stop (like he used to do as a teenager with his Mum), Kelly's screaming and crying were not hurting either of them. It was simply her way of expressing her strong feelings. They were both safe. He knew that his Mum regretted yelling when he was a teenager, and she wouldn't want him to overcompensate Kelly and not comfort her when she needed it. Instead of getting frustrated and doing whatever Kelly asked for when she had a meltdown (like changing her outfit or staying home from work), he practised 'being with her' and letting her know that he understood that it was hard for her to leave him when she just left Mummy yesterday. He practised 'taking charge', carrying her into daycare and handing her care over to Kelly's favourite worker, who would help her join in play with her friends.

As Mark felt more confident 'being with' Kelly when she had strong feelings and 'taking charge' of the situation when Kelly was upset, Kelly started to feel better. Kelly learned that she could trust her Dad. He would comfort her and know what to do when she had a meltdown. Although she still got upset sometimes, especially with difficult transition times, she calmed down much more quickly. Mark and Kelly grew closer in their relationship, and Mark found he was enjoying being Kelly's Dad more as his frustration grew less.

Conclusion

The COS programs are very popular parenting and attachment education and intervention programs used worldwide and particularly in Australia. They are used in child and parent health services, non-government organisations (NGOs), as well as in daycare centres. One of the main benefits of COS is that there are three main packages of the program that can be used, depending on the parent/caregiver's needs. The major focus on attachment theory is another main benefit of this program as it is less emphasised in other parenting programs. Clinicians need to complete the training to help facilitate a group program, and depending on the type of the program, this can be cost and time intensive. The COSI program takes a lot of commitment from the parents; the 20-week group model, in particular, requires about a half-year of engagement. A limitation of the COS programs is that parents often find the COS graphic harder to implement in practice compared with their conceptual understanding of the different aspects of the circle. At the outset, it seems like a simple concept, but for parents to increase their reflective capacity and reflect on their own parenting, it can take a while for them to be able to do so comfortably. This process can be confrontational for some parents/caregivers. Being with a child and responding with empathy are concepts some parents may not be familiar with from their own upbringing, and hence it takes a cognitive shift to understand these. COS theory believes that change in relationships does not occur to its full extent based entirely on a new cognitive understanding. COS assists caregivers to get in touch with their own emotions and their child's emotions, as emotional experiencing also facilitates positive relationship change. Experiencing painful emotions can be challenging for caregivers, although it is positive and therapeutic. It can be challenging for caregivers to hold onto these new emotional ways of relating to their child outside of the COS group, in their moment-to-moment interactions with their child.

Reader's Exercises

The following are examples that invite you to reflect on your own life experience. Participation in a COS program involves participants devoting time to exploring life experiences and invites reflection on how these experiences have shaped their emotional patterns and the way that they relate to others.

As an introduction to how it feels to participate in the type of reflection encouraged in a COS program, meet up with someone who is similarly interested in participating in COS–style reflection. You can talk together about your experiences of emotions in relationships, particularly in caregiving relationships during your developmental years. If you are a parent, you may reflect on your experiences as a caregiver to your children. These exercises mirror those offered to participants during the COSI and other COS programs. The following questions will help guide your reflections:

- What was it like, growing up as a child in your family?

- Who was your main caregiver, and what were they like in responding to your needs?

- How did the adults in your family manage their emotions? Did they share them or keep them private? How did they ask for help with emotional challenges?

- What emotions did the adults in your family encourage the children to share? Happiness? Sadness? Shame? Guilt? Anger? Fear? Love?

- What emotions did the adults in your family encourage the children to keep private and manage on their own?

- How did the children in your family learn about the expectations of how to manage emotional challenges? Was it based on the things their parents said? Or their actions and their body language?

- What are your thoughts, as an adult, about how you were taught to manage your emotions as a child? What would you like to continue, in your relationships as an adult, that you learned as a child about how to manage your emotions? What things would you like to change, as an adult, that you learned as a child about how to manage your emotions?

- When it comes to supporting others with their emotions, which emotions are easy for you to share with and help with? Which emotions are more difficult for you to share and help with? Are some emotions uncomfortable for you and avoided if others bring them to your attention?

- What do you hope that others will learn from their relationship with you in terms of managing their difficult emotions?

- If you have a child, think about where their emotional need is on the Circle of Security at any particular time. Think about whether you find your child's needs easier to meet when they are at the top or bottom of the circle and why?

- If you do not have a child, think about other close people in your life. No matter someone's age, our emotional needs remain. We are all needing something on the Circle of Security, and it changes all the time. Think about how comfortable you are to notice others' emotional needs. Are you more comfortable with others' needs when they are on the top of the circle? Or when they are at the bottom of the circle? Or do you struggle to notice and help people with their emotional needs altogether? If so, you may find it difficult to be the 'hands on the circle'.

- Think about how you might experiment with changes in your relationships to better notice and help people with their emotional needs.

- Think about whether you might like to communicate your own emotional needs to others who you are close to.

If you do not have someone you are comfortable reflecting with, you may like to reflect on some of these questions in a private journal.

Whilst Circle of Security is an intervention for caregivers of young children, the COS concepts apply to everyone in relationships across their lifespan. You can practice COS-style thinking in all of your relationships, whether they are relationships with children or adults. In different situations in your relationships, practice observing the other person and trying to guess their emotional need in that situation, according to the COS graphic.

To get you started, below are some hypothetical situations, and you can make some guesses about the people's emotional needs on the COS:

1. Bill had an exciting day at work, where he was unexpectedly informed that he had been given a promotion and a pay rise. The interaction with his boss went very well, and he is feeling proud and optimistic about the future. He comes home and finds his partner Mary busy trying to

complete her overdue tax return paperwork. Mary has rushed home from work to get the task done before a deadline with her accountant. She is feeling guilty as she left an important work job for her colleague to finish, and she did not offer to stay back at work to help. What are Bill's emotional needs? Where is Bill on the Circle of Security? What are Mary's emotional needs? Where is Mary on the Circle of Security? What challenges do you think Bill and Mary may have in noticing and meeting each other's emotional needs?

2. Garry is a 40-year-old male who was raised by a father who was quite excessive in his physical punishment of Garry and his siblings if they did anything wrong. He would use yelling and hitting them with his hand or his belt to punish them. Garry is less active in parenting his children (aged 4 and 6) and dislikes punishing them for misbehaving. His wife says he is 'too soft' on them. She says it feels like she has to be 'the bad cop, and he gets to be the good cop'. She would like him to be more involved in the parenting of their children, especially in regard to their behaviour management. What do you think Garry's Shark Music might relate to? What emotional needs do you think Garry might struggle to notice and meet for his children? How might Garry make positive changes in meeting his family's emotional needs?

Observations and Reflections: If you have children of your own or spend time with children, watch and see if you notice what part of the Circle of Security they are on. Try to observe what part of the circle is harder for you to respond to. Do you notice any part that gives you Shark Music? Try and observe what happens when you might have it wrong in terms of thinking about what part of the circle they are on. How might you know you have it wrong?

If you have a pet, watch and try and identify where they are on the COS as well. Can you tell when they are coming in on the bottom of the circle for a pat or comfort and when they are on the top of the circle wanting to explore and play in their environment? What happens if you get it wrong? How do you know this? How do they let you know that you have it wrong? How do they let you know that you have it correct? If you have multiple pets, are some of the pets more easily able to tell what part of the circle they are on and give cues? Are any of the pets more difficult to tell what part of the circle they are on and give cues?

References

Ainsworth, M., Blehar, M., Waters, E., & Wall, S. (1978). *Patterns of attachment: A psychology study of the strange situation*. Erlbaum.

Bowlby, J. (1995) [1950]. Maternal care and mental health. *Bulletin of the World Health Organization. The master work series. Vol. 3* (pp. 355–533, 2nd ed.). Jason Aronson.

Coyne, J., Powell, B., Hoffman, K., & Cooper, G. (2019). The circle of security. In CH Zeanah (Ed.), *Handbook of infant mental health* (pp. 500-513).

COS International (2022). *Circle of Security parenting: Evidence guide.* https://guidebook.eif.org.uk/programme/circle-of-security-parenting

https//:wwwhttps://guidebook.eif.org.uk/programme/circle-of-security-parenting

Hoffman K.T., Marvin R.S., Cooper G., & Powell B. (2006). Changing toddlers' &Preschoolers' attachment classification: The Circle of Security intervention. *Journal of Consulting & Clinical Psychology, 74*(6), 1017–1026. http://doi.10.1037/0022-006X.74.6.1017

Huber, A., McMahon, C.A., & Sweller, N. (2015). Efficacy of the 20-week COS Intervention: Changes in caregiver reflective functioning, representations, and child attachment in an Australian clinical sample. *Infant Mental Health Journal, 36,* 556–574. http://doi:10.1002/imhj.21540

Main, M., & Solomon, J. (1986). Discovery of an insecure-disorganised/disoriented attachment pattern. In T. B. Brazelton & M. W. Yogman (Eds.), *Affective development in infancy* (pp. 95–124). Ablex Publishing.

Powell, B., Cooper, G., Hoffman, K., & Marvin, B. (2014). *The circle of security intervention: Enhancing attachment in early parent-child relationships.* The Guilford Press.

Sroufe, L. A., Egeland, B., Carlson, E. A., & Collins, W. A. (2009). *The development of the person: The Minnesota study of risk and adaptation from birth to adulthood.* The Guilford Press.

Stern, D. N. (2018). *The interpersonal world of the infant: A view from psychoanalysis and developmental psychology.* Routledge.

Winnicott, D. W. (1991). *Playing and reality.* Psychology Press.

Yaholkoski, A., Hurl, K., & Theule, J. (2016). Efficacy of the Circle of Security Intervention: A meta-analysis. *Journal of Infant Child and Adolescent Psychotherapy, 15,* 95–103. https://doi.org/10.1080/15289168.2016.1163161

Chapter 5

Tuning in to Kids (TIK)

Ingeborg Stiefel

Tuning in to Kids (TIK) is a group program for parents of preschool-age children based on the concept of emotional intelligence (EI). The program was developed in 1999 by Professor Sophie Havighurst (Clinical Psychologist) and Ann Harley (Teacher) at the University of Melbourne, Australia (Havighurst & Harley, 2010). TIK emphasises the important role of the caregiver in facilitating emotional intelligence in young children through developing their predominately used parenting style to an emotion coaching style. Emotion coaching parenting includes the validation of the child's feelings, responding with empathy, assisting the child in understanding their feelings, regulating behaviour and solving problems with the help of active coaching. The program also emphasises the important role of parental self-awareness so parents recognise their own emotions, express them in appropriate ways and provide a good role model for their child when dealing with challenging feelings. TIK is a manualised program with a semi-structured format conducted by trained facilitators. The standard program consists of 6 weekly group sessions of a two-hour duration, with a possible extension to 8 sessions, if indicated. TIK was the first program developed as part of a suite of emotion coaching programs, which also includes Tuning in to Toddlers (TOTS), Tuning in to Teenagers (TINT), Dads Tuning in to Kids (DADS), and a program for teachers called A Whole School Approach (WSA) which is an adaptation of TINT. Further information on the TIK programs and facilitator training can be found on the TIK website (https://tuningintokids.org.au/). TIK is an evidence-based program, and research findings suggest that TIK increases positive parenting practices, with parents being more involved and less dismissive of their child's emotions. TIK also fosters emotional competence in children and reduces behavioural difficulties (Havighurst et al., 2013; Wilson et al., 2012).

Theoretical Underpinning of TIK

TIK follows early parenting programs based on humanistic theory. The program recognises the important role of emotions in communication and connection between parent and child (Havighurst & Harley, 2010). It is based on the concept of EI and on research that explores different parenting styles and their effect on child development.

Communication Approaches to Parenting

The roots of emotional coaching programs for parents date back to the late 1960s and are associated with Haim Ginott's approach to parenting (Ginott, 1965). Ginott was a clinical psychologist, and he proposed that the primary goal of human beings is to belong, feel connected to others and develop capability (Stiefel & Renner, 2004). Ginott stressed the need for parents to respect their child's feelings but also emphasised their role in setting limits when emotions are expressed behaviourally in inappropriate ways. Ginott's ideas were subsequently taken up and further developed. Faber and Mazlish (1980), students of Ginott, developed parenting self-help books in the 1970s and 1980s, and Gottman and Declaire (Gottman, 1997) outlined their approach to emotionally intelligent parenting in the 1990s. Core parenting skills in these earlier approaches include listening with full attention, acknowledging the child's feelings, talking about the child's emotional state, labelling the feelings, giving the child his wishes in fantasy, and mutual problem solving in which the parent provides scaffolding in the process of generating possible and realistic solutions (Faber & Mazlish, 1980). Faber and Mazlish (1980) proposed that parenting based on a communication skills approach helps children to understand and accept their own feelings, deal with the wide range of their emotions more effectively, trust their own perception, develop the capacity to read the feelings of others and learn to problem solve successfully in conflict situations. They also emphasised that these parenting skills needed to be applied with compassion in a real and authentic way. Further, parents must also be able to deal with their own negative feelings and communicate them when needed.

Emotional Intelligence

The term EI as a trait construct was first used in the 1960s (Roy, 2013) and is based on the assumption that there are multiple aspects of intelligence over and above the theory of cognitive intelligence as measured with standardised IQ tests (Goleman, 1996). In the 1980s, Howard Gardener introduced the concept of personal intelligence, consisting of interpersonal and intrapersonal components (Goleman, 1996). Interpersonal intelligence refers to people skills, such as understanding the motivation of other people, working cooperatively and responding appropriately to others (Goleman, 1996). Intrapersonal intelligence includes the capacity to assess one's own feelings and draw upon them to guide one's behaviour (Goleman, 1996). These early approaches also recognised the essential role of feelings in thinking. Gardner's approach focused more on the cognitive aspects of personal intelligence, the meta-emotions. Meta-emotions can be defined as higher-order emotions or as an organised set of feelings and thoughts about emotions in self and others (Fainsilber Katz et al., 2012).

John Mayer and Peter Salovey co-formulated a theory of EI in the 1990s. They understood EI as a set of mental abilities separate from personality or general intelligence yet overlapping with cognitive intelligence (Graves, 2000). EI, according to these authors, consists of a set of abilities, including the knowledge of one's own feelings (noticing them, monitoring emotional states), managing one's own emotions (self-soothing, self-control, for example, dealing with anxiety, irritability, anger), motivating oneself (managing emotions in the service of important goals), recognising emotions in others (empathy), and social competence in handling relationships (Goleman, 1996).

The term EI gained popularity with Goleman's seminal work on EI in the 1990s (Roy, 2013). Goleman proposed that EI is linked with success in most aspects of life. EI, as a multi-dimensional construct, refers to a set of emotion-processing abilities that, combined, contribute to improved social interaction. EI has been variously defined and includes a set of emotional competencies, including perception, processing and management of emotions both in self and in interaction with others, which includes the ability to recognise emotional states in others and respond appropriately and display empathy if indicated. People with well-developed EI are emotionally aware, tracking and identifying feeling states in themselves and in others, reading non-verbal cues in communication, appraising the emotion in regard to possible responses, and describing emotions using an emotional vocabulary. EI includes the management of one's own emotions and the emotions of others and the ability to regulate states of physical arousal by using self-calming strategies. Goleman's definition of EI is adapted from Salovey and Mayer and includes five basic emotional and social competencies (Goleman, 1999). These include:

- **Self-Awareness**: Emotional awareness and accurate self-assessment. Knowing one's feelings in any given moment and using this information to guide decision-making with a realistic assessment of one's own ability.

- **Self-Regulation**: Handling one's feelings so they facilitate and support the task at hand, recovering from emotional distress and being able to delay gratification to pursue goals. Keeping disruptive emotions and impulses in check.

- **Motivation**: Taking initiative and showing perseverance towards one's goals, dealing effectively with setbacks and frustration.

- **Empathy**: Taking other people's perspectives and sensing what they are feeling. Cultivating rapport and attunement with a broad diversity of people.

- **Social Skills**: Social competence, reading social situations accurately, handling emotions in relationships, interacting smoothly, being able to negotiate and settle disputes and working in cooperation with others.

High EI is associated with a range of personal, health and social benefits, including lower levels of stress, more satisfying relationships, increased ability to concentrate, focus and solve problems, a greater degree of resilience and better health (Gottman et al., 1997). High EI correlates positively with occupational outcome, school-based performance, prosocial development and overall educational achievement (Krauthamer Ewing et al., 2019). Goleman suggests that EI determines who excels in a job, succeeds in leadership positions and works well in teams (Goleman, 1999). The concept of EI has been explored and applied in a variety of contexts, such as leadership in the workplace and performance in educational settings (Costa & Faria, 2020; Shank, 2012). High IQ combined with a high EQ is often found in top performers. People who can read emotions in others are more popular and outgoing, more emotionally adjusted and perform better at school. EI fosters social competence, including the ability to follow display rules. For this to occur, a person must be able to read social, nonverbal cues in others, assess speech quality and body language and display appropriate non-verbal behaviour towards others in social interchanges (Goleman, 1996).

Goleman proposes that EI starts to develop in early childhood, is to a large extent learned, and processes of mimicry and mirroring between caregiver and child are involved. EI continues to develop over time and with maturity (Goleman, 1999). Repeated experiences between child and caregiver affect the formation of neural circuits responsible for emotional development. Goleman refers to critical developmental periods which can extend over several years during which sculpting and pruning of neural circuits is strongly affected by experience. For example, between 10 and 18 months, a time during which the orbitofrontal area of the prefrontal cortex forms connections with the limbic system, the infant, given the correct experience, will gradually learn how to calm themselves when distressed if this has been modelled by the caregiver. Critical areas responsible for emotional development mature slowly and offer the greatest opportunity for optimal outcomes during the early years, middle childhood and adolescence, though neural changes are possible at later stages with the help of corrective experiences such as psychotherapy (Goleman, 1999).

Empathy is an aspect of EI. Referring to Daniel Stern's concept of attuned parenting, early roots of empathy can be found in early childhood (Stern, 1995). An infant or toddler emotionally connected with their caregiver will experience interchanges of matched, reciprocal and empathic social exchanges in which the young child's feelings are responded to and mirrored back to the child by the caregiver, combined with soothing verbal or non-verbal communication if the infant is distressed (Goleman, 1996). Empathy builds on self-awareness of physical and emotional states, and the ability to experience one's own emotions leads to the ability to read the emotions of others. Hence it makes sense to provide parenting interventions to those caregivers that struggle with empathic, attuned and sensitive responses to their young child's needs.

Emotion Coaching Parenting

Emotion coaching programs are based on empirical research exploring the effects of different parenting styles on child development (Gottman, 1997). There is a growing body of scientific evidence that suggests that sensitive, attuned, warm and responsive parenting promotes social-emotional development in children and attachment security (Gottman, 1997). Parents who read their child's emotions, and perceive the adaptive function of emotions, are more inclined to respond empathically, help and comfort their child, but also provide scaffolding that helps the child to deal with the more challenging emotions (Krauthamer Ewing et al., 2019).

The research by Gottman and his colleagues, as evidenced by their longitudinal studies, suggests that there are strong benefits of emotional coaching to several aspects of child development (Gottman, 1997). First, the child learns to deal more effectively with a wide range of different feelings, utilising self-regulatory and self-soothing strategies if needed. Emotion coaching also affects physiological processes in the child, such as reduced heart rate, respiration and quicker recovery from stress. Gottman describes a high vagal tone in these children, referring to the parasympathetic autonomic nervous system, which helps to regulate bodily functions and assists with recovery after stressful events (Gottman, 1997). Emotion-coaching parents in their study reported a reduced rate of infection, increased attention and fewer behavioural problems in their children compared with parents who utilised predominantly other styles. These children experienced fewer negative feelings, performed better academically, related better in social situations, were teased less, had fewer conflicts with peers, and had better problem-solving abilities. Gottman states that emotion-coaching parenting leads to a good knowledge of the world of feelings and social relationships (Gottman, 1997). Emotion coaching is linked with better impulse control and an increased ability to delay gratification, with higher self-motivation and a reduced need for parental discipline. Their research also points to the important role fathers have in providing emotional coaching to their offspring, with strong positive effects on many aspects of child behaviour and development.

Emotion coaching helps parents to develop a style that focuses strongly on the emotional experience of the child, increases the parent's ability to understand their child's feelings, and assists the caregiver in dealing more successfully with situations that caused intense emotions and stress in the child. Emotion coaching parenting is active, structured and supportive, and it is markedly different to critical or punitive parenting, or a relaxed and permissive style, which lacks sufficient structure, guidance and discipline (Gottman, 1997).

TIK is based on Gottman's emotional coaching approach for parents (Gottman, 1997). Gottman and Schwartz-Gottman define Emotion Coaching as a research-based approach that teaches children the skills of regulating behaviour and emotions (Gottmann & Schwartz-Gottman, 2013). Emotion coaching helps children to understand the range of different feelings and why they are feeling a particular way. Gottman's approach underlies empirical evidence gathered in several studies, which assessed, coded and classified parent and child behaviour starting from the preschooler years to adolescence. Emotion coaching is a gradual process that does not happen overnight, and it is a suitable approach for children of all ages. A parent's views and feelings about emotions depend on their meta-emotion, whether they believe emotions should be expressed freely or should be controlled and hidden. There are cultural differences in regard to the expressiveness of emotions. However, most people and cultures express seven basic emotions; these are sadness, anger, contempt, fear, disgust, happiness and surprise. Emotions, according to Gottman and Schwartz-Gottman (2013), serve an important purpose in social interaction, and they act as a body compass to guide and direct thinking and behaviour. These authors also stress that parents only need to coach at certain times, and a rate of 35–40% is optimal (Gottman & Schwartz-Gottman, 2013). Parents should not use this strategy when they are highly distressed themselves or when the parent-child conflict is very tense. Self-soothing or separation from the situation may be indicated. Emotion coaching also assists parents in increasing awareness of their own feelings, including their expression of emotions, as these act as a model for the child.

Gottman and colleagues research explored parenting styles, and their classification overlaps with early categorisations, which assesses parenting based on Baumrind's dimension of parental support versus control (Rothrauff et al.,

2009; Viramontes (2009)). Based on the cross-classification, Rothrauff et al. (2009) list four categories:

- **Authoritative Style**: This style combines reasonable parental demands and expectations with expressed warmth, affection and responsiveness, in which both the parent's and the child's needs are regarded. This style has been found to be conducive to positive child adjustment.

- **Authoritarian Style**: These parents display a demanding style and value conformity and obedience in their child. Parental needs preside over those of the child. These parents can be rigid, show low support and responsiveness, and they can be punitive. This style has been associated with compromised developmental outcomes, including aggression and low social and academic performance.

- **Permissive Style**: This style is characterised by nurturing, closeness and acceptance but at the cost of rules and demands. These parents can be indulgent and overly tolerant of their child's needs and behaviour. This style also compromises long-term developmental outcomes.

- **Uninvolved Style**: This style lacks both of the important parenting qualities, parental demands and warmth. Parents displaying this style can be unresponsive, rejecting and neglectful. This style is associated with a poor developmental outcome.

Gottman and his colleagues exploration also found that most parents use one dominant parenting style, although a mix of styles is possible. Their extensive research included measurement of overt child behaviour and development and physiological measures in the child related to parenting styles (Gottman, 1997). Gottman's four categories are:

- **Dismissive Style**: Parents who predominantly utilise a dismissive style may feel uncomfortable about the expression of emotions and do not attend strongly to emotional expressions in their children, although some parents may respond to positive feelings expressed but not to negative ones, or they disregard or trivialise these states in their child. They may minimise the emotional experience, use humour, make light of the emotion (e.g., calling it 'silly feelings'), ignore or distract, or even believe that focus on negative emotions will increase the emotion's intensity. Further, these parents overall do not use stressful situations as opportunities for coaching and problem-solving. Parents with a dismissive style may believe that it is unhealthy to dwell on negative emotions, or they may fear that the child will lose control over the emotion. Nevertheless, these parents can be warm and loving (Gottman, 1997).

- **Disapproving Style**: Though overlapping with dismissive parenting, parents who are classified as disapproving tend to be critical and judgemental of their child's emotions and related behaviour, may reprimand or punish the child, believe that emotions should be controlled or that the child uses the emotion to manipulate others. Parents may label the behaviour in negative terms (e.g., 'Stop your stupid fear'), tend to focus on child obedience and feel that they need to set firm limits on the expression of negative emotions. Similar to the dismissive style, disapproving parents do not perceive stressful moments as an opportunity for problem-solving in relation to issues that lead to the expression of strong negative emotions. Parents with this style may lack empathy and may state that the child's emotional display is attention-seeking or an expression of immaturity (e.g., describe the child as 'A cry baby') that needs to stop as the child needs to toughen up for the real world (Gottman, 1997).

- **Laissez-faire Style**: Parents with a laissez-faire style are warm and empathic parents who accept and value feelings unconditionally but are overly permissive. They often find it hard to set limits on inappropriate behaviour, have few rules, and generally do not assist the child in solving the problem, which leads to emotional stress. Hence, they do not teach their children strategies on how to calm themselves (Gottman, 1997). This parenting style encourages and allows the expression of all emotions but does not put sufficient limits on how these emotions can be expressed.

- **Emotion Coaching Style**: Parents who frequently utilise emotion coaching have a strong awareness of their own emotions, and they are sensitive to the feeling states in their child and display empathy for their child's distress. They value emotions as an important aspect of life experience, and they can tolerate emotional expression in their child. Overall, they feel confident that they can help their child deal with the different range of emotions. These parents try to understand the link between the emotion and the situation that has led to the expression of strong feelings or behaviour; they will label the emotion and will guide the child to solve the issue that led to the high level of arousal in the child (Gottman, 1997).

Gottman's parenting program (Gottman, 1997) consists of five steps:

1. *Awareness of emotions in self and child*, which requires tuning into and being sensitive to feeling states in both self and others. Feelings may be expressed in different ways depending on variables, such as gender and cultural background, and young children's feelings may not always be easy to understand.

2. *Recognising emotions as opportunities for intimacy and teaching*, usually when emotions are expressed at a lower or mid-range level of intensity and utilising this moment to connect with the child.

3. *Listening with empathy and validating the child's feelings, using simple language.*

4. *Naming the emotion and/or helping the child to verbally label their feeling state.* This process is believed to help increase the emotional vocabulary of the child and calms both the parent and the child.

5. *Setting limits on the expression of emotions if needed.* All feelings are acceptable, but the behavioural expression may not be. Inappropriate behaviours include hitting, breaking toys or verbally abusing others. The parent stays calm while also helping the child to understand and generate ideas for problem-solving, and finding a good solution to the problem. The 'traffic light colours' can be helpful to assess emotional expression according to the three categories, green standing for appropriate and desirable expression of feelings, yellow stands for expression that can be tolerated but behaviour that is not dangerous, and red indicates dangerous or highly unacceptable behavioural expression of a feeling.

Depending on the child's ability and the complexity of the issue, the parent offers gentle guidance in this process. The emotion coaching parent provides scaffolding by helping the child understand the child's goal (what the child's intention was, what the child tried to achieve, how the child perceived the conflict), generate possible solutions as to how to resolve the issue, assists in evaluating each possible solution and selecting the best strategy from a range of possible options. Assistance takes into consideration the developmental age and the cognitive capacities of the child. Some children enjoy getting help from the parent in this process, while others may resent too much parental assistance. Gottman and Schwartz-Gottman (2013) stress the importance of love, affection and connection between parent and child but also emphasise the need for guidance and problem-solving. When problems occur, the authors suggest talking calmly, staying empathic, and stating facts and parental observation without criticism and blame. For example: 'Oh no, it is broken, your favourite toy', 'How upsetting', 'Dad must have driven over it when he reversed the car, he could not see it', 'He may be able to fix it'. 'What could you do next time to make sure it is not left in the driveway?'

The Role of Empathy in Emotion Coaching

Empathic parental responding is a strong focus in emotion coaching parenting programs, such as TIK. Indeed, Gottman states that empathy is the foundation of emotion coaching (Gottman, 1997). Empathy is a multi-layered concept consisting of several components, each involving different brain regions. Elliott et al. (2011) refer to three different aspects of empathy: emotional empathy, cognitive empathy and emotion regulation.

- **Emotional experience**: Empathy is understood as an emotional experience involving shared affect, an emotional/physical experience of the affect state of the other person and may involve automatic and body-based responses (Elliott et al., 2011). It is an emotional stimulation that mirrors the emotional elements of the other person and relies on limbic structures as anatomical substrates. Emotional empathy develops early and consists of a vicarious experience of another person's emotional state, may involve a somatic component (body sensation), can occur at a sub-conscious level, and involves subtle motor responses based on mirror neurons (McDonald & Messinger, 2011).

- **Cognitive empathy**: Cognitive empathy, on the other hand, involves perspective taking, a cognitive and conscious appraisal of the other person's experience, and an imagining of the other person's emotional and situational state. Cognitive empathy requires theory of mind, includes cognitive processing and may include language, describing the perceived experience of the other person in words (McDonald & Messinger, 2011). It involves the younger regions of the brain, the cortex (Elliott et al., 2011).

- **Emotion regulation**: According to Elliott and colleagues, empathy also involves a third component, an emotion regulatory process, which helps soothe or reappraise personal distress states in self and others or mobilise responses. The neuro-anatomical substrate involved in this process is the orbitofrontal cortex (Elliott et al., 2011).

Empathy develops during the preschool years, and even toddlers can display clear awareness of observed stress in other people, for example, by engaging in some form of helping behaviour (McDonald & Messinger, 2011). By the third year of life, most children have established empathy-related behaviours, such as displaying verbal or facial concern or offering some helping behaviour (McDonald & Messinger, 2011). Empathy development is part of the larger personality trait of prosocial behaviour (McDonald & Messinger, 2011) and is based on genetics, neuronal processes, temperament, and socialisation factors. Elliott and colleagues point to the crucial role empathy and mentalising (understanding, predicting action and intention of others) play for effective and successful functioning in social groups and value empathy as a critical factor for the developing affective bond between child and main caregiver (Elliott et al., 2011).

Outline of the TIK Programs

TIK is a manualised program with a semi-structured format consisting of core components, optional segments and some flexibility in the sequential presentation of content. The standard six-week program is presented in a group format to parents and other caregivers of preschool-age children and is suitable for both clinical and non-clinical populations of parents and children. The optimal group size is 8 participants (with one group leader) or 10–14 participants with 2 facilitators (Harvighurst & Harley, 2010). Smaller groups may be indicated for families with more complex clinical issues. A session duration of 2 hours is recommended. However, some parents may benefit from a slightly longer session duration. The program also offers an extension to 8 sessions and can be delivered in individual work with parents. Booster sessions may also be offered to help parents maintain emotion coaching skills, increase their parenting confidence and address any new parenting challenges. The program has been trademarked, and only trained professionals can advertise, deliver the program and access course resources. To facilitate TIK, clinicians need to complete workshops conducted by qualified TIK trainers, and the cost for a three-half-day workshop for certification is $1012. Group leaders should have a background in allied health and related disciplines and have experience with group facilitation. There is a modified program available for fathers only (Dads TIK) of slightly longer duration (7 sessions), TIK for parents of younger and older children (toddlers and adolescents), and an extended version for parents of highly traumatised children (Havighurst et al., 2021).

The aim of TIK is to increase parental competence and help parents to develop new or extend their current set of positive parenting skills, including responsiveness to their child's emotions and expressed empathy (Havighurst et al., 2013). The group format also offers social support and peer learning from each other. The program assists parents in dealing more effectively with their own level of stress. TIK is unique in its focus on the emotional experience of both parent and child. It assists the parent in finding ways to help their child deal more effectively with stressful emotions by developing self-soothing capacity and increased interpersonal skills. TIK has a strong relationship focus aiming at strengthening the bond between parent and child. The program offers resources, including videotaped scenarios of parent–child interaction demonstrating different parenting styles for comparison, which can be purchased by clinicians trained in the model via the website www.tuningintokids.org.au/.

The Six Group Sessions of TIK

Session 1: Setting Out – How to raise emotionally intelligent children

Session 1 starts with common aspects of group work, such as greeting, developing rules for the group, explaining the structure of sessions, and introducing the program (Havighurst & Harley, 2010). Emotional Intelligence and Emotion Coaching are defined and explained in the context of parenting. Facilitators stress the benefits of Emotion Coaching in terms of increasing the bond between caregiver and child, decreasing child problem behaviour and points of conflict (as the parent does not disapprove of the emotional expression of the child), and developing a child's ability to self-soothe or cope with stressful emotions. Gottman's five steps of Emotion Coaching are also presented, and group leaders provide the reasons why Emotion Coaching improves child behaviour. The group explores ways in which parents can connect with their children. Parents are encouraged to complete home exercises during the week (e.g., opportunities for parents to utilise emotional talk to connect with their child and to record these times in a diary).

Session 2: Naming the Emotion

As with all subsequent sessions, Session 2 starts with a warm-up exercise for the parents. This can include a relaxation exercise or the use of emotion stickers for parents to identify their own emotional states. The start of the sessions also offers a review of the week and the parent's homework task. The session then moves to the discussion of typical child development during the preschool years, parenting tasks and challenges (e.g., establishing routines), and the value of descriptive praise as a positive parenting strategy. Parents are encouraged to describe desirable child behaviour and link the behaviour with the positive effects the behaviour has on others. For example, 'You put your plate in the dishwasher, that's great, it saves me so much extra work', or 'You shared your toys with your sister, I am so proud of you, you are so grown up. She looks really happy, and she will not snatch it off you.'

The Emotion Coaching Steps are introduced by a) Noticing/guessing the child's feelings, clarifying with questions if needed, b) Linking the child's behaviour with a feeling state and labelling the emotion, offering examples of possible feeling states if needed, expressing empathy, c) Responding how the parent would feel if in a similar situation, and d) Exploring the stressful situation and feelings further, for example, with questions about the situations, people involved and their behaviour. It can also be helpful to ask the child to locate the emotion in the body. Emotion Coaching is practised in role play. Parents are encouraged to utilise opportunities for Emotion Talking Times and help their child identify feelings aided with the help of a simple visual chart depicting facial expressions. The aim of the session is also to increase the parents' awareness of their own emotions and to understand the role of their meta-emotions. Dismissive parenting is explored further, defined and described behaviourally with concrete examples (for example, by telling the child not to worry or the parent offering distraction).

Session 3: Understanding the Child's Emotional Expression

Ideal conditions and opportunities for Emotion Coaching are discussed, such as low or mid-range stress situations for the child or the parent and when Emotion Coaching should be deferred (e.g., parents are rushed or stressed, high-intensity emotions in the child, fatigue, situations in public). The session then focuses on the concept and language of empathy, helping parents to describe feelings and states in their child using appropriate language (e.g., 'I can see you are feeling frustrated'). Emotion Coaching is role-played using typical situations covering different feeling states. The parents are given a sheet with a large range of feeling states, broadly representing the four categories of Happy, Sad, Angry and Afraid. Homework includes labelling the child's feelings, expressing empathy, and asking the child to draw different emotions. The aim of the session is to help the parents to become more skilled in Emotion Coaching.

Session 4: Self-care, Problem-solving and Coaching Fears and Worries

The aim of the session is to consolidate Emotion Coaching skills related to different feeling states and to increase participants' awareness of the detrimental effects of critical parenting. The different parenting styles (e.g., dismissive and disapproving) are contrasted with Emotion Coaching. Gottman's DVD (2008) offers enacted parent-child interactions, demonstrating each style and summarises the Emotion Coaching briefly (Gottman, 2008). Problem-solving is then role played within the complete Emotion Coaching sequence of the model; listening and labelling emotions, empathy, brainstorming solutions and helping the child to select the most appropriate option to address the stress or conflict. The session emphasises the need for the parent to be aware of their emotional state and to find a solution that is mutually satisfying for both if the conflict is between parent and child. Common fears and worries of preschoolers are discussed, and relaxation exercises for children are introduced, for example, the noodle metaphor: stiff/tense = uncooked spaghetti vs floppy/relaxed = cooked noodles. The program also utilises the character of a turtle in a story and as a simple stress management strategy which involves the image of the child going into the shell and stating, 'I can be calm'.

Emotion coaching during the week involves the utilisation of Emotion Talk Times, the introduction of stress management strategies to the child and for parents to notice when they display critical parenting.

Session 5: Emotion Coaching Addressing Angry Emotions

The session helps parents develop Emotion Coaching skills around anger. The difference between an expression of angry feelings and inappropriate angry behaviour is made to help parents realise that all feelings are acceptable, but not all behaviour is, and also stresses the need for limit setting. The session focuses on both the child's and the parent's emotions. Feelings underlying the expression of anger are explored, such as frustration, jealousy or fatigue.

Emotion coaching for anger has several steps. First, validation of the child's emotion; second, stating the limits (for example, stating the house rules of non-aggression); and problem-solving. Anger management techniques are introduced including physical/emotional outlets (e.g., letting off steam by yelling anger down the plug hole and rinsing the words away; banging a drum) and soothing techniques (e.g., having a bath). The parents are instructed to utilise the Turtle Technique with their child. Examples of anger coaching are given, and parents are encouraged to spot anger referring to a real situation in their child's life. The session progresses with strategies for sibling fighting and problems around eating (optional). Home activities include Emotion Coaching Technique with the child, and the parent's own anger management.

We have found in our own emotion coaching program (Communication & Connection) that questions are an effective strategy for the exploration of the problem situation and for problem-solving in the context of anger (Stiefel & Renner, 2004). Questions have to be tailored toward the developmental and language level of the young child. For problem exploration: 'Tell me what happened, 'Was somebody mean to you?', 'How did it start?', 'What happened next?', 'Did you feel scared or rather angry', 'Did anybody try to help you?'. For brainstorming solutions: 'What would be the best thing to do now?', 'What could you do tomorrow?', 'Do you think that's the best idea?', 'What else could be helpful?', 'Which one might work best, what do you think?', 'Which one would you like to try in the morning?', 'Do you want to test it out?', 'Do you want me to help you?'. The 'W' questions invite the child to think, 'When, where, what, who with' and are usually well tolerated by children with oppositional behaviours.

Session 6: Emotionally Intelligent Parenting Now and in the Future.

The session offers an optional self-care component, and progresses to a review of the week, offers time for role plays of typical problem situations, revision of the parenting styles and a review of the steps of Emotion Coaching. Parents receive a hand-out of a large list of children's books covering typical emotional problems encountered by young children, such as anger, fear, jealousy, loneliness, sadness, anger, and moods. The session offers an opportunity to address any issue not already covered in previous sessions and explores avenues for further assistance should intervention be required in the future.

The following is an example of a parent completing the TIK group program.

Melanie, Karyn and Mick

Melanie and her two children, Mick age 5, and Karyn, age 3, were referred to a child and family counselling service by a paediatrician who had diagnosed Mick with Attention Deficit Hyperactivity Disorder (ADHD). Melanie reported that she had completed a brief parenting program, but nothing had worked. When the clinician asked about the content of the program, Melanie recalled that the group leader had discussed praising Mick when he was behaving well and ignoring minor behaviour issues and meltdowns. Melanie's concerns were that Mick was 'constantly on the go', his 'behaviour was impulsive', 'he disobeyed parental rules', and she felt exhausted trying to correct his behaviour, as he 'did not respond to common sense parenting'. Karyn, on the other hand, was very anxious and clingy, did not mix well with children at her preschool, and had attached herself to one teacher and one slightly older child in her age group. When the therapist asked Melanie to explore what she meant by 'common sense parenting', Melanie reflected upon her childhood. She said she grew up in an immigrant family; both of her parents worked in order to establish themselves financially in Australia, and she and her younger brother became self-sufficient at a very early age. Melanie described her mother as busy, never having time for the children, tired and cranky, but nevertheless, the mother provided healthy meals in line with the family's cultural background. Further description revealed that her mother had a dismissive style, not responding to the children's emotional needs, and a common verbal response was 'Just get on with it' when Melanie or her brother felt distressed. Melanie said you just did what you were told. Her mother also often referred to her own deprived upbringing and stressed how much better Melanie's situation was, and she should not complain. Melanie could not remember times of closeness, moments of being comforted, being read to or doing craft activities together unless she was physically sick, at which time her mother cared well for her.

In the initial joint session with the children, the therapist observed on several occasions that Melanie also displayed a dismissive style of parenting with her two children. For example, when the children approached her during the session demanding help with a toy, she told them to wait but continued with the conversation with the therapist. When Karyn hurt herself, Melanie dismissed the pain and said it did not need a band-aide. When Mick said he was hungry, Melanie stated that he consumed a large breakfast and did not need anything now. The therapist understood from observation and report that Melanie had good rules in place in regard to daily routines such as bedtime, playtime, use of technology and meal times. Her husband was from a similar cultural background and worked 7 days per week, running his own business. Hence, his involvement with the children was limited. Melanie said some months ago, both she and her husband had started praising the children more often after it was suggested by a friend, but Melanie did not think it had made any difference in regard to either Karyn's anxiety or Mick's challenging behaviour, and they were probably doing it less often now.

Melanie accepted the offer to enrol in a TIK course. She attended all sessions, completed all homework and was an active group participant. However, she struggled with the concept of empathy in the beginning but gradually learned to give feeling states a name, and she also started to appreciate that empathy was an important part of bringing up children by reflecting on her own deprivation during her childhood. However, in role-play, her expression of empathy remained at a cognitive level, being able to describe how her children were feeling but lacking the deeper emotional and non-verbal expression which indicates to others, without words, that the parent can put herself into the child's shoes and experience the emotion. When the Problem-Solving components of TIK were introduced, Melanie not only told the group that she liked this approach, but she also reported a great improvement in Mick's behaviour. Instead of directing, shouting, correcting, and reprimanding Mick, she reported that sitting down with Mick and brainstorming ideas together had been hugely successful, as Mick felt he was involved and, to some extent, in charge of finding a solution to the problem. Despite Melanie's somewhat restricted expression of empathy, she reported that Karyn had started to respond to her identifying and naming feelings around her daughter's anxiety. Separation on preschool days though still an issue, was less stressful. Melanie felt the reflection of empathy gave her a tool to use when Karyn showed signs of stress or anxiety, and she herself no longer felt so helpless, not knowing what to do. At the end of the two booster sessions, all group members were invited to contact the centre if further input was needed. At a final telephone check-in, Melanie reported that they were travelling well and she would contact the therapist should further therapy be needed.

Question for Readers: What might be effective and facilitating therapy techniques to help a parent like Melanie, who has experienced very limited levels of empathy during her own childhood, to develop both her cognitive (verbal) and emotional/non-verbal skills to express empathy?

Think about the role of the therapist-client relationship in this process, role plays, therapist feedback techniques, viewing of recordings of role plays, the role of other group members, reflection on culture and Melanie's experiences in her relationship with her own mother that might be relevant in this process.

The Evidence Base for TIK

TIK is based on longstanding research into parenting styles and on Gottman's concept of emotionally intelligent parenting and involves the steps of coaching parents in developing Emotion Coaching competence in their child. While Gottman's model developed out of a longstanding tradition of humanistic parenting approaches, which value the importance of emotions in child development and good communication between parent and child, Gottman's approach is also based on research findings, exploring the effects of different parenting styles on child behaviour and development, specifically the theory of emotional intelligence and Baumrind's categorisation of parenting styles in the 1960s. Research into parenting is ongoing and recent studies have confirmed the findings by Gottman and colleagues, emphasising the link between positive parenting styles and the levels of emotional intelligence in children (Wang et al., 2019).

TIK, as a program for toddlers, preschoolers, school-age children and adolescents, is developing a strong research base with randomised controlled trials into the effectiveness and efficacy of the program. Further information can be found on the TIK website www.tuningintokids.org.au. TIK for parents of preschoolers has undergone several studies to explore the effects of the program on parent and child behaviour. A randomised controlled study with parents of preschoolers, age range 4–5 years, compared TIK with standard paediatric care (Havighurst et al., 2013). Parents in both groups showed a reduced level of dismissive responses to child emotions, and both reported lower levels of child behaviour problems. However, the parents who had completed TIK displayed increased levels of empathy and emotion coaching ability, and the children increased their knowledge of emotions. Preschool teachers also reported a reduction in problem behaviours. The participating parents showed a greater ability to label emotions, and they explored emotional states more often compared with the control group. The caregivers also showed greater improvement in emotion-coaching parenting over time.

There is growing evidence that TIK is an appropriate intervention for anxiety in the preschool years, in particular for separation anxiety and social phobia (Edrissi et al., 2019). A pilot undertaken by these researchers in Iran suggests that the TIK intervention resulted in a significant reduction in the level of anxiety presentations in a group of 4-6-year-old children and that clinical changes remain stable over time.

A large research study has also been conducted by Wilson and colleagues involving fathers (Wilson et al., 2016). The modified program DADS Tuning In To Kids ran over 7 sessions, included content relevant to fathers and allowed more time to process the content of the program, based on the fact that fathers overall have a decreased emotional awareness and lower levels of reading emotions (Wilson et al., 2016). The study indicated a number of improvements, including increased levels of empathy, encouragement of emotion expression and a reduction in emotion dismissive beliefs and practices. There was also a positive effect on child problem behaviour.

There is growing evidence that TIK is an appropriate program for parents from different cultures. Research has been conducted in different countries, including Iran, Germany, USA and Norway, and applied in both community and clinic settings (tuningintokids.org.au; Meybodi et al., 2019) and TIK has been culturally adjusted for mothers of preschoolers in China (Qui & Shum, 2022). There is preliminary support that Trauma Focused TIK, an extended version of the program, is a suitable treatment for children who have experienced complex trauma (Havighurst et al., 2021). This extended TIK program adds three components to the standard TIK, education about trauma, the effects of trauma on children, and how trauma can disrupt the attachment relationship. Treatment with clinical samples indicated that the program helped parents to understand the function of their child's behaviour and that parents changed their parenting response to their child's emotional expression. Positive effects have been found in several areas, including the parent-child relationship, parents' regulation of their own emotions and their overall mental health (Havighurst et al., 2021).

Discussion

Emotion Coaching programs are different from programs based on social learning and behavioural change principles, which focus strongly on reinforcement of appropriate behaviour, effective management of challenging behaviour, and compliance with parental requests. However, many parenting programs include both the structural-behavioural aspects of parenting, including rules and discipline, and the relationship components. Structural aspects refer to the setting of clear and age-appropriate rules, parental consistency, the giving of effective and clear directives, shaping appropriate child behaviour through positive attention and praise, and dealing effectively with problem behaviour through ignoring, distracting, time-out or negative consequences, including punishment or withdrawal of privilege. Relationship components in behavioural parenting programs emphasise the need for the parent to be involved and attentive, listen to their child and engage in joyful interaction. Parents are encouraged to provide a positive learning environment and strongly reinforce desirable behaviour. This is based on the idea that the learning of new skills, but also the application of discipline, is facilitated within the realm of a positive connection between parent and child.

Behavioural programs stress the need for a parental hierarchy in which the parent should be firmly in charge of the child, especially when the child displays intense negative emotions or problem behaviour. While these programs also stress the importance of emotional connection and closeness between parent and child, 'parent management' of the child's behaviour receives stronger emphasis. The parent becomes effective and applies a set of skills that encourages appropriate behaviour by reinforcing it strongly, but also by setting clear limits on problem behaviour by stating rules and ignoring problem behaviour by decreasing attention. Child compliance with parental requests and a reduction in problem behaviour are important outcomes of parent training in these programs.

Emotion Coaching parenting programs, on the other hand, focus first and foremost on the emotional connection between parent and child, and they value the important role of emotions as an aspect of human experience, though structural components of parenting are not disregarded. Emotion Coaching is active, empathic and sensitive and will offer the child an understanding between the emotion and the underlying problem, guiding the child through problem-solving steps to resolve the issue that led to strong negative feelings. The parent is seen as a facilitator, helping the child to recognise challenging feeling states and inviting the child to problem solve in finding good solutions that decrease intra- or interpersonal stress. Emotions and social conflicts are seen as opportunities for closeness and teaching and offer validation of feelings. In this process, the parent provides scaffolding to help the child understand the conflict, followed by finding alternative ways of dealing with difficult emotions or situations. The ultimate outcome of Emotion Coaching is not compliance or obedience to parental requests but responsible child behaviour, a developing ability in the child to make their own good decisions, cope with challenges, enjoy the accomplishments and positive social relationships in life (Gottman, 1997). The parent is strongly involved and applies gentle governance.

Both parenting approaches have an important place in parent training and therapy. Behavioural approaches may suit families who lack in a clear structure. These families may have few, confusing or unclear rules, parental expectations may change ad hoc, requests are unclear and vague, consequences are not explained to the child, or they are inappropriate for the child's age. These parents may be inconsistent in their response to a specific child's problem behaviour, or challenging behaviour is intermittently reinforced. Further, there may be conflict or inconsistency between parents. A parenting approach that helps the parents to establish some basic house rules and routines with clear expectations and a consistent response on the part of the parent and reinforcement of desirable behaviour can be extremely helpful. On the other hand, parents who may be organised and consistent but overly strict, harsh, dismissive or lacking emotional involvement may gain specifically from an Emotion Coaching approach. The overly relaxed parents with a laissez-faire style will also benefit from Emotion Coaching by utilising problem-solving components in addition to their warm and empathic style. The problem-solving component in TIK, which invites mutual involvement, is also a suitable approach for children with developing conduct problems or those who cannot deal well with adult directives. TIK offers gentle adult coaching and stimulation of the child's own resources.

TIK is a fairly young group program for parents, though the concept of Emotion coaching parenting dates back to the late 1960s, as evidenced in a large range of parent self-help books. TIK is in the process of establishing its empirical evidence as a relevant and effective program for parents. We see the value of TIK as a stand-alone program for mild to moderate developmental and relationship issues or as a treatment modality that can be combined with either other parenting approaches in sequential format or as an additional therapeutic approach in the context of family and child therapy or school intervention (Havighurst et al., 2014).

We believe that good clinical assessment is needed to determine which of the available parenting program options should be offered to a family at which time and in which sequence or if other forms of treatment are required. Our clinical experience indicates that highly stressed families, often described as 'chaotic', with limited and confusing rules, may benefit first from the intervention that focuses on a clearer family structure and a firmer parental hierarchy, and once this is established, gain more from the concept of emotion coaching. Some families initially prefer a more skills-based approach, as offered by TIK, whereas others benefit more from a highly reflective program (such as Circle of Security) as a way of addressing parenting struggles and parent-child relationship issues. The opportunity to reflect on the emotions of both caregiver and child makes TIK a potentially suitable model for working with clinical situations where both parent and child have jointly experienced a period of significant stress in their lives, such as situations of family violence, relationship conflict, loss or other trauma. Further, the approach, as represented in the TIK program, offers an attuned and involved approach that will foster attachment and connection between caregiver and child in which emotions of both child and parent are valued as an important aspect of human experience.

Conclusion

Based on longstanding knowledge of the effects of parenting styles on child development, clinical evidence over the past 50 years and a growing body of sound empirical evidence utilising RCTs, there is no doubt that TIK fills an important niche in parent training (Gottman & Schwartz-Gottman, 2013; Havighurst & Harley, 2010; Qui & Shum, 2022). We see the distinct advantage of the program in its specific and focused scope, helping parents become effective emotion coaches, and as a result, the program can be targeted specifically for parent-child issues that require input in the area of sensitive, attuned parenting within a semi-structured group format that helps parents to understand and practice the needed steps towards this goal. Our clinical experience indicates that TIK may not be a sufficient, stand-alone intervention for all complex parenting issues or for severe child and parent relationship conflicts, where additional intervention may be required. However, further research may help to understand the specific needs of these families and the value of the TIK program to address these. Nevertheless, a large population of parents in community and clinical settings will benefit from what TIK can offer and as such, TIK offers a cost-effective and brief group intervention that can address both internalising and externalising problems of early childhood and parenting deficits.

Reader's Exercises

You are planning to run a TIK group for parents of preschool-aged children, and you need to find two more participants in order to have sufficient numbers. You interviewed three families recently referred to your service.

The first family consists of a single mum Judy, age 23, with two children, 5-year-old Emma and a new baby. The children have different fathers, and Judy reports that she struggles relating to her 5-year-old daughter, does not enjoy closeness and describes the child in negative terms. She reports that her older child was the result of a difficult relationship, and there is no contact between Emma and the father. Judy is passive in the session, not sure what to expect from the service. As a reason for referral, Judy states that she wants to improve the compliance of her daughter to requests.

The second family consists of Catherine, the mother age 30, her new partner and her 4-year-old daughter Louise. Catherine has struggled to overcome depression, her GP prescribed an anti-depressant, and Catherine recently started seeing a counsellor. Catherine feels extremely guilty and responsible for Louise's problem behaviours, which include extreme shyness, anxiety and sometimes outbursts of anger. Refusal to go to preschool is a major issue, and she wants to address this issue.

The third family consists of Ching (28) and her child Mei (4). Ching reports that Mei is a very bright, independent and highly spirited child and a 'real handful'. She struggles to cope with Mei's demanding and independent behaviour but jokes that Mei is just like her maternal grandmother. Ching wants to address her relationship with Mei, as they clash in daily arguments, and the intensity of arguments has been increasing over the past 6 months.

Consider the three families. Which family (from the limited information) appears both ready and potentially suitable for a TIK group as the first point of intervention? What other information or intervention may be required for some of these families prior to recommencing a TIK group, and what components of your intervention may be important to consider first? How would you introduce the TIK program to those parents you think may benefit from this intervention?

References

Costa, A., & Faria, L. (2020). Implicit theories of emotional intelligence, ability and trait-emotional intelligence and academic achievement. *Psychological Topics*, *29*(1), 43–61. https://doi.org/10.31820/pt.29.1.3

Edrissi, F., Havighurst, S. S., Aghebati, A., Habibi, M., & Abbas, M. A. (2019). A pilot study of the tuning into kids parenting program in Iran for reducing preschool children's anxiety. *Journal of Child and Family Studies*, *28*(6), 1695-1702. https://doi.10.1007/S10826-019-01400-0

Elliott, R., Bohart, A. C., Watson, J. C., & Greenberg, L. S. (2011). Empathy. In J. Norcross (Ed.), *Psychotherapy relationships that work.* (2nd ed.), (pp 132–152). Oxford University Press.

Faber, A., & Mazlish, E. (1980). *How to talk so kids will listen and listen so kids will talk.* Avon Books.

Fainsilber Katz, L., Maliken, A. C., & Stettler, N. M. (2012). Parental metal-emotion philosophy: A review of research and theoretical framework. *Child Development Perspectives*, *6*(4), 417–422. https://doi.org/10.1111/j.1750-8606.2012.00244.x

Ginott, H. G. (1965). *Between parent and child. New solutions for old problems.* Macmillan.

Goleman, D. (1996). *Emotional Intelligence. Why it can matter more than IQ.* Bloomsbury.

Goleman, D. (1999). *Working with emotional intelligence.* Bloomsbury.

Gottman, J. (1997). *Raising an emotionally intelligent child. The heart of parenting.* Simon & Schuster.

Gottman, J. M., Fainsilber Katz, L., & Hooven, C. (1997). *Meta emotions: How families communicate emotionally.* Lawrence Earlbaum.

Gottman, J. (2008). *Emotion Coaching. Parenting styles and five steps of emotion coaching.* DVD, Talaris Institute, 100-606-08/08. https://www.gottman.com /product/emotion-coaching-the-heart-of-parenting-video-program/

Gottman, J. & Schwartz-Gottman, J. (2013). *Emotion coaching. The heart of parenting.* The Gottman Institute.

Graves, M. L. M. (2000). *Emotional intelligence, general intelligence, and personality: Assessing the construct validity of an emotional intelligence test using structural equation modelling.* [Doctoral Dissertation, California School of Professional Psychology].https://www.proquest.com/docview/304647427/fulltextPDF/DEF7 46AA378A4B4DPQ/1?accountid=166958

Havighurst, S., & Harley, A. (2010). *Tuning in to Kids. Emotionally intelligent parenting. Program Manual.* Mindful. Centre for Training and Research in Developmental Health. University of Melbourne.

Havighurst, S. S., Wilson, K. R., Harley, A. E., Kehoe, C., Efron, D., & Prior, M. R. (2013). 'Tuning into kids': Reducing young children's behaviour problems using an emotion coaching parenting program. *Child Psychiatry and Human Development, 44*(2), 247–64. http://doi10.1007/s10578-012-0322-1

Havighurst, S. S., Duncombe, M., Franklin, E., Holland, K., Kehoe, C., & Stargatt, R. (2014). An emotion-focused early intervention for children with emerging conduct problems. *Journal of Abnormal Child Psychology, 43,* 749–760. https://www.doi.org/10.1007/s10802-014-9944-z

Havighurst, S. S., Murphy, J. L., & Kehoe, C. E. (2021). Trauma-Focused Tuning into Kids: Evaluation in a clinical service. *Children, 8,* 1038. https://doi.org/ 10.3390/children8111038

Krauthammer Ewing, S., Herres, J., Dilks, K. E., Rahim, F., & Trentacosta, C. J. (2019). Understanding of emotions and empathy: Predictors of positive parenting with preschoolers in economically stressed families. *Journal of Child and Family Studies, 28,* 1346–1358. https://doi.org/10.1007/s10826-018-01303-6

McDonald, N. M., & Messinger, D. D. (2011). The development of empathy: How, when, and why. *Free Will, Emotions, and Moral Actions: Philosophy and Neuroscience in Dialogue, 23*, 333–359. https://www.researchgate.net/publication/267426505

Meybodi, F. A., Mohammadkhani, P., Pourshahbaz, A., Dolatshahi, B., & Havighurst, S. S. (2019). Improving parent emotion socialisation practices: Piloting Tuning into Kids in Iran for children with disruptive behaviour problems. Family Relation. *Interdisciplinary Journal of Applied Family Science, 68*(5), 596–607. https://doi.org/10.1111/fare.12387

Qui, C. & Shum, K. (2022). Emotion coaching intervention for Chinese mothers of preschoolers: A randomised controlled trial. *Child Psychiatry and Human Development, 53*(1), 61–75. https://doi.org/10.1007/s10578-020-01101-6

Rothrauff, T. C., Cooney, T.M., & An, J.S. (2009). Remembered parenting styles and adjustment in middle and late adulthood. *Journal of Gerontology: Social Sciences, 64*(1), 137–146. https://doi.org/10.1093/geronb/gbn008

Roy, S. R. (2013). *Leading with trait emotional intelligence in the higher education classroom: An exploratory study investigating trait emotional intelligence in higher education faculty members.* [Doctoral Dissertation, University of Charleston]. https://www.proquest.com/dissertations-theses/leading-with-trait-emotional-intelligence-higher/docview/1399591779/se-2

Shank, J. C. (2012). *Emotional intelligence and educational leadership: Measuring the emotional intelligence of educational leaders and their corresponding student achievement.* [Doctoral Dissertation, Idaho State University]. https://www.proquest.com/dissertations-theses/emotional-intelligence-educational-leadership/docview/1017718068/se-2?accountid=166958

Stern, D. N. (1995). *The motherhood constellation: A unified view of parent–infant psychotherapy.* Basic Books.

Stiefel, I., & Renner, P. (2004). Beyond behaviour — The importance of communication and connection in parenting 'defiant' children: Pilot Study and program. *Australian and New Zealand Journal of Family Therapy, 25*(2), 84–93. https://doi.org/10.1002/j.1467-8438.2004.tb00590.x

Viramontes, M. (2009). *Parenting styles and practices and their impact on school behaviour.* [Masters Thesis, California State University]. https://www.proquest.com/docview/305179826/previewPDF/AC6E945213224AD0PQ/3?accountid=166958

Wang, Y., Li, Z., & Zhu, L. (2019). Emotional intelligence of 3- to 6-year-olds and parenting style: Peer communication ability as a mediator. *Social Behavior and Personality: An International Journal, 47*(12), e8636. https://doi.org/10.2224/sbp.8636

Wilson, K., Havighurst, S. S., & Harley, A. E. (2012). Tuning in to Kids: An Effectiveness trial of a parenting program targeting Emotional socialisation of preschoolers. *Journal of the Division of Family Psychology of the American Psychological Association (Division 43), 26*(1), 56–65. https://doi.org/10.1080/07317107.2021.2024717

Wilson, K. R., Havighurst, S. S., Kehoe, C., & Harley, A. E. (2016). Dads tuning in to kids: Preliminary evaluation of a fathers' parenting program. *Family Relations, 65*(4), 535–549. https://doi.org/10.1111/fare.12216

Chapter 6

Positive Parenting Program (Triple P)

Ingeborg Stiefel

The Positive Parenting Program (Triple P) is a behavioural parenting intervention, developed in the 1980s by Matthew Sanders, Professor of Clinical Psychology, and his colleagues at the University of Queensland, Australia. The program evolved from clinical research and experience with therapy programs run in the Parenting and Family Support Centre and the Behaviour Research and Therapy Centre at The University of Queensland, and the development was supported by various Health Departments within Australia (Sanders et al., 2001). Triple P was initially designed as a preventative program for children at risk of developing behavioural and emotional disorders (Sanders et al., 2002), and typical presentations included children displaying demanding, oppositional and disruptive behaviours. The aim of Triple P is to assist parents in developing effective strategies dealing with a variety of common developmental and behavioural problems, to strengthen the parent–child relationship and to increase the level of parental confidence (Sanders et al., 2002). Triple P is an evidence-based parenting program with a strong research tradition.

Triple P consists of a range of programs with different levels of treatment intensity depending on the needs of the parent and the level of professional support required to address both child development problems and parenting deficits. Online options, separate programs for parents of children and adolescents, and specific program strands for parents of children with developmental disability are available. Triple P also offers program modules for families going through a separation, families with partner conflicts, parental mental health issues and stress, and children struggling with obesity and anxiety. Triple P offers programs for early educational settings, courses for fathers and modules for parents with anger issues. Available is also an Indigenous Triple P version. Each level and program component offers a separate intervention. The standard program is suitable for parents of children up to the age of 12, with a separate program for parents of teenagers (Teen Triple P) within the age range of 12 to 16 years (Triple P International, 2021).

The objective of Triple P is to increase parental competence and confidence, to reduce or eliminate coercive cycles of interaction between parent and child, ineffective forms of discipline, parental stress and child behavioural problems. Further, the aim of the program is to increase effective communication between parent and child and to improve the parent–child relationship (Sanders et al., 2002). The program teaches parents skills that promote positive child development, social skills and self-control and offers clear and practical ideas in responding to the child's needs, including the need for nurturing and parental calmness. Depending on the client population and program strand, the program can be delivered in a group format, 1:1 or as an online course. Where appropriate, both parents and other important caregivers are encouraged to attend the training. Parents set their own goals for treatment. Triple P is a program that can be facilitated by sole practitioners and organisations or applied as a population-based strategy.

The Theoretical Base of Triple P

Triple P highlights that dysfunctional parenting styles, such as harsh and inconsistent parenting, are risk factors linked with compromised development during childhood and maladjustment later in life (Sanders et al., 2002). Insufficient and negative parenting practices compromise social, emotional and behavioural development in children, increase the risk for conduct disorder (CD), depression and anxiety and are linked to lower educational achievements (Gottman, 1997). The first two years of life are seen as the most crucial period for determining outcomes, and parents play an important role in steering the direction of adjustment for their children (Knudson, 2004). Hence, it makes sense to offer interventions to families that assist in preventing childhood maladjustment or, where indicated, to treat the early onset of development issues with the help of effective parenting interventions.

As with other behavioural parenting interventions, such as Parent–Child Interaction Therapy (PCIT), see Chapter 7 in this book, Triple P is based on theories of learning and applied behaviour analysis, including classical conditioning, operant conditioning and social learning theory.

Classical conditioning is associated with Ivan Pavlov, a Russian physiologist who had a special interest in experimental medicine (Clarke, 2004). Classical conditioning considers learning by association, the pairing of two stimuli. The most well-known example of classical condition was Pavlov's experiment with a dog, where a neutral stimulus (a bell) was paired with food, and later the bell itself triggered the salivation response. Similarly, in the context of child psychology, a neutral stimulus (e.g., a familiar object in a child's environment) may trigger a fear response if this object is associated with a fear-inducing or traumatic event. An example might be a child being repeatedly bullied at preschool but only when using the slippery dip, which is in a corner of the play area. Once conditioning has occurred, the presence of the object (any slippery dip) can trigger anxiety or avoidance in the young child. Hence, an association has occurred between a once-neutral stimulus and a response of fear, although the initial fear-inducing situation may no longer be present. Classical conditioning can also be associated with other feelings, including positive ones. For example, a child with a supportive preschool teacher may associate the teacher with the preschool and as a result enjoys preschool.

B. F. Skinner, a North American psychologist, was the founder of operant conditioning (Staddon & Cerutti, 2003). Operant conditioning focuses on the consequences linked with the occurrence of specific behaviours. According to this theory, different consequences can either increase or decrease the likelihood of the behaviour from re-occurring. Positive and negative reinforcements are the processes involved in operant learning. If for example the supportive preschool teacher frequently tells a child how well they can draw people, the likelihood is increased that the child will engage in further drawings depicting people, increase skills and may even develop the belief that their drawing skills are good. If on the other hand the teacher ignores all drawing attempts, the child may develop the idea that drawing is not their strength.

Social learning theory was developed in the 1960s and 1970s and is associated with psychologist Albert Bandura (Nabavi, 2012). Social learning theory adds two additional components to learning. First, learning occurs within a social context, and second, learning also involves cognitive processes that mediate between stimulus and response (Vera-Rios, 2018). According to this theory, children learn from observing actions and interactions of others in real life situations or through media and symbolic presentation. These observations invite modelling, imitation and replication of the observed behaviour.

Sanders, Turner and Markie-Dadds advise that Triple P draws from a large area of research and theoretical models (Sanders et al., 2002), including:

- **Social Learning Models.** In the context of the parent–child relationship, social learning theory takes into consideration the reciprocal and bi-directional nature of interactions between caregiver and child, based on Patterson and colleagues work in the 1980s. Patterson focused on coercive, harsh and confusing parenting practices, in particular, the vicious cycles which can develop between caregiver and child. Coercion theory (Patterson, 1982) describes a process of mutually reinforcing negative and escalating behaviour between parent and child, often triggered by child non-compliance, in which the caregiver unintentionally reinforces the child's challenging behaviour by responding and reinforcing it with negative attention, which then in turn elicits further negative responses in the child with increasing escalation, until the mutual battle ends with one person 'winning' (Smith et al., 2014). The conflict may end with the parent smacking the child, or the child succeeding with the behaviour and the parent saying, 'I don't care', and walking away. Coercive parenting has strongly been linked with the development of childhood conduct disorder (CD) and antisocial behaviour, and the link between negative parenting styles and the development of emotional and behavioural problems in children is now well established (Akhter et al., 2011).

- **Applied Behavioural Analysis.** Applied behaviour analysis (ABA) explores the mechanisms for behavioural change. Applied behavioural analysis developed within the North American pragmatic culture between 1940 and 1960. Its basic science is experimental analysis of behaviour, and the philosophical underpinning is radical behaviourism (Morris et al., 2013). In the context of childhood problems, applied behavioural theory tries to understand both the antecedents to problem behaviour and the consequences that follow the target problem behaviour, especially those which increase the likelihood of the behaviour to re-occur, thus reinforcing it. ABA tries to control behaviour through the application of positive or negative consequences (differential reinforcement), which can strengthen or weaken the behaviour. ABA also tries to understand the triggers, the stimuli that produce the problem behaviour. In the context of child-rearing, antecedents to problem behaviour may be an environment that lacks stimulation and interest or consequences in which the caregiver responds to negative and challenging child behaviour only, with neglect of attention to positive behaviour in the child.

- **Developmental Research.** Developmental research explores how children grow and develop and tries to understand the pathways to normal development. This field of research explores vulnerability, protective and risk factors that impact healthy child development. Though nature and nurture interplay, it is now established that the quality of the early parent–child relationship has a major influence on developmental outcomes, including mental health, speech and language, cognition, and social development. This research also explores the impact developmental issues have on the carer's perception and expectations of what the child can do compared with the child's peers.

- **Paediatric Psychopathology Research.** This area of research tries to explore risk factors, offers an understanding of coercive cycles, and the influence of poor parental mental health, and adult relationship conflicts on child development. Risk factors may include poverty, parental discord and family violence, high levels of stress, parental depression, anxiety, neglect, or poor self-regulation or substance use in the parent.

- **Social Information Processing Models.** This area of research focuses on cognitive aspects and recognises the important role of parental mindsets, including beliefs, expectations, and values, on parenting factors such as parental self-efficacy, decision making and resulting parental behaviour.

- **Population Health Research.** Population health studies explore how childhood adversity can be prevented or addressed in the general population and within the broader social context. This often involves large-scale universal approaches to address social issues.

The Five Core Principles of Positive Parenting

Five positive parenting principles form the basis of Triple P. These principles are based on what is known to constitute protective factors that foster positive development but also address specific risk factors which can compromise the developmental outcome for a child. These principles are:

1. Provision of a safe and interesting environment that is stimulating, encourages learning and positive development and reduces the development of challenging behaviour.

2. Creation of a positive learning environment in which the caregiver is receptive to interaction and communication initiated by the child. Parents respond by attending, engaging in brief interchanges, praising the child, providing physical contact, modelling positive behaviour and using charts as visual aids for behaviour change.

3. Utilisation of assertive discipline, which is consistent, predictable, calm, clear and age-appropriate. This includes the development of ground rules, the use of logical consequences, quiet time or time out to replace the use of threats, and physical or verbal abuse.

4. Development of realistic expectations with developmentally appropriate goals without a strive for perfection.

5. Self-care for parents to reduce the impact of stress, mental health issues or adult social relationship problems, which can impact parenting.

The Five Levels of Intervention in Triple P

Triple P has 5 levels of intervention with increasing degrees of intensity and support to parents (Sanders et al., 2002) (see www.triplep.net).

Level 1. The first level offers a universal communication strategy and is not an intervention as such but offers information and education to the community. The aim of the program component is to increase awareness of parenting issues in the community, to circulate information about positive parenting and to de-stigmatise common struggles parents may face. Level 1 aims to meet the need of a cross-section of the general population, and offers suggestions to address common problems. Level 1 utilises a range of materials, such as tip sheets, brochures, or posters which can be displayed on billboards in strategically relevant areas.

Level 2. This level is a brief preventative strategy and consists of one or two individual sessions or a group seminar for parents, offering developmental guidance for parents addressing common issues occurring during the childhood years, usually at a milder level. This strategy is suitable for parents who are overall coping well in their role but may have one or two concerns about their child. Level 2 aims to prevent the onset of significant child behaviour problems by increasing parental competence and correcting unhelpful parenting practices early. The Level 2 intervention is usually applied in a primary care setting such as a Community Health Centre or a Non-Government agency, which provides a wide range of services at the level of both prevention and intervention.

Level 3. This is a brief intervention of 4 sessions facilitated by a trained professional, targeting mild to moderate problems and involving active skills training for parents. Level 3 Triple P can be delivered in a group or an individual format, in this case with briefer sessions of 30 minutes duration. Every day mild to moderate parenting problems can be addressed. This level also aims at preventing the onset of more significant child behaviour problems.

Level 4. This level targets more significant child presentations and parenting issues. Level 4 is often indicated when children display marked behavioural disorders, such as severe aggression or meet full diagnostic criteria for a mental health condition such as CD or Oppositional Defiant Disorder, and for parents who display significant parenting deficits. Level 4 Triple P can be offered in individual sessions, in a group format or as a self-directed intervention.

The average length for Standard Triple P, the individual program, is 10 sessions of 60-minute duration each, with a range of 6 to 15 sessions, depending on clinician assessment and the needs of the parent. It can be applied in either the home or a clinic setting and addresses parent-selected goals with active practice, observation, training and feedback provided by the clinician and home practices.

Group Triple P at Level 4 usually consists of 8 sessions, of which the first four are conducted in groups. A group number of approximately 8 participants allows opportunities for a rich discussion among parents; however experienced group facilitators may accept up to 15 participants per group. The program offers four 2-hour group sessions with active skills training in small groups. Parents complete homework tasks between sessions, and individual follow-up is offered either in person or over the phone with up to four shorter follow-up sessions.

Self-Directed Triple P is a self-help program in which parents follow the 'Every Parent's Self-Help Workbook' (Markie-Dadds et al., 2000). Self-help Triple P can be enriched with additional weekly telephone consultations. This program is suitable for families who have limited access to services, such as those living in remote areas.

Level 5. Obstacles to successful achievement of goals at Level 4 may be due to severe psychopathology in the parent, extremely challenging child behaviour, or family adversity. In this case, a higher level of intervention may be required (Sanders et al., 2001). Level 5 offers a more intensive family intervention, and indicators for level 5 may be high parent ratings of child behaviour problems on standard questionnaires, issues that complicate parenting such as partner conflicts, communication problems, high level of parental stress, parental anger and mental health issues, risk of harm including abuse or neglect of the child, parental separation and divorce (Triple P International, 2021). This program builds on Level 4 with additional modules, and requires that parents complete Level 4 Triple P first. Parents who report no or little change after completion of Level 4 or have difficulties implementing strategies may also benefit from a more intensive form of intervention. Sessions are tailored to the needs of the family and involve active skills training.

Special Programs

Special Programs within the levels are also available, such as the Stepping Stones program (offered at Levels 2–4) for parents of children with a developmental disability, programs for children with anxiety issues, or childhood obesity. Online options are available for parents of children in the age range 0–12 years or 10–16 years, as a stand-alone treatment or as part of a mixed delivery with additional support. Partners who cannot attend a group may choose to complete the online component. Online Triple P is also a suitable universal strategy to prevent the development of behavioural and emotional problems in childhood. Positive Early Childhood Education (PECE) is a program for early childhood educators based on Triple P principles. Triple P has been translated into different languages, and an Indigenous Triple P Program is available, which has been created in consultation with elders from Indigenous groups within Australia.

Each of the different programs and levels are separate interventions. In the context of this chapter, we will be referring primarily to Level 4 (Individual and Group) intervention as the main focus, interventions for moderate to severe childhood presentations and parenting challenges, as these presentations are the primary focus of this book.

Level 4 – Standard Triple P — Individual Family Intervention
Assessment for Standard Triple P

Triple P starts with an intake interview with the parent or the parenting figures only. The purpose is to understand the reason for referral and to explore parental concerns and expectations. A parent–child or family observation is helpful, and older children over the age of 7 or 8 may also benefit from an individual assessment session to gain a better understanding of the presenting issues. Direct observation offers a good opportunity to gain a better assessment of the nature of the behaviour problems, the parent–child interaction and the parenting strategies employed by the parent. Further, information about antecedents to challenging behaviour, contextual factors and consequences may be obtained in different ways. Clinicians can set up an observation area in a clinic setting or during a home visit and suggest tasks appropriate to the referral issues, such as a meal time for eating problems, or free play with parent-directed play and tidy-up instructions for children with compliance issues. The Practitioners Manual (Sanders et al., 2001) suggests a range of assessment tools and more elaborate coding systems to record the observation. Coding gives more detailed information about frequency, sequences, duration of behaviour and the interaction between child and caregiver and helps refining the clinician's hypothesis as to the nature of the presenting problem.

Triple P recommends the usage of a number of different measures pre- and post-treatment and the completion of family background questionnaires which can be posted to the family prior to the first session. The practitioner's manual contains measures (with scoring protocol) that are free of charge and offers samples of questionnaires that can be purchased (Sanders et al., 2001). Questionnaires prior to the treatment are self-report measures and include family demographics; information about the child's behaviour, such as the Eyberg Child Behavior Inventory which explores presence, frequency and intensity of behavioural problems (Eyberg & Pincus, 1999); the Strength and Difficulties Questionnaire developed by Goodman (Goodman, 1997; https://www.sdqinfo.org), which assesses emotional, behavioural, attention/hyperactivity problems, peer relationship and social concerns; and the Parent Daily Report Checklist developed by Chamberlain and Reid in 1987 (Sanders et al., 2001) which explores behavioural occurrences over a 7-day period.

Questionnaires that explore parenting factors such as parenting style and confidence include the Parenting Style Questionnaire by Arnold and colleagues in 1993 (Arnold et al., 1993) and the Parenting Sense of Competence Scale by Gibaud-Wallston and Wandersman, revised in 1989 by Johnston and March (https://www.bristol.ac.uk). Conflicts over parenting and stress in the parental relationship can be assessed with the Parent Problem Checklist by Dadds and Powell (Sanders et al., 2001), parent relationship issues and parental personal issues with the Relationship Quality Index by Norton, 1983 (Sanders et al., 2001) and parental mental health with the Depression Anxiety Stress Scale by Lovibond and Lovibond (https://maic.qld.gov.au).

As part of the initial assessment and to monitor treatment outcomes, Sanders and colleagues suggest that simple structured behavioural monitoring (recording) can be extremely helpful, and the manual suggests a number of different procedures. These include episodic records of when what and where the behaviour occurs, what happens before and afterwards, tallies of target behaviour with a simple tick list, recording of frequency or duration of problem behaviour, and time sampling. However, they warn that behavioural monitoring can be taxing for some parents (Sanders et al., 2001).

The Functional Assessment outlined in the manual offers two tools. First, a classification system to code parent and child behaviour according to the criteria of excessive, deficient, or asset. Excessive parent behaviour may be a large number of ineffective or vague parental requests, such as repeatedly calling out 'stop it', and excessive child behaviour may constitute repeated outbursts of 'no' in response to the parental request. Deficient behaviour may constitute a lack of descriptive praise by the parent or a lack in the child's response to a parental request. Assets include the presence of effective parenting strategies (e.g., descriptive praise) and developmentally appropriate behaviours in the child.

The second tool available for the functional assessment is the SORCK behaviour analysis which leads to an understanding of the antecedent and consequent events that serve to increase or maintain the target problem behaviour.

SORCK stands for:

> **S** timulus (trigger or antecedent that immediately precedes the problem behaviour)
>
> **O** (rganism) relates to personal variables such as fatigue, hunger, and physical exhaustion, variables that moderate the relationship between trigger and target behaviour
>
> **R** esponse or Target Behaviour
>
> **C** onsequences are either those that have an immediate effect on the probability of the target behaviour re-occurring or which have longer term effects and are indirectly related to the target behaviour, such as context variables.
>
> **K** stands for Contingencies and refers to the hypothesis between S, R and C.

The purpose of the assessment is to arrive at a detailed case formulation and to determine the level, format and type of Triple P required for a particular family. Information from multiple sources may be helpful, such as an interview with the preschool teacher or an exploration of other relevant issues that may need to be addressed in more serious childhood presentations, such as the presence of adult substance issues, family violence, learning problems, serious parental mental health issues or suspected abuse. The aim of the assessment is to understand the child's presenting problem, but also the parent–child relationship, parenting factors and the family's social context. Sanders and colleagues stress that there should never be an intervention without a good assessment (Sanders et al., 2001).

The next stage is the negotiation of an intervention plan with the parents with a clear outline of sessions. After completion of treatment, self-report questionnaires are again administered to explore treatment effects for the family. These include measures of child behaviour, parenting style and confidence, conflicts over parenting, relationship and personal issues for parents, as well as satisfaction with the program.

Session Structure and Content

Triple P is a manualised intervention. The Standard Triple P manual offers detailed and helpful information on conducting a good interview and offers tips and hints to address various obstacles and challenges. These include topics such as maintaining a strength-based approach, responding empathically, effective interviewing, preparedness, addressing issues with data completion, utilising of assessment data in sessions, homework completion, and conducting role plays. The detailed outline is especially helpful to novice or inexperienced clinicians.

The teaching and parent training format for both group and individual intervention includes giving of information and discussion of parenting issues, observation, demonstration, role play and active skills training with feedback to the parent, modelling by therapist, rehearsing, and homework tasks to consolidate skills development. Parents complete tasks in their workbooks in-between sessions.

The manual (Sanders et al., 2001) outlines the content for each of the sessions, session objectives, materials required and preparation needed. The program teaches parenting skills that can be broadly classified as contingent positive consequences to adaptive/prosocial behaviour or to behaviour that is incompatible with the target problem behaviour and strategies for dealing effectively with maladaptive child behaviour. Parenting strategies taught in the program fall into four main categories: skills to develop a positive parent–child relationship, skills that encourage desirable behaviour, teaching new skills, and skills for managing child misbehaviour effectively.

Overview of Standard Triple P over 10 Sessions

Session 1 is the intake interview. The primary objectives are to establish rapport with the parents, understand typical behavioural challenges, and gain an understanding of influences that reinforce the problem behaviour, including current parenting strategies and other influences that may be contributing to the target behaviour. Session 1 also explores the developmental history and the social context of the family, parental adjustment, health and expectations, and finally, one or two target behaviours are selected with an instruction to keep a baseline record. The Every Parent's Family Workbook (Markie-Dadds et al., 2000) offers five optional Homework Monitoring Forms to choose from, these include behavioural records of occurrence, duration, time or frequency, and the parent is encouraged to complete the monitoring exercise as a homework task.

Session 2 includes a structured observation of the parent–child (or family) interaction. The clinician provides feedback to the parents on assessment results from different sources and provides an integrated summary. Causes for child behaviour problems are discussed in general, such as genetic and environmental factors, parenting factors such as beliefs and expectations, and other influences on the family (e.g., peers, media and school). Parents are encouraged to assess whether these factors apply to their own family situation, helping the parents to understand the specific reasons for their struggle. Goals for change are explored and an appropriate intervention is selected. The session ends with instructions for homework, monitoring the child's behaviour with the forms from session 1, and reading from the workbook as preparation for session 2.

Session 3 starts with a recap of session 3, an update on the child's behaviour, and a review of homework. The session then introduces two principles of positive parenting, promoting children's development and developing positive relationships with children. Three parenting strategies are introduced:

1. Quality time: Parents are encouraged to spend frequent but brief amounts of quality time with their child involving a child-preferred activity.

2. Talking to the child: This strategy involves parents utilising opportunities to have brief conversations with their child about the child's activity or topic of interest.

3. Showing affection: Parents are encouraged to show positive affection towards their child in the form of hugs, cuddles or tickling.

The next section focuses on the encouragement of desirable behaviour. To increase desirable behaviour, Triple P introduces three parenting strategies:

1. Descriptive praise: Descriptive praise involves the labelling of behaviours that are desirable and appropriate.

2. Giving attention: This parenting strategy refers to non-verbal parenting behaviour, such as smiling, patting on the back, and watching a child in an activity.

3. Providing engaging activities: Parents are encouraged to provide interesting, age-appropriate activities and play materials, including toys and activities in and outside the home.

The final part of session 3 focuses on teaching of new skills and behaviour with four additional parenting strategies:

1. Setting a good example: This strategy increases the parent's awareness of the effects of parental modelling.

2. Incidental teaching: Incidental teaching involves utilising opportunities for questions and prompts in response to child-initiated interactions.

3. Ask, say, do: Using verbal prompts or gestures, providing help and tactile contact to teach new skills.

4. Utilising behavioural charts: Encouraging new behaviour with the help of reward charts for appropriate behaviour.

As homework, parents will select up to two out of the ten positive parenting strategies introduced in the session and are encouraged to apply them with their child during the week and monitor progress with the charts provided in the parenting book. Parents are also asked to watch a section of a video prior to the next session, either at home or in the clinic. Finally, parents are encouraged to explore with their child possible rewards for desirable child behaviour.

Session 4 focuses on the management of misbehaviour. The session starts with a review of the previous session and a discussion of homework. The session then provides a rationale for seven different parenting strategies introduced for challenging child behaviour. The strategies include:

1. Establishing ground rules: Parents develop a set of specific rules and developmentally appropriate expectations in daily routines.

2. Directed discussion and behaviour correction for rule breaking: This strategy involves open discussion and correction of rule-breaking with identification of the problem behaviour and rehearsal of the correct behaviour.

3. Planned ignoring: Ignoring consists of the withdrawal of attention in response to mild problem behaviour.

4. Clear and calm instructions: Parents give clear and specific instructions to initiate a behaviour or to stop a behaviour.

5. Logical consequences: This strategy teaches parents to apply consequences that involve the removal of a privilege or the removal of an activity.

6. Quiet time: This strategy is a non-exclusionary form of time out and involves the removal of the child from an activity linked with the problem behaviour or prompting the child to be quiet.

7. Time-out for serious misbehaviour: In some cases, the removal of the child from the problematic activity or location is needed for a set period of time, for example taking the child to another room. The manual describes several time-out options and outlines ideas for troubleshooting.

Parents are encouraged to combine positive strategies from session 3 with those that deal with problem behaviour (session 4) into good routines, combining clear and calm instructions with praise or logical consequences, quiet time or time out. A behaviour chart is finalised. Homework for the week includes developing 4–5 ground rules, selecting and utilising strategies to manage mis-behaviour, monitoring behavioural change, starting the behavioural chart and reading as preparation for session 5.

Sessions 5–7 are practice sessions and can be of shorter duration. These sessions offer an application of skills in vivo with the child with the aim for the parent to demonstrate proficiency in using positive parenting strategies with gentle feedback and prompting from the therapist. The session location can be the family home or another appropriate location. The parent sets the goal for the sessions and demonstrates a selected parenting strategy with their child while the therapist observes. Self-evaluation by the parent is encouraged with the help of prompts, but feedback is also provided by the therapist, so both strengths and weaknesses of the parental behaviour can be explored. Parents also set goals for practices in-between sessions.

Session 8 addresses the application of positive parenting in high-risk situations both at home and in the community through planned activity routines that will help to reduce or prevent problems in these situations. Parents will be able to identify high-risk situations, prepare and plan for these events and also implement planned activities for other risk situations so generalisation takes place. Getting ready for work at a specified time may be a highly stressful situation for one parent, while travelling in the car, or outings such as shopping will be highly stressful situations for other parents. Planned activity routines take six steps: preparation, stating rules, selection of engaging activities, encouragement of appropriate behaviour, use of consequences, and follow-up discussion with the child. Parents are advised to practice planned activities during the week and record the routine.

Session 9 involves the implementation of planned activity routines with in vivo skills training with the parent and target child and can take place in the family home or the clinic. Session 9 prepares the parent for a variety of high-risk situations. Therapist prompts are gradually phased out to increase the parent's sense of mastery and generalisation of skills. Children are encouraged to engage in independent play for part of the session while the parent and therapist talk to each other. Homework consists of the implementation of at least two planned activity routines prior to the final session.

Session 10 focuses strongly on maintenance of gains and the generalisation of parenting strategies in different situations. The session also offers survival tips and problem-solving for the future. At the end of this session, parents should feel that they can implement positive parenting strategies with confidence and resourcefulness. The session also offers a review of further goals for change and discusses the required input of other services or programs in the future. Parents complete the final assessment questionnaires.

Group Triple P Level 4

The Facilitator's Manual for Group Triple P (Turner et al., 2000) offers detailed session guidance for group leaders, lists materials needed, and gives helpful tips for planning a group, such as recruitment strategies, venue, date and time planning, protocols for registration of interested parents and strategies of dealing with failure to attend. The manual also offers a wide number of tips for group facilitation, such as managing time, soliciting ideas from participants, validating parents' attempts to solve problems, constructive feedback, use of humour, involving non-engaged parents, dealing with over-talkative participants and therapist self-disclosure. Further, the manual gives suggestions for role play, setting homework tasks, and working with couples. Group Triple P is an active skills training course in which parents practice in small groups, receive helpful feedback and apply new skills between sessions in the form of homework. The manual outlines the advantages of group training, such as mutual support, feedback from others, and normalising the challenges of being a parent.

Group Triple P also involves a comprehensive assessment which includes family demographics, assessment of child behaviour, parenting skills and competence and parental personal adjustment. Post-session assessment also explores satisfaction with the group program, attendance rate, and facilitator's adherence to the program protocol. Ratings of the child should focus on one target child if parents report problems with several of their children. Copies of sample pre- and post-treatment assessment forms are printed in the Facilitators Manual for Group Triple P (Turner et al., 2000) and are similar to those recommended for standard Triple P, although some additional questionnaires may need to be purchased.

Session Structure and Content

Session 1 starts with an introduction and outline of the program, and covers several topics, such as working as a group, information as to what positive parenting is, and causes of child behaviour problems (e.g., accidental rewards for problem behaviour, ignoring desirable behaviour, learning from negative models, parental beliefs, influence of peers). Parents' goals for change are explored, and parents are instructed to keep track of their child's behaviour by utilising checklists, graphs and charts. Homework consists of baseline monitoring over seven days by tracking the child's behaviour. Parents are also encouraged if feasible to watch the Every Parents' Survival Guide video. As with all sessions, instructions for group facilitators are very detailed and specific. The first four group sessions are of 120-minute duration.

Session 2 is a recap and review of homework at the start of the session. The session then focuses on the promotion of positive child development and on the establishment of strong relationships between parent and child. Parenting strategies taught include spending quality time with the child, talking and communicating, showing affection, encouraging desirable behaviour with the help of descriptive praise, paying attention, and providing engaging age-appropriate activities. Strategies for teaching new skills and behaviours are illustrated with the help of brief video clips and slides. For example, video excerpts on incidental teaching, the principle of Ask-Say-Do and the concept of behavioural charts. Homework for the week consists of the selection of two positive parenting strategies taught in the session, application and monitoring progress, and exploring possible rewards with the child. Parents are also encouraged to gather the needed materials for a behaviour chart.

Session 3 starts with a recap and review of homework. The session's main focus is on the management of misbehaviour. Session content covers the establishment of ground rules, direct discussion when problems occur and planned ignoring. The next section helps parents to give clear and calm instructions and to use logical consequences if needed. The session progresses with the concepts of quiet time and time out and the development of parenting routines (both compliance routines and behaviour correction routines when non-compliance occurs). Behavioural charts are finalised, and a homework task for the management of misbehaviour is given. Visual aids are used to illustrate these strategies.

Session 4 recaps previous learning and homework and discusses family survival tips, such as social networks and taking care of one's own needs as parents. The session further shows parents how to utilise strategies from sessions 2 and 3 in high-risk or challenging situations by using planned activity routines, similar to the individual program. Parents design their own planned activity routine in small group exercises. Brief video clips are again used to illustrate the content. The session prepares participants for the upcoming telephone sessions, explaining their purpose and format. The homework task for the week involves the development of planned activity routines and applications at home.

Sessions 5–7 are 15–30 minute phone sessions. Session 5, 6 and 7 focus on the implementation of positive parenting strategies (contents from session 1–4), updates on progress and tackling issues of challenge. The aim of these sessions is to help parents become confident and self-sufficient and to generalise skills, while parents also work through the Every Parent's Workbook.

Session 8 focuses on program closure, offers a review of positive parenting strategies, helps families to identify changes made and discusses the maintenance of gains. Challenging times and development periods are discussed to prepare parents for these special events and encourage independent problem-solving. Post-treatment assessment forms are filled in, and the facilitator uses clinical judgement to assess families where further intervention may be needed, such as a higher level or additional module of Triple P.

Training Requirement, Resources and Ongoing Support

Facilitator training for Standard Triple P Level 4 is strongly recommended but not mandated, and it is further suggested that facilitators have a degree in health, education or social sciences; however, experienced para-professionals working with families may also apply. To become Triple P accredited, training is required. All practitioners should familiarise themselves with the program material but should also undertake background reading to understand the theoretical underpinnings and the research background of the program. They should have a sound grounding on issues of child pathology and the effects of adverse life circumstances on children. Further, they need to know when further assessment and treatment of children with disruptive behaviour may be indicated.

Training for Standard Level 4 consists of 3 full training days, a 1-day pre-accreditation workshop and accreditation (total of 5 days, cost of approximately $2090, or less for agencies who train 10 or more staff). Face-to-face and online training options are available with additional cost for in-house, in-person training at the clinician's facility. Accreditation assures that Triple P is delivered competently and successfully. Training also leads to a better understanding of the utilisation of resources and questionnaires and offers tips for phone consultation sessions with parents and skills for group facilitation.

Triple P offers a variety of support services. An initial Triple P Consultant can give organisations advice on client population and fit of program components for the organisation, can monitor program fidelity and outcome, and help with the selection of clinicians for training and the development of the capacity for effective implementation. Support networks are available for clinicians, and a range of resources are offered, such as tips for delivery, access to questionnaires and scoring programs, peer supervision and participation in a range of workshops such as cultural diversity, hard-to-reach families, group skills for delivery and program flexibility vs fidelity.

The Treatment Program Implementation Framework gives guidance as to the suitability of families for each strand of intervention. Decisions are made on two key principles: self-regulation and minimal sufficiency. Self-regulation relates to the capacity of the parent to resolve the issue at hand independently. Minimal sufficiency relates to the principle of least intensive/just enough intervention for a given family. Triple P offers the guidance of an implementation consultant who can be approached in all matters of application in a given setting, including client characteristics and the appropriateness of a program for the specific agency or clinician. Triple P International provides Training Courses for professionals and offers resources to both providers and to parents. Triple P resources such as parent booklets are required for facilitation of workshops and for individual family intervention, and clinicians or organisations need to budget for this additional cost. Additional videos may also be purchased to demonstrate positive parenting skills. Facilitators and therapists should be familiar with the Every Parent Family Workbook (Markie-Dadds et al., 2000), and each participant requires a copy of the book.

Standard Triple P and Group Triple P (Level 4) provide detailed facilitator's manuals that outline each session. In similar ways, the Every Parent's Family Workbook guides parents through tasks to be completed in or between sessions. Additional visual resources include the Every Parent's Survival Guide, which demonstrates specific parenting strategies, and the Every Parent's Guide to Preschoolers, which shows planned activity routines for this age group. Books are also available for parents who wish to read about Triple P, such as the book 'Every Parent: A positive approach to children's behaviour' (Sanders, 2004).

The Evidence Base for Triple P

Triple P is a well-known parenting intervention supported by a long-standing research tradition into the program's effectiveness (Sanders et al., 2014). The evidence includes theoretical papers, meta-analytic studies, clinical trials and population-based trials. Details can be found on the website https://pfsc-evidence.psy.uq.edu.au/. Outcome studies suggest wide replication of research findings in different countries and good cross-cultural adaptability of the program (Li et al., 2021).

Outcome studies indicate that the program benefits children, parents, and the community at large, and improves maternal mental health and the quality of the parental couple's relationship (Triple P International, 2021). Research suggests that when parents change problematic parenting practices, children will have fewer behavioural problems, both at home and at school, better peer relationships and cooperate better with others. Triple P has been shown to increase parental confidence, improve parenting skills, and increase the positive attitude towards the child. Parents also feel less stressed and depressed (Sanders et al., 2002). Positive treatment effects are evident both in university clinics and in public health settings. A large-scale study in the UK comparing parenting programs in the community setting indicates that level 4 Triple P applied within a group setting shows significant improvement in child behaviour, parenting skills and parental mental wellbeing (Lindsay et al., 2011). A meta-analysis by Sanders and colleagues also reports similar positive gains, however treatment effects were smaller for fathers compared with mothers, and treatment effects that measured changes in the parental relationship were small (Sanders et al., 2014).

There is some indication that the program's content and strategies are acceptable to families from different cultural backgrounds, including families from Vietnam, Africa, Europe and from the South Pacific (Morawska et al., 2011). Further, there is evidence that parents from diverse cultural backgrounds living in rural areas in the US and displaying high-risk behaviour benefit from home-based Triple P with improved parenting skills, reduction in the level of anger, reactivity, hostility and reported improved child behaviour, regardless of cultural background (Abate et al., 2020).

A meta-analysis by Nowak and Heinrichs (2008) of 55 studies confirms that overall, Triple P is associated with positive changes in parenting skills and parental wellbeing and a reduction in child problem behaviour. The treatment effect size increases with a higher level of program intensity, and individual application shows better improvement compared with Triple P group programs. Further, larger effect sizes were found for parents' self-rating of improvement, compared with observational measures, and treatment effects were greater for younger children and those with more severe presentations at the beginning of treatment (Novak & Heinrichs, 2008).

A comparison of Triple P with Parent–Child Interaction Therapy also confirms that Triple P treatment shows positive effects, however treatment outcome varies depending on the length of intervention, components of treatment and source of outcome data, such as external observational measures versus parent report (Thomas & Zimmer-Gembeck, 2007). A systematic review and meta-analysis of high-quality outcome studies using rigorous and randomly designed control protocol during the time period 2012 to 2020 suggests that Triple P can improve social competence in children and reduce social and behavioural difficulties to a certain extent while also addressing negative parenting styles and parental efficacy and confidence (Li et al., 2021). These studies suggest that the age of the child, intervention level, setting and delivery format may be important factors affecting the outcome of the intervention.

A meta-analysis of level 4 Triple P supports the findings of other studies that this intervention produces positive changes in regard to parenting competence and style when rated by parents, with treatment effects maintained 3–12 months post-treatment (de Graaf et al., 2008). In de Graaf's et.al. study, no differences in treatment outcome were found comparing group, individual and self-help Triple P. Positive long-term gains were further demonstrated in a large-scale study, which assessed the sustainability of gains 1 and 3 years post-treatment for parents of preschoolers and all treatment conditions, Standard Triple P, Enhanced Triple P and Self-Directed Triple P indicated sustained gains irrespective of the variant of Triple P program (Sanders et al., 2007).

Considerable critique has been voiced concerning the research into the program's effectiveness, in particular in regard to the quality of data with an over-reliance on underpowered trials, including small sample size (Coyne & Kwakenbos, 2013; Wilson et al., 2012). These authors have argued that these trials are susceptible to risk of bias, rely mostly on maternal assessment of child behaviour, and do not document long-term effects. Several studies do not have a treatment comparison group or do not show significant difference from control group conditions. Further, of the 33 studies reviewed, most studies were not independent of Triple P affiliation by author, and preferential reporting of positive results was noticed in article abstracts (Coyne & Kwakenbos, 2013; Wilson et al., 2012). However, Sanders and colleagues dispute some of these claims referring to methodological, conceptual and interpretational inadequacy in these critiques (Sanders et al., 2012).

Discussion

Triple P is an established and well-researched behavioural parenting program proven to be effective in addressing parenting skills, behavioural difficulties in children and parental wellbeing via parenting intervention (Li et al., 2021; Nowak & Heinrichs, 2008). Triple P is a highly structured, pragmatic and action-centred program with a focus on practical problem solving (Li et al., 2021). Clinicians who prefer manualised and highly structured programs, embrace principles of applied behavioural analysis, and value the scientific practitioner approach may appreciate this model. The very structured format will also assist the beginning therapist in conducting Triple P sessions. Each format, group, individual and self-help has distinctive advantages and disadvantages. While Group Triple P offers social connection, exchange of ideas between parents, group learning and normalisation of parenting experiences, individual Triple P can be more specifically tailored to the needs of each family. If the behavioural analysis is done well, the parent observation and recording can give a good entrance point to the understanding of the child's and parent's struggle and the needed direction of therapy.

The program suggests that presentations of severe disruptive behaviour or features of Attention Deficit Hyperactivity Disorder (ADHD) may warrant further assessment and additional intervention, such as pharmacological therapy or interventions in the educational setting. We would like to add that specific parenting struggles may also need assessment scrutiny. Our clinical experience has shown that Triple P may not be the first and best form of treatment for parents who struggle with an extremely negative perception of their child, high levels of stress, significant unresolved trauma or those who unconsciously project their own unresolved conflicts from past relationships into the relationship with their child. These parents may perceive the child as 'just like his (abusive) father', or they may insist that the child has a condition that needs to be fixed, deflecting from the need to also focus on themselves in the parenting role. In these cases, other forms of therapeutic input may need to be offered prior to a behavioural intervention and may include treatments that offer insight, such as individual adult therapy, or reflective programs such as Circle of Security (see Chapter 3), Psychodynamic child therapy in relational context (see Chapter 14), or Child Parent Psychotherapy (see Chapter 7).

The requirement for parents to complete Level 4 Triple P before moving to Level 5 could be problematic for some highly stressed parents or families with severely impaired parent–child relationships. The manualised format may not be tailored towards their needs, and therapy progress may not be optimal. For some families, their belief that 'nothing will work' may be further reinforced by the lack of progress. If these parents attend a group, they may also compare their own slow progress with that of other participants who gain from the program at a faster pace and, as a result, feel further disempowered. These parents may need a higher intensity program from the start, with a slower pace, repetition of learning, and greater time to absorb and apply components of the program.

The program can be taxing for parents who have a learning disability or who struggle with underlying mental health issues, are extremely stressed, depressed or angry, and as a result lack the energy or competence to complete the written and observational tasks required. Further, Standard Triple P introduces a large number of parenting strategies, particularly in Session 3 and 4. Although parents do not need to absorb all principles, as they will be working on selected strategies only, treatment outcomes may be compromised for families where therapeutic work requires strategies in all or most aspects of the program. Further, the allocated time to master a new skill can be too short for parents who have not experienced positive parenting in their own upbringing and, in our experience, require more intensive teaching and training in developing complex skills.

Like any therapeutic program, statistical data which report average group improvement does not tell us which parent benefits well and which parent does not gain significantly from a particular program. Detailed single case studies of parents who show little or no improvement would be extremely helpful for both clinicians and social policy planners in determining what the needs of these parents are and how intervention could be tailored to address these. Some therapists, especially those whose embrace attachment theory and theories of social and emotional intelligence, may struggle with some of the premises and practices of Triple P. From the corner of the emotional intelligence position, one of the criticisms of the program may be the argument that Triple P teaches children compliance, but not an understanding of their stressful emotional experiences and the skill of problem-solving. Attachment proponents may take issue with the practice of time out when dealing with very young children's emotional or behavioural stress, favouring calm presence or even physical-emotional containment of dysregulation in young children.

Nevertheless, Triple P can function as a stand-alone program or as a component in a comprehensive treatment plan to address parenting skills deficits, parent–child relationship distress and behavioural problems in children. Triple P has a significant research base and has been researched in multiple countries and families across a number of socioeconomic domains. Triple P, especially as a group program or a self-directed parenting program, offers a cost-effective intervention, and the self-directed program can reach families in remote or isolated areas that cannot access face-to-face resources.

Case Example: Tina, Brent and their three Boys

Tina was referred to a Family Support Service for a Triple P intervention by an early childhood nurse. Tina and her husband Brent had three boys, ages 8, 5 and 3. Tina was working part-time as a clerical assistant, and Brent was an electrician who was working long hours which involved driving for up to 4 hours to and from work. Their 3-year-old son just had his developmental check with the nurse, and Tina reported that she felt extremely stressed dealing with her sons' unruly behaviour. Indeed all three boys 'were running amuck', dis-respecting household rules and their home was a mess. Tina explained that things 'got out of hand' when her third son was born, an unexpected and medically stressful pregnancy, although her older boys always had some behavioural problems, being very active, aggressive with each other, not looking after their belongings and simply refusing to obey maternal requests. Tina also questioned if her oldest boys had ADHD.

The early childhood nurse assessed 3-year-old Ben using a developmental assessment scale. Other than some disobedient behavioural issues, the nurse did not feel there were any other developmental concerns. Ben was attending preschool on Tina's working days. The teachers described him as active, boisterous, loving the outdoors, and showing little interest in drawing but developing at a normal rate. He had settled into preschool, had learned to share, wait, take turns, and play cooperatively with his peers and most of the time packed away toys he had used.

The Triple P facilitator met Tina and Brent at their home on their own to discuss concerns and assess the need for intervention. The three boys joined for the second part of the assessment. The facilitator noticed that the house looked extremely messy, with toys, clothes, used crockery, and books covering the floor and the surface of the lounge. Tina said her home was like a 'constant battlefield'. She herself would try to impose rules, but the boys would simply ignore her. She felt frustrated and exhausted, had started to scream a lot, and at times would smack them when she lost her patience. Brent reported similar frustration with their sons' behaviour. Their constant fighting was a particular issue he wanted to address. He also reported that nothing had worked except for threats to take away the Xbox or to give them a smack. Both parents stressed that they believed 'Boys should be boys', but felt the boys were now ruling the parents with their disobedience. The facilitator explored rules in the house, times for positive attention and interaction, and use of consequences and found that very few enjoyable times were occurring between parents and children, parental rules were ad hoc and somewhat unclear (e.g., 'I want them to behave'), parental attention focused mainly on problem behaviour and parenting responses often having a critical tone.

Tina said she had attended a parenting course in the past but could not remember many details of the content, other than sending her children into time-out, which no longer was working as she could not enforce time-out with her older boys. The facilitator's first impression was that a Triple P Level 4 intervention would be extremely helpful to the family, facilitating a more positive parent–child relationship, focusing more strongly on desirable behaviour, having clear routines and expectations, helping the parents to increase effective strategies for problem behaviour and as a result reducing parental stress. Due to Brent's work situation and his wish to be involved in the program, a home-based individual intervention was recommended to the family.

Both parents attended the next session. In session 3, the parents realised that their interactions with their boys were mostly stressful and negative, and their responses as parents focused nearly exclusively on problem behaviour. Therefore, both parents thought descriptive praise would be a helpful strategy to tackle the negativity as a first step. They also wanted to help their children develop the new skill of cleaning up toys and becoming more responsive. Brent felt the task of tidying up a set area in the house could also offer opportunities for positive interaction, with prompting and teaching and positive parental response to compliance. The facilitator suggested that parental instructions should also receive attention, so the children would understand clearly what the parents' expectations were.

However, they all agreed that descriptive praise was the first important step to improve behaviour and the parent–child relationship. The parents were encouraged to complete an exercise in the session, 'How to give descriptive praise' and then to apply the strategy during the week, recording examples on a worksheet.

Session 4 focused on the management of non-compliance. The parents discussed what instruction they wanted to give the boys and role-played this in the session. The session then focused on the management of non-compliance with the tidying-up task, which became the focus of the intervention. Behavioural charts and rewards were discussed, but both parents were unsure if these would be effective. They finally decided to discuss rewards for tidying up with the boys, and the facilitator suggested that the parents decide when best to implement this task.

In session 5, the parents presented their plan. They felt that the tidying up task should occur around 5 p.m. but only on days when the boys would not engage in sport, which would account for 5 days per week, and dinner would be served around 5:30. If the child complied, the child would get a star for the positive performance, and once the child had earned 5 stars, he would receive his reward. The older boy had been very specific regarding the reward, wanting new soccer boots, whereas the siblings expressed a wish for new electronic games. Though the rewards were somewhat expensive, the parents decided that the rewards would be motivating and kick-start the process. The middle child complied with the requested task, earned 5 stickers and received his reward after 5 days, whereas the oldest child refused to comply, and the youngest received 2 stars for compliance on 2 days. However the middle child earning the reward, the new game, and the parents' statement to the other boys that they needed to earn their reward, was a turn-around for compliance. The other two boys earned their 5 stickers during the following week. In a subsequent session, facilitator and parents discussed how they could introduce another reward system that was financially sustainable yet also rewarding and decided that they could extend the time frame for earning a reward or exchange the 5 stars for $5 each week.

The treatment ended with the development of strategies for other problem situations, which included sibling fighting. Parents and facilitator arrived at the conclusion that attention to prosocial and appropriate behaviour and ignoring non-dangerous undesirable behaviours might be the solution to many of the current problems. In-session brainstorming of parental responses to non-fighting and role play helped the parents to develop new strategies which could generalise to other challenging behaviours present or in the future.

Reader's Exercises

In a group Triple P session, it becomes obvious that one of the parents, Betty, a single mum, has difficulties developing good and specific ground rules. The parent states that she wants her two children (aged 3 and 5) to 'listen and behave'. She describes a very large number of situations where problems occur, including at home, at school, on outings, at grandparent's visits, and during after-school activities. She is feeling very overwhelmed and says her boys always fight, never listen, do what they want to do, disrespect her as a parent, help themselves to food in the fridge, then not eat the dinner cooked, go to bed late, and play electronic games all day, don't get up on time, refuse to brush their teeth or complete their homework, and every day is a day-long battle. Their rooms are always a mess. Betty states that she would need to have 100 different rules. The parent booklet suggests that ground rules should be small in number, fair, easy to follow, enforceable, and positively stated.

- How could you help Betty to develop appropriate rules according to the criteria? Would you suggest 4–5 rules, or would you encourage her to start with less? Which rule may be a good start to achieve success?

- How could you utilise ideas from other members of the group to assist with the task of developing ground rules? How would you check with Betty if the ideas of others might be helpful?

- What help and encouragement could you give Betty to practice one or two of the rules during the week?

- What other issues would you take into consideration to help Betty become a more effective parent?

- Are there any other therapeutic tools or ideas from the program that could be helpful to Betty at this stage?

References

Abate, A., Marek, R. J., Venta, A., Taylor, L., & Vele, L. (2020). The effectiveness of a home-based delivery of Triple P in high-risk families in rural areas. *Journal of Child and Family Studies, 29,* 997–1007. http://doi.org/10.1007/s/10826-019-01684-2

Akhter, N., Hanif, R., Tariq, N., & Atta, N. (2011). Parenting styles as predictors of externalising and internalising behavior problems among children. *Pakistan Journal of Psychological Research, 26*(1), 23–41.

Arnold, E. H., O'Leary, S. G., & Edwards, G. H. (1993). The parenting Scale: A measure of dysfunctional parenting in discipline situations. *Psychological Assessment, 5*, 137-144. https://doi.org/10.1037/1040-3590.5.2.137

Clark, R. (2004). The classical origins of Pavlov's conditioning. *Integrative Physiological and Behavioural Science, 39*(4), 279–94. http://doi10.1007bf0273467

Coyne, J. C., & Kwakkenbos, L. (2013). Triple P-Positive Parenting programs: The folly of basing social policy on underpowered flawed studies. *BMC Medicine, 11*, 11. http://doi10.1186/1741-7015-11-11

de Graff, I., Speetjens, P., Smit, H. F. F., de Wolff, M., & Tavecchio, L. (2008). Effectiveness of the Triple P Positive Parenting Program on parenting: A meta-analysis. *Family Relations, 57*(5), 553–466. https://doi.org/10.1111/j.1741-3729.2008.00522.x

Eyberg, S. M., & Pincus, D. (1999). *Eyberg Child Behaviour Inventory and Sutter-Eyberg Student Behaviour Inventory-Revised*. Professional manual. Psychological Assessment Resources.

Goodman, R. (1997). The Strengths and Difficulties Questionnaire. *Journal of Child Psychology and Psychiatry, 38*, 581–586. http://dx.doi.org/10.1111/j.1469-7610.1997.tb01545.x

Gottman, J. (1997). *Raising an emotionally intelligent child. The heart of parenting*. Simon & Schuster.

Knudsen, E. I. (2004). Sensitive periods in the development of the brain and behaviour. *Journal of Cognitive Neuroscience, 16*(8), 1412–25. https://doi10.1162/ 0898929042304796

Li, N., Peng, J., & Li, Y. (2021). Effects and moderators of Triple P on the social, emotional, and behavioral problems of children: Systematic review and meta-analysis. *Frontiers in Psychology, 12*, 1–12. https://doi.org/10.3389/fpsyg.2021.709851

Lindsay, G., Strand, S., & Davis, H. A. (2011). A comparison of the effectiveness of three parenting programmes in improving parenting skills, parent mental wellbeing and children's behaviour when implemented on a large scale in community settings in 18 English local authorities: the parenting early inter-vention pathfinder (PEIP). *BMC Public Health, 11*, 962. htttps://doi.org/10.1186/ 1471-2458-11-962

Markie-Dadds, C., Sanders, M.R., & Turner, K.M. (2000). *Every parent's family workbook*. Families International Publishing.

Morawska, A., Sanders, M., Goadby, E., Headley C., Hodges, L., McAuliffe, C., Pope, S., & Anderson, E. (2011). Is the Triple P-Positive Parenting Program acceptable to parents from culturally diverse backgrounds? *Journal of Child and Family Studies, 20*, 614–622. http://doi10.1007/S10826-010-9436-X

Morris, E. K., Altus, D. E., & Smith, N. G. (2013). A Study in the founding of applied behavior analysis through its publications. *The Behavior Analys*t, *36*, 73–107. http://doi10.1007/BF03392293

Nabavi, R. T. (2012). Bandura's social learning theory & social cognitive learning theory. *Journal of Personality and Social Psychology, 1*, 589. https://www.researchgate.net/publication/267750204_Bandura's_Social_Learning_Theory_Social_Cognitive_Learning_Theory

Nowak, C., & Heinrichs, N. (2008). A comprehensive meta-analysis of Triple P-Positive Parenting Program using hierarchical linear modeling: Effectiveness and moderating variables. *Clinical Child and Family Psychology Review, 11*, 114–144. http://doi10.1007/s10567-008-0033-0

Patterson, G. R. (1982). *Coercive family process*. Castalia.

Sanders, M. R., Markie-Dadds, C., & Turner, K. M. (2001). *Practitioner's Manual for Standard Triple P*. Families International Publishing.

Sanders, M. R., Turner, K. T., & Markie-Dadds, C. (2002). The development and dissemination of the Triple P-Positive Parenting Program: A multilevel evidence-base system of parenting and family support. *Prevention Science, 3*, 173 –189. http://doi10.1023/A:1019942516231

Sanders, M. (2004). *Every parent: A positive approach to children's behaviour*. Penguin Group.

Sanders, M. R., Bor, W., & Morawska, A. (2007). Maintenance of treatment gains: A comparison of enhanced, standard, and self-directed Triple P-Positive Parenting Program. *Journal of Abnormal Child Psychology, 35*, 983–998. http://doi10.1007/s10802-007-9148-x

Sanders, M. R., Pickering, J. A., Kirby, J. N., Turner, K. M. T., Morawska, A., Mazzucchelli, T., Ralph, A., & Sofronoff, K. (2012). A commentary on evidenced-based parenting programs: Redressing misconceptions of the empirical support for Triple P. *BMC Medicine, 10*, 145. http://doi10.1186/1741-7015-10-145

Sanders, M. R., Kirby, J. N., Tellegen, C. L., & Day, J. J. (2014). The Triple P-Positive Parenting Program: A systematic review and meta-analysis of a multi-level system of parenting support. *Clinical Psychology Review, 34*(4), 337–57. http://doi10.1016/j.cpr.2014.04.003

Smith, J. D., Dishion, T. J., Shaw, D. S., Wilson, M. N., Winter, C. C., & Patterson, G. R. (2014). Coercive family process and early-onset conduct problems from age 2 to school entry. *Developmental Psychopathology, 26*(4), 917–932. http://doi10.1017/S0954579414000169

161

Staddon, J. E. R., & Cerutti, D. T. (2003). Operant conditioning. *Annual Review of Psychology*, *54*(1), 115–44. https://doi.org/10.1146/annurev.psych. 54.101601.145124

Thomas, R,. & Zimmer-Gembeck, M. J. (2007). Behavioural outcomes of Parent–Child Interaction Therapy and Triple P – Positive Parenting Program: A review and meta-analysis. *Abnormal Child Psychology*, *35*, 475–495. http://doi10.1007/ s10802-007-9104-9

Triple P International (2021). *Triple P Introductory Guide. Triple P – Positive Parenting Program*, Valid to 30 June 2022, Australia.

Turner, K. M., Markie-Dadds, C., & Sanders, M. R. (2000). *Facilitator's Manual for Group Triple P*. Family International Publishing.

Vera-Rios, J. (2018). *The relationship between parenting styles and conduct disorder in hispanic families*. Dissertation submitted in partial fulfilment of the requirements for the Degree of Doctor of Philosophy Clinical Psychology, Walden University. https://www.semanticscholar.org/paper/The-Relationship-Between-Parenting-Styles-and-in-Vera-Rios/21677c37436c6cb33de87965f738275a8844e365.

Wilson, P., Rush, R., Hussey, S. Puckering, S., Sim, F., Allely, C. S., Doku, P., McConnachie, A., & Gillberg, D. (2012). How evidence-based is an 'evidence-based parenting program'? A PRISMA systematic review and meta-analysis of Triple P, *BMC Medicine*, *10*,130. http://doi10.1186/1741-7015-10-130.

Section III:

Dyadic Approaches

Chapter 7

Parent–Child Interaction Therapy (PCIT)

Tanya Hanstock and Matthew Brand

Parent–Child Interaction Therapy (PCIT) is a structured behavioural treatment program designed for caregivers of young children with emotional and behavioural issues, in particular oppositional and defiant behaviours (McNeil & Hembree-Kigin, 2010). PCIT is a dyadic form of treatment that includes both child and the child's caregiver in the process of therapy. The popularity of PCIT as an intervention is due to several factors. First, PCIT is a behavioural parent training program with a very strong evidence-base on its effectiveness, exceeding the level of treatment effects of many other parent training programs (PCIT International, 2022). A second important factor is that therapy is conducted in real-time with the therapist sitting behind a one-way mirror, observing challenging parent–child interactions from an adjoining room, and offering live coaching to the parent via a bug in ear device (ear microphone). Based on live observations, the therapist encourages the parent to utilise child-centred and positive parenting strategies in response to adaptive child behaviour and guides the parent in addressing challenging behaviour, such as physical aggression or swearing, with very clear and specific parenting strategies. A further important reason for the popularity of PCIT is the fact that there are an increasing number of training opportunities within Australia and worldwide where clinicians can receive high-quality training in the model.

PCIT has two primary and immediate goals; firstly, to improve the quality of the parent and child relationship, and secondly, to improve the child's compliance with the parent's commands. A generalisation of the second primary goal is that children will comply with adults' commands when expressed in a normal tone, such as instructions from a teacher in a classroom. One of the main benefits of PCIT is that it is competency-based in its evaluation and progression. On average, it takes 12 sessions for families to reach competencies and for the child's behaviour to improve on measures when we have used it within our community clinics with children with developmental and/or psychosocial issues. Hence PCIT may be suitable for clinical settings and funding models where session numbers and duration are limited, compared with treatment models that require longer-term treatment (McNeil & Hembree-Kigin, 2010).

PCIT was initially developed for children within the age range of 3–6 years. In addition to the standard application, PCIT has also been adapted for use with specific clinical populations. These include older children (aged 7–10 years), children with Attention Deficit Hyperactivity Disorder (ADHD), Autism Spectrum Disorder (ASD), anxiety disorders, physical abuse, trauma, extreme aggression/explosions, hearing impairments and those who are from different cultural backgrounds. PCIT has also been adapted to be used with siblings and parents experiencing marital conflict. In addition to PCIT being used in the standard form of dyads attending a clinic, it can be conducted in groups, in home settings and via telehealth. Variations of PCIT exist such as Staff-Child Interaction Therapy (STIT), Teacher–Child Interaction Therapy (TCIT) and Intensive PCIT (I-PCIT). Furthermore, PCIT can be used preventatively for externalising problems, child abuse and developmental delay (Lieneman et al., 2017; McNeil & Hembree-Kigin, 2010).

Historical and Theoretical Context

PCIT was established in the 1970s by Sheila Eyeberg (McNeil & Hembree-Kigin, 2010) at the Oregon Health Services University. PCIT is based on Baumrind's (1966) parenting styles, where the authoritative parenting style is encouraged. An authoritative parenting style balances parental expectations and demands with an expression of warm, attuned and sensitive parenting, compared with an overly rigid and authoritarian or overly relaxed (laissez-faire) parenting style. In addition, PCIT also draws from both attachment and learning theories (operant conditioning) and elements of behavioural and play therapy. The unique real-time coaching ('bug in the ear') element was inspired by Constance Hanf's (1969) work with mothers, which focused on improving compliance with their children with disabilities. Hanf's parenting program was named PCIT in 1974 in a grant application to pilot-test it. The first decade of PCIT was focused on standardising the assessment tools and establishing the initial efficacy of PCIT. The second decade was dedicated to efficacy and generalisation studies of PCIT. The third decade resulted in research funding from the National Institute of Mental Health (NIMH) to study PCIT further. PCIT has since been disseminated internationally with the help of the PCIT

International Inc website (http://www.pcit.org/), the biennial PCIT conventions and now by a large number of qualified trainers internationally (Funderburk & Eyeberg, 2011).

Conducting PCIT

The session number in PCIT is not stipulated, but the structure (see Table 1) is. Therapy ends when the parent achieves competency (previously referred to as mastery) of skills and the child's reported behaviour is within normal limits using the parent reports via standardised measures such as the Eyberg Child Behaviour Inventory (ECBI, Eyberg & Pincus, 1999; Eybeg & Ross, 1978). PCIT usually requires weekly one-hour sessions. The first session commences with a pre-treatment interview with the parent/carer and child before moving on to treatment. There are two major therapeutic parts of PCIT: Child-Directed Interaction (CDI) and Parent-Directed Interaction (PDI). Both have equal importance placed on them; however, CDI occurs first, and parents must reach competency in this before PDI can commence. Both therapeutic phases involve a teaching session where parents are taught the skills, ideally without the child present. This is then followed by a coaching phase with the parent and child dyad until the parent meets competency and the child's behaviour improves. A post-treatment interview is then conducted to review and celebrate progress. Follow-up and booster sessions are also available when needed. In cases where two parents attend treatment, one parent and child will be in the therapy room, while the other parent and therapist will sit behind the one-way mirror. Parents then switch roles mid-way through the session. Individual goals are created for each parent.

Pre-Treatment Assessment

The goal of the pre-treatment assessment is to listen to parent concerns, develop rapport and determine suitability for PCIT. The PCIT protocol recommends that pre-treatment assessment involves a discussion of the

Table 1. Structure of PCIT

Step	Assessment/Intervention	Typical Number of Sessions
1.	Pre-Treatment Assessment	1–2
2.	Teaching CDI	1
3.	Coaching CDI	3–4
4.	Teaching PDI	1
5.	Coaching PDI	4–6
6.	Post-Treatment Assessment	1–2
7.	Booster Sessions	As needed

Note: Table adapted from McNeil and Hembree-Kigin (2010).

presenting concerns, an assessment of behaviour, the presence and severity of behaviour problems and an exploration of parent management techniques employed so far, with a particular emphasis on time-out procedures. Sometimes it is beneficial for the parent to attend the first session without the child to enable the parent to openly discuss their concerns about their child and their current parenting strategies. The semi-structured interview provided by McNeil and Hembree-Kigin (2010) takes approximately 45 minutes to administer. Following the assessment phase, PCIT is explained to the parent, and the expectations of treatment are provided. The following standardised measures are implemented at assessment and throughout PCIT.

Dyadic Parent–Child Interaction Coding System — Fourth Edition (DPICS-IV)

The DPICS-IV is a standardised procedure where the dyad is instructed to play together in three structured situations behind the one-way mirror following the manual for the DPICS, which is now in the Fourth Edition (DPICS-IV, Eyberg et al., 2013). The DPICS-IV involves coding the direct observation of the parent–child interaction in each of three scenarios: child-led play, parent-led play and clean-up. The therapist codes each parent statement, as well as whether the child complies with commands or goes to time out. The codes are available in DPICS-IV comprehensive manual (Eyberg et al., 2014) or the Clinical Manual version (Eyberg et al., 2014). Prior to the start of treatment, but also during the treatment phase, the parent–child interaction is coded using the DPICS-IV. Parents are coded for the number of times they make the following verbalisations: Labelled praise, reflections, behavioural descriptions, neutral talk, unlabelled praise, direct commands, indirect commands, questions, and negative talk. The child is coded for the number of times they show the following behaviours following a parent's command: compliance, non-compliance or no opportunity to comply. Where two parents are present, the second parent will also be coded using the DPICS-IV. The DPICS-IV can be administered to one parent alone if only one parent attends or coding each parent one after the other.

Eyberg Child Behaviour Inventory (ECBI)

As part of the initial assessment but also at every treatment session, the child's behaviour is rated by the parent using the ECBI. The ECBI (Eyberg & Pincus, 1999; Eybeg & Ross, 1978) is a brief parent report on their child's behaviour (for children aged between 2–16 years). There are two main scores; the Intensity Score (IS), which assesses how frequently the child displays the behaviours. The Problem Score (PS) asks whether the parent perceives the behaviour to be a problem for themselves. Clinical cut-offs are a T-score of 60 or higher for the IS and the PS (Eyberg & Pincus, 1999), but competency for completing PCIT requires an Intensity T-score of 55 or below. The ECBI is administered at pre and post-treatment as well as at the start of each session to measure treatment progress (McNeil & Hembree-Kigin, 2010). Parents are provided feedback on ECBI scores at regular intervals during treatment.

Sutter-Eyberg Behavior Inventory-Revised (SESBI-R)

Similar to the ECBI, the SESBI-R (Eyberg & Pincus, 1999; Funderburk & Eyberg, 1989) measures the intensity and frequency of a child's behavioural difficulties but in the classroom context. The SESBI-R is completed by the child's school teacher, preschool teacher or daycare educator. Similar to the ECBI, IS and PS T-scores of 60 or greater are in the clinical range (McNeil & Hembree-Kigin, 2010).

Phase One: Child-Directed Interaction (CDI)

The first of the two treatment phases is Child Directed Interaction (CDI). CDI aims to assist in establishing warm, secure parent–child relationships (Lieneman et al., 2017). It focuses on strengthening the parent–child relationship by improving attention to and reinforcement of the child's positive and appropriate behaviour. In this phase, the parent learns to use traditional play therapy skills to follow the child's lead in play. This can be a challenging task for parents who are not used to playing with their child and for parents who tend to lead excessively with directions, questions, criticism, or commands, stifling the child's initiative to be in charge of the toys or direct the play. The overall mission statement of parents learning CDI is that the 'child is in charge of the toys'. Explanation may be required so the parent can understand that attuned and involved parenting will systematically reinforce positive and desirable child behaviour and increases the likelihood that the child will display more of this in the future.

The CDI skills are first taught to the parents at a parent-only appointment, referred to as CDI-Teach. CDI is taught via didactic presentation, discussion, live modelling, and role-playing. CDI provides the foundational skills to help promote a strong and positive parent–child relationship and serves as the foundation for PDI skills. Often when parents come to start PCIT, they want to move straight into the PDI phase (as it may be the skills they are more familiar with). Therapists explain to parents that CDI is taught first because many of the CDI skills are necessary for PDI to work and that we aim for these to become automatic habits, so they will not have to remember as many new things when focusing on the most difficult behaviours. In the CDI-Teach appointment, parents are taught all the skills in the CDI phase, including the 'Don't skills' and 'Do skills'.

In CDI, the 'don't skills' are outlined and explained, and parents are encouraged to avoid saying these things during play as these can lead to negative parent–child interactions and conflicts.

The 'Don't Skills'

- **Avoid Commands**: Commands tell the child what to do. Commands can be indirect commands, such as 'How about you pack away the blocks?' or direct, such as 'Give me that piece'. Commands can cause conflict, stop the play and take the lead away from the child's play.

- **Avoid Questions**: There are several reasons why questions are avoided; they shift the conversation so the parent is leading the conversation, they require the child to stop their play and answer, they are sometimes hidden commands, and it may seem like the parent disapproves of what the child is doing.

- **Avoid Criticism and Sarcasm**: Criticism and sarcasm show disapproval of the child's activities, play and/or speech. Examples might include 'Why can't you do this at home?' and 'That is not the way it goes'. Criticism and sarcasm are avoided because they give attention to negative behaviour, reduce a child's self-esteem, and can increase negative feelings of the child and the parent.

The 'Do Skills'

After the 'Don't skills' are explained, therapists ask the parent to recall the 'Don't skills'. Parents are then taught the 'Do skills', play skills which are referred to by the acronym 'PRIDE' skills (labelled **P**raise, **R**eflection, **I**mitation, behavioural **D**escription and **E**njoyment).

- **Labelled Praise**: Labelled Praise involves parents noticing their child's positive behaviours and telling their child exactly what it is that they like. For example, 'Thanks for sharing' and 'I like it when you use nice words'. This contrasts with unlabelled praise where the child is being told they are being good (e.g., 'Good girl', 'Good job'). With unlabelled praise, the child may be unsure what specific behaviour the praise is connected to. Labelled praise helps the parent communicate clearly what behaviour they like; it increases the likelihood for the behaviour to occur again, shows approval and increases the child's self-esteem.

- **Reflections**: Reflections refer to repeating or paraphrasing back what the child has said. For example, if a child states, 'I am building a tower', the parent repeats back the main content of what the child has said — for example, 'Yes, a very big tower!'. This skill helps the child to lead the play and conversation, shows the parent is interested in what they are doing and saying, and demonstrates that the parent is actively playing with, and giving their attention to, the child.

- **Imitation**: Imitation refers to copying or imitating the desirable behaviour of the child. For example, if the child is sitting at a table playing with blocks, the parent sits near the child at the table and also plays with the blocks. Another example is if the child draws a picture, the parent may say, 'I'm going to draw a picture too', and proceeds to do so. Imitation lets the child lead while the parent follows, shows parental approval, increases the likelihood that they will continue with this play, teaches concepts such as sharing and taking turns, and makes the play more enjoyable. Imitation also helps the parent play with the child at the child's developmental level.

- **Behavioural Descriptions**: Behavioural descriptions involve the parent commenting on what the child is doing. For example, if a child is pushing a car on a track, the parent could say, 'You are pushing the car'. If a child is building a tower, the parent could say, 'You are building a tower'. Behavioural descriptions show that the parent is following the child's play, shows they are interested in the play, can help the child learn concepts (especially for those with a limited vocabulary to describe their play), models speech, can help keep a child's attention on a toy/play sequence and organises the child's thoughts about the activity.

- **Enjoyment**: Enjoyment means that the parent displays pleasure, delight, and warmth and conveys that they are interested in the child's activity and enjoys the interaction with the child. This means that the parent acts happy and warm when playing with their child. For example, the parent may smile, uses a nice tone of voice and makes physical contact (such as giving the child a pat on their arm or back). This helps foster warmth in the relationship between the parent and child and helps make the play fun and meaningful for the child.

Parents are also taught to use two strategies for managing problems that may occur in CDI. The first is ignoring minor misbehaviour or attention-seeking behaviour. Examples of behaviours that can be ignored include screaming, swearing, saying hurtful things, or engaging in play the parent does not like (e.g., the child pretending to fight and kill toy animals). Ignoring requires the parent to look away from the child, show no expression and say nothing to the child. Ignoring serves two purposes; it removes positive attention from the behaviour and, by doing so, does not reinforce the problem behaviour; and it communicates to the child the difference between appropriate and inappropriate behaviour. Ignoring is maintained until the child engages in a positive behaviour. When the child starts behaving appropriately, the parent is encouraged to pay attention to the child's behaviour using labelled praise to reinforce and communicate to the child what behaviour the parent wants to see. Labelled praise becomes particularly powerful when the parent praises the opposite of the negative behaviour that is ignored. For example, if a child swears, the parent ignores the swearing and then waits to praise the child when they speak nicely (e.g., 'I like it when you use nice words'). Parents are also taught that when they start ignoring, children may escalate the behaviour in order to get the parent to respond in previous ways. However, if parents persevere consistently, these behaviours will decrease over time. Many parents find the skill of ignoring negative behaviour challenging and need support with the help of live coaching in the session.

When children engage in aggressive or destructive behaviour, parents are taught to discontinue or stop play. Aggressive and destructive behaviour includes physical aggression (e.g., hitting, biting), throwing toys and breaking toys. When a child engages in any of these behaviours, the parent communicates to the child that playtime is over. This is used because aggressive behaviours cannot be ignored and are dangerous. For example, if a child throws a toy at their parent and hits them, the parent may say, 'Playtime is over because you hurt me'. Even if the child pleads with the parent that they will not engage in this behaviour again, play is discontinued for that day or during homework. In session, however, therapists typically will walk into the playroom and ask the parent to leave, clearly restating the safety rules of the playroom. The parent is then brought back into the room after a minute or two, and coaching resumes.

In the teaching phase, parents are provided education about these techniques, with handouts they are given to take home. They are asked to recall the 'Don't skills' and the 'Do skills' (PRIDE skills) as well as role-playing the skills in the session. The clinician and the parent discuss the importance of practising the CDI skills for 5 minutes every day, the types of toys that are appropriate and inappropriate for CDI and anticipating and problem-solving difficulties around completing the homework task. Parents are also asked to fill in a homework sheet and the ECBI on a weekly basis. The therapist explains that CDI play at home is a highly important part of PCIT to practice and reinforce skills required for consistency and to improve child behaviour. This play usually becomes part of the parent and child's routine at home and is often affectionately renamed 'special time'.

CDI Coaching

Following the CDI Teach session, the CDI treatment phase consists of live coaching of the parent while the child is present. In this here-and-now coaching, the parent is encouraged to apply the PRIDE skills with consistent and constant input from the therapist. At the start of the session, the therapist enquires about homework completion and any issues during practice at home. The therapist also checks in about any stressors unrelated to the child before setting up the bug in the ear device for the parent. The therapist then moves behind the one-way mirror to commence coaching.

The therapist then speaks through the device and asks the parent to play with their children for five minutes while the therapist codes the parent's CDI skills. During the five minutes of in-session CDI coding, therapists tally the frequency of parental neutral talk, behaviour descriptions, reflections, labelled praises, unlabelled praises, questions, commands, and negative talk. The parent is also rated whether they had 'satisfactory' imitation, enthusiasm and ignoring of disruptive behaviour, or whether this skill 'needs practice' or was 'not applicable' (for ignoring only). For competency and 'passing' the CDI phase, in the 5-minute coding, the parent needs to complete 10 labelled praises, 10 reflections and 10 behavioural descriptions. They also need to use less than 3 questions, commands, or negative talk in total and ignore non-harmful but inappropriate behaviour. However, if a parent does reach the above criterion but lacks enthusiasm, warmth and genuineness, CDI should be continued until the relationship improves.

Once the five minutes of coding is completed, the parent is then given feedback regarding their use of CDI skills and is invited to focus on 1 or 2 skill areas for improvement during the session. For example, a parent who has 10 reflections, 14 labelled praises and 2 behavioural descriptions within a 5-minute period may be asked to focus on descriptions. Parents who are just starting CDI typically focus on an area of strength that is closest to competency. For example, for a parent who achieved 7 labelled praises, 2 reflections and 2 descriptions within a 5-minute period of the first session, the therapist may then focus on them gaining competency of labelled praise. This helps build confidence and focuses on what the parent is doing well. Therapists need to be skilled in identifying goal areas to be worked on. This depends on the needs of the parent, their capacity for learning, progress in treatment as well as the strengths and struggles of the parent–child interaction. Some parents learn these skills rapidly (e.g., competency by session 2), while others require substantial practice before competency is achieved (e.g., by session 12 or later).

Once goals are set, the therapist provides coaching to the parent through the bug in the ear device. The therapist as coach provides real-time feedback on what the parent says and how the parent acts towards the child. For example, the therapist may comment, 'Great reflection' and 'Nice use of behavioural descriptions'. The therapist can also provide education about why a child is engaging in a certain behaviour and make a link between the parent's behaviour and the child's behaviour. For example, when a child says, 'Here's a plate, mummy!' and the parent says, 'Thanks for sharing', the therapist can praise the parent's ability to use labelled praise by saying, 'Great labelled praise, she will share with you more often'. Coaches can also make observations of parent and child interactions and changes as a result of therapy. For example, 'Sarah is playing so gently with the toys, she had real difficulty with being gentle when PCIT first started'. This coaching interaction can occur many times between a therapist and a parent within a 30-minute coaching period.

The interaction between parent–child is a parallel process between therapist-parent. The therapist's skill comes from their ability to pay attention to what the parent is doing well, ignore what the parent is not doing so well, and the impact that a parent's micro-behaviour has on a child. For example, when a parent smiles at their child, and the child beams back, the therapist can comment, 'He looks happy playing with you; your smile lets him know this'. For parents with negative thoughts about their parenting capacity, this can be incredibly powerful in helping rebuild their confidence. Many parents do not realise how much their child wants to please them or how much capacity they have to help their child behave appropriately.

Therapists generally ignore most of what a parent does incorrectly in CDI. For example, when parents continue to ask questions, give commands in CDI or do not complete one of the PRIDE skills correctly, this is largely ignored by the clinician, at least in the first couple of sessions. Once rapport has been developed over time, if a parent is still struggling with their DO and DON'T skills, corrective advice may be given if the therapist feels it will be helpful. It is suggested that the positive comments to corrective statements should be given in a ratio of at least 5 positives to 1 corrective (McNeil & Hembree-Kigin, 2010).

When behaviour becomes aggressive or difficult to manage, is starting to escalate, or it becomes clear that a parent is struggling with a particular skill, the therapist may need to become more actively involved. They may provide instruction that helps prevent problems from emerging or offers guidance as to how to handle a particular behaviour (e.g., 'You can ignore him yelling').

This helps maintain a positive parent–child interaction and can be used to educate the parent about potential meltdowns that could be averted. For example, for a young child who appears to be yawning during an afternoon appointment, the therapist may comment, 'He is looking very tired. How about we end in 1 minute?'. Overall, coaching statements need to be as short as possible as the therapist is quickly giving the coaching advice while the child is still playing and also to help model to the parent how succinct the labelled praise is to be to a child.

Phase Two: Parent-Directed Interaction (PDI)

PDI skills are a set of skills to provide structure to young children and to teach parents to be consistent, predictable and follow through with discipline skills. As CDI skills are foundational to PCIT, the use of CDI skills features heavily in PDI. Parents are encouraged to use CDI skills throughout PDI coaching and home-based practice. Specifically, after a command is given and child compliance is achieved, the parent should be encouraged to return to PRIDE skills for at least 20 seconds to 1 minute before the next command is attempted. Skills taught in PDI include giving direct commands (as opposed to indirect ones), praising compliance, being consistent with non-compliance, using time-out for non-compliance and establishing standard household rules (McNeil & Hembree-Kigin, 2010). Parents are encouraged to speak in a neutral manner and to remember several procedures that are enhanced by giving parents clear diagrams of the sequence in time-out. Parents are taught to give single (as opposed to compound) commands that are direct rather than indirect (i.e., giving the child an option of not choosing to do it). If the child is initially non-compliant to the direct command within 5 seconds, they get a time-out chair warning. If the child is still non-compliant, they are directed to the time-out chair. The time-out length is 3 minutes plus 5 seconds of the child being quiet, regardless of the child's age. The time-out chair procedure ends when the original command is obeyed, followed by a second learning command. This learning command is to remind the child to listen and follow commands, or they will have to go back to the time-out chair. A time-out room is used if time-out with the chair has not been successful (McNeil & Hembree-Kigin, 2010).

As with CDI, PDI is also taught via didactic presentation, discussion, live modelling, and role-playing. We find it helpful to say to parents, 'In CDI, the child is in charge of the toys, but in PDI, the parent is in charge of the listening'. PDI aims to assist the parent in giving clear, direct commands and to facilitate compliance (Lieneman et al., 2017). Parents may struggle with the PDI tasks at the beginning, especially if they are not used to enforcing boundaries and compliance. In the first PDI coach session with the child, the time-out procedure can be demonstrated with the assistance of a large doll or toy animal

(Mr. Bear) so the child can see what happens if the doll is non-compliant with the clinician's direct command. Sometimes the child wants to copy this demonstration with the doll.

Commands

Like CDI, the PDI skills are first taught to the parents at a parent-only appointment, referred to as a PDI-Teach. In the PDI-Teach appointment, parents are first taught to give commands to their child, referred to as the eight rules of effective commands. They include:

- **Direct Commands**: Direct commands are clear instructions about what the child should do. They leave no question about what the child is being told to do, do not give a choice, give the idea that the parent will help or do the task for the child and reduces confusion for the child, so it is clear exactly what it is they are supposed to do. For example, a direct command might be 'Please give me the red block' while pointing at the red block. An indirect or unclear command might be, 'Would you like to give me a red block?'. In this case, the child may reply, 'No, I don't want to'.

- **Positive Commands**: Positively stated commands tell the child what to do rather than what not to do. For example, a positively stated command for a child might be 'Please put your hands by your side'. A negatively stated command might be, 'Stop touching that!'. In this command, the child may not know what behaviour to do instead.

- **One Command at a Time**: Parents are taught to only say one command at a time. This helps the parent know when the child has completed a command and helps the child remember what they have been told to do. For example, one command might be 'Put that tissue in the bin'. This contrasts with multiple commands which are harder to remember, such as 'Put the tissue in the bin, tidy up your bag and put your shoes by the door'.

- **Specific Commands**: Specific commands are very clear statements of what the child is supposed to do. Vague and non-specific commands can be difficult to understand and do not give the child clear information as to an alternative behaviour to engage in. For example, a clear command would be 'Please walk' rather than a vague command such as 'Be good'.

- **Age Appropriate**: Commands should be tailored to the developmental abilities of the child. For example, a child who is just starting to draw might be given a command 'Please draw a line here'. The same child would be unable to complete the command 'Please draw a house'. This is a command that the child cannot do and, therefore cannot comply with. These are also referred to as 'no opportunity commands'.

- **Normal Tone of Voice**: Parents are encouraged to give commands in a normal tone of voice. A tentative or quiet voice tone may suggest that compliance is optional, whereas raised voices may create a negative parent–child interaction and may teach children to ignore respectful commands and only comply with an angry voice tone. Using a normal tone of voice also prepares children to listen to the teacher's instructions or to others in different settings. For example, 'Give me the block please' in a normal tone of voice versus 'Give me that block now or else!' in a loud, angry voice.

- **Explanations**: Parents are encouraged to give explanations before a command is given or after they are obeyed. This avoids the child asking why (before a command is obeyed) and avoids children receiving attention using the 'why' delay tactic. For example, a command with an explanation might be, 'I would like to use the blue pencil; please put it in my hand'. This is in contrast to 'Give me the blue pencil' — the child says, 'Why?'— parent says, 'Because I want to use it'. Alternatively, an explanation can be given after the command is obeyed; for example, after the child has given the parent the pencil, the parent can say, 'Thanks for listening to me. I wanted to use the blue pencil, and you shared nicely with me'.

- **Only When Necessary**: Parents are taught to use direct commands when necessary. This means saving direct commands for tasks that are important or that the parent is willing to implement the time-out procedure over. This decreases the child's frustration for small unnecessary commands (e.g., 'Please get me a glass of water' when the parent is next to the sink) and makes it easier for the parent to follow through when giving a direct command. For example, 'Please come and sit here' might be important when a child is standing on the table. The command 'Please get me a tissue' may not be an important or necessary command to be given in the rush of the morning routine.

Time-Out Procedure

Parents are taught a sequence for children who do comply with commands and who do not comply, resulting in a time-out. Non-compliance with time-out includes the use of a time-out room.

- **Compliance**: If the child complies with a command, the parent is taught to use labelled praise for compliance rather than labelled praise for the specific behaviour the child is doing. For example, in the original command 'Please put the wrapper in the bin', the parent would be taught to give the labelled praise 'Thanks for listening to me' rather than 'Thank you for putting that in the bin'.

- **Warning Command and Time-Out Warning**: If the child refuses to comply within 5 seconds of the command, the parent is asked to give a warning command with a time-out warning 'If you don't put that in the bin, you'll have to sit on the time-out chair'. If the child complies, the parent provides labelled praise, 'Thanks for listening to me'. If the child does not comply, the time-out sequence is then implemented.

- **Time-Out**: If the child does not comply with either the original command or the time-out warning, the parent instructs the child, 'You didn't do what I told you to do, so you have to sit on the time-out chair'. The parent is then instructed to take the child to a time-out chair, back away from them and say, 'Stay on the chair until I say you can get off'. The child is then on the time-out chair for 3 minutes plus 5 seconds of quiet (in case the child yells and screams continuously), and the parent is instructed to ignore anything the child does while sitting on the chair. After three minutes plus 5 seconds of the child being quiet, the parent says, 'You are sitting quietly on the chair. Are you ready to (what I previously told you to do) put the wrapper in the bin?'. If the child says 'No', the parent repeats the time-out sequence until compliance is achieved. For example, the parent will say, 'Stay on the chair until I say you can get off,' and then leaves the child on the chair for another 3 minutes plus 5 seconds of quiet. If the child says 'Yes', the parent takes the child over to where the command was given, points to the item and then waits for the child to comply. If the child complies within 5 seconds, the parent gives an acknowledgement or unlabelled praise (e.g., 'Okay') and gives another command, referred to as a learning command. For example, 'Now please put this piece of paper in the bin'.

- **The Learning Command**: The learning command is to teach the child that compliance is required to avoid the time-out chair. If the child complies, the parent is instructed to give enthusiastic labelled praise for compliance, 'Thanks for listening to me' and return to CDI skills. If the child refuses, the time-out sequence is then repeated until compliance is achieved.

- **Time-Out Room**: In some situations, the child may get off the time-out chair, scoot, stand on the chair, or rock the chair before the three minutes are up. If the child does any of these behaviours, parents are instructed to place their child back on the chair. Please see the protocol for instructions on what is a safe and suitable time-out (McNeil & Hembree-Kigin, 2010). The parent then gives a 'Once in a lifetime warning' for the behaviour that the child engaged in. For example, 'You got off the chair before I said you could. If you get off the chair again, you will go to the time-out room. Stay on the chair until I say you can get off', and the standard time-out sequence is restarted. If the child leaves the chair again, the child is told, 'You got off the chair before I said you could, so you have to go to the time-out room'. The child is then placed in the time-out room for 1 minute plus 5 seconds of quiet. After this time, the parent then puts the child back on the time-out chair in the playroom and says, 'Stay on the chair until I say you can get off'. If the child gets off the chair again, the time-out room sequence is repeated until compliance is achieved. If the child complies, the standard time-out sequence is completed. The child receives a once-in-a-lifetime warning for each of those four behaviours (escapes, stands, scoots or rocks), but if the child engages in one of these behaviours again after the lifetime warning has been given, the child is placed immediately in the time-out room.

In the teaching phase, parents are provided education about these techniques, handouts to take home, as well opportunities to role-play. Parents are instructed not to use time-out or commands until after the first PDI coach session, including the importance of scheduling extra time at the first PDI-Coach session if the child does not comply. The parent must be committed to following through with the time-out procedure. The PDI sequence will be explained to the child at the beginning of the first PDI coach session. A description of the first PDI coaching session is also given. Parents are instructed to continue to use the 5 minutes of CDI practice at home, fill in their homework sheet, as well as the ECBI on a weekly basis (McNeil & Hembree-Kigin, 2010).

PDI Coaching

The first PDI coaching session occurs at the clinic. Children are told about the 'new rules' involving listening to their parents and responding to their commands. Other aspects of PDI, such as the time-out chair and the time-out room, are role-played to help the child understand them. Parents are advised that therapists will initially be 'In charge' of the commands and will be coaching everything the parent says. Therapists generally start with 'play commands', which are simple commands that the child is either likely to do anyway or that involve the parent's cooperation in play (e.g., 'Please put that Lego piece on your tower next' or 'Please give me a pencil so I can draw too'). If the child does not comply, the therapist coaches the parent to give the time-out chair warning command, followed by either compliance or follow-through with the time-out procedure (if required). The end of the session involves a debrief, and depending on therapist and parent confidence, parents are asked to use commands after the 5 minutes of CDI homework each day and use the time-out procedure for non-compliance. Parents are also instructed to call if there are any issues during the week.

PDI coaching sessions occur initially in the clinic setting and move beyond 'play commands' to 'running commands' (2–3 commands given in succession) and 'pack up commands'. As the parent's confidence and PDI competence increase, as part of their homework, parents are instructed to use more challenging commands at home, from play commands to pack up commands in CDI, 2–3 real-life commands at home (e.g., 'Put your plate in the sink'), and then commands as needed through the day. House rules are also introduced in later sessions where any instance of non-adherence to a house rule results in a time-out without a warning. This is usually reserved for difficult or aggressive behaviours (e.g., hitting, swearing). Parents are then provided information on using time-out in public settings such as a grocery store and potentially with siblings.

Depending on the PDI session, PDI coaching sessions start with a family check-in and review of homework, administration of standardised measures, and whether there have been any problems with either CDI or PDI homework practices. The clinician will typically continue to code the parent's CDI skills (PRIDE skills) to ensure the competency level is maintained, provide some brief CDI coaching if required and then code their PDI skills. Coding of PDI skills assesses whether a parent was able to give a direct or indirect command and whether the parent provided effective follow-through, including praise for compliance, a time-out chair warning, or following through with the time-out chair and time-out room procedure correctly if required. PDI competency requires the parent to give at least 4 commands, of which 75% must be effective (e.g., direct and single commands) and show at least 75% correct follow-through. If time out is required, the parent must successfully follow through with the time-out procedure without the therapist's input (McNeil & Hembree-Kigin, 2010).

Post-Treatment Assessment Session

Once a parent has met competency for PDI skills and the child's behaviour is within the normal range, the parent and child have completed the requirements for PCIT. A post-treatment session is held where all of the pre-treatment measures are re-administered. Feedback about the assessment results and treatment is explained to the family. Upon graduation, the parents receive a certificate, and the child receives a prize (McNeil & Hembree-Kigin, 2010).

Booster Sessions

Booster sessions are also available to parents and children who require a top-up or reminders of skills used in PCIT. They can occur as needed within a 3-month period. The overall length of treatment is stated to be 3 months or 12 weeks of weekly sessions; however, the length of treatment is dependent on the parent meeting competency criteria, and as a result, some families may move through PCIT quickly, while others may require a longer treatment duration.

Resources Required for PCIT

PCIT requires 3–5 sets of toys. Construction toys without rules are recommended. Good examples of toys include pretend food, cars, blocks, Lego, Mr. Potato Head, farm animals and doll houses. Toys that encourage rough play, require limit setting and do not require high levels of interaction are avoided. Examples include pretend guns, painting and watching TV. The PCIT room and time-out rooms require a specific set-up (see McNeil & Hembree-Kigin, 2010), ideally with a one-way mirror, a bug-in the earpiece and a sound system. There are also adaptations for in-room coaching and where a time-out room is not available. Publications to assist clinicians in conducting PCIT include the PCIT Protocol Manual (available from www.pcit.org) and the Dyadic Parent–Child International Coding System (DPICS): Comprehensive Manual for Research and Training (available from www.pcit.org) and the fourth edition of its Clinic Manual (available from www.pcit.org), as well as McNeil and Hembree-Kigin's (2010) book on PCIT.

Qualifications and Training Required

To become a certified PCIT therapist, clinicians must have recognised graduate or university qualifications in a mental health field as well as complete basic and advanced PCIT training, undergo PCIT consultation with a PCIT trainer for a period of 12 months and have seen two cases to completion meeting a number of therapist competencies. PCIT clinicians can then complete a further recognised training to become a certified PCIT trainer (see the PCIT International website for PCIT therapist and trainer requirements, which may change over time). PCIT International, Inc oversees the fidelity and research of PCIT internationally (Lieneman et al., 2017). It also provides training and certification for clinicians to use PCIT. There are also free training modules online, including PCIT for children who have experienced trauma. Therapists can complete self-assessments to determine whether they have understood the model and are competent in their coaching steps.

Case Example 'Emilia'

Emilia was a 6-year-old girl who displayed a lot of externalising problems in the home environment, including screaming, physical aggression, and defiance. At school, she was the 'ideal student' and was 'perfectly behaved'. She had an older sister, Mackayla (10 years), who had significant anxiety of her own but would often provoke Emilia to react. Emilia and Mackayla lived with their mother, Katie, and father, David. Katie had significant mental health difficulties but was currently accessing appropriate treatments and had been relatively stable over the last few years.

During the initial assessment, Katie reported feeling like she did not know how to handle Emilia's outbursts and often felt overwhelmed when the girls fought. David was working full time and was often home in the afternoon and weekends, where the children's behaviour was significantly better. He reported no concerns with behaviour and felt that things were ok. In the DPICS-IV observation with Katie, Emilia was well-behaved and compliant. She engaged in imaginative and cooperative play with her mother during child-led play, followed her mother's lead in parent-led play, and packed up all the toys when requested in pack up. She acted similarly to her father. Katie commented that Emilia's presentation was typical for situations in which others were present. At the initial assessment, Katie's ratings of Emilia's behaviour on the ECBI corresponded with an Intensity score of 174 (t-score 74) and a Problem score of 20 (t-score 67). The DPICS-IV coding for Katie is displayed in Table 2.

Both Katie and David attended the CDI-Teach and were receptive to the 'Do' and 'Don't' skills. They felt confident that the PRIDE skills would be helpful for Emilia and commented that Emilia is always wanting one on one time. In CDI session 1, Katie reported that play had been received well. Despite this, there had been minimal change in behaviour as rated on the ECBI, with the Intensity score being 166 (t-score 70) and Problem score 25 (t-score 73). In the CDI coding, Katie's skills had improved significantly (see Table 3).

Table 2. DPICS-IV Coding for Katie During the Initial Assessment

Parent Code	Child Led Play	Parent Led Play	Pack Up
Neutral Talk	20	14	15
Behavioural Description	0	2	0
Reflection	4	2	3
Labelled Praise	0	0	1
Unlabelled Praise	2	3	6
Questions	22	8	10
Negative Talk	0	0	0
Direct Commands	0	2	2
Indirect Commands	3	6	10

Table 3. DPICS-IV Coding for Katie in the CD-1 Session

Parent Code	CDI-1
Neutral Talk	13
Behavioural Description	2
Reflection	19
Labelled Praise	8
Unlabelled Praise	3
Questions	6
Negative Talk	0
Commands	2

The goal of the CDI-1 session was to increase labelled praises. As expected, Emilia was very settled and showed no aggression, obnoxious or attention-seeking behaviours. Katie reported feeling some anxiety due to the one-way mirror, but by the end of the session, she felt that the play was much more natural and relaxed.

Treatment progressed through CDI coaching sessions 2 and 3 when Katie met competency for her CDI skills. See Table 4 for the results of the DPICS-IV Coding for Katie in sessions 2 and 3. See Figure 1 for treatment progression during CDI.

Table 4. DPICS-IV Coding for Katie in CDI-2 and CDI-3 Sessions

Parent Code	CDI-2	CDI-3
Neutral Talk	13	15
Behavioural Description	8	11
Reflection	9	14
Labelled Praise	14	10
Unlabelled Praise	3	2
Questions	6	2
Negative Talk	0	0
Commands	2	0

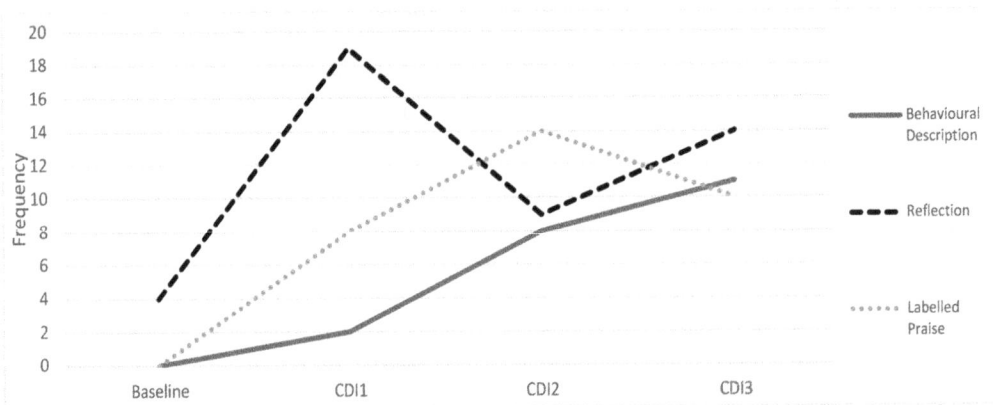

Figure 1. PRIDE 'Do' skills required for competency. The x-axis refers to the session number, while the y-axis refers to the frequency of coded behaviours. Competency for Behavioural Descriptions, Reflections and Labelled Praise is at least 10 of each behaviour in 5 minutes coding on the DPICS-IV.

At CDI-3, the ECBI also showed significant improvements, with the Intensity score reducing to 125 (t-score 58), but the Problem score showed a small decline at 20 (t-score 67). Katie reported feeling closer to Emilia. However, the screaming and fights between sisters continued to be an ongoing problem. Katie was keen to move to the PDI phase to address some of these negative behaviours.

In the PDI-Teach session, Katie was receptive to the 8 rules of effective commands but reported some anxiety about putting Emilia in time out. She reflected that her main discipline strategy is often to distract Emilia to something else or negotiate with her. She felt that the time-out procedure was a necessary next step, and although she anticipated it would be difficult, she nevertheless felt that this was what she needed to work on the most. The clinician reassured her that we would practice simple commands first and work our way up to more real-life commands. The clinician also advised he would be coaching all the commands and follow through in the first session.

In the first PDI coaching session, Katie felt that she was committed to completing PDI that day and the time-out procedure if needed. Emilia initially complied with the first five play commands. However, she appeared to become a bit annoyed in completing the commands. Katie was coached to provide another play command 'I would like the red block, please put that red block (point) in my hand'. Emilia acted as if she did not hear her mother and did not comply with the command. Katie was coached to provide a warning statement 'If you do not put the red block in my hand (point), you will have to go to time out'. Emilia did not comply. Katie was coached to take her by the hand and lead her to the time-out chair and say, 'Stay on the chair until I say you can get off'.

Of note to the clinician, this was the first time Emilia had demonstrated any defiance or oppositionality. When she was put in the time-out chair,

Emilia screamed a high-pitched scream and continued to do so for several more minutes. She also made statements such as 'You don't love me' and 'Why do you hate me?'. The clinician provided a lot of reassurance to Katie during this three-minute time-out as she was very close to the verge of tears. Following the 3 minutes plus 5 seconds of quiet, Emilia then came back to the table and complied with the original command and a backup learning command. Emilia then gave Katie a big hug, and they continued to play as if nothing had happened.

PDI-2 and PDI-3 continued in much the same fashion, with Emilia complying with most commands but occasionally refusing to complete a command resulting in having to go to the time-out chair. No time-out rooms were required in session. At home, during PDI homework, Emilia was reported to have about 3–4 time-outs a week and once had to go into the time-out room at home.

At PDI-2, the ECBI problem score had reduced to 115 (t-score 56), and the Problem score had finally shown a significant decline below the cut-off to 12 (t-score 56). At this stage in the treatment, Katie's coding of commands was at 55% effective commands and 64% effective follow-through.

PDI continued for house rules at PDI-4, and public behaviour was discussed at PDI-5. However, this had never been a problem as Emilia generally behaved well when others were around. By this stage in treatment, Katie had met competency for PDI, with 83% effective commands and 100% effective follow-through. The Intensity score had reduced to 82 (t-score 46), and the Problem score had reduced to 8 (t-score 52). See Figure 2 for ECBI results during treatment. Katie felt more confident and able to complete

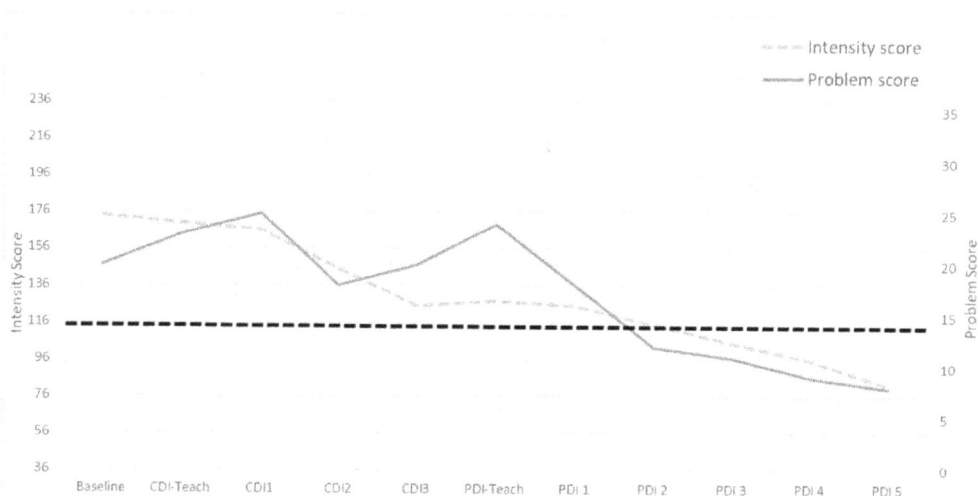

Figure 2. Treatment progress in PCIT. The x-axis refers to the session number. The y-axis (right) is the Problem score, and the y-axis left) is the Intensity score. To achieve competency, an ECBI t-score of 55 (intensity score of 115 or below) is required, as indicated by the horizontal line.

commands and felt she was ready for discharge. A follow-up session was offered in several months' time, but the family felt that their treatment goals had been met and did not feel further intervention was necessary.

This case was a relatively straightforward case where parents completed homework regularly, showed rapid competency in skills and demonstrated reductions in behaviour early in treatment. Emilia was relatively compliant in session, which made it easier for her parents to learn and apply the new skills they had learned. Katie was also quite open about her feelings and experiences, which made it easier for the therapist to address any concerns she had.

Case Example of 'Jarvis'

Jarvis was a 5-year-old boy who displayed a lot of externalising behaviours at home and school, with his behaviour at home being much worse. He had an older brother, Justin (8), who struggled with some mild anxiety but was reported by his school and parents to be 'relatively well behaved'. Jarvis and Justin lived with their biological parents, Karen and Jacob. Jacob presented as a very placid, consistent and gentle father. Karen presented as committed to her children and having a good sense of humour however was more extroverted and confessed openly to having 'a bad temper'. When Jarvis first came to PCIT, he would happily play with Jacob, but when it was Karen's turn to engage in special play with him, he would say, 'I don't want to play with you'. Despite him saying this, he would continue to sit and play with Karen and appeared to enjoy their one-on-one time together. Jarvis appeared to enjoy PCIT. He would often say to his parents in the car park when walking to the clinic room, that he did 'not like special play' and that he did not want to do it; however, once again, his behaviour did not match his vocalisations. His father noted that he never refused to get out of the car or to come into the building. He would improve his behaviour when he was reminded that 'special time' would have to end if he engaged in dangerous behaviour such as banging on the one-way mirror or climbing on the furniture.

As part of therapy, we encouraged Karen and Jacob to watch Jarvis' behaviour at times, as often what he said and what he did were conflicting. For example, despite verbally rejecting Karen, he would sit close to her and continue to play beside her. The same with special play. He said he did not like it when walking into the clinic but appeared to enjoy it when doing it and changed his behaviour if he was warned it would end if his aggressive or dangerous behaviour continued.

The family progressed through the PCIT structure initially. They appeared quite motivated at first, as they had tried a number of other interventions without success. While supportive of each other, they were also interested in seeing if the other parent was reaching competency of CDI before they did. They both were interested in starting the PDI phase soon. However, the parents were not consistent with doing the 5-minute homework exercise. Hence their time to reach competency for CDI took longer than normal.

During the PDI phase, one memorable session with this family was when Karen acted quickly to non-compliance with a command for Jarvis. He had not complied with a command within the required time, so Karen was instructed to place him onto the time-out chair. When they returned, and she gave him the next command, he complied immediately. His compliance with commands became much better after this exercise, and Karen did not have to use time-out chair sequences in future PCIT sessions. Karen said afterwards she had thought she did respond quickly and consistently to Jarvis' behaviour that she did not want to positively reinforce undesirable behaviour. However, she realised she had been giving him multiple commands. She said carrying through with the time-out was harder than she thought, and she was glad of the coaching through the bug in the ear device during this time.

With live coaching and the strong focus of the therapist on Karen's appropriate parenting behaviour, Karen's confidence increased, and she reached competency of CDI in session 8. Homework was completed on a more regular basis, though still not consistently.

Jacob discontinued attending the session as he felt he was coping well as a parent. Jarvis' compliance with commands, even indirect ones, improved greatly. His mismatch in expression also changed, now clearly stating that he enjoyed special time with his mother. The teacher noticed his behaviour had also improved at school.

In PDI session 6, Karen revealed that she had had a very difficult relationship with her own mother, who she described as highly critical and judgemental of Karen, negatively impacting her self-esteem as a parent. She explained that PCIT had helped her to gain confidence in her parenting and had decided to seek personal therapy to address relationship problems of the past.

The case is interesting in that Jarvis was responding to PCIT. However, his parents needed to commit to homework practice in order to gain more consistency in the new parenting skills. While homework takes 5 minutes per day, the case highlights how challenging this requirement can be for working parents caring for two school-age children. Also of interest was the mismatch between Jarvis's verbal statements and positive behaviour and the powerful effect on Karen when realising that her son enjoyed closeness and quality time with her. The case also highlights the fact that parents often believe that they are implementing a time-out chair sequence correctly but claim that it does not work. At closer observation, it often becomes evident that parents are not responding quickly and consistently to non-compliance from the child. Finally, the case illustrates that during the course of PCIT, especially when treatment progress is slow, additional assessment and subsequent treatments may be indicated to address parental mental health issues that hamper treatment progress.

Special Considerations: Use of Time-Out

PCIT's unique therapeutic techniques involve live coaching sessions with parents, preferably with a bug-in-the-ear device, although coaching and feedback can be delivered with the therapist in the room. Often parents will say that other behavioural parenting programs they have completed before did not work, but we have noticed that one of the possible reasons is that some parents believe that they have changed their behaviour. However, in the therapy room, it can be quite evident that they are still reinforcing problematic behaviour interactions. This model retrains the parent to change the behavioural interactions that do occur in a more positive and consistent way. PCIT achieves this through its use of live observation, live coaching, and collection of measures that the parent can also see.

One of the most criticised parts of PCIT is the use of time-out. Time-out is considered a controversial practice by some clinicians, especially when used with children who have a trauma background. PCIT International released a statement in 2018 justifying the inclusion of time-out in PCIT. They highlighted a meta-analysis by Kaminski et al. (2008) that showed that parent training programs with a focus on positive caregiver–child relationship and teaching parents the effective, consistent use of time-out are more effective than programs without these components. They also pointed out that trauma symptoms have been found to decrease for children who have completed PCIT. Parents with a history of physical abuse learn how to use time-out in a safe and effective manner and are less likely to use physical punishment. Finally, they point out that time-out helps children learn emotion regulation and self-control. Dadds and Tully (2019) also have highlighted how the time-out procedure can be a helpful and non-harmful parenting strategy used in behaviour management.

Evidence Base

Currently, PCIT is the most evidence-based parenting program with over 50 years of research (https://www.parentchildinteractiontherapy.com/pcit-research). Lieneman et al. (2017) recently conducted a meta-analysis of the research on PCIT in the previous 10 years. The authors concluded that the efficacy for PCIT has been well established, with most of the research focusing on community settings and families with complex personal and contextual challenges. PCIT has been found efficacious with several child presentations, including externalising disorders, ASD, anxiety disorders and children who have experienced trauma, to name a few. A summary of the latest research findings for PCIT is provided on the PCIT international website (http://www.pcit.org/pcit-research.html).

PCIT has been rated as having Level 1 evidence, which is based on strict criteria such as at least two Randomised Control Trails across two different sites, with improvements demonstrated after one year, according to the California Evidence-Based Clearinghouse for Child Welfare. It has been demonstrated to be an effective and powerful treatment for children, with an effect size of 1.65 (Lieneman et al., 2019). Several meta-analyses have been conducted to suggest that PCIT is effective in reducing externalising behaviour problems in children (Ward et al., 2016) and parental stress (Thomas et al., 2017), with PCIT effectiveness not differing on session length or location (Thomas et al., 2017). In their meta-analysis on younger children (children under 5 years), Phillips and Mychailyszyn (2022) found that PCIT had a large effect size in improving internalising and externalising symptoms and also improved caregiver distress. PCIT has also demonstrated cost-effectiveness with the Washington State Institute for Public Policy (2019) identifying a 15:1 cost-benefit ratio; that is, every $1 spent on PCIT services resulted in $15 savings. PCIT has lacked some diversity in samples, with Ward and colleagues suggesting that most of the samples in their analysis were conducted with white males. There is limited evidence to suggest that PCIT is an effective or appropriate intervention for Aboriginal and/or Torres Strait Islander families, and further research is recommended in this area.

Conclusion

PCIT is a well-researched and theoretically informed parenting program that is well-received by clinicians who are trained in using it (Christian et al., 2014; Niec et al., 2018). The clear and consistent structure of PCIT, combined with the standardised measures, lends itself to be easily researched. Well-defined parenting skills are taught via real-time coaching. Real-life coaching is a unique feature of this parenting program. It is successful in helping families improve their parenting skills as well as interactions with their children more quickly than programs relying on parental reports of their child's behaviour and parenting skills. However, training can be expensive and time-consuming with strict requirements of being a qualified clinician, such as providing recordings of sessions and demonstrating coaching of the various parenting skills. There is a commitment to training and supervision for clinicians wanting to become qualified PCIT clinicians; however, with the wide spread of qualified PCIT trainers internationally, this training and supervision is becoming more accessible. Parents involved in PCIT have to commit to weekly 1 hr sessions for around 12 weeks or until competency is reached, as well as daily homework practice of their skills. Despite the resources and time required for both the clinicians and parents, PCIT continues to be popular internationally and is a successful dyadic treatment of young children.

Reader's Exercises

What theoretical models are PCIT based on? What are the two main parts of PCIT? What are PRIDE skills?

Turn the following behaviours into labelled praise:

- Asking nicely
- Using manners
- Taking turns
- Sharing
- Listening to commands
- Speaking nicely

What would be appropriate commands in response to the behaviours and situations below?

- A child is jumping on the table.
- The child says, 'I am going to steal all these animals' (pointing to the animal figurines).
- A child threatens to hit a parent.
- A child screams at their parent.

How would you coach a parent who did not know how to handle the following behaviours?

- A child holds up a toy and threatens to throw it at the parent.
- A child says, 'You are not the boss; I am the boss', but complies with the command.
- A child calls out from the time-out chair, 'You don't love me!'.
- A child tells their parent, 'Stop talking to me like that'.
- A child hits their parents.

References

Baumrind, D. (1966). Defiant children: Effects of authoritative parental control on child behaviour. *Child Development, 37*(4), 887-907.

Christian, A.S., Niec, L.N., Acevedo-Polakovich, I., & Kassab, V.A. (2014). Dissemination of an evidence-based parenting program: Clinician perspectives on training and implementation. *Children and Youth Services Review, 43*, 8–17. http://dx.doi.org/10.1016/j.childyouth.2014.04.005

Dadds, M. R., & Tully, L. A. (2019). What is it to discipline a child: What should it be? A reanalysis of time-out from the perspective of child mental health, attachment, and trauma. *The American Psychologist, 74*(7), 794–808. https://doi.org/10.1037/amp0000449

Eyberg, S.M., Nelson, M.M., Ginn, N.C., Bhuiyan, N. & Boggs, S.R. (2014). *The Dyadic Parent–child International Coding System [DPICS]: Comprehensive Manual for Research and Training Fourth Edition.* PCIT International.

Eyberg, S. M., Nelson, M. M., Ginn, N. C., Bhuiyan, N., & Boggs, S. R. (2013). *Dyadic Parent–Child Interaction Coding System, 4th Edition (DPICS-IV) Comprehensive Manual for Research and Training.* PCIT International.

Eyberg, S.M., & Pincus, D. (1999). *Eyberg child behaviour inventory and Sutter-Eyberg student behaviour inventory-Revised. Professional manual.* Psychological Assessment Resources.

Eyberg, S.M., & Ross, A.W. (1978). Assessment of child behaviour problems: The validation of a new inventory. *Journal of Clinical Child Psychology, 7,* 113-116.

Funderburk, B.W., & Eyberg, S.M. (1989). Psychometrics of the Sutter-Eyberg student behaviour inventory: A school rating behaviour scale for use with preschool children. *Behavioral Assessment, 11,* 297-313.

Funderburk, B.W., & Eyberg, S. S. (2011). Parent–child interaction therapy. In J.C. Norcross, G.R. VandenBos, & D.K. Freedheim (Eds.), *History of psychotherapy: Continuity and change (pp. 415-420).* American Psychological Association.

Hanf, C.A. (1969). *A two-stage program for modifying maternal controlling during mother-child (M-C) interaction.* Paper presented at the meeting of the Western Psychological Association. Vancouver, Canada.

Kaminski, J.W., Valle, L.A., Filene, J.H., & Boyle, C.L. (2008). A meta-analytic review of components associated with parent training program effectiveness. *Journal of Abnormal Child Psychology, 36*(4), 567-569. https://doi.10.1007/s10802-007-9201-9

Lieneman, C.C., Brabson, L.A., Highlander, A., & McNeil, C.B. (2017). Parent–child Interaction Therapy: Current perspectives. *Psychology Research and Behavior Management, 10*, 239-256. https://doi.org/10.2147/PRBM.S91200

Lieneman, C. C., Quetsch, L. B., Theodorou, L. L., Newton, K. A., & McNeil, C. B. (2019). Reconceptualising attrition in Parent–Child Interaction Therapy: 'dropouts' demonstrate impressive improvements. *Psychology Research and Behaviour Management, 12*, 543-555. https://doi.org/10.2147/PRBM.S207370

McNeil, C.B., & Hembree-Kigin, T.L. (2010). *Parent–Child Interaction Therapy (2nd Edition)*. Springer.

Niec, L.N., Abrahamse, M.E., Egan, R., & Coelman, F.J.G. (2018). Global dissemination of parent–child interaction therapy: The perspectives of Dutch trainees. *Children and Youth Services Review, 94*, 485-492. https://doi.org/10.1016/j.childyouth.2018.08.019

Phillips, S. T., & Mychailyszyn, M. P. (2022). *Parent–Child Interaction Therapy for preschool-aged youth: A meta-analysis of developmental specificity*. Child & Youth Care Forum, 2022. https://doi.org/10.1007/s10566-022-09694-w

Thomas, R., Abell, B., Webb, H. J., Avdaic, E., & Zimmer-Gembeck, M. J. (2017). Parent–child Interaction Therapy: A meta-analysis. *Pediatrics, 140*(3). https://doi.org/10.1542/peds.2017-0352

Ward, M. A., Theule, J., & Cheung, K. (2016). Parent–Child Interaction Therapy for child disruptive behaviour disorders: A meta-analysis. *Child & Youth Care Forum, 45*, 675-690. https://doi.org/10.1007/s10566-016-9350-5

Washington State Institute for Public Policy. (2019, December). *Parent–Child interaction therapy (PCIT) for families in the child welfare system*. In Child welfare benefit-cost results. https://www.wsipp.wa.gov/BenefitCost/Program/77

Chapter 8

Child–Parent Psychotherapy (CPP)

Matthew Brand

Child–Parent Psychotherapy (CPP) is an evidence-based intervention for children aged 0–5 years who have been exposed to traumatic experiences, such as physical abuse, a life-threatening event and/or domestic violence. CPP is also an indicated intervention for young children presenting with other mental health difficulties, such as behavioural problems and for children with attachment disorder or dysfunction. CPP involves both the child and the parent or caregiver, and the dyad is the unit of treatment. One of the primary assumptions in CPP is that strengthening the caregiver–child relationship will result in improvements in children's mental health.

CPP evolved from Infant Parent Psychotherapy, a psychoanalytic treatment developed by Selma Fraiberg (Fraiberg, 1980). Fraiberg involved parents and their young children (0–3 years), using 'Ghosts in the Nursery' as a way to understand and prevent the intergenerational transmission of relationship patterns. The Ghost in the Nursery metaphor offers a language to acknowledge how unresolved conflicts, emotional hurt and mental representations of past maladaptive relationship patterns, usually developed during a caregiver's growing up years, infiltrate the current relationship between a caregiver and a child, unintentionally and unconsciously. It is assumed that insight and awareness of these intergenerational patterns enable a shift in parent behaviour. The primary means of addressing maladaptive parent–child interactions and mental health difficulties occurs through interpretations and gentle confrontations made by the therapist helping the parent to gain insight into their own unresolved childhood conflicts and how these are played out in their own parenting behaviour and in their interaction with their young child.

CPP broadens its scope to also consider psychodynamic, developmental, trauma, social learning and cognitive behavioural theories of change across early childhood. Unlike infants, toddlers and preschoolers bring their own unique experiences and behaviours to the therapeutic room and play an active part in therapy. In addition, focusing only on the parent may discount the young child's experience, which may be quite different to that of the parent. For example, a child's hypervigilance and sleep difficulties may be their reaction to a stressful life event, such as domestic violence, unrelated to a parent's re-enactment of intergenerational behaviours.

Adaptations to Infant–Parent Psychotherapy were initially made with Toddler Parent Psychotherapy (Lieberman, 1992) and then with preschoolers and their parents (Lieberman & Van Horn, 2005, 2008; Lieberman et al., 2005; Toth et al., 2002). CPP is a collective term that refers to the relational treatment of infants, toddlers and preschoolers between the ages of 0–5 years.

Theoretical Underpinnings and Assumptions

CPP is based on six main concepts and assumptions, which are echoed throughout therapy. They include:

1. **Attachment**: Attachment is considered the main organiser of the child's response to safety and danger. Exposure to trauma can influence a child's belief or expectation that their parents are able and/or willing to look after and protect them.

2. **Problems are addressed in the context of an attachment relationship**: Healing a child from trauma is most effective in the context of their primary relationships. CPP aims to create a safe environment with increased protective caregiving practices, helping parents to become more able to read and interpret their child's cues so that they can meet the needs of their children.

3. **Socioeconomic and cultural factors influence mental health**: Problems in a young child's life exist in the context of a child's environment, including cultural beliefs, their neighbourhood, and systems around them (e.g., schools, legal systems). People from different cultures and marginalised groups (e.g., Aboriginal and Torres Strait Islander peoples) often have poorer health outcomes compared with the general population, with higher rates of substance use, violence and chronic health conditions. Socioeconomic factors may limit a parent's ability to respond to their child's needs or protect them. CPP aims to help parents in practical ways to address these socioeconomic inequalities (e.g., advocating for housing, employment, access to education).

4. **Domestic Violence is a traumatic stressor**: Many children and parents referred to services have been exposed to some sort of trauma. Young children are more likely to experience maltreatment

and domestic violence than older children. This may be because of the young child's dependence on a caregiver and often being in close proximity to them, being unable to anticipate danger or know how to keep themselves safe. Alternatively, their parent may not accurately understand the impact of traumatic events on their child because young children are unable to express themselves in words. Trauma can result in a set of emotional and behavioural symptoms that negatively affect children's emotional health and the parent–child relationship. The parent's own behaviour (e.g., yelling at the child for not cleaning up) may be a traumatic reminder for the child who experienced verbal abuse. The child's behaviour (e.g., characters or superheroes fighting or hitting each other) may also be a traumatic reminder for the parent who experienced physical assault.

5. **The therapeutic relationship is critical**: Relationships affect relationships, and a primary assumption of CPP is that the clinician can only bring out positive change if the clinician interacts with the parent–child dyad in a positive way. Therapists work together with the child and parent to develop shared and agreed-upon treatment goals. A trauma frame is created, which aims to be non-judgemental and that understands that a) traumatic events cause strong emotions, b) young children and parents may express strong emotions through a number of ways, and c) the clinician is helping the parent create a safe environment to support the parent and child in managing these emotions.

6. **Therapists 'speak the unspeakable'**: CPP acknowledges how adversity and traumatic events affect young children and their parents and how these may be related to the presenting problems. Therapists shift away from 'what is wrong with you' to 'what happened to you', and trauma narratives are always reframed back to safety and repair narratives. Therapists must be tactful, not diving into unconscious processes too quickly. When the dyad is ready, the therapist works towards open discussion of traumatic events which are acknowledged by adults for their children, helping correct false attributions or interpretations of events that are common in young children (e.g., that they are to blame, they caused the trauma, because they are bad). A balance is also sought between negative and positive events and relationships.

Goals of General Trauma Interventions

In many interventions, one of the primary assumptions from recovery of trauma is the establishment of safety. This can be difficult when the parent is the cause of the traumatic event, the family is still living in a traumatic or threatening situation, or when the parent or child is still significantly affected by their own trauma symptoms and so do not feel safe. The therapist's goal is to help the parent engage in self-protection and protective practices for their child. Common goals for treatment in trauma include:

- Return to normal, healthy development.
- Respond realistically to threat.
- Maintain normal levels of emotions rather than under- or over-arousal (e.g., emotional numbing versus hypervigilance).
- Trust bodily sensations.
- Restore reciprocity in close relationships.
- Normalise the traumatic response.
- Differentiate between reliving and remembering.
- Putting trauma in perspective.

Goals of Intervention in CPP — Recovery of trauma in the context of the relationship.

CPP is different from other trauma interventions because of the need to balance the needs of both child and parent in therapy. They are two different people who are at different developmental stages and interpret the same thing differently. CPP requires the parent to become actively involved in helping the child recover from traumatic events. CPP encourages the goals of trauma-focused interventions as above, but the goals of CPP also include:

- Relieve stressful bodily experiences.
- Learn that adults can support and protect children.
- Help children understand that they did not make the event occur, nor are they to blame.
- Strong negative feelings can be managed in a non-harmful way.
- Life contains positive feelings.

There are six major intervention modalities of CPP.

1. **Promoting developmental progress through play, physical contact, and language**: Young children depend on relationships for emotional health. This can be achieved through responsiveness to a child's signals, safe physical contact, appropriate play and the use of language to explain things. For example, therapists encouraging play by having developmentally appropriate toys and supporting parents to play with their children (e.g., the therapist may state 'all children value their parents playing with them'), encouraging emotional expressions (e.g., the therapist stating 'there are a lot of big feelings in the room') or re-explaining adult comments in a child-friendly way (e.g., 'your mummy was really sick but instead of going to the doctor's to get medicine, she got medicine that the doctor didn't give her and it made her more sick' — to explain a parent's substance use).

2. **Offering unstructured reflective developmental guidance**: This intervention provides parents with information about children's needs, as well as appreciating how children perceive their world. It does not follow a particular format but aims to promote a parent's reflective functioning and encourages parents to understand what is happening to them, so they can understand what is happening to their child. If possible, this is framed in the parent's own experiences. For example, the therapist may state, 'I wonder what he is thinking about right now', or 'If you had to guess, what do you think he is saying he needs from you right now?', or 'I wonder if this ever happened to you as a child — what do you think you needed at that moment?'. Therapists may also be more practical in their advice (e.g., 'All children value their parents playing with them').

3. **Modelling appropriate protective behaviour**: This involves the therapist taking action to stop unsafe behaviour (e.g., a child about to climb up and jump off a filing cabinet). When modelling, therapists explain their actions and reasons why (e.g., 'I think you need to get down off there because I am afraid you will fall'). Parents are encouraged to reflect on dangerous events, keeping in mind that they care for each other (parent and child), but everyone needs to be safe. The clinician may also discuss with the parents the decisions and actions they have made, which might be risky.

4. **Interpreting feelings and actions**: Interpretations help parents and children understand difficult-to-explain and unknown feelings and behaviour. It can involve speaking the unconscious, 'speaking the unspeakable' or attaching meaning to behaviour. Careful timing of

interpretation is required, for example, when the child repetitively plays hitting or fighting between people over several sessions. The therapist might initially say, 'Oh, they are fighting with each other!' and if the play is repeated over several weeks or the therapist is confident of the meaning of this behaviour, an interpretation may be made — 'I think he is showing us that he remembers when you had the fight'.

5. **Providing emotional support and empathy**: All therapies are built on a positive relationship. In CPP, this can be achieved by conveying an attitude of hope, sharing achievements, noticing positive changes, and encouraging the parent and child to express themselves and challenge themselves. For example, the therapist commented (with enthusiasm), 'How he responded to you! It was beautiful to watch you picking him up when he needed it'.

6. **Providing support through crisis intervention and case management**: This means being available when stressful events arise during treatment. This can often be needed at the start of treatment or when new traumas or crises occur. This might include liaising with support services, daycare, child protection and the legal system, or other services as required.

Therapy Environment and Materials

CPP can be delivered in the home or in an office setting. Treatment can be weekly 1–1.5 hour appointments for 6 to 24 months. Sometimes twice weekly appointments may occur when a second session with the parent only is required. Developmentally appropriate toys and toys that are linked with traumatic experiences are also required. For example, children who witnessed a stabbing would have access to a toy knife, whereas a child who witnessed domestic violence would have access to a doll house and family figures. Reflective supervision or consultation is essential, including access to a supportive, reflective supervisor.

Phases in Therapy

CPP is structured in three primary phases: Assessment and Engagement, Core Intervention Phase, and Recapitulation and Termination/Closing. The main conceptual assumptions, aims and goals of treatment, and change processes are echoed throughout these phases. A brief overview of each phase is provided below, as well as examples of how this might be achieved.

Phase 1: Foundational Phase

The foundational phase begins with the development of rapport and a working relationship. This phase generally lasts four to six sessions but can be increased depending on the amount of information gathered, current stressors or crises, and assessment measures used. An outline of a possible format is provided below.

Session 1

The first session is a background gathering session, often with the parent alone to fill in paperwork and discuss any urgent issues. Reasons for referral and/or seeking treatment, areas of concern for the family, background information (such as who is in the family, developmental concerns etc.), and child symptoms can be completed at this session.

Session 2

The second session involves direct observation of the child and parent, observation of the child in interaction with others, and assessment of developmental functioning and functioning in various settings. This may include the parent and child, the child and therapist, and assessment of a child in other settings (e.g., preschool), with formal observational assessments or questionnaires. Structured observational measures may include the Crowell Procedure (Crowell & Feldman, 1988; Larrieu et al., 2018), which assesses several aspects of the parent–child relationship. Measures of behavioural functioning may be the Child Behaviour Checklist and Teacher Reporting Form (Achenbach & Rescorla, 2000), and a measure of developmental functioning may be the Ages and Stages Questionnaire third edition (Squires & Bricker, 2009).

Session 3

The third session is an evaluation of the child's trauma history and trauma symptoms, to be conducted with the parent alone. Parents can have a range of strong emotional reactions to this session. For example, it may trigger their own traumatic experience or strong feelings of guilt for not having protected their child. This is softened by stating that this exploration is part of the standard procedure, hoping that it will normalise the parent's reaction. By speaking with the parent alone, the parent is free to speak without fear of the child overhearing, allowing the parent to start to make connections between what a child experiences and how this has affected her, as well as normalising and educating trauma responses. It is recommended that structured instruments are used in this session, such as the Traumatic Events Screening Inventory, Parent Report Revised (Gosh Ippen et al., 2002) to assess for traumatic events, and the Diagnostic Infant and Preschool Assessment (Scheeringa & Haslett, 2010) and

Trauma Symptom Checklist for Young Children (Briere, 2005) to assess for trauma symptoms.

Session 4

The fourth session is an assessment of a parent's trauma history, trauma symptoms and mental health symptoms. This session is completed with a parent alone and not with their partner, other family members or with the child being present. Some caregivers are open to thinking about how their past has affected them, others are confused about why they are asked these questions, or they may be reluctant to disclose any of their own experiences. This session helps therapists develop empathy for parents and explores how a parent's experiences may affect the current parent–child relationship. Recommended measures may include the Life Stressors Checklist-Revised (Wolfe & Kimerling, 1997) and PTSD Symptom Scale Interview for DSM-5 (Foa et al., 2016).

Session 5

The fifth session is the feedback session, where clinicians review the information available and make a treatment plan, emphasise the need for regular appointments, introduce the dyadic nature of the treatment and discuss beliefs about trauma and parenting. A joint narrative is developed with the parent alone that will be shared with the child. This starts with a description of what the child experienced, their current feelings and/or behaviour that occurred after the event (often the reason for referral) and an explanation that treatment is a place where they can play and talk about their experience.

> **Example**: A 3-year-old girl Emily had experienced multiple traumatic experiences, including domestic violence by her father towards her mother at 12 months of age, and her mother being physically attacked and sexually assaulted. Emily had also been unintentionally hurt by her father in one episode, hitting her head on the wall. Emily had symptoms of being physically aggressive towards her mother, head banging when upset and hitting babies and then cuddling them. Physical aggression was observed in the initial assessment when discussing concerns with her mother. Emily did not seek any support or comfort from her mother and played independently for 60 minutes during the initial assessment. Her mother also reported concerns that included nightmares, night terrors and regression in behaviour when they accidentally bumped into her father at the shopping centre. The mother avoids all places where Emily's father may be. Her mother's self-rating of Posttraumatic Stress Symptoms was high.
>
> In the observational assessment, Emily was keen to play with toys. She did not show any distress upon separation or reunion with her mother but did get upset when she could not reach a certain toy. When she became

distressed, her mother turned away from her quickly and attempted to distract her with toys.

Emily's mother had been raised in a domestic violence situation, and her father left when she was 4 years old. Her mother remarried, but she never got along with her stepfather. She expressed a desire to stay in the relationship with Emily's father because 'I know what it is like to not have a father growing up'. She also thought that her daughter did not love her and deliberately did things to upset her.

After this information was gathered in the assessment sessions, the therapist developed a joint narrative with the mother about what Emily would be told about why she was coming to the centre, as well as providing an overview of treatment and obtaining permission to introduce her to trauma toys. Emily's mother was uncomfortable with the idea of telling her daughter what had happened but agreed to share the experience. Her mother also expressed concern that Emily 'doesn't talk about it' and 'didn't want to dig up old memories' that would upset her. The therapist assured her that Emily might be uncomfortable but was unlikely to be re-traumatised by things she has witnessed and remembers.

Phase 2: Core Intervention Phase

The core intervention phase begins with the child being introduced to treatment. The child is told about the joint narrative developed between parent and therapist, and this gives the child permission to discuss and communicate her past experiences. Many parents fear that they may re-traumatise their child, and although children may show discomfort, Lieberman, Ghosh Ippen and van Horn (2015) advise that children do not become re-traumatised by mention of an event that they remember. Clinicians should be mindful that avoidance is a trauma symptom but that most young children want adult explanations of scary events. Clinicians may also track the parent's response to traumatic events being discussed.

Example: In the first session of the Core Intervention Phase, the therapist introduced Emily and her mother to the playroom. He showed the toys that had deliberately been chosen in the playroom, including babies, family members, a small doll house and hospital equipment. When Emily had finished exploring the room, the therapist then told Emily the joint narrative: 'Emily, you are here because you saw your mum get hurt by your daddy. You also hit your head on the wall when they were fighting. Now you hit your mum, hit your head and hurt babies and then hug them. This is a place where you can come to talk and play about what happened. Your mum is here to keep you safe and make sure that these things do not happen again'.

After being told this information, Emily did not display any recognition of what the therapist told her. She continued to play with the toys and did not seek any comfort from her mother. After 30 minutes of play, Emily took out the doctor's kit and started telling her mother what to do and how to look after her. 'No! You are the baby,' she told her mother and proceeded to check her all over and make sure she did not have any bumps and bruises. The therapist wondered if the play was linked to Emily's experience of physical violence but was holding off with an interpretation as it might have been too early in treatment, instead staying factual and commenting, 'Emily is checking her mum is ok with the doctor's equipment'.

The core intervention phase outlines 12 *Domains of Intervention*, or 'ports of entry'. When intervening, clinicians are guided by two principles: try the most direct and simple intervention first; and encourage the parent to intervene rather than the therapist, where possible. What port of entry to take depends on the therapist, the family's culture and values, therapeutic alliance, progress in therapy, safety (i.e., the therapist may need to act if the parent cannot act), therapist experience and the level of functioning of the child and parent.

1. Play

Play is a core feature of child development. Play is a way children communicate, manage anxiety and make meaning of events. The therapist may help the parent understand the child's play and/or interpret play in the context of past experiences and the child's developmental capabilities. Some children may play out traumatic events repeatedly or appear 'stuck' in traumatic play, may play in isolation, or play with the therapist over preference for the parent. The main goal of play is the involvement of the parent and child in mutually rewarding joint play without the therapist. Some parents may interpret play as 'just playing' without therapeutic value. Education and developmental guidance are recommended at this stage.

> **Example**: In one family, the parent and child had never played together. The parent was sitting on a high chair while the child was busy playing on the floor. This continued for twenty minutes. The therapist felt very uncomfortable but then realised that this was how the child and mother probably normally interacted — he was also aware that the mother's own mother never played with her and so never had the opportunity to learn. The clinician simply commented, 'All children value their parents playing with them'. This was sufficient for the parent to get on the floor and play with their child but also spoke to the mother's own experience of not having her mother play with her. The parent reflected several months later, 'I never realised spending time with my children was that important' and now spends 'quality time' together every day, even months after treatment ended.

2. Sensorimotor Disorganisation and Biological Rhythms

As they develop, children learn to organise their sensorimotor experiences and develop routines with toileting, sleeping and feeding. Most parents find this normal developmental stage difficult and, at times, distressing. Children who experience trauma may have disruptions to this normal developmental process and may display emotional dysregulation, difficulty settling and soothing, body rigidity, irritability, head banging, eating, sleeping or toileting difficulties. The primary goal of this domain is to help the parent to respond in an empathic way that supports the development of these skills. At times, education and guidance are sufficient for improvement. At other times, parents can become 'stuck' and may interpret their child's behaviour as deliberate and intentional. Therapists may need to spend some time exploring a parent's perceptions of their child's behaviour before the parent and child can work it out.

> **Example**: In one dyad, a three-year-old boy was living with his mother and grandmother. His mother moved out, taking him along with her. He was toilet trained at this age. At age five, his mother returned him back into his grandmother's care while she entered a drug and alcohol program. His grandmother was unsure exactly what happened during the past 2 years but suspected domestic violence and drug use.
>
> Back in his grandmother's care, his toilet training regressed with regular accidents. He was soon also suspended for hitting a child who called him 'stinky'. His grandmother was frustrated that he used to be toilet trained and was no longer, causing extra work for her and problems at school. She interpreted his behaviour as 'lazy' and that he was doing it on purpose because he used to be able to use the toilet.
>
> In the assessment phase, the therapist understood that the boy, while living in his mother's care, was often blamed for having the occasional accident. The mother called him 'stinky' and 'disgusting' and would blame his toileting problems for the problems in her life. The therapist wondered if the two events were related. He asked his grandmother if he was possibly being reminded of his mother calling him 'stinky' and that this was one of the possible reasons why he hit the child. He also wondered about the reason why toileting regressed after being in his mother's care.
>
> His grandmother realised that his behaviour may have been a response to his mother's comments. The therapist then provided developmental guidance and suggested that 'the doctor might be able to help with poos', which revealed constipation from holding on. He was prescribed medication. It was hypothesised that he was holding on to prevent accidents and avoid subsequent feelings of shame and embarrassment.
>
> In the joint narrative, the child was told: 'You are here because your mum used to get angry when you had an accident with poo. Now you hold on to the poo, and it makes your tummy hurt, and the poo comes out in accidents.

This is a place you can play and talk about what happened. We also talked with the doctor to get you some medicine'.

3. Child-Fearful Behaviour

Young children show a range of fears, and these may be triggered by changes in routine, unfamiliarity with places or objects or response to sudden noises. Fears may be both rational and irrational (based on an adult's perception of the world) but are considered a normal part of child development. Two primary childhood fears are fear of separation from their parent and losing a parent's love. Children who experience safe and predictable caregiving can generally depend on their parents for safety, whereas those who experience fear at the hands of their parents may have difficulty doing so.

The primary goal of this phase is to facilitate the child's expression and resolution of feelings, even if these feelings are painful for the child and/or parent. Education and reflective developmental guidance about the child's fears may be a sufficient intervention. However, for children in a dangerous situation, it is important not to de-legitimise the child's fear but also to communicate that the adult is trying very hard to keep things safe. Case management may also be required at this stage to help provide resources for the parent that will promote safety (e.g., food, shelter).

> **Example**: In one dyad, a 4-year-old girl would follow her mother around everywhere. She could not sleep in her own bed, had to be in the same room as her to shower and toilet, and became extremely distressed when separated (e.g., when the mother had to go shopping). The mother commented that she feels like she has a little shadow, and is being controlled and manipulated by her 4-year-old.
>
> This 4-year-old girl had experienced multiple losses in her life, as well as temporary foster care between the ages of 12–19 months. The family had moved 9 times in 4 years, and her father committed suicide when the child was 12 months old. Her mother had been raised in foster care in approximately 8 placements and felt like these changes were 'nothing like what I had experienced'.
>
> In several play sessions, the child would play hide and seek with her mother but tell her mother where to hide. The child was never allowed to hide, only her mother, and would resist attempts for her mother to take the lead in the play. The clinician commented several times, 'all children fear losing their parent's love' and 'all children want to be with their parents'.
>
> In collateral (parent-only) sessions with the mother, the therapist talked about her being looked after in foster care. The mother commented that she was terrified of living with someone else, and she could remember wanting to go and find where her mother was. After multiple 'expeditions' to find her

mother, her foster carers told her that her mum was 'on holiday' and that she was never coming back. She remembers thinking that her mother's holidays were more important than looking after her. When asked what that was like, the mother said 'abandoned', and 'lost' but 'hopeful' of finding her mother. The therapist empathised with the mother but then asked, 'That was your experience of being abandoned — I wonder how your daughter feels about foster care and her father killing himself?'. The mother made the connection 'She must feel lost, abandoned and like it was her fault'.

In the following sessions, the child played hide and seek. The therapist commented again, 'All children fear losing their parents'. Instead of rolling her eyes, the mother got on the floor and found her daughter. When she found her, she gave her a big hug and said, 'I will always be here to look after you'.

4. Reckless, Dangerous and Accident-prone Behaviour

Young children who experience trauma may engage in self-endangering behaviour, for example, running away from familiar caregivers, ignoring caregiver cues for comfort, head banging, biting themselves or expressing a desire to die. Some children seem too emotionally dysregulated to protect themselves or seem unaware of cues for danger. When this occurs in the presence of a caregiver, it may represent an attachment disorder. The child is not using caregivers as a secure base to explore, seek comfort and monitor cues for danger. Children with these attachment disorders are stuck in a double bind — they engage in self-endangering behaviour but know the parent will not respond with safe behaviour. It seems that children escalate in increasingly severe behaviour, seeming to ask the question, 'What do I have to do to get a protective and comforting response?'.

The goal of this phase is to help the child understand that an adult understands the meaning of their behaviour and that an adult will take charge of caring for them. Interventions may be targeted at helping parents become aware of recognising danger, educating caregivers about ways to protect their child, or in cases of more imminent danger, therapists engaging in protective behaviour (e.g., physically blocking/grabbing hands of children who are about to run into the carpark).

Example: In one dyad, the child would become increasingly distressed for no obvious reason, and rather than seek comfort or use his mother to regulate his emotions, he would run out of the room. His mother would then proceed to run after him. On one occasion, the child was about to run into the carpark, and the therapist quickly grabbed the child's hand to prevent him from running away.

In subsequent sessions, the therapist problem-solved with the mother ways to identify early warning signs that would indicate that he was about to get overwhelmed. The therapist also problem-solved ways to keep him in the room, including holding the door closed and making sure he was holding hands before they left the room.

5. Aggression to Parents

Child aggression is common in children who have experienced domestic violence, particularly towards mothers. There are several possible reasons for this, including blaming their mother for past events, observing physical aggression towards their mother, identifying with a perpetrator of domestic violence (e.g., father), copying or modelling excessive physical discipline (e.g., smacking), misperceiving other's behaviours as hostile, carer helplessness or difficulty putting in appropriate boundaries for aggression. Aggression towards a parent can also represent a fear of their attachment figure (i.e., fighting off fear-inducing attachment caregivers).

The primary goal of this phase is to help the child understand difficult feelings and develop alternative behaviours to physical aggression. Parents may have a range of reactions to their child's aggression, such as shame, humour or anger and may wish to retaliate. Clinicians can also have strong feelings, but therapists need to have the ability to contain negative reactions and convey calmness. However, to do nothing may imply that aggression is ok.

A minimalist approach is taken, preventing aggression if possible (by distraction or redirection). If a parent responds positively to the child's emotions, the clinician can highlight this. If this fails, the clinician may encourage the parent to respond to the child in a certain way. If unsuccessful, therapists may take action if the parent is unable or unwilling to, particularly if the therapist is at risk of being the target of aggression.

> **Example**: In one dyad, the parent and child had ongoing difficulties with emotional dysregulation. For example, when upset or frustrated about his inability to master a difficult task (e.g., build a tricky tower), he would throw things in the room towards his mother. The mother's reaction to this physical aggression was to let him hit her. The therapist watched and noticed this interaction and commented, 'You have some big feelings right now, and you are throwing things at your mum and hitting her', wondering if this would be enough for the mother to act. However, when the child picked up a chair to throw it at her, the therapist took action because he thought the mother might be seriously hurt — he stood up, held the chair so his mother could not be hurt and said 'this is a safe place where we do not hurt others'.
>
> The therapist was unsure how to proceed, as the mother was unable to prevent herself from being hit and may have been sending a message to her child that it was ok to hit others he loves. This lack of boundaries was also likely to be scary for a child.

The therapist completed several 'collateral sessions' which are sessions with the parent alone to better explore the mother's feelings and perception of these situations. The mother said she felt powerless and helpless. They discussed how her own mother would have reacted if she had done this as a child — the mother said her own mother would have done nothing. By the age of 5, she was required to look after herself, feed herself and look after her mother.

The therapist encouraged the mother to think about how she wished her mother would have acted. Her response was that she would have wished that her mother had taken charge and taken care of her instead of her taking care of her mother. With lots of support and practice, the therapist encouraged the mother to be bigger, stronger and take charge of these incidents. The therapist was amazed when in a subsequent session, the boy attempted to hit her again, and the mother said out of the blue, 'We do not hit others' and 'It is not ok for you to hit me'. The boy listened.

6. Aggression to Others

Children who experience aggression often demonstrate aggression towards peers, siblings or other family members. There are likely overlapping mechanisms between aggression directed to parents and aggression directed to others, but additional factors may include peer rejection and competition between siblings. Similar to when dealing with aggression directed at parents, the primary goal of this phase is to help children with their negative feelings, engage in alternative behaviours to physical aggression and develop appropriate relationships with siblings and peers. Therapists may notice and highlight the meaning of a child's behaviour and alternative ways of expressing anger, encourage a parent to respond in a particular way or take action and/or model alternative behaviours if the parent is unable or unwilling to do so (e.g., when the child is throwing blocks at the therapist).

Example: In one dyad, both the referred child and his 3-year-old sister were present due to childcare difficulties. Sibling aggression was a concern for the parent. The boy became increasingly frustrated when his sister would snatch or take toys out of his hand. He would grab his sister's face, push her face away and pinch his sister's cheeks. His mother would say 'stop', but he persisted with the behaviour. His sister would cry and snatch again.

The therapist commented to everyone, 'I can see there are some big feelings in the room', and then to the parent, 'I can see you noticed when he was angry; I wonder what you have noticed that helps him when he is upset or angry?'. His mother noted that taking some deep breaths and hugs helped him, so she then told him, 'come here...' and put him on her lap while she hugged him. 'I know you are angry because your sister is taking your toys. I will make sure she does not snatch the toys off you, but you cannot hurt her'. He appeared to listen to her instructions, got off her lap and proceeded to play nicely with the toys. When his sister went to take another toy, his mother stepped in and said, 'That is your brother's toy, you can play with this one'. The therapist commented, 'You could see big feelings were about to come out again, and you were able to help everyone get along'.

7. Parental Physical Punishment

Physical punishment by parents can include slapping, smacking/spanking, pulling hair, biting, hitting using an object or any other means to cause pain to their child. Although physical punishment is common, it is generally not recommended. This is particularly salient for children who have experienced physical violence and may be hypervigilant or reactive to physical threats. Discussions around physical punishment can invoke strong feelings in parents and therapists. The overall goal of this phase is to reduce parental physical punishment, help the parent develop alternative ways of managing strong feelings towards their children and use other discipline strategies with the aim of helping their children learn new behaviours. Therapists may provide education and guidance about physical discipline, discuss a parent's cultural and child-rearing beliefs about what is acceptable and unacceptable, or explore alternative parenting behaviours with the parent.

Example: In one dyad, the mother of a 4-year-old frequently used smacking as a primary means of discipline, and this also occurred in the therapy sessions. The boy was also starting to hit and bite other children at preschool. The therapist commented, 'I wonder how you feel about managing his behaviour?'. The mother responded, 'This is the way I've always done it, this is the way I was raised, and it turned out fine for me'.

In the collateral session, the therapist asked what it was like to live in a house where she was smacked for misbehaviour. The mother commented, 'I hated it, but at least I respected my parents'. The therapist commented 'Sometimes parents say they learned to respect their parents but were also scared of their parents. I wonder if that happened to you also?'. The mother took a second to think. 'I hated being smacked. I remember it didn't matter what I did; I would always get smacked with a wooden spoon or a belt. I was always scared of my father'. The therapist asked, 'Do you feel a similar thing is happening here'. The mother took a moment to consider. 'Actually, yes, sometimes I think he is scared of me, and I don't want him to feel that way'.

In the next session, the boy started to test the limits, banging the toys together. His mother started to get an angry tone in her voice, and he looked at her, scared. She sensed his fear, got down to his level and said, 'Please be gentle with the toys,' and then started to play with him.

8. Parental Negative Talk

Parental negative talk can include name-calling, teasing, laughing/mocking and threats towards their children. Therapists need to balance the needs of the parent with the needs of the child in crafting a therapeutic response. Ideally, this is a response that shows empathy for the parent's feelings of frustration or anger and a reflection of the child's feeling of being emotionally hurt or alone (e.g., 'There are big strong feelings in the room right now'). The goal of this phase is to help the parent express more appropriate ways of dealing with difficult feelings or behaviour in a way that is more positive and meaningful for the parent and child. Therapists may empathise with the parent's frustration, providing reflective guidance or information about normal child behaviour, helping the parent make sense of the child's behaviour or modelling alternative behaviours.

> **Example:** In one dyad, a mother would often call her 3-year-old son 'aggressive' and a 'little psycho'. He was starting to stamp on bugs and ants, which the mother took as a sign that he did not have empathy. The therapist did not know what to say about this, but after 5 minutes of observing them play, he asked: 'I wonder what we could do to help him learn empathy?'. This was not an easy question for the mother to answer but one that she had held onto. In the week between appointments, his mother had talked to his preschool about stopping him from killing bugs. She told him, 'When you kill the bugs, you are hurting them'. She then told him when he pulled his dog's tail, 'That hurts him when you do that,' and when he grazed his knee, she patched him up and said, 'It hurts when you graze yourself. It also hurts bugs when you squash them'. The therapist congratulated the mother for taking the initiative to teach him empathy. The therapist asked her how she knew how to do that. She said, 'I don't think he really understands when people or animals are hurt'.
>
> In the subsequent weeks, the mother continued to prevent him from killing bugs and saying 'that hurts' when he stomped on them. A few weeks later, he visited his aunty on her farm. When she suggested that she kill a chicken for dinner, the boy became distressed, crying and screaming, 'You can't hurt the chicken!'. Despite being an upsetting event for him, his mother secretly laughed and realised he was learning to understand how others were feeling through her intervention.

9. Relationship with Absent Parent

Following traumatic experiences, children often experience the loss of a parent. For example, in domestic violence, the mother may leave the father. In this situation, children may be torn between love and fear of their parent — a mother who was needed at that moment by the child but was unavailable and unable to protect themselves, as well as love towards the father who also engages in terrifying behaviour and causes pain. When a parent dies, children may express a mixture of sadness, anger towards the remaining parent, or feeling responsible for what occurred, among other common grief reactions (Lieberman, et al., 2003). Therapists are encouraged to help the child facilitate an ongoing relationship with the absent parent. This requires that the remaining parent respects the child's relationship with the absent parent and is able to separate this relationship from the couple's relationship; for example, parents may still fear the absent parent or become angry that their partner committed suicide and left them alone to look after their child.

The goal of this phase is to help the child to form a balanced view that incorporates both positive and negative feelings about the absent parent. Therapists may achieve this goal by encouraging the child and parent to speak about the absent parent, clarify misperceptions about events that occurred, and give permission for the child to have conflicting feelings. Given the relationship between domestic violence and co-occurring child abuse, therapists need to be mindful of the ongoing safety of the child when visiting the absent parent.

> **Example**: In one dyad, a 5-year-old boy was living with his grandmother due to parental substance use and domestic violence. He would continually play out the desire to be with his biological mum and dad. He would talk about how great they were and that he couldn't wait to get his licence and drive to their house. The therapist wondered how this affected his relationship with his grandmother, who was doing all the work.
>
> The therapist asked his grandmother one day, 'What is it like for you to see him express a desire to live with his parents?'. She said that she has a stepson that she helped raise. She could identify that no matter what she did, there was always a desire for him to live with his 'real mum'. This helped her to understand and tolerate the boy's idealisation of his parents. The therapist felt free to talk about all the things the boy wished he could do with his parents and also re-iterated the reality of why he couldn't live with them and that his grandmother was here to care for him.

10. Ghosts in the Nursery

Ghosts in the nursery refers to the parent's re-enactment of their repressed experiences of helplessness and fear. The parent re-enacts how they were parented in an effort at self-protection by becoming like their abusive parent. Instead of seeing child behaviours for what they are, parents may interpret the behaviour based on their own experiences of being raised.

Transference of relationship experiences into the child can occur in several ways. For example, a parent may unconsciously transfer an unwanted or unacceptable aspect of themselves into the child but then resents it in the child and may become critical of the child's behaviour. Or a parent may interpret the child's behaviour in distorted ways, adhering meaning to the behaviour that stems from the parent's own experience during their childhood and projecting it into the child. Parents may repress the emotional content of these frightening memories but express them towards their child.

Children raised with these sorts of parental distortions may internalise their sense of self as unworthy and undeserving of love. In CPP, parents may act like a young child, scared and terrified, but attempt to manage these feelings by modelling abusive behaviours from figures in the past. In domestic violence, for example, a mother may perceive her child's aggression as abusive, something that belongs to the adult abuser.

The goal of this phase is to identify how ghosts in the nursery are alive in the current parent–child interaction, those that lead to stressful parent behaviour or relationships. Therapists generally use this approach when previous and simpler interventions have not worked, such as reflective developmental guidance. These conversations may be best had in a collateral parent-only session.

> **Example:** In one dyad, the mother was noted to be overly focused on academic performance, and interaction between mother and child appeared more like a classroom setting. When the child was upset, his mother would engage him in learning instead of meeting his emotional needs (e.g., when he was crying, she would say, 'What colour is this block?'). The clinician commented on the mother finding education important. She was studying full time, working full time and raising three young children.
>
> Over several weeks, the boy had started to comment that his mum was always busy and added that she doesn't love him because 'she doesn't spend time with me'.
>
> In collateral sessions with the mother alone, we talked about the importance of academics. She talked about her mother emphasising academics at the expense of anything else. Her mother worked full time, her father worked full time, and she described her parents as 'professionally neglectful', prioritising their careers over her and her brother. She was also constantly compared to her smarter and more academically-minded brother. The clinician asked her about her experience of living in a house with such a strong focus on learning and achievement, and how that was for her as a child to focus on learning. She said, 'I hated it' and 'I always wished they spent time with me instead of me looking after myself'.
>
> The clinician used this piece of knowledge at challenging points in the current relationship — when the boy was upset or engaged in one activity and the mother engaged in a teaching task, the therapist would sometimes comment, 'All children need their parents just to be there for them'. As time went by, the mother started to become more aware of how she was repeating a pattern she had experienced with her own mother. A turning point

occurred in session 15. The mother and child arrived late to their appointment and still catching their breath from a trip to the beach for 'us time', something that had never happened before.

11. Angels in the Nursery

Angels in the nursery refers to parents' re-enactment of caregiving practices stemming from childhood experiences where the parent felt understood and accepted. The goal of identifying angel moments or memories is to enhance the parent's sense of self, optimism and hope in the future. Helping parents understand the value of angel moments in their own lives can help them recreate these positive experiences with their own children.

Example: In one dyad, a father was having difficulty knowing how to respond to his son when he was crying. He often said he did not know what to do and often attempted to distract him by interesting him in toys when he would get upset or cry.

When asked, the father said that when his mother and father would find him crying or upset, they would tell him to be quiet. Instead, he went to his aunt, who was a very important person in his life, and he often spent a lot of time with her after school. The clinician asked 'Can you remember a time when your aunt found you crying?'. The father replied, 'Yes. She gave me a hug and said, 'It's ok,' and that made me feel better. I'd never really had that before'. The clinician wondered if that would work with his son.

At first, the boy was not used to this new response from his father, but the clinician encouraged him to persist. After a few weeks, the boy started to accept hugs and contact from the father when he was upset. The father was also feeling more comfortable and able to identify and respond to his son's feelings. Several months into treatment, his son was starting to trust his father enough to tell him about things that had upset him during the day. These are examples of creating 'angel moments' for this boy with his father that the boy can recall throughout his life and serve as a positive example through which he can interact with his children if he were to become a father himself.

12. Separation and Loss Reminders

Losing an important person is one of the most difficult experiences a person can endure, particularly early on in life. For children exposed to traumatic events and loss, everyday events may remind them of loss. Young children also tend to believe that they are responsible for events in the world and may take the blame for the loss. The goal of this phase is to help children and parents understand that separations can be followed by reunions and that separations and loss do not always mean loss of love. Therapists can achieve this by giving warnings about sessions ending, games that encourage separation and reunion (e.g., hide and seek), discussion of separations and maintenance of the relationship, and/or goodbye rituals.

> **Example:** A 5-year-old girl and her mother had both experienced significant losses in their lives, including the girl's grandmother dying, the child being physically abused by her father and her mother being assaulted by her grandfather before he was taken away by police. She was also separated from her mother for several weeks while in temporary foster care until her mother was able to find a stable home environment.
>
> The girl would often play hide-and-seek with the clinician and her mother and would often run away and hide when discussing difficult topics, which stopped during treatment. Coming towards the end of treatment, the clinician introduced the idea of not coming here anymore as things were getting better. This resulted in increased anxiety for the girl and discussion of a new theme in therapy, their dog dying. The first time she talked about her dog, she stared angrily at her mother and said, 'It's your fault'.
>
> During the weeks that followed, the clinician discussed whether saying goodbye reminded her of the other losses in her life, losses that she may blame herself or others for. In these situations, the goodbye was painful, unexpected and unplanned. The clinician worked over a long period of time to help prepare her and her mother for this new and planned 'good goodbye' or 'better goodbye' as well as a celebration of gains and acknowledgement of disappointment. The clinician read the book, 'The Invisible String,' to discuss that the loss of someone does not always mean the loss of feelings. We marked it on the calendar for when they would eventually stop coming, practised saying goodbye, played some games of hide-and-seek as well as reaffirmed her mother's commitment to do whatever she could to be there for her despite past separations.

Phase Three: Recapitulation and Termination/Closing Phase

The final third phase involves a focus on the end of the intervention and saying goodbye. It focuses less on problems and more on the positives and what has been achieved. This phase aims at preparing both parent/carer and child for the upcoming termination of treatment. Many people who have experienced trauma have had very unexpected and sudden experiences of loss, may have had multiple losses in their lifetime, and in some situations, were unable to say goodbye. This can create negative feelings or anxiety, especially for dyads where saying goodbye can cause parents and children to re-experience these negative feelings. This is a chance to create a more positive experience of saying goodbye.

Ideally, termination begins a couple of months before the end of treatment. The parent and therapist meet alone to discuss treatment ending, and the therapist completes an evaluation, which may include re-administering psychometric measures used in the assessment phase. Developmental guidance or psychoeducation is also provided to the parent about how the meaning of trauma may change as the child develops and that symptoms may return with new trauma or reminders.

Children are given notice about treatment ending approximately six sessions before the end of treatment so that they have enough time to prepare themselves and process reactions to separation. It is recommended that this is done in a concrete way to aid in understanding (e.g., marking days off on a calendar). Occasionally, children or parents may start to develop symptoms again in an unconscious way to show treatment is still needed or to prevent saying goodbye. However, with enough preparation, this is usually short-lived. In the last session, it is recommended to do something unique that is symbolic of the feelings of saying goodbye. This may be a celebration, or it may be something that captures the complex mix of positive and negative feelings when saying goodbye.

The Evidence Base of CPP

CPP has been demonstrated to be effective in five randomised trials. Research samples have been completed with infants, toddlers and preschoolers with a range of experiences, including domestic violence, physical abuse, emotional abuse, sexual abuse, neglect and parental mental health difficulties. CPP also has evidence of being an effective approach when working with families from culturally and socioeconomically diverse backgrounds (Lieberman et al., 1991).

Positive gains have been demonstrated in general behavioural problems, trauma symptoms and diagnostic status (Lieberman et al., 2005), with some gains demonstrated 6 months post-treatment (Lieberman et al., 2006). Toth et al. (2002) also found preschoolers had a greater reduction in negative representations of themselves and their mothers.

Chicchetti et al. (2006) found changes in attachment classification, with 0% of infants having a secure attachment pre-treatment compared to 60.7% of infants post-treatment. Cicchetti et al. (1999) found that 16.7% of children had a secure attachment pre-intervention compared to 67% post-intervention. Some improvements have also been found in maternal functioning, including their own PTSD symptoms (Ghosh Ippen et al., 2011). The results of these studies indicate that CPP is considered to be supported by research evidence based on the California Evidence-based Clearinghouse for child welfare, with high relevance to child welfare.

CPP has only started to be investigated in an Australian context, with the first training group completed in 2016. To our knowledge, CPP has not been explored as a suitable model for families identifying as Aboriginal and/or Torres Strait

Islander (e.g., see Hooker et al., 2022). We believe that CPP could potentially be a powerful and tailored intervention for families who have experienced significant inter-generational trauma, present with high levels of reported family violence, stress and mental health issues, and are over-represented in statutory child protection systems. CPP not only helps caregiver and child to process traumatic life experiences but also addresses the need for parenting intervention within the realm of a sensitive and trusting therapeutic relationship, with gentle guidance in the development of appropriate parenting skills.

Conclusion

CPP is an intensive, challenging, but rewarding treatment that focuses on the relationship between a parent and child as a way to heal from traumatic experiences. It involves the parent and child equally where possible, and there are multiple 'ports of entry' or avenues that can be taken through which to intervene. The primary mechanism of change is within the attachment relationship between parent and child. It is a developmentally sensitive, trauma-informed and multi-theoretical approach. It is a highly valuable treatment. However, it has an intensive training requirement which requires three residential schools over 18 months, and a hundred hours of reflective supervision, with a cost of at least $5,000 per clinician. Ongoing reflective supervision or consultation is necessary but can be difficult to obtain, and CPP recommends the development of learning collaboratives rather than sole providers. It is hoped that agencies and governmental departments will recognise the long-term benefits of CPP and be able to advocate that the healing from trauma takes a considerable investment of time, energy and resources, but the benefits for change in the parent, child and the relationship outweigh the costs. Child–parent psychotherapy can have a positive intergenerational impact by breaking the cycle of maladaptive and, at times, harmful patterns rooted in parents' past, such that both the parent and the child can move forward in healthy ways, creating transmission of protective, adaptive beliefs and behaviours in child–parent relationships henceforth.

Reader's Exercises

Read again through the case example of Emily on pages 200–202.

- What are the possible meanings of Emily hitting babies on the head?

- What do you think Emily's play might indicate? How responsible do you think Emily feels about what occurred? How powerless might Emily's mother feel? Imagine Emily's mother described this doctor play as 'controlling'. How might Emily's 'controlling behaviour' be re-interpreted?

References

Achenbach, T. M., & Rescorla, L. A. (2000). *Manual for the ASEBA Preschool Age Forms and Profiles.* University of Vermont, Research Center for Children, Youth and Families.

Briere, J. (2005). *Trauma Symptom Checklist for Young Children (TSCYC): Professional Manual.* Psychological Assessment Inc.

Cicchetti, D., Rogosch, F. A., & Toth, S. L. (2006). Fostering secure attachment in infants in maltreating families through preventive interventions. *Development and Psychopathology, 18,* 623–650. https://doi.org/10.1017/S0954579406060329

Cicchetti D., Toth S. L., & Rogosch, F.A. (1999). The efficacy of toddler–parent psychotherapy to increase attachment security in offspring of depressed mothers. *Attachment and Human Development 1,* 34–66. https://doi.org/10.1080/14616739900134021

Crowell, J., & Feldman, S. (1988). Mothers' internal models of relationships and children's behavioural and developmental status: A study of mother–child interaction. *Child Development, 59,* 1273–1285. https://doi.org/10.2307/1130490

Foa, E. B., McLean, C. P., Zang, Y., Zong, J., Rauch, S., Porter, K., Knowles, K., Powers, M.B., & Kauffman, B.Y. (2016). Psychometric properties of the Posttraumatic Stress Disorder Symptoms Scale Interview for DSM-5 (PSSI-5). *Psychological Assessment, 28,* 1159–1165. https://doi.org/10.1037/pas0000259

Fraiberg, S. (1980). *Clinical studies in infant mental health: The first year of life.* Basic Books.

Gosh Ippen, C., Ford, J., Acker, M., Bosquet, K., Ellis, C., Schiffman, J., Ribbe, D., Cone, P., Lukovitz, M., & Edwards, J. (2002). *Traumatic Events Screening Inventory — Parent Report Revised (TESI-PRR).* National Center for PTSD and Dartmouth Child Psychiatry Research Group.

Ghosh Ippen, C., Harris W. W., Van Horn, P., & Lieberman, A. F. (2011). Traumatic and stressful events in early childhood: Can treatment help those at highest risk? *Child Abuse and Neglect, 35,* 504–513. https://doi.org/10.1016/j.chiabu.2011.03.009

Larrieu, J. A., Middleton, M. A., Kelley, A. C., & Zeanah, C. H. (2018). Assessing the relational context of infants and young children. In C. H. Zeanah (Ed.), *Handbook of Infant Mental Health, 4th Edition,* (pp. 279–295). Guilford Press.

Lieberman, A. F. (1992). Infant–parent psychotherapy with toddlers. *Development and Psychopathology, 4,* 559–575. https://doi.org/10.1017/S0954579400004879

Lieberman, A. F., Compton, N. C., Van Horn, P., & Ghosh Ippen, C. (2003). *Losing a parent to death in the early years: Guidelines for the treatment of traumatic bereavement in infancy and early childhood*. Zero to Three.

Lieberman, A. F., Ghosh Ippen, C., & Van Horn, P. (2015). *Don't hit my mommy! A manual for Child–Parent Psychotherapy with young children exposed to violence and other trauma, Second Edition*. Zero to Three.

Lieberman, A. F., & Van Horn, P. (2005). *Don't hit my mommy! A manual for Child–Parent Psychotherapy with young witnesses of family violence*. Zero to Three.

Lieberman, A. F., & Van Horn, P. (2008). *Psychotherapy with infants and young children: Repairing the effects of stress and trauma on early attachment*. Guilford Press.

Lieberman, A. F., Van Horn, P. J., & Ghosh Ippen, C. (2005). Toward evidence-based treatment: Child–parent psychotherapy with preschoolers exposed to marital violence. *Journal of the American Academy of Child and Adolescent Psychiatry, 44*, 1241–1248. https://doi.org/10.1097/01.chi.0000181047.59702.58

Lieberman, A. F., Ghosh Ippen, C. & Van Horn, P. J. (2006). Child–parent psychotherapy: Six-month follow-up of a randomised control trial. *Journal of the American Academy of Child and Adolescent Psychiatry, 45*, 913–918. https://doi.org/10.1097/01.chi.0000222784.03735.92

Lieberman, A. F., Weston, D. R., & Pawl, J. H. (1991). Preventive intervention and outcome with anxiously attached dyads. *Child Development, 62*, 199–209. https://doi.org/10.2307/1130715

Hooker, L., Toone, E., Wendt, S., Humphreys, C., & Taft, A. (2022). *RECOVER – Reconnecting mothers and children after family violence: The child–parent psychotherapy pilot*. ANROWS.

Scheeringa, M. S., & Haslett, N. (2010). The reliability and criterion validity of the Diagnostic Infant and Preschool Assessment: A new diagnostic instrument for young children. *Child Psychiatry and Human Development, 41*, 299–312. https://doi.10.1007/s10578-009-0169-2

Squires, J., & Bricker, D. (2009). *Ages & Stages Questionnaires®, Third Edition (ASQ®-3): A Parent-Completed Child Monitoring System*. Paul H. Brookes Publishing Co., Inc.

Toth, S. L., Maughan, A., Manly, J. T., Spagnola, M., & Cicchetti, D. (2002). The relative efficacy of two interventions in altering maltreated preschool children's representational models: Implications for attachment theory. *Developmental Psychopathology, 14*, 877–908. https://doi.org/10.1017/S095457940200411X

Wolfe, J., & Kimerling, R. (1997). Gender issues in the assessment of posttraumatic stress disorder. In J. P. Wilson, & T. M. Keane (Eds.), *Assessing psychological trauma and PTSD* (pp. 192–238). The Guilford Press.

Chapter 9

Integrated Family Intervention for Child Conduct Problems (IFI)

Tanya Hanstock

Integrated Family Intervenion for Child Conduct Problems (IFI) is a parenting program based on behaviour, attachment and family structure theory that is suitable for parents of young children within the age range of 2–8 years. IFI was developed by Mark Dadds and David Hawes (Dadds & Hawes, 2006), Australian clinical psychologists and researchers. IFI was designed as a tertiary treatment for children displaying severe conduct problems, including aggression, non-compliance, rule-breaking, tantrums and fighting with siblings (Dadds & Hawes, 2006). It has since been applied to families who often do not benefit from mainstream parenting programs, families where the child is presenting with severe conduct problems with comorbid callous-unemotional traits (CU), which includes limited empathy, lack of guilt and shallow affect (Hawes et al., 2014). The main focus of IFI is on altering parents' behaviour that maintains aggression and conduct issues in children through having a high number of coercive parent–child interactions (Dadds & Hawes, 2006; Patterson, 1982). IFI helps to encourage parents to be more aware of how their own behaviour impacts their child's behaviour (particularly how they may be unintentionally rewarding undesirable behaviour and ignoring desirable behaviour) and promotes warmth and boundary setting to improve the parent–child relationship (Dawes & Dadds, 2006). IFI also encourages parents to engage in self-care and to seek help from external resources. The focus on the younger age range of children for this program was due to the fact that time-out, when applied in a calm and non-punitive way, is considered to be an essential component for effective treatment of conduct problems in young children, however is less applicable and appropriate once the child becomes old enough to attend primary school (Dadds & Hawes, 2006). IFI is a relatively brief form of treatment delivered in a structured format and includes an assessment and up to nine treatment sessions. The program involves face-to-face sessions with the child–parent dyad as well as separate sessions with the main caregiver/s. Although initially designed as a family intervention for child conduct problems, IFI can also be offered in a group format and as a universal preventative intervention (Dadds & Hawes, 2006). IFI has also been adapted and delivered as an online program called ParentWorks (Piotrowska et al., 2020) and a therapist-assisted online program called AccessEI (Dadds et al., 2019). IFI is considered an evidence-based family-based treatment (Hawes & Dadds, 2005).

The History and Theoretical Base of IFI

History

IFI was originally developed by Mark Dadds and David Hawes at the University of New South Wales. IFI has been researched most extensively in the tertiary treatment setting at the Sydney Child Behaviour Research Clinic at The University of Sydney, which Professor Mark Dadds and David Hawes co-founded. This clinic also provides training to clinical psychology students. As well as being adapted in a number of different formats, parts of IFI were demonstrated on the television show 'Kids on Speed' with families of children with Attention Deficit Hyperactivity Disorder (ADHD) produced in Australia by the Australian Broadcast Corporation (ABC) in 2014 as a three-part documentary. IFI was originally developed for parents of children with severe conduct problems. The original IFI manual was published in 2006, and the principles of IFI have been adapted to various parenting programs. ParentWorks was developed in 2016 as a universal, online, father-inclusive parenting program that is suited to a broader community sample of parents who have concerns about parenting and their child's behaviour. ParentWorks was offered to Australian families as a freely available parenting program in 2016 (Piotrowska et al., 2020). AccessEI is a therapist-assisted adaptation of IFI and ParentWorks and was researched in 2019. AccessEI was found to be as effective as a face-to-face parenting intervention for Oppositional Defiant Disorder (ODD) or Conduct Disorder (CD) (Dadds et al., 2019). This chapter focuses on the version of IFI published in the manual by Dadds and Hawes (2006).

Theoretical Basis

IFI can be classified as a Behavioural Family Intervention (BFI). BFI is an 'umbrella term' referring to behaviour programs for families that have been developed from social learning theory and behaviour theory, specifically operant conditioning (Dadds & Hawes, 2006). It involves primarily modifying parent behaviours that are maintaining their child's aggressive and antisocial behaviour through frequent coercive parent–child interactions (Patterson, 1982). BFI has become a commonly used therapeutic approach for children and their families with ODD and CD. In addition, IFI is also based on Attachment Theory, Family Systems Theory, in particular Structural Family Therapy, and Cognitive Attribution Theory.

Behavioural Theory

There are three models of learning and behavioural change used within the theoretical base of IFI. They are:

Operant Conditioning

Operant Conditioning is a method of learning that is attributed to the work of B.F. Skinner (1957), an American Psychologist. Operant Conditioning's main premise is that the consequence of a behavioural response determines the probability of whether the behaviour will be repeated or not. A behaviour that is positively reinforced will most likely be repeated. Behaviour that is punished or ignored will be less likely to reoccur. Operant conditioning includes positive reinforcement where a reward (natural, tangible, social or token) is given when desirable behaviour is displayed (e.g., giving positive verbal praise to a child for complying with instructions) (Dadds & Hawes, 2006). Negative reinforcement is when a behaviour is strengthened or encouraged by the removal or stopping of an aversive stimulus (e.g., removing crayons to prevent a child from drawing on the wall). Positive punishment is when a negative consequence is given to unwanted behaviour (e.g., asking a child to apologise to another child they have hurt). Negative punishment is when something desirable is taken away to reduce the likelihood of that behaviour reoccurring (e.g., leaving an outing the child enjoys when they misbehave) (Dadds & Hawes, 2006).

Social Learning Theory

This approach explains how learning extends from a purely behavioural explanation to include cognitive theories of learning to provide a comprehensive model accounting for a range of learning experiences. Social Learning Theory was initially outlined by Bandura and Walters (1963), and they emphasised the role of imitation in learning. Bandura (1986) progressed to a more cognitive view of Social Learning Theory and explained how learning occurs firstly by a cognitive process that takes place within a social context. Secondly, learning can occur by observing a behaviour as well as observing the consequence of the behaviour (called vicarious reinforcement). Thirdly, learning involves observation, extraction of information from observations, and making decisions about the performance of the behaviour (modelling). Fourthly, reinforcement plays an important role in learning but is not the only reason to explain learning. Finally, the person learning is not a passive recipient of information. Cognition, the environment and behaviour all influence each other (reciprocal determinism) (Bandura, 1986).

The Coercion Model

In IFI, Dadds and Hawes (2006) focus on the role of the Coercion Model (Patterson, 1982) in explaining how children develop antisocial behaviours. Coercion theory was developed by Gerald Patterson, a child psychologist, and his colleagues at the Oregon Social Learning Center (OSLC, 1982). Coercion theory arose from extensive behaviour research on the interactions of families. This theory explains how ineffectual parental responses to problem behaviour escalate aversive and aggressive behaviours in children in the short term. It also describes how frequent repetitions of these coercive cycles result in a progressive worsening of aggressive behaviours in both type and intensity, corresponding with increasingly less parental control over the aggression (Dadds & Hawes, 2006).

In the coercion model, negative reinforcement explains how the coercive behaviour of the parent or the child may be reinforced when it results in the removal of an aversive event being applied by the other (Dadds & Hawes, 2006). For example, if a child shows a negative behaviour (e.g., whining) in response to an adverse stimulus (parental command), and the parent withdraws the command in response, the child's whining may be negatively reinforced (Dadds & Hawes, 2006). If the parent escalates their command to a threat (e.g., 'I will throw your toys in the bin') and the child withdraws their negative behaviour (whining) and complies, the parent will be negatively reinforced for providing a verbal threat (Dadds & Hawes, 2006). Eventually, the parent learns that the child will eventually stop negative behaviours and comply if the parent becomes more negative or threatening, which can escalate to more aggressive behaviours such as smacking. Meanwhile, the parent is also modelling a coercive interaction style which the child may also adopt. The child can also escalate their own behaviours, such as displaying physical aggression, running away or breaking items, which may also be negatively reinforced through the coercive interaction process (Dadds & Hawes, 2006).

Families with children with conduct problems initiate and reciprocate aggressive behaviour and persist in aversive behaviour such as arguing, yelling and smacking more than families who do not have children experiencing conduct issues (Dadds & Hawes, 2006). Patterson (1982) explains that via operant conditioning, parents in these families reinforce conduct problems in two ways. Firstly they role model more antisocial and aggressive behaviours. Secondly, they unintentionally reinforce difficult and unwanted behaviour by paying more attention to the child's negative behaviours and ignoring the child's positive, prosocial and compliant behaviours (Dadds & Hawes, 2006).

Attachment Theory

Attachment Theory states that young children have an innate drive to attach to their significant, main or important caregiver (Ainsworth et al., 1978; Bowlby, 1969). When the caregiver reciprocates with predictable nurturance, children develop a secure and positive attachment. Attachment theory differentiates between four different attachment styles: Secure, insecure-anxious, insecure-avoidant and disorganised. Children with a secure attachment feel more confident to explore their environment as they feel secure that their attachment figure is going to consistently respond helpfully to them when needed. Insecure attachment develops based on a repeated experience in which the caregiver lacks sensitivity, attunement and predictability to the young child's needs. Children with an anxious attachment style tend to be clingy to the caregiver or demand attention. Whereas avoidant children tend to withdraw from an unpredictable or frightening caregiver and display an over-reliance on themselves when dealing with frightening or uncertain situations. Children with disorganised attachment display a combination of insecure and avoidant behaviour. A secure attachment is associated with more positive outcomes for children. Please refer to Chapter 4 on the Circle of Security program for a more detailed outline of attachment theory.

Attachment threat causes proximity seeking in children. However, some children have learned that negative behaviour, such as being clingy, whining, crying and screaming are the most useful ways to get the caregiver's attention, as positive behaviours are often ignored (Dadds & Hawes, 2006). To resolve the misdirected attempt for a positive connection with the parent, Dadds and Hawes (2006) recommend attachment-rich rewards for behaviours the parent wants to increase (differential attention, one-to-one time with parent/s etc.) and 'attachment neutral' discipline techniques for behaviours the parent wants to reduce (ignoring and neutral emotions). These new strategies can be challenging for parents, requiring role play and practice in sessions to replace their previous way of responding to their child.

Family Structure Theory

Family structure is also an important part of IFI as problematic family structures, such as a poorly defined family hierarchy and parents in conflict, are two risk factors for conduct problems to develop and can lead to inappropriate and/or inconsistent reinforcement of child problem behaviour. Structural family systems therapy derives from the work of Minuchin (1974), also discussed in Chapter 14. Healthy family structures are one where there are clearly defined, yet not too rigid subsystems of parents, children and extended family members, with boundaries and defined roles that assist the family to adequately function but also ensure closeness and connection between all family members (Dadds & Hawes, 2006). In such a system, the parents work as an executive system or 'parenting team' in effective problem-solving and also have a positive relationship independent of their parenting role. Targeting the teamwork aspect of the parent role helps to improve conduct issues in children (Dadds et al., 1987). However, in children with ODD and CD, the typical family structure can contain poor boundaries as well as unclear rules and roles. Typically, parents act less as the executive system in the family compared to families with children without conduct issues (Dadds & Hawes, 2006). For example, this may include instances where the 'child is in charge' more so than the parents and have a lot more say regarding daily activities and routines (such as bed and screen times). Alternatively, this may include parents who are not aligned in their parenting views or work together as a team, for example, where a maternal grandmother and the mother are more aligned and have more input into daily household routines and child behaviour management compared to the father (Dadds & Hawes, 2006).

Cognitive Attributional Theory

Attribution theory describes how people try to understand why others behave the way they do by attributing causes to their behaviour. Attribution theory evolved from the work of Fritz Heider in the early 20th Century, looking at the locus of causality (such as internal or external locus of control) (Ryan & Connell, 1989). It was also influenced by Harold Kelley's interdependence theory, which looked at how interacting people can influence one another's experience (Van Lange & Balliet, 2014). Finally, Bernard Weiner (1992) proposed that people have initial affective responses to the potential consequences of the internal and external motives of the person, which therefore shapes their own future behaviour.

In IFI, Cognitive Attributional Theory is used to explain how parents of children with conduct issues develop problematic attributions about the meaning of their child's behaviours. Parents can misinterpret the child's problematic behaviour as being purposeful and deliberately directed towards them (such as thinking the child is doing the behaviour to directly upset the parent), or that the child can behave in a way that they are not developmentally capable of (such as expecting a child to not have tantrums when they are still preschool age). Unhelpful attributional styles include the parent feeling the child's behaviour is a sign that they have a mental health issue (such as a diagnosis they have not been assessed for or been given), is inherited from a disliked family member (such as an abusive separated parent) or possibly as a punishment that the parent deserves (such as if the parent was depressed when the child was younger or they were ambivalent in keeping the pregnancy and/or child in their early years) (Dadds & Hawes, 2006). Parents can be shocked, horrified and ashamed by their own thoughts of rejection and dislike of their child at times (Dadds & Hawes, 2006). Some parents describe 'loving' their child but sometimes not 'liking' their child during stressful times. They may have thoughts about hurting them or thoughts that they could never have imagined having before becoming a parent (Dadds & Hawes, 2006). They may have never told others about such thoughts and continue to be distressed by them.

Parents may also hold incompatible thoughts about parenting strategies taught in evidence-based parenting programs and instead be more influenced by how they were parented, by personal beliefs, what they have read online about parenting, or by what they have been told from relatives and friends (Dadds & Hawes, 2006). This may include beliefs such as yelling and smacking is necessary for a child to learn how to behave. The goal of treatment in IFI is not to change attributions but to identify them and allow the parent/s to talk about them. Sometimes the parent has not reflected on where their beliefs about parenting have come from. However, any unrealistic expectations of a child's development or unsafe parenting practices are discussed with parents (Dadds & Hawes, 2006).

The Assessment and Treatment Process of IFI

Two assessment sessions and 7 treatment sessions form part of the IFI program. Sessions 3–6 are standard sessions offered to all families, whereas sessions 7 and 8 (parent care modules) are specific to the parent's needs. Table 1 shows a summary of the assessment and treatment sessions from the Dadds and Hawes (2006) IFI manual. However, the complete details of how to implement the IFI assessment process and treatment program can only be obtained by accessing the manual.

Table 1. Session Summary of IFI

Session Number	Session Content
1	Parent Interview
2	Assessment with Parent and Child
3	Core Strategies Taught: How to respond to good behaviour and misbehaviour.
4	Continue-Review-Fine-tune Strategies
5	Contextual Issues: Managing sibling conflict, high-risk situations
6	Midpoint Review of Strategies
7	Parent Care Module
8	Parent Care Module
9	Review and Relapse Planning

Source: (Dadds & Hawes, 2006)

Session 1: Parent Assessment

The main purpose of the first parent assessment session is to explore each parent's explanation of their child's problem behaviour. The therapist's goal is to integrate both parents' conceptualisation of the problem into a shared understanding of it. In IFI it is recommended that the first session is for the parents only so they can openly discuss their concerns about their parenting relationship and their child and also that plans for treatment are established by the adults in the team (the clinician and the parents) (Dadds & Hawes, 2006).

It is important that in the first session the therapist establishes good rapport and a trusting relationship with both parents (when there are two parents). The manual recommends the clinician pays close attention to each parent, helping make them both feel heard and respected when integrating each of their views into the case conceptualisation (Dadds & Hawes, 2006).

The parents are encouraged to work as a team. In these assessment sessions, clinicians need to be aware of any gender bias they have around parenting and how this can impact the attention they give each parent during the assessment session (Dadds & Hawes, 2006). Equal attention and focus on both parents helps to show that they are equally important in solving the problem. The formation of a trusting therapeutic relationship is stressed in this model. This is facilitated by empathy displayed by the therapist, non-judgemental exploration of parental concerns, warmth, paraphrasing involving positive reframes, which emphasises the positive intention in the parent's behaviour and neutrality with each parent (hence not taking sides) (Dadds & Hawes, 2006)

Information gathered in this session includes details about the child, parents, family structure, family members and childcare arrangements. In terms of presenting problems, the parents are asked about their main concerns and understanding of the child's problems (Dadds & Hawes, 2006). The therapist tries to gain an understanding of issues around the onset and history of the problem, contextual factors, duration and specific presentations. Further information is sought about the child's health and developmental history, including information about pregnancy, infancy, toddlerhood and the preschool years (Dadds & Hawes, 2006). The clinician tries to gain an understanding of the child's general functioning, including their social and school functioning. The therapist further collects information about the child's treatment history, family relationships and psychosocial details such as parent health and wellbeing, parent social support and the childcare contributions from each parent. The parents' feelings and thoughts about the child are also enquired about. Additional information sought includes information about the parent's own childhood, the parent's relationship, the child's relationship with siblings and significant others, financial and environmental stressors and family history of mental illness and alcohol and substance use. Any further assessment that will occur is explained to the parents (Dadds & Hawes, 2006).

Sensitive information that also needs to be explored includes information about any experiences of domestic violence, abuse of the child, how family members feel about each other, parental attributions about their child and their behaviour, parental drug and alcohol use and the role of the extended family members (Dadds & Hawes, 2006). Parents are asked sensitive questions about things they may not have voiced to anyone previously, such as 'What are you most worried about for your child?', 'What is the most upsetting thought you have had about your child?' and 'What is the hardest day you have ever had with your child, and what did you think about them during this?'. All of these issues are raised sensitively and are incorporated into the case conceptualisation (Dadds & Hawes, 2006). The parents are informed that they will receive assessment feedback and discussion of treatment options in the next session (Dadds & Hawes, 2006).

Session 2: Parents and Child Dyad Assessment
Assessment of the Child

The aim of session two is to observe and assess the child and the parent–child interaction. Assessment of the child involves direct observation of the child and an interview (if they are old enough) as well as an assessment of their cognitive and emotional functioning (Dadds, 2006). The child assessment includes observations about their general presentation, health and wellbeing, assessing their cognitive and emotional state and when developmentally appropriate to ask the child their views of the problem, social adjustment and additional problems that their parents may not be aware of (Dadds & Hawes, 2006). Commonly used checklists and measures for children and their behaviour are administered, and information is gained from other clinicians and services who have been involved with the child's care (Dadds & Hawes, 2006).

It is helpful if the assessment of the parent–child interaction is directly observed and recorded, and if accessible, this can occur behind a one-way mirror. In clinical settings, oppositional behaviour can occur when a parent tries to engage their child in a structured teaching task or when compliance is required, such as the parent telling the child that it is time to pack up the toys (Dadds & Hawes, 2006). To assist with this assessment, the manual suggests the following semi-structured format to assess the parent–child interaction: free play between the parent and child, a drawing task (asking the parent to lead the child in a writing or drawing task) and a separation from the parent (Dadds & Hawes, 2006). The clinician can make qualitative observations of both the parent and child's behaviours or also use the more formal coding procedures such as Waugh and

Sanders's (1993) Family Observation Schedule. Usually, any non-compliance of the child or coercive parent–child interaction will become evident in this section of the assessment. This forms the basis for a functional assessment to understand how the parent and child may unintentionally negatively reinforce each other's negative behaviour (Dadds & Hawes, 2006).

At the end of the assessment session, the therapist and parent/s will also agree on specific treatment goals which are clearly defined in behavioural terms. One goal may be that the child goes to bed at a certain time without complaining. This goal setting involves sharing the understanding of the assessment data with the parents and explaining what it means, the parent's perception of the child and the main presenting issues as identified by the parents (Dadds & Hawes, 2006). Language sensitivity is required, and the clinician is encouraged to use appropriate similar language used by the parents to summarise the assessment. At the end of the session, the therapist thanks the parents for expressing their concerns and doubts (Dadds & Hawes, 2006).

Session 3: Strategies

In the third session, the therapist starts by asking the parent for a review of how their week has been and asks them to also describe any major events or challenges that have occurred with their child and their parenting. The third session has two main goals. Firstly, to help the parents understand the cause of their child's problem behaviours the negative reinforcement trap of conduct is explained to the parents. Secondly, to introduce attachment-rich positive reinforcement strategies and attachment-neutral discipline strategies (Dadds & Hawes, 2006).

Psychoeducation introduces the different influences on problem behaviour in young children by outlining the different contributing factors such as genetics and biology (such as activity and impulsivity levels), parenting behaviour and characteristics of the parent–child interaction (such as accidentally rewarding misbehaviour and ignoring desirable behaviours), conflicts and struggles between parent and child, and stressors that affect the family life or the parent's coping ability, such as work stress, health issues, conflicts with the extended family or financial stress (Dadds & Hawes, 2006). Parents are taught to understand the importance that parental attention plays in perpetuating oppositional behaviour (Dadds & Hawes, 2006).

Positive reinforcement is explained so parents understand that behaviour that is given attention (positive or negative) will either continue or even increase, whereas behaviour that does not receive attention will gradually decrease. The clinician explains that parents often ignore children when they are behaving well as it gives the parent a chance to rest and relax or to attend to other parenting duties. Parental attention is often triggered when the child misbehaves. As a result, instead of giving attention when the child's behaviour is desirable, attention is mostly given to negative behaviour, reinforcing it with negative attention (Dadds & Hawes, 2006).

Stressful interactions between parent and child are also explained within an attachment framework. When parents accidentally reinforce problematic behaviours in their child, the interaction also establishes physical and emotional contact and closeness between the parent–child dyad, though of a negative quality. In highly stressed families, these contact moments may be the only opportunity a child has to direct their parents' attention to themselves (Dadds & Hawes, 2006).

Following the psychoeducation phase of this session, the parents are asked to identify four specific behaviours that they want to see their child engage in more. Examples are given when parents need help generating ideas, such as; playing well with others, playing independently, speaking nicely to others and accepting when told 'no' (Dadds & Hawes, 2006). Planned ignoring as a way to manage oppositional behaviour is explained to parents.

Throughout the week, parents are encouraged to try and 'catch' the child displaying desirable behaviour and to show excitement to the child about this (Dadds & Hawes, 2006). Parents are helped to come up with rewards for these behaviours, including (1) descriptive praise, (2) tangible rewards, (3) time spent with the child (attachment-based reward) and (4) physical affection (attachment-based reward) (Dadds & Hawes, 2006). IFI stresses the importance of non-tangible, attachment-rich rewards and encourages the parents to replace tangible rewards such as stickers, money, toys, and lollies with attachment-rich reinforcers (such as special time with the parent, going to the park together, observing a child's play). Parents are to use a variety of these strategies (Dadds & Hawes, 2006). Planned ignoring is also introduced to parents when a child displays negative behaviours. 'Attention pop-ups' are also introduced, which involves the parent seeking out the child when they are playing nicely and providing descriptive praise to them (such as 'I love seeing you play nicely with your toys'). If the child wants the parent to stay, the parent responds by saying, 'I have to go and do something, but please keep playing well', then leaves and comes back ('pops back') and praises them again before the child's attention span runs out (Dadds & Hawes, 2006).

The second group of child-management strategies are the attachment-neutral responses to misbehaviours. To minimise attention to misbehaviour, parents are asked to use boring, predictable and attachment-neutral approaches. This parenting strategy is role-played in the session, and the parents often realise how difficult it can be to maintain attachment neutrality when responding to misbehaviour (Dadds & Hawes, 2006). The parents are asked to lower the volume of their voices and speak in a serious tone. Parents are encouraged to use a voice that is boring, calm and neutral (Dadds & Hawes, 2006).

Four steps for responding to misbehaviour are also taught, which is referred to as the 'behaviour-correction routine'. The first is to get the child's attention (such as touching the child's arms and establishing eye contact with them). The second step is to use a clarifying statement (which is naming the misbehaviour and saying what the preferred alternative behaviour is). The next step is to use a firm instruction (such as 'Pick up the toys in the dining room'), and the fourth step is to use time-out if the child does not comply with the instruction (Dadds & Hawes, 2006). The therapist asks if the parents already use time-out and then asks them what that entails. The parents then set up a time for a time-out rehearsal. Rehearsals and role plays are used in this session. The clinician reviews the behaviour-correction routine steps to see if the parent is following the steps correctly. This involves telling the parent to go through the four-step process (outlined above) in 15 seconds (Dadds & Hawes, 2006). Time-out consists of around one minute where access to reinforcers is ceased. The child spends quiet time on a chair or in a separate room that is safe, neutral and boring. Time-out is complete when the child is quiet and is back in control of themselves. Time-in is then initiated, which is fun, loving and contains a lot of positive reinforcement (Dadds, 2018).

Session 4: Continue-Review-Fine-tune

The fourth session starts with a review of the week and explores how the parents were able to implement the behavioural change techniques taught in the previous session and discusses any successes and challenges they have experienced (Dadds & Hawes, 2006). The parents are asked to give detailed examples of the behaviours they rewarded and which rewards they used. The parenting approach is then 'fine-tuned' in preparation for the coming week. This includes a discussion of desirable behaviour, what are the most effective rewards they noticed that their child responded to, ways to increase parental attention when positive behaviour is occurring, and exploring ways to increase opportunities for positive behaviours in order to 'set up the child (and parent) for success', such as setting up situations where it is easier for the child to perform desirable behaviours (such as taking the child shopping when it is not a busy time and when the child is not tired, sick or hungry) (Dadds & Hawes, 2006). Advanced reward strategies are also discussed, including planned 1:1 child-focused time. The clinician then reviews the behavioural-correction procedures and makes any needed adjustments to the time-out sequence. At the end of the session, short homework tasks and goals are collaboratively agreed upon between the therapist and the parents, with the focus being on improving the use of reward and discipline strategies (Dadds & Hawes, 2006).

Session 5: Contextual Issues

This fifth session focuses on child management strategies that help compliment the basic reward and discipline program. Strategies to manage sibling conflict are discussed, including praising positive play and dealing effectively with arguing. Parents are also taught how to deal with boredom (called 'Boredom busters' in the manual), which is a preventative strategy of identifying situations that the child finds most boring (such as waiting for an appointment) and difficult to behave in and having a plan for what they can do during these times (such as bringing along a colouring-in a book or a toy for them to play with the parent during this time). The implementation of boredom-busters is discussed using praise, novelty, joining in with the child and providing children with immediate feedback about their behaviour. The importance of family rules is also discussed; house rules are written down and agreed to, and strategies are taught to maintain these (Dadds & Hawes, 2006).

Session 6: Midpoint Review of Strategies

A review of parenting goals occurs in session six. The clinician summarises the relevant issues and asks parents about what changes have occurred, positively reinforcing parents for their hard work and for any successes they have reported. If no or minimal progress has been made, the clinician refers them back to the plan of action to see whether it is being performed as they were taught (Dadds & Hawes, 2006). Renegotiation of the plan of action for problem areas and goals is facilitated using a problem-solving approach with parents. Problem-solving is broken down into five steps: Step 1, define the problem; Step 2, brainstorm solutions; Step 3, narrows down the potential solutions, Step 4, select the most appropriate solution, and Step 5, consider how the chosen solution could be implemented (Dadds & Hawes 2006). Homework is provided, which focuses on the parents using the strategies they have learnt and taking a problem-solving approach when they are not working (Dadds & Hawes, 2006).

Sessions 7 and 8: Identifying and Planning Supports

Sessions 7 and 8 offer additional therapy components based on the family's specific needs. The aim of these sessions is to identify barriers related to heightened parental stress that reduces the parent's ability to effectively use the parenting strategies (Dadds & Hawes, 2006). The therapist helps the parent to identify stressful situations such as time management, anger management, problem-solving skills, lack of pleasant events and social support, compromised cognitive coping skills and the need for partner-support training (Dadds &

Hawes, 2006). These can be delivered over these two sessions depending on which ones the parents need and request (Dadds & Hawes, 2006).

Session 9: Review and Relapse Prevention

In the final session, parents are asked to report on the aspects of treatment they have found helpful as well as those that have been less helpful. The clinician asks the parents what they think are the possible reasons that they have found some of the strategies have been less helpful. Then the clinician collaboratively works with the parents to identify long-term goals and develops strategies for issues that require more work or for specific situations that are challenging for the family (Dadds & Hawes, 2006). For some families, it can be helpful to revisit specific parts of the program. Role plays can be helpful in assisting the parent in understanding the parenting strategy more, refining their skills or dealing more competently with a common challenging behaviour displayed by their child (Dadds & Hawes, 2006). A problem-solving approach can also be helpful if there are problems with parents achieving their goals. The clinician reviews each strategy covered in the program with a special focus on success, and the therapist asks parents to think of other situations where they could use these approaches (Dadds & Hawes, 2006).

Finally, the ending of treatment is discussed. The clinician asks the parent if they have any worries about implementing the strategies once treatment has ended. The therapist explains that the problems may reappear or even change in nature and severity over time; however, positively reinforcing that the parents have the skills to manage this (Dadds & Hawes, 2006). The clinician presents parents with hypothetical scenarios and asks them how they would respond based on the strategies they have learnt. Lastly, parents are reminded of 'positives before negatives' in choosing a strategy to use in any future parenting scenario (Dadds & Hawes, 2006).

Clinical Examples

The Case of Ellie

> Ellie was a 5-year-old girl who her parents, Karen and Joel, described as 'strong-willed'. Ellie was an only child. From age 1.5 years, Ellie was very determined and assertive, and at both home and at her daycare centre, she often questioned rules and was not always compliant with parental and daycare educators' requests. She would sometimes respond to limit-setting or being told 'No' by either ignoring the adult giving the instruction or by replying, 'You can't tell me what to do' and 'Adults can't boss little kids around'. She was described as a 'busy and curious girl' who was 'confident and brave'. Ellie liked to 'go first' and 'to be the winner' and found it hard to take turns. She found sharing very difficult and would become frustrated and

physically lash out or bite if another child took a toy off her. So eventually, the other children did not want to play with her in case she hurt them. Ellie was still described as being caring with others and animals and changed her behaviour around the babies in the daycare centre, and was quieter and more patient with them. Ellie was mostly egocentric, and her impulse control and emotional regulation appeared to be at a younger age than her chronological age. The biting behaviour was a major concern for both parents and childcare workers, as several parents had complained about Ellie's behaviour and felt she should leave the centre and threatened to remove their children if something was not done about her behaviour.

On the Child Behaviour Checklists (Achenbach, 2009), Karen and the Day Care Educators rated Ellie as having symptoms in the clinical range for ADHD and ODD. In contrast, Joel rated Ellie as being in the subclinical range for ADHD and ODD symptoms. Karen and Joel separated when Ellie was 1 year old, and they had shared care of her. While Karen and Joel prided themselves on having an amicable relationship with a strong focus on consistency for Ellie, they acknowledged she found the transition between two homes and daycare confusing, as in 'Who was the boss?' and 'What the rules were' at each place. Ellie was always trying to work out the hierarchy of who was in charge at each place. She was the only child in both households. She was anxious regarding which parent was picking her up from daycare each afternoon as she did not yet understand the days of the week and the pattern of parental care. Therefore she often asked who was picking her up each afternoon. Joel and Karen would get into arguments with Ellie, which was unhelpful and led to more non-compliance from Ellie and frustration for the adults.

Joel said Friday evening, when he had to pick Ellie up from Karen's place, was the most stressful for him. Ellie would argue that she did not need to leave her mum's house and would scream and yell at Joel, telling him that she did not like him, and would lash out when Joel tried to force her into his car. Both parents and Ellie would engage in endless verbal arguments, leading to an escalation, and often, this would end with Joel forcefully dragging Ellie to his car.

Karen said dinner time and bath time were the most stressful times for her as Ellie would refuse her cooked meals, insisting on junk food or dessert, throwing her cooked meal on the floor and yelling at her. Karen often responded by yelling back at Ellie. When asked to have a shower, Ellie typically refused, which often resulted in Karen yelling and smacking Ellie. Karen said she did not like yelling or smacking Ellie, but it was often the 'only thing that seemed to work' with getting her to do things.

Karen and Joel decided not to pursue a diagnosis for Ellie. However, Karen was worried that Ellie was showing 'some selfish and stubborn traits just like her father'. She was worried Ellie 'may accidentally hurt another child and cause permanent damage to them'. Karen and Joel agreed to pursue the IFI program with a private clinical psychologist to try and prevent Ellie's behaviours from getting worse and leading to a diagnosis of ADHD and ODD.

During sessions 3–5, the clinician helped the parents to increase their focus on positive behaviour, such as talking nicely and doing what she was told. Parents also practised ignoring dinner refusal and not giving in by feeding her dessert or treats instead, just stating clearly and calmly what was for dinner and leaving it up to Ellie to eat it or not. Similarly with the shower, they found it helpful to turn off the TV and remove any stimulation, telling her it is time for her shower and that if she wanted help, they were happy to help. The first night, Ellie went without a shower, even though she eventually went to bed a little later than normal. However, the second night, Karen repeated the instructions calmly, and Ellie went to the bathroom straight away, even asking for help in the shower. Karen said she tried to make this shower time an attachment-rich experience by quietly singing and using Ellie's favourite shower wash and sponge to help her. With the handover, Joel and Karen agreed to make some changes to help Ellie with the transition. This involved Joel picking up Ellie from daycare on Friday afternoons. Joel would talk about all of the fun things he and Ellie will be doing on Saturday (such as gardening and jumping on the trampoline together). Joel was happy with this arrangement and felt that it would help Ellie understand that she would be going to his house at the end of the day.

Both parents learnt to increase attachment-based positive reinforcement activities (such as physical contact and joint play) instead of material ones (such as toys). Attending the sessions together helped them discuss what was happening in each household and to work out ways to be more consistent in their parenting approach (cooperative parenting). Sometimes each parent was confused as to what either of them should do when Ellie did something they did not like (such as calling her parents 'stupid') and this was problem-solved between both of them. It helped them have more consistent rules (such as a consistent bedtime on weeknights and weekend nights) and consequences for not complying with these (time-out).

The daycare centre educators saw an improvement in Ellie's behaviour and improved compliance with their requests. Her social play even improved, and there were fewer dangerous incidents towards other children. She also appeared less tired at daycare. Both Joel and Karen agreed to work more as a parenting team and worked hard to reduce verbal arguments in front of Ellie. Throughout the program, they also identified more social support, as they did not have extended family living close by to help with their care, such as asking their friends for childcare help at times. Both Joel and Karen were satisfied with the program and felt there was a reduction in their own personal stress and an improvement in their communication.

The Case of Susie

Susie was a Master of Clinical Psychology student who was administering the IFI program to families in a psychology training clinic at a university campus. She was not sure why sometimes the families did not return after a few sessions of IFI (mostly after session two). Her supervisor watched a recording of her first sessions and noticed she appeared to show more empathy for the mothers in the sessions compared to the fathers. She appeared to have a bias for not encouraging the fathers to explain their frustrations with their parenting role, especially if they said anything negative about the child's mother. She had not been allowing the fathers the same amount of time as the mothers to talk, and she was mostly looking at and agreeing (using more minimal counselling skills) with the mothers in the assessment sessions. Susie was shocked when she realised she was doing this. In supervision, she reflected on her strong feelings towards mothers and felt she understood how stressful it was for the mother in families. By contrast, she noticed that she felt very uncomfortable when fathers complained about what the mothers were doing and not doing, particularly if the father was doing this in front of the mother in the session. Susie disclosed she had been raised by a single mother and did not have much contact with her own father, and did not have a lot of exposure to fathers who were actively involved in the parenting role or how the two roles may differ. Susie's supervisor asked her to try and give both parents the same amount of time (and to be conscious of the time using her watch subtly), attention and positive regard in the sessions, and they would review her recordings of her next sessions to see if this had improved.

Susie benefited from ongoing supervision sessions in her IFI delivery and recording each session and watching for any more unaware biases coming through in her clinical work. For example, she was more aware of her eye contact and minimal counselling skills used with each parent.

The above case vignette highlights how we may hold a gender bias around caring and parenting roles and need to be empathic and engaging to all our clients equally, including those less like ourselves or who have had similar experiences to our own. Most parenting programs involve a high number of mothers, but the inclusion of fathers is very important, especially in the above scenario where Joel had shared care of Ellie. We have seen many families where fathers would also like to be included in all or at least some of the sessions. It is important we treat all parents with the same level of warmth and respect and be aware of any known or unknown biases that may prevent this. The issue of working with fathers in parenting programs is an important one for all clinicians working with families. An Australian Study of child mental health practitioners found participants noted that father participant was important;

however, a third reported they had low confidence in working with fathers (Tully et al., 2018).

Training

The content of IFI is offered in the form of a treatment manual (Dadds & Hawes, 2006) which can be purchased from its publisher, Australian Academic Press, at the cost of $70.00 (Australian dollars in 2023). Therapists delivering IFI need to be experienced clinicians with training in psychology or related disciplines, such as social workers, family counsellors, paediatricians and psychiatrists (Dadds & Hawes, 2006). Prerequisites for conducting effective therapy based on the program include knowledge and skills in clinical family consultation, child development and psychopathology, assessment methods for assessing child problems, and at least a rudimentary knowledge of the coercion model, attachment, family systems and cognitive attributional theories (Dadds & Hawes, 2006). Once these prerequisites are fulfilled, there is no formal training required to be able to deliver IFI besides fidelity to the treatment manual. The therapy manual has detailed information for each session and also contains the handouts for parents. Mark Dadds and David Hawes also run workshops on this program nationally and internationally that help clinicians use the program and enhance the effectiveness of family-based intervention in real-life settings. These workshops help the clinician expand their knowledge of IFI beyond the manual.

Evidence Base

IFI has been well-researched. However, it has evolved over time, and the research includes different formats of this program. The majority of research has been produced by the founders Mark Dadds and David Hawes and psychology students at The Sydney Child Behaviour Research Clinic. Many of the research studies of IFI have been supported by the National Health and Medical Research Council of Australia (NHMRC), the main Australian government funding body of human research.

IFI has been shown to be effective in reducing child externalising problems in a face-to-face format (Dadds & McHugh, 1992; Dadds, Schwartz, & Sanders, 1987; Hawes & Dadds, 2005; Hawes, Dadds, Brennan, Rhodes, & Cauchi, 2013). It has also been evaluated via children's pre and post-family drawings (Kloff et al., 2017). Fifty-three children with conduct issues had their family drawings evaluated before IFI and also 6 months post-treatment using a modified version of the Family Drawing Paradigm (FDP; Fury et al., 1997). Post-treatment, there was an improvement in family functioning but not in language (indicated by written descriptions). Children with high levels of CU demonstrated greater change in FDP dysfunction than a lower level of CU group, resulting in similar levels at follow-up. Increased FDP warmth was more strongly related to improved conduct issues in the high versus low CU group.

An open trial of ParentWorks by (Piotrowska et al., 2021) with 338 families demonstrated a significant decrease in child emotional/behavioural problems, dysfunctional parenting, inter-parental conflict and parental mental health issues post-treatment. Children with initially higher levels of problems benefited more from being in the program. Parent sex did not affect the program outcome. An earlier evaluation of ParentWorks (Dadds et al., 2018) examined child and parent demographics predictors of treatment attrition. They found parents with the greatest need tend to engage with online parenting programs, and online programs appear useful for fathers, single parents and those in conflicted relationships. AssistEI has been shown effective in multi-site trials to be as effective as face-to-face in reducing conduct problems, and large treatment effects across families living in rural and urban communities have been reported (Dadds et al., 2019).

Conclusion

IFI (Dadds & Hawes, 2006) is a structured and helpful parenting program for parents of children aged between 2 and 8 years with conduct problems and it has a strong theoretical and empirical base. IFI's strength is in the multiple theoretical influences on its development, particularly the importance of coercive cycles in the development and maintenance of conduct problems and its use of evidence-based behaviour management strategies, strategies that foster attachment between parent and child as well as highlight the importance of the family structure or parenting team in addressing oppositional and conduct problems in young children. IFI is an easily accessible treatment for clinicians who work with children and families, is cost-effective to set up and deliver, and has minimal training requirements before qualified and experienced clinicians can use the treatment manual. IFI is a fairly new program, and compared with highly established programs, the research base is developing. Nevertheless, IFI includes a wide range of well-established and researched parenting strategies based on behaviour and social learning theory, which are known to be effective components in parent education and in the treatment of behavioural problems in children. IFI comes in a face-to-face format for parents of children with conduct problems, and the newer adapted online, more general parenting version ParentWorks and the therapist-assisted version called AccessEI. Given the stability of conduct problems in early childhood over time, the cost to society for antisocial behaviours in adolescents and adults, and evidence of the effectiveness of interventions to address these concerns, IFI is likely to be an important treatment approach for clinicians working with families.

Reader's Exercises

- How would you explain the different types of reinforcement and punishment to parents with practical parenting examples of each one?

- What are some attachment-enriched rewards you could suggest to parents to try using?

- How would you describe to parents what attachment-neutral responses are to use when a child misbehaves?

- How would you advise a parent to pay more attention to desirable behaviours and to ignore low-risk misbehaviour?

- What are some parent self-care techniques that could be helpful to suggest to parents?

- What are some common parental external resources that you can encourage parents to access?

References

Achenbach, T. M. (2009). *The Achenbach System of Empirically Based Assessment (ASEBA): Development, Findings, Theory, and Applications.* University of Vermont Research Center for Children, Youth, & Families.

Ainsworth, M.D.S., Blehar, M.C., Waters, E., & Wall, S. (1978). *Patterns of attachment: A psychological study of the strange situation.* Erlbaum.

Bandura, A. (1971). *Social learning theory.* General Learning Press.

Bandura, A. (1986). *Social foundations of thought and actions: A social cognitive theory.* Prentice-Hall, Inc.

Bowlby, J. (1969). *Attachment, Vol.1 of attachment and loss.* Hogarth Press.

Dadds, M. (2018, March 8). *How to do family therapy well: A personalised stage model* [Conference Presentation]. Central Coast Local Health District.

Dadds, M., & Hawes, D. (2006). *Integrated family intervention for child conduct problems: A behaviour-attachment-systems intervention for parents.* Australian Academic Press.

Dadds, M.R., & McHugh, T.A. (1992). Social support and treatment outcome in behavioural family therapy for child conduct problems. *Journal of Consulting and Clinical Psychology, 60(2)*, 252–259. https://doi.org/10.1037/0022-006X.60.2.252

Dadds, M., Sicouri, G., Piotrowska, P.J., Collins, D.A.J., Hawes, D.J., Moul, C., Lenrrot, R.K., Frick, P.J., Anderson, V., Kimonis, E.R., & Tully, L. (2018). Keeping parents involved: Predicting attrition in a self-directed online program for childhood conduct problems. *Journal of Clinical Child Adolescent Psychology, 48(6)*, 881–893. https://doi.org/10.1080/15374416.2018.1485109

Dadds, M.R., Sanders, M.R., Behrens, B.C., & James, J.E. (1987). Marital discord and child behaviour problems: A description of family interactions during treatment. *Journal of Clinical Child Psychology, 16(3)*, 192–203. https://oi.org/10.1207/s15374424jccp1603_3

Dadds, M.R., Schwartz, S., & Sanders, M.R. (1987). Marital discord and treatment outcome in behavioural treatment of child conduct disorders. *Journal of Clinical Child Psychology, 55(3)*, 396. https://doi.org/10.1037/0022-006X.55.3.396

Dadds, M.R., Thai, C., Mendoza Diaz, A., Broderick, J., Moul, C., Tully, L.A., Hawes, D.J., Davies, S., Burchfield, K., & Cane, L. (2019). Therapist-assisted online treatment for child conduct problems in rural and urban families: Two randomised controlled trials. *Journal of Consulting and Clinical Psychology, 87*, 706–719. https://doi.org/10.1037/ccp0000419

Fury, G., Carlson, E.A., & Sroufe, L.A. (1997). Children's representations of attachment relationships in family drawings. *Child Development, 68*, 1154–1164. https://doi.10.2307/1132298

Hawes, D.J., & Dadds, M.R. (2005). The treatment of conduct problems in children with callous-unemotional traits. *Journal of Consulting and Clinical Psychology, 73*, 737. https://doi:10.1037/0022-006X.73.4.737

Hawes, D.J., Dadds, M.R., Brennan, J., Rhodes, T., & Cauchi, A. (2013). Revisiting the treatment of children with callous-unemotional traits. *The Australian and New Zealand Journal of Psychiatry, 47(7)*, 646–653. https://doi.10.1177/0004867413484092

Hawes, D.J., Price, M.J., & Dadds, M.R. (2014). Callous-unemotional traits and the treatment of conduct problems in childhood and adolescence: A comprehensive review. *Clinical Child & Family Psychology Review, 17*, 248–267. https://doi:10.1007/s10567-014-0167-1

Minuchin, S. (1974). *Families and family therapy*. Harvard University Press.

Patterson, G.R. (1982). *A social learning approach: 3. Coercive family process*. Castalia.

Piotrowska, P., Tully, L.A., Collins, D.A., Sawrikar, V., Hawes, D., Kimonis, E.R., Lenroot, R.K., Moul, C., Anderson, V., Frick, P.J., & Dadds, M.R. (2020).

ParentWorks: Evaluation of an online, father-inclusive, universal parenting intervention to reduce child conduct problems. *Child Psychiatry Human Development*, *51*(4), 503–513. https://doi.1007/s10578-019-00934-0

Ryan, R.M., & Connell, J.P. (1989). Perceived locus of causality and internalisation: Examining reasons for acting in two domains. *Journal of Personality and Social Psychology*, *57*(5), 749–761. https://doi. 10.1037/0022-3514.57.5.749

Skinner, B. F. (1957). *Verbal behavior.* Prentice-Hall.

Snyder, J., & Stoolmiller, M. (2002). Reinforcement and coercive mechanisms in the development of antisocial behaviour. The family. In J. Reid, G. Patterson, & J. Synder (Eds.), *Antisocial behaviour in children and adolescents: A development analysis and model for intervention* (pp. 65–100). American Psychological Association.

Tully, L.A., Collins, D.A.J., Piotrowska, P.J., Mairet, K.S., Hawes, D.J., Moul, C., Lenroot, R.K., Frick, P.J., Anderson, V.A., Kimonis, E.R., & Dadds, M.R. (2018). Examining practitioner competencies, organisational supports and barriers to engaging fathers in parenting interventions. *Child Psychiatry & Human Development*, *1*, 109–122. https://doi.10.1007/s10578-017-0733-0

Van Lange, P.A., & Balliet, D. (2014). *Interdependence theory.* American Psychological Association. https://doi.10.4135/9781446201022.n39

Waugh, L., & Sanders, M.R. (1993). *Family Observation Schedule: Observer training tape* [videotape]. Behaviour Research and Therapy Centre. The University of Queensland.

Weiner, B. (1992). *Human motivation: Metaphors, theories and research.* Sage Publications.

Chapter 10

Dyadic Developmental Psychotherapy (DDP)

Sian Phillips

Dyadic Developmental Psychotherapy (DPP) is a relationship-focused therapy for parents and caregivers of children who have experienced developmental trauma. It is also a model that can support and strengthen relationships in all families. It is based on attachment theory, interpersonal neurobiology and the concept of intersubjectivity. DDP was developed by Daniel Hughes, a clinical psychologist in the USA, during the 1980s and 1990s and formally became known as DDP in 2000. DDP grew out of clinical experiences, which showed that there was a group of children who did not benefit from mainstream contemporary psychotherapies. These were children who had experienced developmental trauma, lacked an experience of attuned, synchronised and secure relationships with main caregivers and were often removed from their parents and placed into alternate care. Given their experiences, these children lacked trust in relationships with others, which made it hard for parents or other adults to influence them, guide them or find comfortable connections with them. Dyadic Developmental Psychotherapy and then later Dyadic Developmental Practice and Dyadic Developmental Parenting provide a model to invite these children to move from mistrust to trust so that they can benefit from healthy, reciprocal relationships and begin to resolve past traumatic relational experiences. The DDP practitioner provides support to the parent and other caregivers to understand and respond in ways that increase a felt sense of safety for the child. The practitioner then works dyadically: the parent is helped to provide the safety the child needs to accept their comfort, love, guidance and limit setting, and the child is helped to trust that support. With increased safety, the child is helped to understand and resolve their past traumatic experiences, find less shame-based narratives and start to be open to new learning. DDP is currently undergoing a randomised control study to contribute to anecdotal and qualitative research that shows the efficacy of DDP.

DDP grew out of clinical experiences that showed that mainstream contemporary psychotherapies were not helpful for children who learned to mistrust their primary caregiver given experiences of abuse, neglect, lack of attunement or multiple separations early in life. Nor were they helpful in supporting the adults who tried to care for this group of children. DDP, whether in its original psychotherapy form or in practice form, focuses on creating the safety in relationships that children need to move from mistrust to trust. They then can make use of relationships in ways that strengthen their resilience and help them integrate past traumatic experiences. Hughes (2000) integrated into the therapeutic relationship between the child and their main (and often new) caregiver the following types of interactions: Playfulness, Acceptance, Curiosity and Empathy (PACE). When adults respond to children (or other adults) with PACE, the individual learns that they are seen, heard and valued. They learn that they are loved unconditionally.

History and Theoretical Basis

Dyadic Developmental Psychotherapy (DDP) was first developed by Dan Hughes, a Clinical Psychologist in the US, during the 1980s and 1990s in response to his observation that traditional psychological interventions were not as helpful as needed for some of the children who had experienced abuse and their parents/caregivers who he was working with at the time (Hughes et al., 2019). There were a group of children who had learned not to trust adults, given that their first relationships with parents or caregivers created experiences of fear, loneliness, terror and shame more than they allowed for experiences of safety, comfort and joy. Often these children required out-of-home care where other relatives, foster or adoptive parents were unsure of how to care, comfort and influence children who brought with them the expectancy that all adults would cause harm to them. What worked with their own children was not working with these mistrusting children. Parents and caregivers also struggled with how to keep going in the face of persistent mistrust and would feel shame about their desire to 'give up' or struggle with painful feelings of inadequacy. Dan needed a way of working that could support parents in the difficult job of parenting children who were fearful of being parented, as well as a way to make it safe enough for the children to give up their effective adaptive strategies to avoid and control relationships so as to mitigate the anticipated harm and find new ways of being that could tolerate, and then welcome, connection. Although it is relationships that have caused great harm to this group of children, it is only through the establishment of safe relationships that they can begin to heal.

Many researchers have identified that healthy child development occurs within safe and attuned relationships (e.g., John Bowlby, Mary Main, Mary Ainsworth, Jude Cassidy, Daniel Stern, Peter Fonagy, Edward Tronick, and Susan Woodhouse). Parent responsiveness to their 4-month-old infant is correlated with optimal cognitive development at one year (Jaffe et al., 2001), secure attachment (Beebe & Lachmann, 2013), development of neuronal connectivity (Bernier et al., 2019), capacity to regulate stress (Feldman, 2007), child and adolescent capacity for empathy (Feldman, 2007), adolescent capacity to engage in reciprocal, intimate relationships (Pratt et al., 2019) and reflective capacity as an adult (Fonagy et al., 1991). The parent's ability to notice, respond sensitively, co-regulate the baby's distress and help organise the baby's experience is critical to all aspects of their development across the life span.

DDP was first conceptualised as a therapy that could mirror what responsive parents did with their infants to promote healthy child development. Dan integrated into the therapeutic relationship the Playfulness, Acceptance, Curiosity and Empathy (PACE) that good enough parents demonstrate as they teach their infants about what it means to be in a safe relationship with them (Hughes, 2000). He attended to the frequency and prosody of their voice, their nonverbal facial expressions and body language, as well as the stories they would tell to their infants to help them make sense of what was happening in their internal world and the external environment. This attuned and repetitive co-regulation of their baby's affective experiences gradually led to the ability to self-regulate and a sense of relationship security that freed them up to learn about their world. When adults respond to children (or other adults) with PACE, the individual learns that they are seen, heard and valued. They learn that they are loved unconditionally. A 'PACE-ful way of being' allows individuals to lean into relationships because what they expect to find there makes them feel good. They also learn that they have the ability to make others feel good. They learn that they are loveable and worthwhile (Hughes, 2020).

Unfortunately, not all infants are responded to in ways that help them develop in healthy ways. Parents can be overwhelmed emotionally and cognitively with their own attempts to survive relationships that have and continue to hurt, substance abuse issues, mental health issues, poverty, racism and other forms of marginalisation. When parents are focused on their own survival, there is little energy left over to notice and respond to their infant or child's needs. The infant's needs can easily overwhelm their already fragile sense of coping, and parental responses can become harsh and abusive, too infrequent, or the child is attended to but without the 'heart and mind' of the parent. If such parental responses are persistent, the infant experiences an unresolvable dilemma: they need to be close to adults in order to survive, yet also need to avoid the intense pain inflicted by frightening adults.

Psychiatrist Van der Kolk and colleagues coined the term 'developmental trauma' to describe the pervasive impact this dilemma has on all aspects of a child's development. They also use the term 'complex trauma' to describe the dual problem of children's exposure to traumatic events and the impact of this exposure on immediate and long-term outcomes (Cook et al., 2003). Children with developmental trauma learn that they must be bad, unlovable, too much or frightening to their parents. They learn to become transactional in relationships. Rather than developing the skills to interact or 'dance' comfortably with adults, the infants learn to take from adults what is needed for their survival and to avoid any intersubjective interactions for fear that their pain, loneliness, fear, anger and shame will be exacerbated and overwhelm them. The experience of being in relationships does not feel safe and comfortable.

Abused children's chronic lack of safety makes it difficult to develop the nervous system and neuronal connectivity that allow for effective regulation of emotions, thinking and behaviour (Porges, 2011). It takes enormous energy for a child with developmental trauma to manage the competing need to keep adults close enough to survive but far enough away to avoid further harm. As a result, there is little energy left over for learning, exploring, and caring for themselves and others. Survival for children with secure attachments is about engagement and collaboration. No matter what stage of development, we all do better when working together in a responsive, supportive, helpful and trusting relationship (Hold-Lunstad et al., 2010). Survival for children (and adults) with developmental trauma is a lonely endeavour. Trauma operates on the principle of 'I have been fooled once, so never again'. Relationships continue to be frightening and interactions transactional, making it difficult to establish reciprocally enjoyable and meaningful connections.

Our therapeutic goal for children with developmental trauma then is to help move them from their understandable mistrust of relationships to trusting that connections with others can be safe and pleasurable. In DDP, the *relationship* between the child and caregiver becomes the client or therapeutic focus. DDP helps both partners in the dyad find more comfortable and enjoyable ways of being together. Once relational safety is experienced, the child is helped to resolve past traumatic experiences (Hughes et al., 2019). The child can open to new ways of seeing, being, hearing and doing, and the developmental trajectory can be changed to a healthier one for the child, dyad and family.

Theoretical Underpinnings in DDP

DDP borrows from three comprehensive and integrated bodies of literature; attachment theory, intersubjectivity theory and interpersonal neurobiology.

Attachment Theory

Attachment theory recognises the critical role of safe relationships for healthy social and emotional development. John Bowlby, a British psychologist and psychoanalyst, documented the deleterious effects of separation and loss from primary caregivers for children (Bowlby, 1969). Ainsworth (Ainsworth et al., 1978) and Main (Main & Soloman,1990), also child psychologists, later described patterns of attachment that develop in response to parent's sensitivity to their experiences and needs.

Secure attachments arise from relationships that are responsive and adequately contingent. Secure attachments do not guarantee positive mental health, but they are definitely correlated with positive developmental outcomes across domains. Insecure attachments are a response to parents who can notice and attend to their child but not necessarily in a timely way or in a way that allows for a sufficient sense of safety. One solution is to coerce their parent into connection for fear of not being noticed while also being worried about whether the parent will be angry. Being with, or too far away from, their parent causes anxiety. Ainsworth called this pattern an ambivalent attachment. Another insecure attachment pattern is to suppress emotional needs so as not to overwhelm the parent. Although desperately wanting to be noticed, the child believes that not being noticed or taking care of the parent is the best way to stay safe (avoidant attachment). Disorganised attachment (Main & Solomon, 1986) describe a child's response to parents who are frightening to the child or who seem to be frightened of the child. There is no painless solution to being with such parents. These children bounce between strategies that reflect mobilised stress responses such as fight and flight and immobilised, freeze responses as their stress response systems stay activated in response to the fear of being with parents who hurt or who are clearly not in a position to create safety because of their own fear.

Given that healthy development can only occur in safe relationships, DDP focuses on the relationships that support the child. The DDP therapist ensures that the adults are supported to understand and respond sensitively to the child with developmental trauma. If the adult is overwhelmed, anxious, resentful or lacks knowledge about how trauma impacts the developing child, they will not be in a position to create the safety the child needs to learn new expectancies about or ways of being in relationships. A dysregulated adult will never be able to regulate a dysregulated child.

Initially, the DDP therapist's work may be with parents and caregivers. Even skilled, securely attached parents will struggle with the powerful resistance and ongoing rejection that is motivated by a child's fear of connection. Dan Hughes and Jon Baylin, in their book *Brain-Based Parenting; the Neuroscience of Caregiving for Healthy Attachment* (Hughes & Baylin, 2012), outlined how parents can develop *Blocked Care* when their child does not know how to engage reciprocally with them. It is very hard to keep going in non-reciprocal relationships, and parents can become reactive and defensive or disengaged as a result of the pain of their child's rejection. Parents often express a great deal of shame about their parenting. As therapists, our first job is often to remove the block and integrate the shame with PACE. As parents develop a felt sense of safety and trust that they are accepted and that the therapist is truly interested in their experience and has empathy for their struggles, they become more open to learning about how their child's rejections are an adaptive strategy, how their own attachment strategies, or expectancy for relationships, maybe making it more difficult to parent and eventually have more openness to learning ways of responding that can create more emotional safety for the child.

Intersubjectivity Theory

Intersubjectivity theory integrates what we know from attachment theory and interpersonal neurobiology. The relationship between self and others has long been studied by philosophers and increasingly so by psychology researchers (Stern, 1985; Trevarthen & Aitken, 2001) and neuroscientists (Shore, 1994). Intersubjectivity theory helps us understand that we develop a sense of self by being held in mind and experienced by our parents and then by others. We learn to see ourselves the way that others see us. If our parents truly experience us with delight, we will feel delightful. If they experience us as a burden, we will feel unworthy. This is what DDP understands as primary intersubjectivity.

The DDP therapist must be able to accept, like and delight in both parent and child if change is to occur. They must be able to experience the child's courage for the child to learn he or she is courageous. They must fundamentally experience the child's 'goodness' to re-structure the child's shame-based narrative. The therapist helps the parent see what lies behind the child's challenging behaviour, encouraging empathy and respect for the child's enormous struggle to survive in a world that feels frightening and confusing. As the parent accepts the child's underlying experiences, the child is better able to integrate their shame and develop a sense of being worthy. If the parents focus only on behaviour and the need to change it, emotional experiences will not be mirrored, and behavioural manifestations of trauma will continue.

Intersubjective relationships also help us learn about others. When parents can experience their children as separate beings with their own intentions and motivations, the child can eventually come to experience others as separate beings with their own perceptions, motivations and intentions. This capacity for mentalisation — seeing mental states in self and others (Fonagy et al., 2002) — is so essential for the building of healthy reciprocal relationships. That reflective capacity can only emerge in the context of the attachment relationship. The more accurate the parent is at mirroring their infant's internal experiences, the better the baby will become at regulating their own emotional states and understanding others (Fonagy et al., 2002). This reflective capacity is poor in children who have not been mirrored in this way. They struggle to understand why they do what they do or why adults do what they do. Other people's intentions and motivations are also understood poorly (e.g., 'My parent sets a limit because they are not interested in what I want' or 'My parent is angry because they hate me'). Such concrete and inaccurate interpretations make it difficult for either partner in a dyad to feel understood, and the relationship tends to remain unsatisfying.

DDP, through the establishment of safe relationships, creates a foundation to start to build the child's reflective capacity. Through repetitive synchronised mirroring of the child's experience, curiosity and storytelling, the DDP therapist introduces the child to a new way of understanding himself, his parents and his world.

Example of Intersubjectivity

> Therapist: Hey, I noticed when your dad was telling me about how he enjoyed spending time with you last night you made a face — something like this (therapist looks down and purses her lips). It seemed like you had a hard time believing that he enjoyed spending time with you. I wonder if I am right about that. Dad, you probably didn't notice because you were delighted about telling me how much you enjoyed your daughter last night. If I am right, your daughter seems to be unsure whether to believe you. She isn't sure that she is an enjoyable kid.

The therapist immediately notices the child's change in state and tries to make sense of it. She mentalised that the look meant the child was struggling to believe she was enjoyable and tried to organise the child's experience through her curiosity and telling a story about what it might mean. If she had asked, 'What are you feeling right now?' the child would probably have answered, 'I don't know.' As Fonagy et al. (2002) and Stern (1985) outline in their work, to know oneself, one first has to be known. The therapist's guessing helps organise the child's experience, build reflective capacity and helps the child talk about their emerging sense of self.

> Annie: (shrugs her shoulders).

Therapist: It makes so much sense that you don't know! Thanks so much for telling me that you don't know if I am right. Your face may have meant something totally different, couldn't it? It might mean that you were tired of your dad talking (playful) or that you had a toothache, or were bored. Shall we ask Dad what he thinks you were feeling when you made that face? He knows you well, let's ask! Dad — when you were talking about the fun you had with your daughter last night, she made that face, and my guess was that she was having a hard time believing you. She might have been thinking you were making it up because deep down, I think she may feel like a rotten kid, like a kid who has done something wrong and who must somehow be a bad kid. Why else would she be in foster care and not live with her first parents?

Dad: I do think Annie feels like she is a bad kid a lot of the time. I wish she didn't. I try telling her often that I think she is a terrific kid and we are so glad to be looking after her.

Therapist: I wish that Annie could believe you when you tell her that. I wish she could learn just by you telling her. It is so very hard to feel like a no-good kid, and you see her pain and want to make it go away. My guess is that when you have fun together like last night, Annie might think for a moment that she is wrong about being a rotten kid — how can a dad have so much fun with her if she is rotten? Then when we are talking about it now, she is not so sure. The part of her that is convinced she is rotten is big and loud. The voice that says 'Maybe not?' is little, and it gets drowned out by that big loud voice.

Dad: I do love it when we laugh together. She is so fun to be with.,

Therapist: Could you look at Annie and tell her that?

Dad: (Turns to his daughter). I am sorry that you don't see yourself the way I see you. I love having fun with you and looking after you. (Smiling), 'I hope one day you will see that I am right — you are a terrific kid!

Annie: (She doesn't look at Dad but leans into him, and he puts an arm around her shoulder).

The therapist continues to organise Annie's experience. Her playfulness, acceptance, curiosity and empathy (PACE) are continuously present and communicate without telling her that the therapist also experiences her as a 'good kid'. The storytelling makes explicit both Annie's emotional experience and how she might be thinking about herself. The story is informed by the therapist's attunement, her capacity to mentalise and her knowledge about how trauma impacts a child's development.

Interpersonal Neurobiology

Our parent's responsiveness and mirroring drives brain development (Shore, 2013). Without that responsiveness and corresponding intersubjective experiences, the architecture of the brain becomes specialised to handle threat (Baylin & Hughes 2016). The chronic stress that results from disconnection and harm impairs the development of neuronal connectivity that allows for effective executive function, regulation of attention and emotion or theory of mind and reflective capacity. When threat or the expectation of threat is persistent, the stress system stays active. The brain regions that develop are the ones lower and back in the brain that facilitate hypervigilance and reactive defences that promote survival. Children with developmental trauma do not *choose* their behaviour. Their behaviour reflects an underlying physiology that is responding to threat and a lack of brain connectivity that would allow for regulation.

Stephen Porges's Polyvagal Theory (Porges, 2011) further illustrates how our autonomic nervous system allows for social or defensive responses depending on whether we feel safe, in danger or in a life threat. Optimal responsiveness to a situation is only possible when we feel safe. If we start to experience danger, our vagal tone decreases, and we shift into mobilised defensive fight or flight behaviours. If we experience a life threat, our nervous system moves us to immobilised or freeze defence. These defensive behaviours emerge from our rapid — less than 20 milliseconds (Porges, 2011) — assessment of safety, danger or life threat. Choosing or making conscious decisions about how we behave is a longer process that requires the integration of higher brain regions, especially the pre-frontal cortex. If we are in danger of being eaten by a crocodile, there is no time for thinking. We react and then think later. For so many children with developmental trauma, they act and do not know why and then when there is time to think, the story they tell themselves is that they are a bad or crazy kid. Part of any trauma work is to help the child, as well as their parents, understand that their nervous system has decided for them in the service of protection.

The only way then to change defensive behaviour is to change the underlying felt sense of safety. Behaviours consistent with social engagement are not voluntary. The softness around the eyes that communicate warmth and interest, the voice prosody, the ability to recognise perspectives and hold differences in opinion with interest, and the ability to collaborate and negotiate are not voluntary. They emerge only from an underlying sense of safety. We cannot punish or incentivise that behaviour into existence. If we want behaviour consistent with social engagement, we have to increase the *felt* sense of safety.

Inviting a child with developmental trauma to move from mistrust to trust requires this change in physiology. That change must first come from the experience of co-regulation. Self-regulation, thinking through a problem, and remembering what the therapist taught about relaxation or breathing is not available to a child whose nervous system registers constant danger or life threat. Imagine reciting a poem or remembering your times tables if you believe you will at any moment become a crocodile's next meal.

To co-regulate the client, the therapist has to stay in their social engagement system while their client may be stuck in defensive responding. This is not always easy as our brains are also in the business of survival, and our physiology will move towards defensive responses when we don't feel safe. Being well ourselves, having knowledge about trauma, good supervision, and a map for responding helps us stay regulated. DDP's — PACE and Affective/Reflective (A/R) dialogue provides us with that map.

Being PACE-ful is only possible when we feel safe. When in the social engagement system, the therapist or parent can be optimally responsive, communicate that they pose no threat and recognise that the child is not a threat. Adults and children can be close without fear (Porges, 2011). DDP, in essence, is rehabilitation for the nervous system (Phillips, 2020).

Attachment, intersubjectivity and interpersonal neurobiology all highlight the essential experience of a felt sense of relational safety for wellbeing. DDP aims to first establish safety. Once safety is more accessible, then the DDP therapist can work towards increased reflective capacity, regulation, and relational engagement. Experiences of trauma can then be integrated and positive affect enhanced.

Core Concepts of DDP

Our therapeutic goal for children with developmental trauma then is to help move them from their understandable mistrust of relationships to trusting that connections with others can be safe and pleasurable. In DDP, the *relationship* between the child and caregiver becomes the client or therapeutic focus. DDP helps both partners in the dyad find more comfortable and enjoyable ways of being together. Once relational safety is experienced, the child is helped to resolve past traumatic experiences (Hughes et al., 2019). The child can be open to new ways of seeing, being, hearing and doing, and the developmental trajectory can be changed to a healthier one for the child, dyad and family. DDP aims to achieve this goal through two primary means, 'PACE' and A/R dialogue.

PACE

PACE is an acronym for **P**layful, **A**cceptance, **C**uriosity and **E**mpathy. PACE is an attitude and a way to communicate to others that they can be close to us without fear. When we provide these safety signals to children, we co-regulate their affect, help them find emotional equilibrium, and gradually make sense of their lives. PACE is not a way of *doing* to be applied in a linear or template fashion. Acceptance of underlying experience must be a constant. Empathy can be used liberally but may not always be tolerated by the child. Sometimes curiosity and playfulness must wait until the child is more regulated. How we respond is informed by the child. Our attunement guides how we learn to find a rhythm with the child and create safety for the child to dance reciprocally. All elements of PACE are a way of communicating safety, and together, they flow naturally from the attuned and responsive adult.

Playfulness: When we play with another person, we experience enjoyment. The mirror neurons in our brains help us experience ourselves the way that other people see us, so when an adult enjoys a child, the child feels that they bring joy. This is a new experience for children who have been hurt. Abuse and neglect create shame, and their experience of themselves is typically one of being unlovable, a nuisance, disgusting or unwanted. It is really hard to play with someone you do not like, so when we can be playful with hurt children, we are communicating — without telling them directly — that they are enjoyable and likeable. Being playful also communicates confidence and hope that the child's life will improve. Play is also a crucial component of learning how to get along with others. In DDP, it is as essential to help children learn to play and have enjoyment, delight and joy as it is to reduce anger, shame, anxiety and other painful emotions. Learning how to play is a really important step towards healing.

Playfulness is so dependent on the developing relationship between the child and therapist. As we come to know someone, we learn how their sense of humour works, and we become more attuned to when our client can tolerate a gentle tease or invitation into silliness. Playfulness as a safety signal also depends so much on what we as adults find uniquely playful. Playfulness in DDP tends to be spontaneous and communicated nonverbally in our tone of voice, the twinkle in our eyes, and the twitching of our facial muscles that all say I am SO enjoying being with you right now! Because it is so spontaneous and emergent between two individuals, it's hard to provide examples as they may not feel right given the unique relationship between a child and therapist.

Acceptance: Acceptance is the child's underlying emotional experience that leads to behaviour. Acceptance makes us feel safe. It communicates that support is unconditional, and the behaviour is less important than the relation-ship. It can be difficult for adults to accept the underlying deep sense of self-loathing, rage or despair that children with developmental trauma experience. Adults like to argue with, reassure, minimise or distract children from painful feelings. As DDP therapists, we need to challenge ourselves to accept all parts and all experiences of our clients so that they can begin to integrate those parts themselves and begin to heal. If we can accept the child underneath the behaviour, the child can experience that we do not turn away from them. If adults can stay connected to those painful experiences, then children can learn to do the same, and healing can begin.

Acceptance is communicated in our nonverbal messages, in our tone of voice, our facial expressions and gestures. We do not judge the emotional experience that child is having even though we may have things to say about their behaviour. For example, we might say things like:

> 'Daniel, you are so very angry right now! You want to explode. I know you do! Let's figure out a way to let me know you are angry with me without throwing things! I know you know it's not okay to throw things at your therapist! We have to figure out what is making you so angry!'

Adults like to reassure or argue with kids who express painful emotions. When a young person says, 'I'm stupid', 'I'm just a bad kid', and 'I can't do anything right', most adults will say, 'No, you are not! Or that's not true!' or to a child who claims that everyone hates them, adults might say something like, 'That is not true! I saw you playing nicely with Jenny earlier.' As hard as it is to stay with a child's painful emotional experience, it is so important for that student to know that we are not afraid of their pain and want to talk them out of their experience. For a child who says, 'I'm stupid!' acceptance may be expressed by 'Oh, how hard that is to feel stupid. I'm sorry you carry that feeling with you.' For the child that says everyone hates them: 'Ahh, that must be so hard and probably makes you feel lonely.' Your acceptance and empathy will communicate, much more than any reassuring words or arguments, that you do not hate that child.

Curiosity: When the therapist is curious, it helps us stay in an understanding stance and explore what might be causing the challenging behaviour. As mentioned earlier, children with developmental trauma have poor reflective capacity. They typically do not have any idea why they do what they do or why adults do what they do. The story they make up is usually that they are bad kids or that adults are mean. The therapist's curiosity invites the child to also be curious, and it helps build reflective capacity. Trauma makes it so very difficult to be interested in anything other than survival. Our curiosity also communicates intersubjectively that the child is worth understanding and that they are interesting, challenging their core narrative that there is nothing about them worth knowing. We do not have to know the answer; we just want to discover and then delight in the discovery.

'I wonder' statements are a great way to express curiosity. For example, 'I wonder if you are upset right now because I asked you to do something that feels too hard?' or 'I wonder if you are worried that Joey doesn't like you when he said no to playing basketball?'. Often the child will say 'I don't know' to which the adult can delightfully exclaim 'Then let's figure it out!' Together the adult and child can guess, stretching the child's understanding of their own and others' motivations and intentions.

Curiosity also reminds us to stay focused on what is causing behaviour rather than focusing on the consequences. Until we know what's causing the behaviour, we do not know how to proceed with the consequences. A child who is aggressive because he is scared and in a full sympathetically driven fight reaction needs a response to calm his fear rather than a punishment of the behavioural outcome. Once feeling safer, the child will be able to enter into a discussion of how to repair any physical or relational damage that occurred while their anger masked their fear. For example;

> 'You were really angry this morning and had such a hard time listening to me. You were so mad! I was wondering if, underneath that anger, you were feeling scared that your mum and dad may not show up for your visit today. I know sometimes they do and sometimes they don't, and it's so very hard when they don't. Funny how worry can lead to anger, isn't it?'

If the child is regulated, we can use our curiosity to determine what, if any, consequence is necessary. For example,

> 'You said some pretty mean things to your friends while you were angry. Do you have any ideas about how you might make things better with your friends? Don't worry if you don't, I have some ideas. Let me know if you need my help.'

Empathy: Empathy helps us feel 'felt.' It is not sympathy, pity or reassurance. It can communicate that we understand and are with our clients. When we feel others are with us in our experience, we can do more and feel braver or stronger (Coan, 2016). We can express empathy for any emotional experience, not just sadness. We can communicate our empathy verbally and nonverbally through our tone, intensity, rhythm of our voice, soft gaze, open body posture and, when safe, through touch. Having empathy for a client's experience does not mean that there will be an absence of limits or consequences for the behaviour. We maintain acceptance and empathy for the underlying emotional experience while also providing necessary consequences — also given with empathy.

Some examples of empathic responses include:

- 'It is so hard right now.'
- 'I am so sorry this is so tricky.'
- 'Oh boy, you really wished you could have done what you wanted in the way you wanted to.'
- 'It is so very hard when adults tell you to want to do.'

- 'Ahh, your anger is SO big. I know you know that it isn't okay to hurt others. It is so very hard to be in control of your hands and words when you are so angry, isn't it?'

Empathy helps the other person know that they are not alone in their experience. Matching the vitality of our client's emotional experience increases the likelihood that they will feel us with them. If a child is sympathetically driven and in a fight or flight mode, our energy must match the heightened state; otherwise, it can be experienced as mis-attuned. If our client is more para-sympathetically driven and in a shutdown state, our energy must match theirs and be less exuberant. Empathy may not be available to us if a client is aggressive towards us or if we are frightened by their behaviour. We might have to rely more on our cognitive understanding of what is happening and remind ourselves to remain compassionate to the sadness, loneliness, and shame that might be precipitating the aggression.

Affective/Reflective Dialogue

Once we have established a sense of relational safety through PACE, the DDP therapist shifts to help the client make sense of their experiences through engaging in an A/R dialogue. When individuals encounter people and events, we integrate both our emotions (affective) and the story we tell ourselves (reflective) about that interaction or experience. Children with developmental trauma struggle to recognise and articulate their emotional experiences and are poor at reflecting or making sense of why they do what they do or why others do what they do. Engaging with the therapist in the A/R dialogue helps develop that reflective capacity and helps the client develop a more coherent and less shame-based narrative.

As therapists guide the conversation, the child may experience intense emotions. The therapist must co-regulate that distress. In addition to PACE, the therapist can direct the rhythm of the conversation from serious to lighter topics, allow the child to avoid or distract to ensure a break from the emotional intensity, may at times talk for the child or about the child, encourage the parent to use touch or physical contact for comfort and initiates repair of the relationship if the child becomes dysregulated. The therapist stays active and attuned to the child's verbal and nonverbal communication to ensure that there is enough safety to engage in the hard conversation.

Co-regulation skills within the A/R dialogue

Follow-Lead-Follow: This principle helps the therapist engage in reciprocal conversation, at times initiating and at times responding in ways that are similar to how parents respond to their infants and young children. The therapist, with curiosity, may initiate a conversation or exploration of an emotion to encourage a deeper emotional experience or, if the child is in danger of becoming overwhelmed, initiate a lighter topic of conversation. It is important that the therapist initiate a conversation about all aspects of a child's experience, not always the difficult ones (Hughes et al., 2019). This way, the child comes to find all aspects of their heart and mind in the heart and mind of their parent and therapist.

Leading can feel foreign to therapists who may have learned to wait until the client is ready to discuss their trauma before engaging in conversation. For children with developmental trauma, however, if we wait, we may never have the conversation. Avoidance and dissociation are powerful strategies for avoiding pain. With limited ability to be aware or express their experiences, children with developmental trauma are stuck in not knowing. Open-ended questions are generally too difficult for children with developmental trauma and are usually met with the answer — 'I don't know'. In DDP, the therapist is active in helping the child discover what they know as well as discover new ways of knowing using curiosity and story-telling to find and organise the child's experiences.

> Child: We went to the beach yesterday, and I found all kinds of crabs and little fish. I even got to bring some crabs home in a bucket! They are out in the garage right now with some rocks and water. I am going to check on them later today.
>
> Therapist: (following).... You did! Wow, that sounds like a great day at the beach. What kind of crabs were they, do you know?
>
> Child: No: just little ones
>
> Therapist: Maybe it might be easier to care for little crabs rather than the big ones with big crab claws! What do you think?
>
> Child: Maybe. We have to figure out what they eat, I guess, and make sure we can give them the right food.
>
> Therapist: (leading) Good thinking! I love seeing how you are thinking about what the crabs need and having some help from your mom to get them what they need to eat. You are taking good care of them. I wonder if you are learning how to care for the crabs because you are starting to let your foster mom take care of you! I wonder! It hasn't always been easy for you to let your mom care for you. When you were little, I think you decided adults were no good at caring for kids, and you would just stop relying on adults. You did all the hard things all by yourself, didn't you?
>
> Child: (looking down, looking sad)
>
> Therapist: I see that even just remembering those times when you didn't have anyone to notice what you needed and wanted makes you sad. Maybe you even wondered if people weren't helping you because somehow you were not

a good enough kid to help.

Child: I want to read a book now.

Therapist: (following): Ahh, I love how you are telling me that thinking about when you were not cared for is hard work, and you need a break now! Good for you for letting me know a book is a better idea than thinking about all those times when you thought you might be a kid that is not worth looking after! What book will you pick? I wish I had one on crabs!

Talking for: Children with developmental trauma often lack the awareness or the skills to articulate what they might be feeling. They also carry with them the anxiety of what will happen in the relationship if they were to be vulnerable and speak their mind. In DDP, the therapist might *talk for* the child in such situations. The therapist first asks permission to speak for them and then adopts the child's voice — a first-person voice — to articulate what they might be thinking or feeling. The child can then experience how the therapist understands them as well as witness how their parent (or therapist) responds with understanding or empathy rather than the expected anger or indifference to their needs that may have been their experience in the past. The therapist is careful to express the child's experience in a way that the child is free to agree or disagree with it. In DDP, it is not the getting things *right* that is therapeutic, but the motivation and intention to understand the child. When we are curious about the child's inner life, it helps the child become aware of their thoughts and feelings and learns to feel that they are worth understanding. The adult is providing an experience of organisation.

If we return to the above example at the time when the child looks down, the therapist may have wanted to highlight the developing relationship between the child and the foster parent.

Therapist: Your mom has been telling me that it has been easier for you to let her take care of you lately. I imagine that might feel good and scary all at the same time. Could I take a guess at what you might want to say to your mom if you had the words?

Child: (nods)

Therapist: Okay, listen and let me know if I get anything wrong…. 'Mom, Sian is right. I do like it when you take care of me. But sometimes I get really scared that you will discover that I am just a bad kid and you won't want to take care of me anymore. When I get scared, I get mad at you and scream and yell. I think it's a way to make sure you don't get too close to see that I am just not worth being taken care of.' Did I get that right?

Child: (nods)

Therapist to foster parent: Could you just let your boy know right now how much courage he has to let you know about that huge worry? Can you also give him empathy for how hard it is to have that huge worry?

Talking About: Talking tends to increase the emotional intensity of a conversation. The child's inner world is expressed, which can create anxiety and fear. *Talking about* allows the therapist to continue the conversation or story-telling in a way that promotes reflection. The therapist might summarise what everyone has learned so far in the exploration of the event, highlight the child's courage in letting the adults know about his experience and add some meaning without expecting the child to engage in that conversation. The child is free to listen or play with one ear open to how the adults have come to understand them and learn something from the conversation. If emotion is too high, the capacity for reflection is diminished. Talking is a way to decrease the intensity and create safety for new learning when needed.

Therapist: Wow, we talked about some hard things today! First, we learned all about how fun it was on a beach and how tricky it was to look after crabs, and then your boy let us know that he has had times in his life when he wasn't looked after properly by the adults in his life. And that made it hard for him to trust you when he came to live with you. He thought you wouldn't be good at looking after him either and remember when he first came, he had to do everything by himself! Everything! Even when it was too hard for a kid who was only 6 years old. Then today, he let us talk about how he is learning to trust and then used that incredible courage he has to let us know he is really scared that if he lets you take care of him, you will discover that he isn't worth taking care of! Wow, what courage he has to take the risk to find out whether you will be like the first adults in his life or whether you might be different. Did you know your boy had so much courage?

Parent: (smiling) I am learning more about him every day, but yes, I knew he was a brave kid. I can't wait until he knows he is brave.

Therapist: Me neither!

Initiating Repair: Whenever two people are in connection, there will be times when we fall out of connection. It is unrealistic to maintain a connection at all times. We may fall out of connection when the therapist or parent fails to notice a need or change in emotional state quickly or sensitively enough, when the parent or therapist moves too quickly or too slowly, enters into problem-solving before a child is ready, or the parent or therapist gets defensive or loses acceptance for the child's experience. In healthy relationships, the parents recognise quite quickly — often unconsciously — the loss of connection and work hard to come back into synchronised and reciprocal interactions (Feldman, 2007; Stern, 1985). For many of our clients who have experienced developmental trauma, parents were too unwell themselves to notice when their child's needs were not being expressed or met and when there were ruptures in the relationship, parents may have blamed their child or been angry or uninterested, causing prolonged periods of disconnection. As mentioned earlier, disconnection creates trauma because it threatens our ability to survive.

It is always the adult's responsibility to initiate repair. In DDP, the therapist remains alert for times of disconnection, notices them, names that disconnection has occurred and initiates repair over and over again. In this way, the child learns that they are being noticed and that the therapist will slow down and not proceed further with any exploration until connection has been maintained. This repetitive process allows the child to develop trust in the therapist and parent that the state of distress that occurs from disconnection is noticed and addressed, and the relationship is brought back into a harmonious state.

> Child: (As the therapist is talking with the parent about his early experiences of neglect, the child crawls behind the chair).

> Therapist: Oh, I am so sorry, you are telling me, 'Stop having this conversation. It's too hard!' and I didn't stop in time, did I? You gave me some cues that you had had enough, and I missed them. I am so sorry. I need to work harder to see when you have had enough of talking about hard stuff!

> Child: (mumbling) It's okay.

> Therapist: I think you might want to say to me, 'Sian, I am upset with you, but I also don't want to make you angry, so I am going to say, 'It's okay'. Thank you for telling me you had enough. You might not be quite ready for my apology yet. Upset feelings can hang around for a while, can't they? I am going to work really hard not to miss those cues again'.

Touch as a tool for regulation: Providing comfort is often provided through touch. For many of our clients, touch has been painful or painfully absent and certainly not associated with comfort. Some clients engage physically with others in ways that make adults or peers uncomfortable or just stay away from physical interaction altogether. How can we help our clients receive a corrective experience of physical comfort without jeopardising their or the therapist's psychological safety?

Working dyadically allows the therapist to help the child receive a hug or physical comfort from their parent. This may be incremental — parents moving closer, putting a hand on their child's shoulder, holding their hand, giving them a hand or foot massage, arm over their shoulder and finally drawing them into a hug. The therapist asks for permission and monitors the child's ability to tolerate their parent's touch. The therapist helps organise for the child the deep desire for comfort coupled with the fear of such vulnerability and co-regulates the arising emotions with PACE.

If the child engages in promiscuous or inappropriate touch with others, the therapist notices, sets a limit and then wonders about what the child may be trying to communicate by their behaviour, using acceptance, curiosity and empathy. Often children have learned to keep adults happy by engaging provocatively, or they may be indiscriminate in their affection because they have never had a chance to develop a felt sense of safety with any one attachment figure.

Touch can also be introduced safely through play. When we work dyadically, we want to bring all aspects of a child's experience into relationships, not just the tough experiences. Playing together and enjoying each other is just as important as integrating traumatic experiences. The therapist may engage the parent and child in games where the child receives touch as an inherent part of the play. The therapist and parent may play tug of war with the child, always ensuring that the parent wins the fight; the parent might be asked to blow raspberries on the child's stomach if appropriate or draw on their back for the child to guess what is being drawn. So many of our clients have missed out on the somatic experiences and coordinated movements that are involved in how we play with infants, toddlers and young children. Theraplay (Booth & Jernberg, 2009), a model of child and family therapy, aims to strengthen the child's attachment to their parent through playful, nurturing, physical and mutually enjoyable activities. It can be a wonderful way to help a child and parent learn how to engage with one another in safe, enjoyable ways and can be integrated very successfully with DDP.

We might also imagine comforting touch. If the therapist does not have another adult in the room to ensure safety or the child is not yet comfortable enough to receive physical touch, the child or dyad may be asked to close their eyes and imagine the interaction. We can explore quite effectively through imagination, and it has a reciprocal effect on parent and child. For the child, they can have the safety to just imagine and can be in control of how much or little they want to think about receiving touch. For the parent, it allows them to complete their intention for caring. A child's rejection of a parent's attempt to offer care can lead to blocked care. Imagining the how, when and where of providing physical comfort can help the parent sustain hope and lessen the pain of the rejection.

In summary, DDP is a framework that focuses on first creating relational safety using nonverbal communication such as tone, frequency, rhythm of voice, facial expressions and body language. The therapist creates the safety in the same way good enough parents do. Once that safety is established, the child is more open to making sense of their experiences, whether past, present or future. PACE is a way of being that says we can be close without fear, and the invitation into an A/R dialogue deepens the intersubjective experience allowing the child to learn more about themselves and others. DDP allows for the integration of different therapy modalities (e.g., neurofeedback, Eye Movement Desensitization and Reprocessing [EMDR], theraplay, and trauma-informed cognitive behavioural therapy). It provides the foundation for healing through the relationship.

Dyadic Developmental Psychotherapy Practice

Over the past 10 years, DDP has developed as a Practice. DDP Practice is an application of the core principles of the DDP therapeutic intervention, applied to different settings and for different adults who come into contact with children who have experienced developmental trauma but do not necessarily see the child in a therapeutic setting (e.g., teachers, doctors, health professionals). Children with complex needs are in connection with many different adults, not just therapists. DDP Practice aims to help all of those adults understand how trauma impacts a child's development and current behaviour and respond in ways that co-regulate the child rather than in ways that add stress. Both PACE as a way of being and the creation of intersubjectivity through the A/R dialogue are useful in classrooms, day-care centres, residential treatment programs, emergency departments, and hospital programs where adults can be therapeutic in their interactions without engaging in therapy.

The focus in DDP Practice is helping adults create safety and provide co-regulation while also providing limits and consequences that help the child learn what it means to be in healthy relationships. The way we help adults create safety and set limits is similar to the ways described below in DDP-Informed Parenting, when the therapist or practitioner helps a parent respond in ways that prioritise the relationship and feel a sense of safety.

DDP-Informed Parenting

DDP-Informed Parenting is an extension of the DDP therapeutic intervention that provides a framework for parents using DDP principles in the day-to-day parenting of their child. Just like in Dyadic Developmental Practice, helping parents parent with a PACEful attitude is also an important part of creating environments that feel safer so that new behaviours can emerge. Parents are helped to understand the necessity of parenting with 'two hands'. The first hand provides the PACE that is needed to communicate that the parent understands and empathises with the child's distress. PACE helps the parent co-regulate the child, bringing them back into connection and preparing them for any follow on that might be required regarding their behaviour. The second hand is the limit-setting/consequence-giving hand. Parents are helped to understand that limits and consequences are an essential part of helping children learn but not what is going to change the behaviour. So often, parents believe that consequences have to hurt to *teach* kids to do or not to do something. The DDP-Informed therapist helps the parent understand that discipline is about learning and does not have to hurt.

When limits and consequences are given, we want them to create greater success and safety for a child. For example, a parent may tell their toddler that they can not go to the park as planned because they are having a hard day, and the fear would be that when they are having a hard day, it is harder to listen. The parent would stress that listening is so important for keeping them safe, and it would be better to wait until the parent is sure that the toddler can listen to the rules about crossing the road, climbing and swinging. The parent stresses that the outing would not be successful for the child, versus the child can't go to the park because they are being punished. In the latter version of this particular consequence, the child may feel that the problem lies with them and their experience is not important to the adult. They are then likely to respond negatively or experience more shame in the face of the parent's disapproval. In the first version of the example, the parent wants the child to succeed and makes the decision that going to the park would lead to additional trouble, which would not be good for their child. The child then learns that adult limit setting is in their best interest and begins to trust the parent's intentions and motivation. With many repetitions, the child hopefully can feel safe enough to relinquish the control they believe is essential to their survival.

Secondly, we want our consequences to be reparative and help the child return to connection with others. For example, a parent might say, 'When you were upset just now, you said some really hurtful things to your brother, and I think he may not want to play with you for a while. Do you have any ideas about how to apologise when he is ready to accept an apology? Don't worry if you don't have an idea; I can help you.' If a child has broken something, how can they contribute to fixing it? Children with developmental trauma have no practice in making things better. We can use DDP principles to help them learn that mistakes don't have to lead to loss of a relationship and that relationships can withstand disagreements and hurts.

Thirdly, we want consequences to be relational. Wherever possible, we encourage parents and other adults to make both incentives and consequences relational. Children will be most successful when their parents provide more supervision and more co-regulation. Children with developmental trauma do not yet have the capacity for effective self-regulation, so asking them to figure it out themselves is likely to be a distressing experience for the child who wants to do better but can't and for the parent who might feel inadequate because they can't make their child listen. The DDP-Informed parenting practitioner or therapist helps parents recognise that if kids could do better, they would and that the child needs to rely on their parent's skill at co-regulating their emotions.

For relational consequences to work, the parent obviously has to be regulated themselves. A dysregulated adult will never regulate a child. The parent may need to initiate a time-out for themselves first before offering a time-in for their child. This may sound like, 'Oh wow, we are really struggling, aren't we? You want to have more screen time, and I feel like you have had enough, and more isn't good for you. We are really disagreeing, aren't we? Give me 5 minutes to figure out how to help us figure this out. Let me see what I can come up with to help.' This statement conveys that the relationship is strained at that moment, and it is the parent's intention to help the relationship come back to a more comfortable experience. It gives the parent time to regulate so that they are in a better position to co-regulate their child's upset. It also prioritises connection over compliance, which will, with repetition, make it more likely that the child wants to comply.

In summary, whether in DDP Practice or DDP-Informed Parenting with DDP principles, the caregiver is helped to:

1. Use two hands for caring responses: PACE and limit setting in balance communicates, 'I understand, value, and have empathy for your experience, *and* I will help you follow the rules or expectations.'.

2. Understand and accept the emotional experience that lies beneath behaviour rather than focus on the behaviour.

3. Understand that the child's underlying intention is to be well. They are not 'choosing' to behave inappropriately when their nervous system has decided they are threatened.

4. Prioritise connection before correction or compliance (unless there is an immediate safety issue where compliance is essential).

5. Understand that co-regulation must precede self-regulation.

6. Repair the relationship with the child following any upset, limit setting or consequences.

7. Help the child repair relationships or contribute to fixing what is or feels broken with others who may have been impacted by their upset.

Cultural and Relational Humility

Establishing a felt sense of safety is at the core of DDP. PACE and A/R dialogue gives us a map of how to create that relational safety. However, DDP has historically been very euro-centric and based on research that prioritises a Western way of knowing. This has caused harm to children, families, therapists and practitioners who are not part of the white, privileged culture. One of the responsibilities of the DDP clinician is to understand how the clients and families they work with may have experienced generations of oppression, discrimination and marginalisation that is inherent in colonised countries. Great harm continues to be perpetrated when we do not understand how the white way of knowing and being discounts and devalues any other ways of knowing or being.

In Canada, as in Australia, we struggle with the great harm white people have inflicted on Indigenous people and communities. What must it be like to be Indigenous and seek help from a white clinician that represents the culture and systems that have caused the trauma that they suffer from? Similarly, black people or people of colour have experienced implicit and explicit forms of racism every day, many times a day, by those of the privileged white culture. Individuals who have been marginalised for their culture, gender identity, sexual orientation, religious beliefs and practices, and cognitive or physical abilities will be sceptical that clinicians who represent the people and systems that have caused harm can be helpful and will likely implicitly, if not explicitly, expect that further harm will come from being in relationship with their clinician who clearly has a different lived experience.

Creating safety for all clients will require the clinician to commit to learning about their own implicit biases that get in the way of creating safety. Our practice must be an anti-discriminatory and anti-oppressive practice. We must make it safe to explore and accept all ways of knowing and ensure that intervention is sensitive to each client's lived experience.

Evidence Base

As a relatively new model of therapy for families struggling with developmental trauma, DDP does not yet have the support of a randomised control study. This is currently underway in the United Kingdom, spearheaded by Patricia Minnis, a Professor of Child and Adolescent Psychiatry at the University of Glasgow. The clinicians that practice DDP provide many anecdotes about the power of this model to help children and parents find more pleasure in each other and find new expectancies for relationships. A qualitative study indicates that DDP is a powerful way of working with families (Wingfield & Smith, 2017). Other studies have identified a positive impact of DDP Practice in education (Phillips, Melim & Hughes, 2020) and in DDP-Informed Parenting groups (Golding & Alper, 2016).

Who DPP Suits

DDP, whether psychotherapy, DDP Practice or DDP-Informed Parenting, is suitable for all families, not just those struggling with developmental trauma. It will, however, not work well as a family therapy when the parent or parents are unresolved in their own trauma and are not yet able to respond to the therapist's attempts to provide emotional safety. Without that safety, the therapist would not invite the child into the work. The therapist may work with another adult — an auntie, a key residential worker or a teacher — as an attachment figure for the child or work with the child individually. DDP may also not be possible for children who are still so dysregulated and fearful of relationships. For these children, we may need to start with more bottom-up approaches such as neurofeedback, sensory integration work with an occupational therapist or Sensorimotor Psychotherapy. Relational safety with the therapist will be essential in any therapy.

Training

Training in DDP is provided by trainers who have been certified by DDP-WorldWide (formally known as Dyadic Developmental Psychotherapy). There are two levels of training; the first level introduces the trainee to the basic principles of DDP and gives the opportunity to learn DDP Practice and DDP-informed Parenting during the 28-hour course. A second level of training provides the opportunity to become more proficient in the model, utilising role-plays, clinical videos and discussion to build the trainee's knowledge and confidence in using the principles of DDP. The second level of training is also 28 hours and provided over four days if training is in person and 5 days of online training. Training groups are small (24–27 participants for level one and 15–18 for level two) so that participants can access effective feedback from the trainer. In Australia, DDP is championed by Compass Australia, and training is provided regularly throughout the year. The cost of this training in Australia is typically $2000. Other one-day trainings may also be available as a brief introduction to the model. There are trainings provided worldwide, and these trainings can be found on the website DDPnetwork.org.

After 56 hours of training, a clinician may apply to a practicum process. Currently, this involves working with a certified DDP consultant in a competency-based process — akin to having a personal trainer. With consent of the client and organisation, the clinician videotapes their work to review with their consultant. The consultant provides feedback that helps the trainee develop a greater understanding of the principles of DDP and greater confidence and independence in the use of the model. At the end of this process, the trainee is certified as a DDP practitioner. This process typically takes between 12 and 18 months. Individuals may continue to deepen their learning through the consultant practicum, where they begin to provide support to practitioners. Certification is also available for trainers and organisations. Not everyone may wish to enter a formal practicum process. Supervision is available to any clinician at any point of learning — both individually or through study or supervision groups. Consultants can be found on DDPnetwork.org. Given that DDP is a relational model, the learning of this therapy model is best done in a relationship with a mentor or others who are learning and practising.

Conclusion

DDP, whether in its traditional psychotherapy form or utilised in its practice form or by parents, provides a framework for creating the relational safety needed to develop trust and greater security in attachments with caregivers. With greater safety, the child is helped to integrate past traumatic experiences so that those experiences no longer inhibit learning in all aspects of their development. The experiences and needs of children with developmental trauma are complex. DDP works well as a foundation for treatment and can also be integrated with other models of treatment such as theraplay, Sensorimotor Psychotherapy, Neurofeedback, EMDR, art and movement therapies and, when the child is ready, Cognitive Behaviour Therapy.

DDP is in the early stages of building a body of empirical research. Information about the journey towards this goal can be accessed in Hughes et al. (2019) and on the website DDPnetwork.org. Clinicians who practice DDP are also expanding the use of the model beyond children with developmental trauma to ensure that the model provides safety for LGBTQIA+, BIPOC (Black, Indigenous, and people of colour) individuals and communities, Indigenous youth and families and individuals from all cultures and religions.

The efficacy of DDP is dependent upon having adult caretakers that are sufficiently regulated so that they can recognise and be responsive to the child's needs, either independently or with the help of the therapist. Parents who remain unresolved in their own trauma will continue to be focused on potential threats to their own survival and be unable to meet their children's needs.

DDP as a psychotherapy also works best for children who are three years and over and who cognitively are able to engage in ways that allow for a co-creation of a more coherent narrative. For the child who is two and under, the focus may be more on helping parents parent from a DDP perspective, focusing on meeting the emotional needs that are informing the behaviour. DDP Practice may also be a focus to help day-care providers, educators or other caregivers to provide the safety in the child's environment that the child needs to learn.

DDP principles and interventions are grounded in the theoretical underpinnings of attachment theory, neuroscience research and intersubjectivity theory. The model continues to be responsive to the growing literature that discovers how trauma impacts all aspects of our humanness and ensures that the interventions reflect the theoretical underpinnings as well as responsive to the uniqueness of every individual and relationship.

Reader's Exercises

Practice leading with acceptance of the child or parent's emotional experience and empathy for the struggle. What do you notice in your child or client when you slow down in this way and delay problem-solving? What do you notice in yourself?

A parent says to you: 'My child deliberately makes me mad. I think he hates me.' How might you respond PACEfully?

1. 'Oh, I don't think he hates you. Kids love their parents. They don't always show it.'

2. 'Really? Are you sure?'

3. 'That must be so hard to feel your kid hates you. I can't imagine that was what you hoped for in your relationship with your son.'

4. 'When he makes you mad, what is happening in the family? Is there something that makes him upset?'

5. 'How do you respond when he provokes you?'

The parents of a 5-year-old have recently separated. There were many verbal arguments in the family leading up to the separation, which the child witnessed. The family sold their home and each parent lives in an apartment and shares custody of the child who spends Monday, Wednesday and Thursday with their mother and Tuesday , Friday and Saturday with their father. Sundays alternate between parents. The parents report to you that their child, who was once 'easy-going', has become 'anxious' and 'difficult' and needs therapy. How might you use PACE to help the parents become more aware of the child's emotional experiences that underly behaviour? Write some possible responses using each letter of PACE as your guide.

Try your phrases with a colleague paying attention to how your voice sounds and whether you have soft eyes and relaxed facial expression. Have your colleague give you feedback on how our delivery feels to them.

References

Ainsworth, M. S., Blehar, M. C., Waters, E., & Wall, S. (1978) *Patterns of attachment: A psychological study of the strange situation.* Lawrence Erlbaum.

Baylin, J., & Hughes, D. A. (2016). *The neurobiology of attachment-focused therapy: Enhancing connection and trust in the treatment of children and adolescents.* W W Norton & Co.

Beebe, B., & Lachmann, F. (2013). *The origins of attachment: Infant research and adult treatment.* Routledge.

Bernier, A., Dégeilh, F., Leblanc, É., Daneault, V., & Beauchamp, M.H. (2019). Mother–infant interaction and child brain morphology: A multidimensional approach to maternal sensitivity. *Infancy, 24,* 120–138. https://doi.org/10.1111/infa.12270

Booth, P. B., & Jernberg, A. (2009). *Theraplay: Helping parents and children build better relationships through attachment-based play.* Wiley.

Bowlby, J. (1969) *Attachment and Loss: Volume 1 Attachment.* Basic Books.

Coan, J. A. (2016). Towards a neuroscience of attachment. In J. Cassidy & P.R. Shaver (Eds) *Handbook of Attachment (3rd ed).* Guilford.

Cook, A., Blaustein, M., Spinazzola, J., & van der Kolk, B. Eds., (2003). *Complex trauma in children and adolescents: White paper.* National Child Traumatic Stress Network. Retrieved July 2005 from http://www.NCTSN.org/

Feldman, R. (2007). Parent-infant synchrony and the construction of shared timing; physiological precursors, developmental outcomes and risk conditions. *Journal of Child Psychology and Psychiatry, 48* (3–4), 329–354. https://doi.org/10.1111/j.1469-7610.2006.01701.x

Fonagy, P., Gergely, G., Jurist, E., & Target, M. (2002). *Affect regulation, mentalisation and the development of self.* Other Press.

Fonagy, P., Steele, M., Steele, H., Moran, G.S., & Higgitt, A.C. (1991). The capacity for understanding mental states: The reflective self in parent and child and its significance for security of attachment. *Infant Mental Health Journal, 12,* 201–218.
https://psycnet.apa.org/doi/10.1002/1097-0355(199123)12:3%3C201::AID-IMHJ2280120307%3E3.0.CO;2-7

Golding , K.S., & Alper, J., (2016) *A quantitative and qualitative evaluation of the Nurturing Attachments group work programme across four geographical sites* (Summary Report). Retrieved from http:/tiny.cc/mywafy

Holt-Lunstad, J., Smith, T. B., & Layton, J. B. (2010). Social relationships and mortality risk: A meta-analytic review. *PLoS Medicine,* 2010. https://doi.org/10.1371/ journal.pmed.1000316

Hughes, D. A. (2000). *Facilitating developmental attachment: The road to emotional recovery and behavioural change in foster and adopted children.* Jason Aronson Inc.

Hughes, D. A., & Baylin, J. (2012): *Brain-based parenting: The neuroscience of caregiving for healthy attachment.* Norton Professional Books.

Hughes, D.A., Golding, K.S., & Hudson, J. (2019). *Healing relational trauma with attachment focused interventions: Dyadic Developmental Psychotherapy with children and families.* W.W. Norton & Co.

Jaffe, J., Beebe, B., Feldstein, S., Crown, C., & Jasnow, M. (2001). Rhythms of dialogue in infancy. *Monographs of the Society for Research in Child Development, 66,* 1–132.

Main M., & Solomon J. (1986). Discovery of a new, insecure disorganised/disoriented attachment pattern In Yogman M. & Brazelton T. B. (Eds.), *Affective development in infancy* (pp. 95–124). NAblex.

Main, M., & Solomon J. (1990). Procedures for identifying infants as disorganised/disoriented during the Ainsworth strange situation. In: Greenberg MT, Cicchetti D, editors. *Attachment in the preschool years: Theory, research, and intervention* (pp. 121–160). University of Chicago Press.

Phillips, S., Melim, D., & Hughes, D. (2020). *Belonging: A relationship-based approach for trauma-informed education.* Rowman and Littlefield.

Porges, S. W. (2011). *The Polyvagal Theory: Neurophysiological foundations of emotions, attachment, communication and self-regulation.* Norton Professional Books.

Pratt, M., Zeev-Wolf, M., Goldstein, A., & Feldman, R. (2019). Exposure to early and persistent maternal depression impairs the neural basis of attachment in preadolescence. *Progress in Neuro-Psychopharmacology and Biological Psychiatry 93,* 21–30. https://doi.org/10.1016/j.pnpbp.2019.03.005

Shore, A. N. (1994). *Affect regulation and the repair of the self.* Norton Professional Books.

Shore, A. N. (2013). *The science of the art of psychotherapy.* Norton Professional Books.

Stern, D. (1985). *The interpersonal world of the infant.* Basic Books.

Stern, D. (2004). *The present moment in psychotherapy and everyday life.* Norton Books.

Trevarthen, C., & Aitken, K. J. (2001). Infant intersubjectivity: Research, theory, and clinical applications. *Journal of Child Psychology and Psychiatry, 42,* 3–48. https://doi.org/10.1111/1469-7610.00701

Wingfield M., & Gurney-Smith B. (2019). Adoptive parents' experiences of dyadic developmental psychotherapy. *Clinical Child Psychology and Psychiatry, 24*(4):661–679. doi:10.1177/1359104518807737

Woodhouse, S. S., Scott, J.R., Hepworth, A. D. & Cassidy, J. (2019). Secure base provision: A new approach to examining links between maternal caregiving and infant attachment. *Child Development, 91*, e249-e265. https://doi.org/10.1111/cdev.13224

Chapter 11

Watch, Wait, and Wonder (WWW)

Denise Guy and Marion Doherty

Watch, Wait, and Wonder (WWW) is an infant/child-led dyadic psychotherapeutic intervention drawing on attachment research and relational theories derived from the field of psychoanalysis. It uniquely places the infant/child in an active central role in every therapy session. Parents are supported in observing, to become more knowing of them. In the first part of the session, the parent is given a number of instructions about following their child's lead and not taking over the child's activity: to be attentive and non-intrusive. This is followed by a discussion with the parent supporting them in noting their observations of the child's play, their responses to the play and the child's relationship with them. They are invited to wonder about the communication from their child, the experience and the anxieties felt when following their child's lead. The child remains in the space with ongoing access to the toys and to their parent.

The intervention is used when the difficulties for the child, the parent and the relationship are distressing and serious, and developmental progress for the child and the relationship is compromised. Offered in the office/clinical setting, in the home and more recently online, weekly or fortnightly, beginning with eight sessions and finishing after sixteen to eighteen sessions. Where parents come to this work with their own significant childhood adversity, therapy may continue through twenty-four to thirty sessions. WWW has an evidence base supporting its capacity to improve the child's self-regulation, cognitive development and attachment security, and parents' levels of depression and sense of competency in their parenting (Cohen et al., 1999; Cohen et al., 2002). The dyadic parent–child relationship is the focus of the work described, but the influence of culture, social environment, biological factors and the parental relationship are considered and incorporated into assessment, formulation and intervention planning. In this chapter the clinical work is typically describing mothers and young children. However, WWW has been successfully implemented with fathers, grandparents, kin and non-kin caregivers. The intervention has also been used with older children (5–9 years) (Muir et al., 1999).

History

Jerry Dowling, a Psychiatrist and Clinical Director of an Infant/Toddler program in Milwaukee writing in 1985 to Elisabeth Muir, a Child Psychotherapist, shared the three articles describing the origins of the infant/child-led dyadic work that became WWW. Dowling and his team were interested in the Mahrer, Levinson and Fine (1976) review of the available infant therapy literature. These authors had produced intervention goals for the infant that they felt were not being attended to because the parent/therapist was typically initiating and would at times over-ride the infant. They suggested the infant be the stimulating, activating resource for parents and set up instructions to prioritise the infant's initiatives. Johnson et al. (1980), Wesner et al. (1982), and Ostrov et al. (1982), clinicians working in Milwaukee, Wisconsin, developed this into the dyadic technique they called WWW.

They tried to keep the instructions simple for their parents. 'Don't start anything and don't take over any infant and/or child activity; observe and follow your child's lead.' The children were aged from 3 months to 3 years. Play sessions varied in number, typically twice a week and from 5–90 minutes, depending on the age of the child (Dowling, 1985). There was no formal evaluation of the outcome but the majority of over one hundred mothers self-reported benefiting from their participation. Verbal responses (Wesner et al., 1982) included being comfortable with their child developmentally, enjoying the activity, infants and toddlers becoming less demanding, less clinging, and parents learning about development from their child.

Muir and Stupples (1986), child psychotherapists working in the Under Fives Service in Dunedin, New Zealand, were interested in the potential for work with young children and their parents where there were worries for the relationship. At that time, the Queen Mary Research Project in Dunedin (Monaghan et al., 1986) was successfully identifying vulnerable/at-risk families and directing them to group programs (Squirrel and Acorn Clubs) with some encouraging results. These programs did not include interventions focused on the parent–infant relationship.

Muir looked to WWW as a possible intervention. It seemed to be a simple technique, easy to conduct, potentially brief, portable, and economical to set up. It made use of a setting such as a playroom where the activity could approximate the natural activity of the child within the home setting. Although intervention could happen at different points in the system, it seemed appropriate systemically that the parent, generally the mother, was provided with the means to be the agent of change. This was an intervention that took place directly within the interactional processes between mother and child (Muir et al., 1989).

With the support of Dowling, a pilot study following guidelines set up by the Milwaukee team was planned. Weekly sessions were filmed with a maximum of 30 minutes in child-led play. It also introduced a critical change to the WWW approach developed by Johnson and colleagues (Johnson et al., 1980; Ostrov et al., 1982; Wesner et al., 1982).

A discussion with the parent, with their child present, was deliberately added. This phase in the intervention was at least as long as the child-led play part. Other programmes within the Under Fives service offered opportunities for mothers to watch their children through the one-way screen. Muir and Stupples consistently observed how anxious mothers became when observing their children's play and behaviour with other children and staff. The experience raised anxieties about their mothering and what the child might expose about them in the play. The opportunity to discuss what they had seen had been helpful in containing these anxieties and a space for this was easily incorporated in the study. It also provided an opportunity to review this new intervention. Mothers were asked what their impressions of the session had been, what they had observed in their children's play and whether any changes were occurring in their child's relationships and/or their symptomatic behaviour.

There were cogent learnings that guided the development of the intervention. Therapists needed to follow the parents' observational lead — to see the child the parent saw. In one of the first pilot cases the toddler was described by his mother as having little concentration and not able to play constructively. The therapist had observed the toddler to be building block towers in a focused way and commented on this to his mother. When asked to share what she had seen, the block towers had not been noticed, and she did not respond to the therapist's comments. She was not able to see this capacity in her child until later in the therapy. Our therapeutic role was to keep our observations to ourselves. This was one aspect of the WWW stance which emphasised not getting in the way of the parent–child relationship, following and not impinging.

The pilot study was run beginning with six sessions with the option of a further six, and by the fourth session there were consistent reports of improvements in the presenting problems. The mothers expressed increased satisfaction and pleasure in their children (age range 18 months–4 years) and more confidence in their maternal role.

The findings from the pilot study launched the clinical developments described in the WWW Manual (Muir et al., 1999), addressing this child-led approach to problems in infancy and early childhood and underpinned the focus of the research evaluations.

Theory of Change

As with other infant parent interventions, the theoretical and research frameworks around caregiving behaviour and representations and the developing attachment relationship of the infant and young child, have been central to understanding the clinical process of the intervention and the research findings. A key research finding was that WWW was effective in facil-itating significant change from a disorganised to an organised attachment pattern and that improvements were sustained at 6-month follow-up (Cohen et al., 1999; Cohen et al,. 2002).

It was hypothesised that the instructions for parents to follow their child's lead and that supporting a therapeutic space that made this possible initiated parental change at the behavioural level. Progress in watching and observing in the 'here and now' of the room, at the pace of the dyad, sees parental improve-ments in tracking sequences of play and being with their child for longer periods. There is a reduction in withdrawn or disengaged behaviour. These changes, along with less intrusiveness, supports improved attunement and less abrupt misattunement, and is seen in improved sensitivity in care.

Ainsworth et al. (1978) postulated that maternal sensitive responsiveness to the infant's signals and communications was critical to the development of secure attachment. However, a meta-analysis of over four thousand mother-infant dyads (De Wolff & Van Ijzendoorn, 1997) found the link between maternal and infant attachment that is transmitted via maternal sensitivity/responsiveness was small ($r = 0.24$). Furthermore, the subsequent meta-analysis looking at parental sensitivity and disorganised attachment (Van Ijzendoorn et al., 1999) found a very small effect size. It seems unlikely therefore, that improved maternal sensitivity is a complete explanation for the efficacy of this interven-tion and the changes noted in children, parents and the dyadic relationship.

Cohen et al. (2002) additionally hypothesised that the changes in WWW may occur at the representational level as a consequence of the discussion with the parent of the observations and experience. They noted that this discussion supported parents to reflect on their child's inner experience, a process that would allow the development of reflective capacity. There was no formal assessment of parental reflection pre-and post-intervention.

The possibility that parental reflective function (RF), to think reflectively about their child, themselves as a parent and the relationship with their child, is improved with WWW is pertinent. RF was the term introduced by Fonagy et al. (1998) and developed from their research addressing intergenerational transmission of attachment and parental capacity for understanding mental states. The capacity to interpret behaviour in light of underlying mental states such as needs, desires, feelings, beliefs, goals, purposes and reasons, is mentalising. RF is mentalising in an operationalised form, and the two terms are often used interchangeably. Mentalising is necessary for optimal social relationships, is central to an individual's ability to regulate behaviour and emotions and is a determinant in the development of an integrated sense of self. Mentalising makes other people's behaviour understandable and predictable and is protective in managing traumatic experiences. Higher levels of maternal RF are associated with secure infant attachment. Lower levels of RF are associated with insecure organised attachment patterns, and the lowest levels of RF are associated with disorganised attachment in infants (Grienenberger et al., 2005).

Findings from the WWW research lend support to the hypothesis that this intervention improves parental RF, specifically the shift in attachment from disorganisation to an organised secure or insecure pattern. The significant improvement in children's self-regulation and cognitive development may also be a consequence of parents' enhanced capacity to think about the child's internal world; to mentalise. There are aspects to the clinical practice of WWW that allow a parent to develop their capacity to mentalise their child, themselves and the relationship. As noted by Barlow et al. (2021), the intervention specifically encourages a parental reflection stance but this theorising requires further research. A beginning was made when Guy et al. (2014) looked at transcribed discussions from eight completed interventions and highlighted increased examples of RF from that seen at the first session and then at the last session.

Giving the child the opportunity to experience himself feeling and thinking in his mother's presence without having to react to external impingements, as Winnicott described 'to flounder' (Winnicott, 1958), and, to then see in the play that develops, the child communicating to their parent something of the relationship problem (Muir, 1992), is a stance focused on the child's mind, on their intentionality. The child has the opportunity in session after session to develop the stories they want their parent to understand.

Alongside this, the parent is developing their capacity to wait, to self-regulate, and in doing this, becomes less reactive. Many parents highlight finding this place of slowing down and waiting as a key learning with the WWW work. Therapists support waiting by attending to the instructions and, over time, focusing on those that are hardest for a parent to follow, finding words that help the parent to persist.

The therapeutic work is in the 'here and now', what is being observed and felt within the session. The regulated parent observes more of what has happened in the play and their observations are richer and more balanced. Parents are attuning to their child's interests. This allows the child, over time, to be without the impingement and/or need to be vigilant to their parent's dysregulation. The relationship between the parent and their child is protected. It is not the therapist's knowing/not-knowing about the child's mind but the time given to supporting a parent to observe, become curious and wonder about their child's thoughts, feelings and intentions that is critical.

Clinical Illustration: Lily and her Mother

The following description is provided to indicate the way in which a parent moves into reflection that hypothetically drives some of the changes in the intervention, including reducing disorganisation. During the discussion in the middle phase of therapy Mum was talking about the play her daughter (3.5 years) had done, and it led her to connect what she had seen in the session with behaviour at home and whether that behaviour had any relationship to her own mood and her daughter's mood. This puzzling potentially led to more attuned and less scary care of her daughter. She had described her daughter's play as 'more organised'. Her daughter had set up the doll's house with two dolls in a room with a table and chairs, one chair being placed in a corner facing away.

> Mother: Sometimes at home Lily goes away and curls up on a chair in the corner. I wondered if she does it when she's worrying about me, cause I've been so upset these last few months cause she's not very old and she doesn't know why I'm crying she just gets worried I guess...

And later in the same discussion there is a direct interaction with her child who has approached her twice with irritable vocalisations 'ahh, ahh, ahh'. Mum had moved off the floor onto a chair during the discussion. There is another approach, and Lily has hold of her mother's hand.

> Mother: (lets go of her daughter's hand) What do you want me to do? Why are you pulling me? What do you want me to do? Where do you want Mummy to be. Talk to me sweetie.
>
> Lily: (really pulling) Urghh.
>
> Mother: Eh?
>
> Lily: (has moved away but looking back at Mum, comes back and grabs both of Mum's hands) URGHH.
>
> Mother: Talk to me. What are you feeling angry about? What's the matter L, what's the matter? You're frustrated aren't you? Want Mummy to play do you?

Lily: Want you to play Mummy. (almost completely settled)

Mother: Oh, okay.

Lily: There. Mummy, Mummy here.

Mum moved to the floor, positioned herself close to her daughter, where she was able to have direct eye contact with her and talk with the Therapist. L was singing. This mother's capacity to keep puzzling about her daughter's irritable vocalisations and pulling behaviour, allowed her to identify different feelings her daughter was having and what they might mean so that between the two of them they found a solution that shifted her daughter's emotional distress to enjoyment (singing) and she could find her words.

Assessment

Assessment typically begins with sessions including all family members, and interviews are designed to firstly understand the current concerns the parents have about their infant or young child. Secondly, the family relationships are explored, and we obtain a developmental history of the referred child and family histories for each parent. Finally, a structured assessment of the parent-child interaction is filmed. Depending on the presentation and concerns raised, each parent may be filmed separately in interaction with their child. This assessment, when the WWW intervention is being considered, begins, like many filmed assessments, with 5 minutes of unstructured play. For an older child (5–8 years) we extend this to 10 minutes. The parent is asked to play with their child as they would at home, so we get a sense of how their child plays and a picture of how they interact. We acknowledge that filming makes it different and it may feel stressful. This captures the nature of the relationship at the time of assessment. It is these first five minutes of play along with the history that enables clinicians to complete the Axis II Relationship Classification using the Diagnostic Classification of Mental Health and Developmental Disorders of Infancy and Early Childhood: Revised Edition (DC: 0-3R; Zero to Three, 2005) and/or the Zero to Five: Diagnostic Classification of Mental Health and Developmental Disorders of Infancy and Early Childhood (DC: 0-5 ; Zero to Five, 2016).

Parents are then asked to be on the floor with their child, to follow their child's lead, not initiate or take over the play. This gives us information about the parent's capacity to allow the child to initiate, whether they can follow even for a short time, and what does this parent's following look like? What does the child do when able to lead, do they show what may be missing in the relationship? Do they play out anything that relates to their symptoms? In attempting to follow their child, what seems to be the more difficult play or behaviour for this parent?

Parents are then asked about each 5-minute sequence separately and this is also filmed. For example, the parent is asked to think back to the first 5 minutes when asked to play as they usually would at home and answer a series of questions, including whether this 5 minutes was how it usually would be and if not, in what way was it different? What did they observe about their child's play, and what did they think their child was feeling? The second sequence of play is asked about, including differences between the two episodes and whether this parent was aware of any difficulty following the instructions.

This discussion is a shift from the assessment described in the Manual. It allows clinicians to think about the parent's capacity to observe (watch), to follow at least for a short time (wait) and to think about mental states in their child and themselves (wonder). There is no requirement for the parent to be managing watching, waiting and wondering at this time. We may hear one observation and it may not be congruent with our own but it is a beginning. We may see 30 seconds of following before a parent intrudes or absents herself and it may be very difficult for a parent to think about the feelings. This information guides formulation and intervention planning.

Clinical Case Assessment: Gai and Clare

Gai, and her 3-year-old daughter Clare were referred by a community adult mental health service. Gai was worried that her mental health difficulties were impacting her child. She did not want to repeat the parenting she had had as a child which had been frightening with lots of anger, family violence and abuse, and no memories of being cared for and thought about. The first year was difficult, with Gai having post-natal depression and Clare not sleeping well. Support for Gai was primarily from friends.

Gai was Māori, and the cultural advisor working on the case noted that although she knew her iwi affiliation, she quickly changed the topic when asked about it. When this was explored further, it became clear that she had lost practical support from both immediate and wider whānau as well as a sense of connection and identity — whanaungatanga (a glossary of Māori words and phrases is included on page 298).

She described spending a lot of time thinking about how to respond to her daughter, to not react and repeat her own parenting and that her parenting felt mechanical as a consequence. Within this preoccupation over how to parent, Gai noted that her daughter was having more tantrums and being put in her bedroom to calm her down was more distressing for her daughter. Gai was not sure she was the best person to be parenting her daughter.

The WWW interactional film was the opportunity to observe and talk about the relationship. It had been difficult to attend to Clare before this with Gai's story dominating the assessment. Gai had struggled with describing her daughter and their relationship. Clare was in full time day care and the Early Childhood staff described her as 'bright, helpful and developing well'.

In the 'Play as you would at home instructions.' (The first 90 seconds)

Clare: began saying *baby* as she sat by the cot containing two dolls.

Gai: *Is there a baby? ... Do you think the baby wants a bottle?*

Claire:. *Yeah*

Gai: (moving to the head of the cot).

Clare: (Holding the bottle and waving it towards mum)

Gai: *And what does the baby say*?

Clare: (Waved the bottle uncertainly). *Here.*

Gai: *Just pretend, you don't need real milk in it. Just pretend. It's not a real baby. Shall we put the bottle down here?* (she tapped the floor).

Clare: (Turned and looked at the therapist and then sat with her back to her mum in front of the tea set).

Gai: (leaning forward over her with more questions). *Shall we have a cup of tea?... Can you make me a cup of tea? There's the teapot.*

Clare: (Found a cup, pretended to pour from the teapot, and handed mum the cup).

Gai: (suddenly pulled back) *It's boiling.*

Clare: (Looking worried, dropped her head and pushed the cooking utensils around the mat in an unfocused way).

There were further examples of this Mum's struggle with pretend and real; the plastic knife became real 'Cut, cut, cut' she said in a harsh whisper. She asked to be fed on another two occasions when Clare had just moved to pick up different toys and this brought her daughter's focus back on her.

Gai thought this was like play at home. 'Yes, she was playing as in real life. A bit different cause I let her play more on her own'. 'She wanted to keep me involved by keeping looking back at me. Normally she would go from one thing to another.' She thought her daughter was 'probably a bit unsettled' because 'She sat straight on me and normally she'd be into the toys.' She described herself as 'Happy to let her have a play.'

We noted that the child began play with the baby dolls in the cot and the bottle and appeared to want to give her Mum the bottle to feed the baby doll. Mum at this time was not able to see this request and did not take the bottle. There was a lot of talk from Gai, questions both directing play and cutting across her daughter's play. There was not much space for this child in the relationship. It was hard for this mother to support and sustain reciprocal interactions and she was not predictable. There was definite interest in each other but limited pleasure. Clare was careful and compliant and went with her mother's direction. Gai's description of her appeared to prioritise independence and her language development. We thought there was some role confusion/reversal with Gai's repeated requests to be fed. On a couple of occasions, the struggle with real/pretend had frightening content and appeared to confuse or frighten Clare.

With the history and 5-minute film of play as you would at home, provisional Axis II Relationship Classification (DC:0-3R) and Axis II Relational Context (DC:0-5) diagnoses were made.

Axis II, DC:0-3R (2005). The Relationship Problems Checklist (RPCL) indicated definite Over Involvement with little space for this child and definite Under Involvement which seemed to happen when Clare needed to be closer to her mother. There was some evidence for the category Angry/Hostile with abrupt interactions and a child who was fearful, vigilant and avoidant. It also appeared that attending to her daughter's needs was seen by Gai as Clare being demanding. The rating given on the Parent-Infant Relationship Global Assessment Scale (PIR-GAS) was Disordered with a rating of 35.

Axis II, DC:0-5 (2016) — On the Caregiving Dimension for Levels of Adaptive Functioning (Levels 1–4), the relationship was understood to be at Level 3 — Compromised to Disturbed. This rating takes account of the child's contributions to the relationship as well as parental caregiving. Gai was parenting alone so the Caregiving Environment was not included.

In the WWW 'Follow your child's lead instructions.' *(The first 90 seconds)*

Clare: (started to move the cot into the middle of the mat)

Gai: (immediately) *What's your baby doing?*

Clare: (holding the baby doll over the potty) *Pot.*

Gai: *Clever Baby.*

Clare: (jumping up, picking up a ball and throwing it towards her mother, smiling and looking at her).

Gai: *Awesome.* (throwing ball back).

Clare: (throwing the ball back towards her mother)

Gai: (throwing the ball back a bit fast)

Clare: (dropping the ball. Moved closer to her mother, and threw again).

Gai: (throwing the ball back to Clare).

Clare: (caught the ball. Gave her mother a big smile. Held onto the ball for a bit before throwing it very fast towards her mother).

Gai: (nearly dropping ball).

Clare: (smiling at her mother and then at the therapist. Throwing and catching continued through 3 more cycles.)

Clare: (a truck on the mat got in Clare's way, and she moved it with her foot, coming closer to her mother. She placed the ball, which was very soft, on her mother's head).

Gai: *Ohhh, gentle please.* (pulling the ball off her head and handing it back to Clare).

Clare: (putting the ball on her own head. As the ball rolled off, she was leaning in a little closer to her mum).

Gai: (Leaning forward and looking as if she was going to kiss her daughter)

Clare: (pulled back, moving out of touching range from her mother. The ball play resumed but then the ball fell out of Clare's hands into the cot)

Gai: *Just as well the baby wasn't there.*

Clare: (Stopped this play. She returned to feeding the baby doll and her mother returned to asking more questions.

When asked what she had noticed in the play during this second five minutes Gai paused 'Probably … umm … that she enjoyed playing again. More relaxed, less looking back at me and saying things that required me to respond to. I think she played longer with the toys than in the first part.' Gai thought she was 'Happy to play. She didn't do any of the not-happy things, no whinge, whine, no climb on me for cuddles, no tantrums. Nice body language. Not stiff and rigid.' Clare approached her mother at this point with the ball again and was told 'I'm not playing now, I'm talking.'

We noted that Clare was quick to engage with her Mum again with the baby doll, but then there was a shift into reciprocal ball play initiated by Clare in response, it seemed to us, to praise for the baby doll that perhaps felt like praise for Clare herself. Then she was directly praised for her throw to Mum — 'Awesome'. Smiles and direct gazing were seen, a little tricky throwing by Clare and playfulness. This play was stopped by Clare in the face of a possible shaming comment. Gai was able to follow her daughter's activity for longer and to reduce her intrusive talking. However, as with the first five minutes, Gai struggled to provide specific observations of the activities/play her daughter engaged in. There were no references to the ball play. We observed in that play Gai had capacity to wait and to adjust her throws so that her daughter had more catching success. We also observed Gai move closer to her daughter as if to kiss her and her daughter moved away. There was a parallel poignant sadness in Clare's pulling away from her Mum's attempt to be closer and to Gai's lack of response to Clare's attempts to have her Mum take the bottle and feed to the baby in the first 5 minutes.

It was difficult for Gai to keep her daughter in mind and we observed the abrupt rebuff of her daughter when Clare wanted to resume the ball play when Gai was focused on talking to the therapist. Gai was able to use the here and now of the interactional assessment to find some words to describe her daughter and to think about her in relation to herself.

It is not unusual in the assessment to get very few observations about what the child does and/or to be left as clinicians feeling we had observed a different child to that observed by the parent. This mother noticed what her daughter didn't do and that is also relatively common.

Indications and Contra-indications for WWW

Having completed the assessment, thought is given as to whether this intervention is indicated and whether there are any contra-indications to WWW. This intervention is worth considering when there is a concern about the relationship between the child and the parent. A parent may not feel bonded to their child, that they do not understand their child, and/or, do not know how to play with them. They may feel their child is in control of them and/or struggle not to be harsh or emotionally negative with their child. Parents may talk about the relationship having got off to a difficult start with problems that have become persistent, as may happen after traumatic births and perinatal depression. Their child may have difficulties with sleeping, eating, tantrums, irritability and/or aggression. There may be problems with regulation, difficulties soothing and settling and a child who is easily dysregulated. There may be anxieties around separation and effects related to loss, grief, and/or trauma and developmental difficulties. The assessment may have highlighted problematic caregiving and significant attachment difficulties for the child.

There are no absolute contra-indications for WWW, but care needs to be taken when there are preoccupying external stressors, including impending death, illness, couple conflict and family violence. How much might these stressors impede a parent's capacity to focus in the session and on the child, and is the child adequately protected. The filmed assessment will give some indication and a discussion with the parent may lead to delaying the work or beginning with 8 sessions and reviewing progress.

Again, where there is evidence of severe parent psychopathology, such as complex trauma, depression and anxiety, priority is given to careful assessment and formulation. There is no contra-indication to parents having individual therapy and WWW concurrently. This intervention is helpful for parents with moderate to severe mental health problems. Getting it right for their young child is a potent motivator for parents. Our clinical experience is to err towards concurrent therapy if available rather than waiting while the parent has individual therapy. Waiting six, twelve, or eighteen months is often too long for the young child.

Where there is significant couple conflict and opposition to addressing the conflict, clinical judgement is required, and again a trial of therapy may be a better approach. On occasion, one parent may be actively hostile about the therapy; perhaps deeply anxious about the impact on their relationship with the other parent if the young child starts to have a closer relationship with that parent. The worry for this parent needs to be understood by the therapist and it may not be appropriate to use WWW.

Formulation and Contract Setting with Parents

Having completed the assessment, typically over three or four sessions, a provisional formulation that addresses the centrality of the relationship difficulty can be made. A discussion with parents about the assessment process and its influence on their understanding of the concerns they presented with, underscores working together. Using the parents' words, it is generally possible to find a point of entry for a formulation that connects these concerns with the intervention being offered. It can be difficult for some parents to understand how an intervention that asks them to follow their child's lead as their child plays could be helpful. Allowing time for this discussion is important.

Regular appointments are set, preferably weekly and no more than fortnightly, preferably at the same time and, if possible, at a time that best suits the child's schedule. Typically beginning with eight sessions and then a family review before continuing with a further eight sessions. On occasion the work finishes after eight sessions, more often continuing through sixteen to eighteen sessions. Where presentations are more complex, including when parents have problematic childhood histories of abuse and loss, the work continues through twenty-four to thirty sessions.

Clinical Case Study: The Clinicians' Formulation Gai and Clare

Gai was bothered about her parenting, worried that she was damaging her daughter and was not the right person to mother her. Her daughter was having persistent tantrums at home. Gai struggled to think about her daughter and to think about Clare as separate from herself and this was seen in the film with repeated intrusions from Gai directing play and over-riding her daughter's initiatives. She recurrently requested nurturance for herself from Clare.

The film had shown Gai could briefly follow her child's lead and could observe a little of Clare's behaviour with her. Clare used the toys to show something of the relationship problems; the doll needed nurturance and was ignored. She also took the opportunity of engaging her mother in a brief piece of reciprocal ball play. This was accompanied by smiles and direct looking at each other but not recalled by Gai when given the opportunity to discuss her observations.

Clinically, Clare's attachment relationship was significantly compromised with observations of vigilance, avoidance, some fearfulness and caregiving in her interactions with her mother.

It was concluded that WWW was an appropriate intervention for this dyad and it was positive that Gai was engaged in ongoing individual therapy given her history of depression and childhood trauma. She consented to the respective clinicians being in contact to support collaborative care and clarity around the boundaries of the adult and dyadic therapeutic work.

The Watch, Wait, and Wonder Setting

Setting up the space in which WWW takes place requires thoughtful planning by therapists and services. It is an investment to provide a consistent setting that the young child can use to be with their parent. This setting promotes the frame that 'holds' the dyad and the therapist.

The space may be in a clinic or office setting or be created within the family's home. The 'mat' sets the primary space for the work, and we have continued to suggest practitioners use a heavy-duty blue polythene mat. This is portable and neutral. The mat needs to be kept clean and the surface comfortable and not slippery either on the floor underneath or for the dyad.

The therapist needs to be in a chair off the mat, preferably a little way away so that it is clear they are not part of the child-led activity and where they do not feel they are intruding on the dyad. Typically, a chair is not provided for the parent. Many individuals and teams have a bean bag as one of the 'toys', and this may be used by some parents, but they would not be directed to sit on it. On occasion, parents have physical difficulties that prevent being on the floor and we suggest therapists talk with parents about what sitting arrangement best meets their need for comfort and allows them to observe and be available for their child's approaches. Being in a wheelchair is not a contra-indication to the work.

Clinical Illustration: Tilda and her Son

Tilda was in the late stages of her pregnancy and sitting on the floor had become difficult and painful. She and her therapist talked and decided to move a chair into the room for her. At this time in the work, her 3-year-old son was increasingly approaching and wanting to spend time on her lap. He continued to approach her and they managed cuddles in the chair. Interestingly, Tilda felt that the chair had made it more difficult for her son, and she decided she would rather manage her own physical discomfort and be back on the mat where they could look at each other with ease.

The toys provided for WWW need to be safe, clean, and in good order. If the intervention is happening in the home, the therapist will provide the toys. The therapist takes responsibility for the same toys being consistently present and for arranging them in a predictable order around the mat. This changes when delivering WWW online. These factors are critical because young children become interested in specific toys, which they rely on using from session to session to work out the problems they are experiencing. Young children use certain toys to represent themselves and/or their parents, and to enact events, especially traumatic situations.

While some thought is given to the use of developmentally appropriate toys, primarily the toys used offer an opportunity for the child to play out family/relational themes, concerns about illness and death, hospitalisation, aggression, and nurturance along with blocks, stacking and construction toys. For example, we use the baby dolls and small family dolls with children from 4 months to 9 years. Over the length of an intervention, as the child grows, one or two new toys that have a fit with this older child may be introduced. Table 1 gives an idea of the toys used but is not complete.

Therapists need to allocate time either side of a session for setting up the space and then leaving the room as it has been before the session. Certainly, setting up does not involve the dyad. When working in the home, the therapist takes

Table 1. *Toys and Considerations for WWW*

Toys	Considerations
Two sets of small family dolls, of different ethnicities and covering three generations.	Consider how the dolls represent the ethnicities of the family and the community served.
A doll house and furniture	Simple, sturdy and of a size that the dyad can comfortably sit alongside each other.
A Medical Kit	Containing a stethoscope, thermometer, syringe, bandage(s), auroscope and now, a mask.
Family sets of tame and wild animals	1–2 different sets of animals of each sort.
Emergency vehicles	An ambulance, fire truck, and police car.
A train set	
Doll's cot	Large and strong enough to hold the young child safely as they often want to get in the cot themselves.
Two dolls	Boy and girl dolls placed in the cot
A real baby's bottle, with replaceable teats, and dolls.	
A bean bag	

time ahead of beginning the intervention to talk with the family and settle on an approach to setting up that keeps the space consistent and predictable.

The Watch, Wait, and Wonder Session

Typically, sessions are described as having two components — the activity/play time when the parent is asked to observe and follow the child's lead and the discussion when the parent is asked in the first instance about their observations and wonderings. There is a dynamic sequence to how these two components shift as the therapeutic work continues.

Over time, therapeutic attention is also directed to two other components. The first is settling the dyad into the space and giving them the instructions to guide the session. These instructions are modified to fit the dyad's therapeutic progress and struggles and ultimately simplified to 'you are watching, waiting and wondering'. The second is to manage the transition between the child-led play and the discussion with the parent.

The Watch, Wait, and Wonder Instructions

The Manual (Cohen et al., 1999) sets out instructions that were given through the first years of implementing the intervention. They were not necessarily all given to a parent or repeated over sessions. In the last twelve years these original instructions have been modified, and most importantly a complete set is delivered clearly at the beginning of the first three to four sessions. Several of the instructions are discussed here to give the reader a sense of the way the frame is established for the child, the parent and the therapist.

The suggested beginning is as below:

> (First session) 'Jane and Sam, I'm going to start with some instructions about Watch, Wait and Wonder and it will take me a little while to read them out. You don't have to remember them all as I'll be repeating them again for at least the next 3–4 sessions.'

Each instruction needs to be clearly said as it is not predictable as to which will have particular salience for the mother and the dyad. For example, the following instruction may have been omitted:

> 'It's important that you don't tell Sam what to do, teach or stop him or show you are unhappy with what he is doing. This is a different time you will be having with him'

A parent, anxious in this different time of being with her son, may start teaching him and persist with this through the session. The therapist needs to acknowledge her mistake in not giving this mother the full information. This mother may then feel undermined, set up or let down. It becomes somewhat harder to begin the conversation that asks her whether there were times in the activity when she found it hard to just watch and not direct when the full instructions have not been given.

The wording of the instruction around safety has been changed to —

'Whatever Sam does in the child-led activity (play) time is fine unless something happens that's unsafe and we will manage that together.'

This instruction is more specific and allows for the therapist to be alongside the mother around the safety concern. Sometimes mothers do not recognise a situation is unsafe or they may become harsh and frightening in response to their child's behaviour. The therapist can refer back to the instruction to say this is one of those safety times and let's deal with this together. Where possible talking with Mum about her thoughts and ideas for managing the specific issue.

The instructions around timing have become more flexible, allowing for changing dynamics through the intervention.

'This time will last for _____ minutes [between 5–15 minutes depending on the age of the child and the capacity of this dyad to be together in this different way], and after this time I will ask you about your observations of Sam's activity (or play when the child is playing), your observations of Sam, and how he has been with you. In time, I'll ask about your thoughts and feelings during the first part of the session. I'll also check in with how it's been following these instructions.'

For dyads beginning with more than 15 minutes is problematic and for many, impossible. In general, 20 minutes would be a maximum. The interactional filmed assessment will provide guidance as to how much time the young child can manage and how much time the parent can tolerate in this different way of being together. These may be different for each, and not unusually, we begin with 4–5 minutes because that is the limit for this dyad at this time. Gradually, as a parent builds their observational skills (Watching) and their capacity to regulate themselves (Waiting) this time can be extended. Many mothers through the beginning phase cannot tolerate being asked directly about their feelings and thoughts, especially their feelings. The question is best left, and the focus kept on the observations of their child.

Over these first three to four sessions the therapist will begin to observe some of the patterns of this particular dyad when this mother is beginning to watch and follow her child's lead. Then the instructions that are being followed can be omitted and those that are proving more problematic to follow can be highlighted. The therapist may have a little more information that allows for reformulating an instruction in a language that is shared or that has more meaning for this mother. On occasion it may be necessary to reintroduce an instruction to maintain the frame of WWW.

The Therapeutic Process of Watch Wait and Wonder

In the beginning, both child and parent are anxious. The child may be so preoccupied with negotiating a relational connection with his mother that he struggles to play and may frequently look at, and even try to engage the therapist. His mother is learning to be with her child in a different way, to watch and follow her child's lead. Her discomfort may also result in hesitancy, distracting her child to her activity, teaching, or becoming unresponsive. The therapist occupies a seat off the mat, quietly and actively observing the interaction without intruding or intervening. This parallels what is being asked of the mother, with the stance that the most important relationship is between the parent and their child; the primary task of the therapist is to make it possible for the parent to follow their child's lead.

Through the first four to eight sessions, the discussion with the parent is unlikely to include much reflection and indeed the therapist's focus is directed to fostering observation — the watching and waiting. What has this mother observed of her child's play or activity with the toys, what has she observed about her child today in the room, and what has she observed about her child and his behaviour with her today. Using the parent's words, the therapist assumes a not-knowing stance, respectfully listening and checking they have understood the observations a parent has made. What has been this mother's experience of letting her child take the lead? It is essential to get observations first, to allow time, to follow the parent's lead. It is important to avoid pointing out something the child did do as a reaction perhaps to the parent's discomfort, or to the therapist's anxieties. The goal is to support this parent to become a sensitive observer of their child.

WWW with children through to 6 years follows the therapeutic process outlined for younger children. Their capacity to express thoughts and feelings verbally means language has more focus. They may comment through the discussion, adding to their parent's observations and, at times correcting them. The therapist still maintains a relationship that supports the parent to observe their child and does not initiate direct interactions with the child. For older children, the relational patterns are generally more entrenched, and the therapy may take longer than sixteen to eighteen sessions.

Clinical Case Study: Gai and Clare

In session one with Gai and Clare, the instructions were carefully gone through over a number of minutes.

> Clare: (Clare sitting alongside her mother, pulled the medical kit close, removed the syringe, opened her mouth and pretended to give herself some

'medicine'. She looked at the therapist, then her mother).

Gai: (opened her mouth, took the syringe, gave herself a little medicine and then said to Clare) *Here is your medicine, take it.*

Clare: (took the syringe giving herself medicine and then some for her Mum.)

Gai: (pretended she had got some in her eye and laughed)

Clare: (Laughed. Then repeatedly pretended to get her mother in the eye with the medicine.)

Gai: *Just pretend.*

Clare: (Put the syringe back in the medical kit and removed the scissors.)

Gai: *Don't cut your fingers off...* (and soon after) *Shall we put these away?* (She stopped this play).

As in the assessment, Gai's response to the question 'What did you see Clare do with the toys today?' was to talk about her daughter's mood as she perceived it. Gai could not recall the specifics of this play. 'She was very happy playing. She really enjoyed herself.' She continued, 'I was allowed to play and usually I'm clearly excluded. She turned to me. There were moments she wanted to show me something.' Gai could not recall the specifics of this play.

She did recall Clare getting into the cot. 'The first time it overbalanced and she managed. The second time she was a bit more wary and when she overbalanced again, she got really frightened. I am trying less to run into things with her. She knows I'm right here, I'm not very far and she did right herself.'

Then Clare did hurt herself and we observed Gai 'Not running into her'. Clare was crying, and Gai invited her to 'Come to Mummy'. Clare was saying, 'Come here', and for some time there was a standoff, then Gai sighed and moved closer. 'What's going on?' she said. 'Use your words.' She did pull Clare into her arms, but Clare continued to cry and Gai continued to ask her to use her words. 'Shall we have a cup of tea' said Gai, and she shuffled Clare out of her lap.

Clare used the time to again bring a theme of nurturance and care, who looked after who, and who was sick and needed medicine. She could play symbolically but it was not easy sustaining this play at this time, when Gai struggled to follow. We saw the beginnings of some provocative and possibly scary play, putting medicine in her mother's eyes, play hinting at blindness, which had been initiated by her mother.

When we ask parents to follow their child's lead in the play, placing the child 'in charge', we are asking them to place themselves in the hands of a child they do not know; to be potentially exposing some shameful, bad, destructive essence of their selves. Showing and being seen, hiding and not being able to see, were recurrent themes throughout the work with Clare and Gai.

As the dyad moves into the middle phase of therapy (from around session six to ten) the play becomes more complex and the content and interaction more central to the relational struggle. Parents become more comfortable and are likely to notice and/or correct themselves when intruding or taking over, except when the specific relationship anxiety is activated, and then they may be more intrusive or unresponsive.

From session six, the instructions needed to focus on Gai watching her daughter, quietly waiting and not interacting unless invited by Clare. Gai found it very difficult to wait and continued to talk and direct the play. It seemed that when there was space and quietness, she no longer felt connected to her daughter. This possibility was supported when Gai made the observation that her daughter was not talking to her as she played with plates and food. 'She's excluding me'. It was as if she was abandoned and possibly not existing or going on being. This was a frightening/disorganising experience, and it was not surprising then that Gai became reactive and would lose being able to watch and wait. In thinking more about a space that was quiet and calm, Gai connected quietness in her own family as being a warning, a signal for potential violence.

We now understood two significant anxieties/fears driving this mother's reactivity. From session ten the therapist overtly set up with this mother a word she would use to support Gai to pause. Additionally, she would check in during the child-led play as to whether Gai's capacity for watching and waiting was okay for a few more minutes. The watching therapist would keep this mother in her mind.

In session eleven Gai was more at ease, actively sitting on her hands and smiling at the therapist as she kept quiet. Clare chose to play a version of 'What's the Time Mr Wolf' — overtly bringing being frightened by her Mum into a game. Gai was able to pretend to be a bit scary and Clare could pretend to be scared. They could both smile and then laugh together and after some time with this Clare moved into a hiding piece of play.

> 'It was definitely a different playtime', said Gai. 'The play hiding behind me to surprise me' 'She found it so funny, so hilarious ... much funnier than I thought she'd find it, and she did it for quite a long time.' ... 'I thought alright, I'll give her a bit more space' and as she talked she caressed the top of Clare's head 'I'll see what it is she wants to be doing with this' and later 'it was alright ... Not too hard but a little strange. I'm very much a talking person'. Clare had approached her mother, placing her hands on her mother's cheeks 'Can you see me in your eyes' she said to her mother. Her mother responded,

'I can see myself in your eyes' and then, 'Do you want to climb on my back and have a cuddle?'

Clare's closeness, her demand to be seen, to be separate and connected was perhaps too intense at this time for Gai but she stayed there and offered her back for a cuddle. Later in the discussion Gai was talking about looking outside of the WWW space.

'I'll look and say yes and continue with what I'm doing and she'll say you have to look Mum. So I've been learning that I have to stay looking until she looks at me to see that I'm looking.'

Gai continued to grapple with watching and waiting.

'I was trying to think have I been invited into the play or not, so I waited. No need to feel guilty that I should be doing more. She really enjoyed building the train track on her own and having a captive Mummy audience. I think she liked it much more here because whenever she turned to me, I was watching, I was watching.'

As the dyad moves into the end phase of therapy (the last six to eight sessions), decisions about finishing are determined by the child's readiness to finish. Children play in a concentrated way, (most of the time), independent of the need to elicit active involvement from their parent. There is shared pleasure in the play, and parents are more confident and positive about their children. Parents may also express their anxiety about managing once WWW finishes. Therapists need to hold the stance and allow the parent to recognise that they have internalised repeated experiences of working to understand their child and competently parent.

Clare was spending much more time in Gai's lap, some of the time lying across her mother as if a baby. The hide-and-seek play shifted from being scary and anxiety provoking to warm and sensitive.

Clare giggled from under the bean bag. 'That sounds just like my daughter', said Gai and she gently lifted the bean bag. 'I found you, I found you,' she said.

Towards the end of the work, Gai talked about an incident at home when Clare had kicked a ball and upset a jug of water, and she got very angry with her daughter. She looked at her, and 'She looked frightened. I looked and said I'm so sorry.' There had been two more episodes of 'spilling' and Gai said they had been okay. She had not got angry, she had stayed settled and she looked after Clare. 'She's a really good kid.' We were observing Clare to be happier, to play alone with her mother watching and to invite her in to play, and the role reversal caregiving was significantly reduced. In parallel, we noted that Gai's observations of her daughter became more detailed and she recurrently moved between: What am I seeing? What does it mean? What does my daughter need?

The Axis II relationship assessment (PIR-GAS) was completed by an independent clinician at the end of what was a 26-session intervention. The rating was 70, which represents a substantial improvement from 35.

At the review interview held a few weeks after completion of the intervention work Gai commented: 'It's easier to accept I have to look after her first when she's upset.' And later, 'I've learnt to be more patient with myself, I've learnt to wonder about what's going on in myself, it's been really good for my mental health.'

Language and the Delivery of Watch, Wait, and Wonder

Practitioners are seeing families with infants and young children who have diverse language and ethnic backgrounds. Decisions about what language is to be used in therapeutic work to promote optimal communication typically include matching the therapist's language(s) with parents, or the use of trained interpreters, with a fallback to the therapist's language.

When parents speak more than one language, they not uncommonly choose to use these different languages with their children. This potentially offers a valuable developmental experience for their child. We are interested in supporting a parent's language choices. Some parents choose to use the language they grew up hearing and then speaking, from infancy, with their child. That language holds their 'mothering' experiences and is so much part of what is between them and the baby/child. Addressing the parent's language choices and integrating the language of the parent's early caregiving experience into dyadic therapy is worthy of attention.

The difficulties for a parent with talking to their young child may be present across all the languages used, and/or there may be differences that importantly hold a parents' experience of care in the past. In our assessments, coming to understand the mother's developmental history, the 'Ghosts' (Fraiberg et al., 1975) and 'Angels' (Lieberman et al., 2005) are leading to more intentional support for multi-lingual parents to use their nursery language with their young children (Guy & Galgut, 2021). The Ghosts and the Angels will be held in the 'mothering tongue'.

We have a small number of dyads (age range 6–48 months) — who have completed WWW using one language during the child-led play and another (usually English) in the parent's discussion with the therapist. In all but one case the mother has chosen to use the language of their infancy. One mother chose after four sessions to use the language of her nanny — a deliberate move to hold an 'Angel' relationship experience in the therapeutic work with her child. Her thoughtful therapist followed this parent's lead watching this mother become tender, interested in her child and using affectionate words.

WWW prioritises building observational skills, and sessions are filmed. The mother's developing skills sit alongside everyone's attention to the communications of the young child with the toys, in their relationship with the parent and themselves. There are no changes to the intervention frame and no requirement for parents to provide any translation of what they are saying. The attention to the moment-to-moment non-verbal interactions, attunement and repair, is critical. WWW work is a mode of helping families perhaps discover another language in their relationship with each other. It aids development of an emotional language, and a language of connection.

Culture and the Delivery of Watch, Wait, and Wonder

Alongside the work supporting parents to use their language of choice, typically their 'Nursery Language' with their children, we have understood culture to be integral to engaging parents in this intervention and supporting the relationships. There are elements of this intervention that allow and hopefully invite culture to be wrapped around as a parent might want and as an indigenous clinician might want to support.

Wilson et al. (2021) state: 'Relational approaches to engaging with Indigenous peoples and their families are cultural imperatives for accessing health services.' (page 3540). The WWW intervention is based first and foremost on building a strong and respectful therapeutic relationship with the parent and the wider whānau or family where possible. It is imperative that, in working with whānau Māori or families from Pacifica or other indigenous or minority communities, cultural advisors are sought out and brought into the assessment from the beginning. Love (2004) defines the important Māori concept of mana as empowerment rather than 'power over'. As WWW places the parent in a position of becoming more knowing of their child and privileges their understandings of this relationship, it has the potential to be more mana-enhancing than didactic approaches which may privilege eurocentric views of parenting.

Māori clinicians have trained in WWW and the intervention has been successfully used with whānau Māori, but further work needs to be undertaken in order to both develop a Te Ao Māori perspective on WWW and to understand how this intervention is experienced. This is especially important as the majority of the workforce currently are Pakeha and will come to any intervention with their own implicit biases.

Online Delivery of Watch, Wait, and Wonder

The Covid-19 coronavirus pandemic has led, amongst many changes, to restrictions in clinicians' capacity to work face-to-face with families in Australasia and across the world. Considerable thought has been given to ways in which we can modify our practice in general and specifically how we can continue to support the provision of the intervention Watch, Wait and Wonder. For some dyads it has been possible to provide WWW online via technology that enables the therapist to still be present and the session to be recorded.

For these families/dyads it has offered a way of working that maintains the therapeutic connections we have, and where feedback from parents and film review is supporting the clinical effectiveness of online delivery. This is promising and opens up possibilities for delivering the intervention to families and communities who are unable to access the intervention face-to-face.

Currently we have experience across the following situations: a full assessment has been completed face-to-face and the WWW intervention work moves online, the intervention work has begun face-to-face and moves online, and when online work begins during the assessment phase.

Planning needs to incorporate organisational issues such as consent, ensuring appropriate cover for online work that includes filming. The technology needs to meet standards around information/data security with tele-mental health care.

Clinicians need to address whether a family can support and manage working with/being with the clinician online, and we have taken a collaborative approach to this with parents, typically suggesting a trial with a review after four sessions. Therapists additionally need to feel they can hold and contain the dyad with an online presence. Supervision of this work is recommended.

There is a discussion with parents about setting up the space, the toys and the device. It takes three to four sessions for the dyad to settle into working in this way. The sessions are kept shorter and more time is taken to welcome the dyad into the space and acknowledge its difference, and then to finish, checking how it was having the clinician be with the dyad in this different way.

There are some families and/or clinicians for whom this approach is not suitable and/or practicable. There must be some space without too many impingements for a parent to commit to consistently setting up the mat area as well as engaging in the work. We have been able to manage safety issues, and it is likely this is helped by having at least one of the assessment sessions being face-to-face. This is another initiative that warrants further clinical work and research.

Evidence Base

The research on WWW has primarily focused on infants and young children, 6 months through 3 years. The Manual (Cohen et al., 1999) has a chapter addressing the use of WWW with older children from a clinical perspective with a case study of a 9-year-old and her mother.

The findings from the pilot study (Guy, 1988) provided some guidance for the decisions regarding data collection in the research testing effectiveness of the WWW intervention (Cohen et al., 1999, 2002). Parents were reporting a reduction in their young child's (18 months – 4 years) presenting problems around the fourth session, increased satisfaction and pleasure in their children, and more confidence in their maternal role. Fathers spontaneously used the word attached to describe the positive changes observed in the relationship between children and their mothers. Both parents noticed improvements in their child's confidence, concentration and expressive language. The clinicians noted that these young children used the sessions to interact with their mothers and that their activity shifted in time to more prolonged and symbolically developed play. There was more joint pleasure. The surge in language development was striking and seemed more than could be expected with normative development over the sessions.

The research involved an alternate treatment design with random allocation to WWW or Infant–Parent Psychodynamic Psychotherapy following Fraiberg et al., 1975 (Lieberman et al., 1991), referred to as PPT in the research at the time, which would now sit under the umbrella of Child Parent Psychotherapy (CPP). Sixty-seven toddlers/young children, aged between 1 and 3 years, and their mothers participated in the intervention study. Attachment and development were key factors assessed pre, post and at 6-month follow-up. Measures addressed included attachment security (Strange Situation Procedure), qualities of the mother–toddler interaction, toddler's cognitive development (Bayley Developmental Scales) and affect regulation. Data on the mother's perceptions of parenting, depression and parenting stress was also collected.

The research found WWW and PPT to be effective, with both interventions reducing the severity of the toddler's presenting symptoms and parenting stress. Observations of the relationships found significant reduction in conflict and improved interactional reciprocity. However, there were differential effects with the WWW intervention group. Here, mothers had more significant improvements in their levels of depression and sense of competency in their parenting role. They were significantly less intrusive. Only children in the WWW group had improved emotional regulation and significant improvements in cognitive development at the end of therapy. One-third of the children in the WWW group shifted from a disorganised pattern of attachment to secure (20.6%) or to an organised insecure attachment compared to one-tenth of the PPT group.

At 6-month follow-up both groups had maintained or made further gains. Mothers in the WWW group had further gains in their comfort in dealing with their child's behaviour. Both groups reported less parental stress, but the differential between the two groups with the more significant reduction for the WWW group was maintained. Mothers in the WWW group had further improvements in mood. The mothers in the PPT group had a significant reduction in depression over the 6-month post-treatment period. The WWW intervention was significantly more effective for those young children who had a disorganised insecure pattern of attachment.

Bakermans-Kranenburg et al. (2005), in their review and meta-analysis of disorganised attachment and preventative interventions looked at interventions that focused on sensitivity and began with infants from 6–24 months. Their conclusions noted that studies with children at risk were more effective than studies with parents at risk and that it seemed difficult to bring about changes in disorganised attachment in clinically referred groups. In this review the most successful intervention was WWW which instructed the parent to follow the infant's lead.

Subsequently there have been clinically focused papers and presentations, but no further research of the quality of Cohen et al. (1999, 2002), and WWW has less of a presence in the intervention literature. In 2016 the Early Intervention Foundation (EIF) published an assessment of seventy-five early intervention programmes directed at improving child outcomes by improving parent–child interactions. EIF has a robust methodology for rating the evidence and costs of programmes. They found seventeen programmes were well evidenced and this included WWW rated at Level 2+.

Further research is needed addressing, for example, effectiveness across a wider age range and incorporating assessment of reflective capacity and parental representations. The latter would examine the hypothesis that some of the therapeutic change seen with WWW is the result of its capacity to support a space for developing parental reflection to promote change.

Training

In order to use this intervention, practitioners must complete a recognised training programme. Lojkasek et al. (1999) documented recommended standards for independent practice which outlined the training programme that had been developed in Toronto. Complete training programmes are currently offered by Wait, Watch, and Wonder (www.watchwaitwonder.com) and Incredible Families Charitable Trust (www.watchwaitwonder downunder.com). The latter training has been developed by Guy, Stevens and

Robinson with the support of Muir and Stupples and is primarily for Australian and New Zealand clinicians.

Practitioners attend an Introductory Course, typically run over three days, and then study the WWW Manual. Individuals then take on one to two WWW cases. These are supervised by an approved supervisor knowledgeable in the practice of the WWW intervention. Moving forward, practitioners attend an Advanced Course, present a case and receive group supervision. Further knowledge is gained through exposure to the work of others in the Advanced Course. Subsequently, two or more supervised cases are completed and depending on the clinician's workplaces, they are encouraged to see infants across the age range from 0–4 years.

The 1999 recommended standards (Lojkasek et al., 1999) supported additional supervision of cases for clinicians working with older children. In Australasia there is support for work with older children (4–8 years) in discussion with the training team. Having completed a minimum of three supervised cases and the Introductory and Advanced Course, clinicians have a final case-based interview before Accreditation for Independent Practice.

Conclusion

WWW is an intervention that directly involves the young child in the therapy and gives them a space and toys to communicate to their parent something of their particular relational struggle. Parents are asked to get down on the floor with their child and to observe the activity and play of their child. They are to interact when they think they have been invited to interact and have some understanding of what their child wants from them. This time of following is then discussed with the therapist taking a parallel stance, asking the parent what they observed. As sessions continue, this is developed into a more reflective time with the therapist interested in what meaning the parent makes from the observations and what that contributes to being with their child.

The intervention is used where young children present with a range of behavioural, regulatory and relational difficulties that have often been present for some years. There is an evidence base supporting its use in children from 12 months through to 3 years and clinical use through 4–6 years. Further research is needed in a number of areas, including its use with older children. This is important given the significant mental health problems in children 3–6 years and the gains in supporting these children to get back on track developmentally and relationally. There is a comprehensive training programme offered in Australasia and Canada. We anticipate and hope for further research and training in this model across the world. WWW is an effective intervention to support the relationship between parent and young child, with improvements in attachment security, emotion regulation, parental mental health and overall development.

Reader's Exercise

You may like to do this alone but we suggest doing this in pairs with a colleague.

Either; take a 5-minute film of a parent and child (3–6 years) with the request that they play as they do at home. Have toys available that potentially allow the child to tell a story. Make sure you have appropriate consents to share the film with a colleague. At the end of filming ask the parent about the play together. 'Is that how it would usually be?'. If not, 'What were the differences?'

Or, find a photograph or painting of a parent and child, the child being 3–6 years. We ask you to look at the picture or the film, then without conferring, write down your observations, giving yourselves at least 5 minutes. Then together share your observations and note when either, in the writing or in the sharing, an observation has expanded to an assumption, inference or judgement.

Ask your colleague what it is that they have observed that led them to this perspective —highlighting this piece of 'wondering' and then ask if there could be another possibility or a different perception.

For example, one clinician may note, 'This mother is looking at her son and he's looking off to the right, not at her'. The other clinician, 'this mother is looking tenderly at her son and he seems to be avoiding her gaze'. What has this clinician observed to support the view that the mother's looking is tender and the son's not looking is avoiding? What might be an alternative possibility and what observations would support that?

It is important for clinicians working with young children to build their observational skills and develop the capacity to separate the assumptions and wonderings, whatever interventions are being considered. Regular review of films with a colleague is useful, even more so with supervision.

Glossary of Māori Words and Phrases

Iwi — tribe, tribal base of which one has genealogical connections.

Mana — prestige, authority, control, power, influence, status, spiritual power, charisma — mana is a supernatural force in a person, place or object.

Pakeha — New Zealander of European descent

Te Ao Māori — the Māori world view — this acknowledges the interconnectedness and interrelationship of all living & non-living things.

Whānau — extended family, family group

Whanaungatanga — relationship, kinship, sense of family connection — a relationship through shared experiences and working together which provides people with a sense of belonging.

References

Ainsworth, M. D. S., Blehar, M. C., Waters, E., & Wall, S. (1978). *Patterns of attachment: A psychological study of the strange situation.* Lawrence Erlbaum Associates.

Bakermans–Kranenburg, M. J., Van Ijzendoorn, M. H., & Juffer, F. (2005). Review and meta-analysis of disorganised infant attachment and preventative interventions *Infant Mental Health Journal, 26*(3), 191–216. https://doi_ 10.1002/imhj.20046

Barlow, J., Sleed, M., & Midgley, N. (2021). Enhancing parental reflective functioning through early dyadic interventions: A systematic review and meta-analysis. Infant Mental Health Journal, 42(1), 21–34. https://doi.org/10.1002/imhj.21896

Cohen, N., Muir, E., Lojkasek, M., Muir, R., Parker, C., Barwick, M., & Brown, M. (1999). Watch, Wait, and Wonder: Testing the effectiveness of a new approach to mother–infant psychotherapy *Infant Mental Health Journal, 20,* 429–451. https://doi.org/10.1002/(SICI)1097-0355(199924)20:4<429::AID-IMHJ5>3.0.CO;2-Q

Cohen, N., Muir, E., Lojkasek, M., Muir, R., & Parker, C. (2002). Six-month follow-up of two mother–infant psychotherapies: Convergence of therapeutic outcomes. *Infant Mental Health Journal, 23*(4), 361–380. https://doi.org/10.1002/imhj.10023

De Wolff, M. S., & Van Ijzendoorn, M. H. (1997) Sensitivity and Attachment: A meta-analysis on parental antecedents of infant attachment security. *Child Development, 68,* 604–609. https://doi.org/10.1111/j.1467-8624.1997.tb04218.x

Dowling, J. (1985). Personal communication with E Muir.

Fraiberg, S., Adelson, E., & Shapiro, V. (1975). Ghosts in the nursery: A psychoanalytic approach to the problems of impaired infant–mother relationships. *Journal of Child Psychiatry, 14,* 387–421. https://doi.org/10.1016/S0002-7138(09)61442-4

Fonagy, P., Target, M., Steele, H., & Steele, M. (1998). *Reflective Functioning Manual, version 5.0, for application to adult attachment Interviews.* University College, London.

Grienenberger, J.F., Kelly, K., & Slade, A. (2005). Maternal reflective functioning, mother–infant affective communication, and infant attachment: exploring the link between mental states and observed caregiving behavior in the intergenerational transmission of attachment. *Attachment and Human Development, 7*(3), 299–311. doi: 10.1080/14616730500245963. PMID: 16210241.

Guy, D. (1988). *The mother–infant relationship.* Unpublished Dissertation. The Royal Australian and New Zealand College of Psychiatry.

Guy, D., Furstenburg, T., Lam, M., & Muir, E (2014). The Watch, Wait and Wonder Intervention: Therapeutically supporting the space to promote a parent's capacity to mentalise. *Proceedings WAIMH Congress, Edinburgh 2014.*

Guy, D., & Galgut, S. (2021). Language in the Nursery — Watch, Wait, and Wonder supports a mother's first language experience into the relationship with her baby. *Proceedings WAIMH Congress, 2021*

Johnson, F., Dowling, J., & Wesner, D. (1980). Notes on infant psychotherapy. *Infant Mental Health Journal, 1,* 19–35. https://doi.org/10.1002/1097-0355(198021)1:1<19::AID-IMHJ2280010105>3.0.CO;2-S

Lieberman, A. F., Weston, D. R., & Pawl, J. H. (1991). Preventative intervention and outcome in anxiously attached dyads. *Child Development, 62, 199–209.* https://doi.org/10.1111/j.1467-8624.1991.tb01525.x

Lieberman, A. F., Padron, E., Van Horn, P., & Harris, W. W. (2005). Angels in the nursery: The intergenerational transmission of benevolent influences. *Infant Mental Health Journal, 26(6),* 504–520. https://doi.10.1002/imhj.20071

Lojkasek, M., Cohen, N.J. & Muir, E. (1999). *Recommended standards for independent practice of the Watch, Wait, and Wonder Intervention.* http://www.watchwaitwonderdownunder.com/wp-content/uploads/2014/05/Standards-for-Practice-WWW-2014.pdf

Love, C. (2004) Extensions to Te Wheke (Working Papers No. 6–04). *The Open Polytechnic of New Zealand* https://repository.openpolytechnic.ac.nz/handle/11072/182.

Mahrer, A. R., Levinson, J. R., & Fine, S. (1976). Infant psychotherapy: Theory, research and practice. *Psychotherapy: Theory, Research and Practice, 13, 131–140.* https://doi.org/10.1037/h0088326

Monaghan, S. M., Gilmore, R. J., Muir, R. C., Clarkson, J. E., Crooks, T. J., & Egan, T. G. (1986). Prenatal screening for risk of major parenting problems: Further results from the Queen Mary Maternity Hospital Child Care Unit. *Journal of Child Abuse & Neglect, 10, 3, 369–375. https://doi.10.1016/0145-2134(86)90012-8*

Muir, E. (1992). Watching, waiting and wondering: Applying psychoanalytic principals to mother–infant intervention. *Infant Mental Health Journal, 13, 319–328.* https://doi.org/10.1002/1097-0355(199224)13:4<319::AID-IMHJ2280130407>3.0.CO;2-2

Muir, E., Lojkasek, M., & Cohen, N. (1999). Watch, Wait, and Wonder: A manual describing a dyadic infant-led approach to problems in infancy and early childhood. *The Hincks-Dellcrest Centre and The Hincks-Dellcrest Institute.*

Muir, E., Stupples, A., & Guy, D. (1989). *Mother–toddler psychotherapy and change in patterns of attachment: Some pilot observations.* Unpublished Manuscript.

Ostrov, K., Dowling, J., Wesner, D., & Johnson F. (1982). Maternal styles in infant psychotherapy: Treatment and research implications. *Infant Mental Health Journal, 3,* 162–173. https://doi.org/10.1002/1097-0355(198223)3:3 <162::AID-IMHJ2280030305>3.0.CO;2-9

Van Ijzendoorn, M., Schuengel, C., & Bakermans-Kranenburg, M. (1999). Disorganised attachment in early childhood: Meta-analysis of precursors, concomitants, and sequelae. *Development and Psychopathology, 11*(2), 225–250. doi:10.1017/S0954579499002035

Wesner, D., Dowling, J., & Johnson, F. (1982). What is maternal–infant intervention? The role of infant psychotherapy. *Psychiatry, 45,* 307–315. https://doi:10.1080/00332747.1982.11024163.

Wilson, D., Moloney, E., Parr, J. M., Aspinall C., & Slark, J. (2021) Creating an Indigenous Māori-centred model of relational health: A literature review of Māori models of health. *Journal of Clinical Nursing, 30*(23–24), 3539–3555. https://doi.org/10.1111/jocn.15859

Winnicott, D. W. (1958). *The capacity to be alone. Maturational processes and the facilitating environment* (Third Edition). Hogarth Press.

Zero to Three. (2005). *Diagnostic classification of mental health and developmental disorders of infancy and early childhood. Revised Edition (DC: 0-3R).* Zero To Three Press.

Zero to Five. (2016). *Diagnostic classification of mental health and developmental disorders of infancy and early childhood. Revised Edition. (DC: 0-5^{TM}).* Zero To Three Press.

Section IV:

Systems-Focused Approaches

Chapter 12

Narrative Therapy (NT)

Ingeborg Stiefel

Narrative Therapy (NT) was developed in the late 1970s and early 1980s by Michael White, a social worker from Australia and David Epston, a social worker from New Zealand. NT can broadly be defined as a Postmodern model of therapy. NT has become a recognised model of therapy in Australia and worldwide. It offers clinical value yet has not fully been integrated into the funding landscape for therapy services, which we believe is due to the lack in developing a rigorous research base into the effectiveness of NT using quantitative and high qualitative research design. NT especially in the early years of development, questioned many assumptions of the then-contemporary models of therapy, opposing diagnostic mental health labels and reflecting on power in the client–therapist relationship and the use of language in therapy. In the early literature, proponents of the model sometimes made sweeping, undifferentiated statements with a lack of scientific rigour in reference to the mainstream approaches at the time.

However, NT has developed and has become a model frequently utilised in various therapeutic settings, and training is being offered at both undergraduate and postgraduate levels. The model has clinical value and attraction as a suitable model for many client groups, including children, adolescents, adults, couples and families, in particular those that are in positions of least power, including Aboriginal people in Australia, people who have experienced violence and abuse, or who struggle with chronic mental health conditions.

The main assumption of NT is that people create narratives (stories) about themselves, and these stories shape their identity and influence the person's behaviour, beliefs, emotions and interactions with others. People seek therapy when problem stories dominate their lives and cause distress, unfulfilled goals or conflicts with others. The main task of therapy is to challenge the problematic stories and assist the client in recognising their full range of abilities, skills and potential. With the help of powerful questions and reflections, alternative narratives will emerge, assisting the person to develop stories of strength that are consistent with their goals in life and improve their psychological well-being and positive interactions with others. In the context of child psychotherapy, we see the value of NT in its refreshing interviewing and questioning style, which allows the therapist to work from a purely narrative perspective or integrate NT ideas with other approaches, such as cognitive behaviour therapy.

Theoretical Underpinning of NT

NT is a conversational form of therapy that can broadly be defined as a postmodern form of psychotherapy. Postmodernism is a zeitgeist, a major philosophical shift away from modernist ideas, which dominated thinking and therapy practices in the previous decades of psychology and family therapy. Rasheed et al. (2011) and Goldenberg et al. (2013) provide good summaries of the model. In contrast to modernism, which assumes that knowledge is objective, value-free and can be explored utilising precise observation and measurements, postmodernism takes a radical departure from these modernist ideas. Postmodernism considers subjective experience, multiple meanings, ambiguity, pluralism, local knowledge and participation. Related and partially overlapping philosophical ideas that have informed NT are constructivism, social constructivism, second-order cybernetics, post-structuralism, feminist critique and critical theory. Constructivism, in its most radical form, proposes that an objective reality does not exist; knowledge evolves in the space between people and is mediated through language. Beliefs about the world are social inventions dependent on culture, time and context. Social constructivism stresses the inter-subjectivity and context dependency of meaning-generating systems and the perception of the world and also strongly considers the influence of culture, gender, age, race, power and language on our understanding of the world and our viewpoints. Knowledge is never valued free, and 'truth' is inter-subjective and context-dependent (Freedman & Combs, 1996). What one person sees as truth, acceptable norm, or reality may depend on their upbringing and personal experiences. Second-order cybernetics, a term introduced to family therapy, focuses on the role of the therapist and the therapist–client system. Departing from a first-order position of outsider and observer, second-order cybernetics postulates that the therapist is also part of the system, an insider, and therapy approaches at the time started focusing more strongly on the role of the therapist, encouraging increased self-awareness and self-reflectivity as part of the process of change. Critical theory and post-structuralism explore the interlink between wider social structures and the use of power. Post-structuralism is rooted in the 1960s post-Marxist era and stresses that forms of knowledge derive from political practice. Finally, feminist critique proposes that therapy is never gender-neutral, value-free and that issues of power and control need to be considered and addressed from a gender lens.

Narrative theory proposes that reality is socially constructed and both communicated and influenced through language. Hence NT focuses on 'meaning constituting language systems', which are embedded in social, political, cultural and historical structures of society. NT encourages clients to question assumptions, positions of power, common values, views and positions people take in society, including the role of the therapist and the therapy setting. Botella and Herrero (2000) point to the relational aspect of NT and define the model as a relational constructivist approach with a focus on shared discourses and collaborative dialogue in the generation of new meaning to people's lives. A central task of therapy is to help clients evaluate and re-evaluate their own situation critically with the aim of reaching greater choices and options.

The model proposes that lived experience, which includes our social and cultural position in society and our interaction with the non-human environment, is represented in the form of narratives and stories about self and relationships with others. Stories give meaning to our experience, but they also act as a schema for new life experiences, expectations and behaviours. These narratives do not fully represent all aspects of lived experience, and significant experiences may be filtered out or ignored. Life is multi-storied, and the narratives can lead to an adaptive, open lifestyle, or they can narrow down and restrain life experience. Negative and narrow narratives can seriously limit an individual's quality of life and can lead to problematic developments, including the full range of psychological and relationship issues. Societal norms, social systems and practices can additionally reinforce non-adaptive personal narratives leading to further restrictions in perception and a person's potential for future development.

NT is a strength-based model which opposes the practice of pathologising people's experiences through labels and verbal descriptions, including diagnostic categorisations. The narrative therapist has a deep respect for the client's situation; the therapeutic stance is non-judgemental, empowering and change-facilitating. In NT, problems are perceived as existing separate from the person, hence allowing clients to view themselves as distant from the problem and gaining control over its negative influence. The core task of therapy is to explore and understand (deconstruct) the dominant/problematic stories, so the client and therapist can explore the developments leading to the problem narrative and appreciate the current influence of the story on the person's life and then gradually develop (re-construct) alternatives stories that are consistent with the client's wished-for change and which increase possibilities and choice for new behaviour. NT sees clients as the experts of their lives, with the therapist adopting a respectful stance and working in collaboration with the client, the client determining the direction, course and tempo of therapy. The therapist's role is to be respectful and reflective and ask model-specific and highly relevant questions, and at times challenge the client by pointing out dilemmas, options and choices. Therapeutic questions allow the client to explore whether the current story has outlived its usefulness, if the client is ready to explore different pathways, or if readiness and change are still issues that need further understanding and consideration.

At any given time, people are confronted with a large amount of information, but certain information is filtered out. People organise the complexity of life experiences by translating them into text, language, words, symbols, stories and narratives. Some aspects of lived experience are neglected or overlooked. Stories give coherence, they determine the meaning people ascribe to their experience, and they also determine which aspect of life experience is selected out. Stories are constructed and negotiated in a social context, and they are open to change. People can get caught in negative stories about themselves through a variety of means, including societal expectations and norms, culture, social position, life events, language practice, coaching and accidental triggers. NT is about re-telling and re-writing of stories. The use of language is heavily emphasised in this model, especially how the use of language can inadvertently invite negative life descriptions and problem stories. Hence, language sensitivity is paramount for effective therapy.

Often presented as a therapeutic approach with a political and social edge, NT is a suitable model for a wide range of child, adult and family issues, where the generation of new meaning and empowerment plays an important role. NT is also seen as an appropriate model for working with Aboriginal people in Australia due to its storytelling approach, which is seen as being part of the Aboriginal culture (Australian Psychological Society, 2018). O'Connor et al. (1997) describe NT as a co-constructed conversation in which both therapist and client are viewed as being experts in the area of their experiences. The therapy process assists the client in constructing an alternative view of the problem, exploring solutions that have not been tested before or which have been tried but have not fully been recognised by the client as possible options. In successful therapy, the client will experience a feeling of agency in the process of change. Therapy excerpts, especially of working with adults, often represent the conversational style of NT with, at times, dense, metaphorical language, long sentences and a fairly high degree of abstraction. Hence it may not be immediately obvious why NT may be a suitable model for working therapeutically with young children and their families.

NT Process

The process of NT consists of several phases, which do not necessarily flow in sequential order. NT starts with the telling of the reasons for seeking therapy. In NT terms, this is understanding the problematic story (or narrative). The problem is then externalised by the therapist, followed by a mapping of the influence of the problem on the person's life, such as the person's beliefs, feelings and behaviours, including interaction with others. This exploration may also include an understanding of the early roots of the problem narrative, if relevant. This first phase is referred to as the 'deconstruction' of the dominant story. Next, the therapist will notice and highlight exceptions to the problem narrative (unique outcomes) and encourages an exploration of these to increase the client's awareness of these alternatives. Naming of alternative story potentials and inviting the person to take a position and evaluate if these alternatives hold value for him or her is the next step of therapy. Alternative stories are then mapped out with a network of questions and feedback responses. These can include an exploration of possible roots to these alternative potentials, for example, ways in which alternatives are already taking an active part in the person's life, people who recognise these potentials and encourage the development of alternative narratives.

1. Engagement and understanding the problematic story

The first part of therapy is for the therapist to understand the reason why the client is seeking therapy. Generic therapist variables are employed, including empathic listening and reflective responding. Part of the initial therapy process is to allow for a respectful appreciation of the client's problem situation so the client feels understood and acknowledged and a safe therapy environment is created.

2. Deconstructing the dominant story and mapping the influence of the problem on the person's life

The aim of the deconstruction of the problem story is to develop a good understanding of the powerful influence that the narrative has over the person, how the narrative developed and how it is maintained through client behaviour and beliefs or through the input of other people. The understanding of problem stories explores and utilises three-time dimensions, including past influences, present effects and sometimes anticipated future impacts on the person. It considers both the cognitions the client holds in regard to the story, such as assumptions, core beliefs, and presuppositions, but also their own behaviours and interactions with others that contribute to the life of the story. Significant others can include family members, friends, work colleagues and people representing social institutions.

Michael White (White, 1991) stresses that the deconstruction of the problematic story:

> has to do with procedures that subvert taken-for-granted realities and practices; those so-called 'truths' that are split off from the conditions and the context of their production, those disembodied ways of speaking that hide their biases and prejudices, and those familiar practices of self and of relationship that are subjugating of persons' lives (p. 27).

The aim of the first phase of therapy is for the client and therapist to gain a mutual understanding of the issues that are reasons for the client to seek help.

3. Re-naming, re-labelling, reframing and starting an externalising conversation

The deconstruction of the dominant story starts with a re-labelling of the problem in externalising language. Externalisations are reframes of the problem, often embedded in metaphoric language. Externalisations involve re-naming, and applying a different lens or viewpoint to the problem, using unique, even unusual, language that offers alternative descriptions of the problem and often leads to a cognitive shift in the perception of the problem. Externalisations create a distance between the problem and the person, allowing more freedom to explore and evaluate the problem's influence and alternative options. Reframes facilitate a change in the conceptual or emotional setting and encourage the client to consider alternative descriptions of the problem. In the work with children, externalisations are often personifications giving the problem a character quality.

In the externalising conversation with the client, the externalised problem is explored at least over the two time zones of past and present, and in some instances, also projected into the future. Typical questions relating to the past may be phrased, such as, 'When did you first receive coaching lessons in self-defeat? Who was the most influential coach in the early days? When did you start adopting the view of yourself? How did it affect your relationships at your work? How did you notice that self-defeat was taking hold of you?'.

Questions relating to the present may be phrased, such as, 'At what time in the day or in what situation does self-defeat manage to get a strong hold of you? How do you know it is active, playing havoc with your view of yourself and undermining your self-worth? How do others respond when this happens? What are the first warning signs when it is about to take hold of you?'. At the end of this phase, both client and therapist arrive at a good understanding of the problem, mapping its historical roots and current influences in the person's life and possibly exploring a future in which the problem still holds control over the person. Examples of questions are 'If fear and worry were to continue holding such powerful control over your daily life, how would your situation look in, let's say, 10 years' time from now?'. Future prediction of the problem story, however, should be used with caution as it can discourage the client and restricts the shift towards more hopeful alternatives.

A good example of an externalising conversation with a child presenting with fears can be found in White and Morgan (2006). The child is encouraged to characterise the fears and map their current effect on the child. Michael White's responses emphasise the externalised position of the fears by using language such as 'the fears running around', 'taking away the boy's sleep', 'they are up to something' and 'have plans for the child's future'. He further suggests that the fears need a good education as they should not roam around at night. There is drama and acting involved on the part of the therapist (White & Morgan, 2006, page 7).

4. Exploring unique outcomes

Throughout the conversation with the client, the therapist will maintain an astute awareness of any reference made by the client that points to alternatives and contradictions to the dominant narrative. NT therapy refers to these instances as 'Unique Outcomes' (also referred to as 'Exceptions' in Solution-Focused Therapy). When instances of these occur, the therapist will alert the client that these contradictions have occurred and invite the client to explore the meaning and relevance of these. The therapist may also more actively encourage the client to consider whether or not the dominant story has taken over his or her whole life, or if there are situations where the problem has no or lesser influence, if exceptions have occurred in the past, or could even occur again in the future given a different situation. The exploration will encourage the client to appreciate that exceptions are already occurring, increase awareness of these instances in everyday life, and increase the client's level of hopefulness and motivation to strive towards integrating these instances into rich tapestries of resourceful alternative stories that will guide the client's behaviour in the present and in the future.

5. Reconstruction of a new story: Re-authoring narratives

The development (reconstruction) of the alternative story is a gradual process, and often, reconstruction and deconstruction create a pattern of 'weaving in and out' with each other, with a conversation about dominant themes and problems alternating with the emergence of alternative options. However, the creation of the alternative narrative is strongly enhanced by therapist-specific questions which draw out unrecognised potential, lived experience, behaviour, beliefs and interactions that point to an alternative. The process of reconstruction of an alternative story is again mapped across the three different time zones of past, present, and this time more strongly on future behaviour, cognition, emotions and interactions with others. At any stage of therapy, the client can be invited to weigh up, to consider which way is the preferred way, the old story, the alternative, or neither, but something else.

6. Anchoring and strengthening the story within the social environment

The final part of NT consists of anchoring the new experiences and behaviours socially within the relevant environment, with family, friends, and people in authority, and considering what type of beliefs and social interactions would achieve this goal. One aim of this phase is for the client to realise and then to experience consciously the changed interaction with others, which in turn will reinforce the new narrative. This final stage of NT consists of consolidation, a firmer grounding of new beliefs, and application of new knowledge to different and relevant life situations so that change can be noticed by others. The client is encouraged to circulate the new story within his or her social network to consolidate the change.

Therapy Techniques in NT

Empathy and Reflective Listening

Although a generic therapy variable and not heavily focused on in the NT literature, it should be stressed that successful therapy requires a respectful therapeutic environment, which values the client in unconditional ways and offers empathic and reflective listening so the client feels heard and understood. NT is not a technique but a sensitive and respectful conversation in which challenging topics will be addressed, which requires a secure base as a starting point. There is a danger that the therapist tries to move to alternative stories too quickly instead of staying with the dominant problem story sufficiently long enough. Reflective listening may include paraphrasing and verbal tracking of content, and empathy can be expressed in both non-verbal and verbal ways.

Self-reflection and a NT Consistent Therapy Environment

To be consistent with the main premises of the model, therapy is enhanced by the ability of the therapist to be open and self-reflective, to consider the client–therapist relationship and the therapist's own strength and vulnerabilities. This can be fostered by encouraging clients to comment on and evaluate the therapy process to ascertain that client's expectations are being met. There should be a good match between model/therapist and client preference. Language appropriateness may need to be scrutinised inside and outside of therapy, including reference to negative labels about the client, and supervision can be helpful in this process.

Personification and Externalisation (Reframing)

Reframing is a powerful therapeutic tool utilised in many forms of therapy and was first introduced to the field in the 1960s by the Mental Research Institute in the USA (Mattila, 2001). Though there are many definitions of reframing, a useful definition describes this variable as a therapist suggestion, question, comment, re-description of a statement or issue, offering an alternative way of perception (Mattila, 2001). Externalisations and personifications in narrative child therapy re-describe the presenting problem in externalised language and introduces externalised characters that assist with change.

Narrative Questions

Narrative questions map out the influence of the problem over the person, and they assist in developing an alternative narrative. NT therapy employs two major forms of questions, '*landscape of consciousness questions*' and '*landscape of action questions*' (White, 1991). The first category, *landscape of consciousness questions*, refers to the client's cognition, such as beliefs, assumptions, and perceptions about the problem and about alternatives, whereas *landscape of actions questions* refer to behaviour, experience and interactions with the social world. Nicholson (1995) refers to this questioning process as a 'narrative dance', shifting between action/experience and meaning (attributed to experience) and moving between the three time dimensions, past, present and future.

The questions at the beginning of therapy often focus strongly on the dominant story, exploring and gently confronting cognitive states, beliefs, attitudes, inter-actions, experiences and behaviours that reinforce the problem narrative. This question style in itself can create new insights and encourage new action/behaviour and interactions with others. Entry points into an alternative are often inconsistencies that do not fit with the dominant narrative. The role of therapy is to explore the significance of these exceptions, again using the same questioning process and inviting the client to evaluate the likely future should these alternatives gain stronger influence over the person's life. Hewson (1991) points to the power of future prediction questions in generating an alternative story. These questions are solution-focused and elicit future scripts, emphasising what action or processes are required for the client to achieve an alternative outcome. Narrative questions are also often circular questions (Brown, 1997), linking client behaviour with observations or beliefs of other people and may involve the time dimensions of past, present and future, such as 'Of all the people who have known you during your growing up years, who would be the least surprised to discover that you have been able to take this important step during last week?'. 'What would they notice first if you would meet them today?'.

Past and present focused questions referring to the dominant story

Examples of therapist questions referring to the past and present may be phrased such as 'What were the situations in the past when the depressive blackness took a strong hold of you? What was happening for you at the time? What sense do you make of the experience? When this blackness invites itself now, what do you first notice that it is happening? Are there situations when you are especially vulnerable to its invitation, places, people, and times of the day? Do thoughts come first or feelings? Which ones are more powerful and harder to stop? You said you really got dragged down yesterday, what was happening?'. The therapist can utilise future prediction questions. However, there is a danger that these questions reinforce increased negativity and pessimism.

Past, present and future questions referring to the alternative story

Examples of therapy questions referring to the past are 'Who in the past would have supported the view that change is possible? Who would have noticed and commented on your changed behaviour last week? What would they say if they had seen it? You have been telling me of three instances in the past where self-defeat played no part. What do you make of it?'. Present-oriented questions may be phrased, such as 'What do you think I just noticed? Do you realise what you are saying right now? How does it fit with self-defeat? If we compare it with 3 months ago, what do you believe is different? What does it tell us about you? How do you describe yourself now? What could I find in the past that would have predicted that you could do this today?'. Future-oriented questions can be extremely powerful and may be phrased in the following way 'When you are ready to undertake this journey, what small steps will you have taken between now and then to have achieved this readiness? Using three words, how will you describe yourself when you achieve this goal? Who in your culture or social group will support this view of yourself? What will they say or do to support you on this journey? What will have changed, the way you look, the clothes you are wearing, the way you walk, talk, sleep, or work?'.

NT with Young Children

NT with children dates back to the 80s (White, 1989; White & Morgan, 2006), and these earlier approaches combined NT with what we believe are strategic and developmental ideas, often leading to refreshing and unique therapeutic applications. NT has been applied to a wide range of childhood problems, including learning problems (Stacey, 1997), behavioural problems, including tantrums, aggression and anger (Stiefel, 2018; Stiefel et al., 2017; Walters, 2011; White, 1989; Wood, 1988), anxiety and fears (Epston, 1986; White, 1989; White & Morgan, 2006), encopresis (Heins & Ritchie, 1985; Silver et al., 1998), attention-needy behaviour (Walters, 2011) and social skills deficits (Beaudoin et al., 2016).

Yet NT with children needs adaption and consideration of the child's age, cognitive and language ability, and also the child's social environment, especially when working with young children who will not attend the therapy session without their parents, carers or families. Therefore, family factors will also need to be considered.

The Therapy Process When Working with Young Children

The Therapy Environment

Therapy with young children (age range 3–6) requires a therapeutic setting in which children can express themselves in developmentally appropriate ways. Toys should be age appropriate and capture the child's interests (Barker & Chang, 2013). However, they should also have therapeutic value and utilisation. Toys can include puppets, a doll house with content, a range of toy animals, various craft and stationery items, toy cars, small toys which represent kitchen items, police cars, ambulances, fire engines or hospitals, especially if emergency themes are relevant to the symptom presentation of the child. A whiteboard or poster stand is helpful for illustrations created by therapist, family member or child. The toys should be appropriate for children within the age range but also for older siblings who may attend the appointment. There should be chairs of various sizes and a small table ready for use by the child.

Therapy Phases of NT with children

1. Referral and invitation of the family

Therapy usually starts with a telephone call made by the carer, explaining the reason for referral and giving relevant demographic information, such as who lives in the family and other relevant details. In the author's experience, it is wise to invite the complete family (family members who live together in the household) to the first interview. The reasons are several. Most importantly, the first family appointment offers an opportunity to meet and engage with all family members, understand important roles each family member may take during the course of treatment, and explore other family dynamics or circumstances as they may be relevant to the problems. Older siblings can be extremely helpful contributors to the therapy process (Stiefel et al., 2017). Once all family members are engaged, more flexible arrangements can be made with the therapist and family working out the best, most practical and effective ways to continue with therapy. Parental employment and the needs of older siblings working or attending high school may be factors to be considered in the planning of further sessions.

2. Engagement of the referred child and family

Active and positive engagement of children in NT is desirable and often essential. Engagement of the referred child can be direct and immediate or slow if the child is shy, anxious or hesitant. The therapist needs to be an astute observer and explorer, as one of the tasks of NT is to find anchoring points for the later introduction of themes, the development of stories, externalisations of problems, and discovery of characters that can act as helpers in the process of therapy (Stiefel et al., 2017). Therapists can utilise their full creative potential with words at an appropriate cognitive level, non-verbal engagement and expression, refreshing ideas and their rudimentary drawing skills consisting of stick figures and simple illustrations. The child may offer clues of likes and dislikes, for example, in the form of clothing they wear, toys they bring to the appointment, games they play with friends or siblings and topics of interest, including TV shows. The Batman shirt may indicate that Batman is the child's favourite hero, or the parents may offer relevant information on favourite TV shows, cartoon characters or forms of play, and the response by the child to these comments may offer important feedback as to the relevance of these themes.

3. Exploring the problem

Problem talk is essential to allow the family to report their concerns and for all to get a good understanding of the presenting issues, the developmental roots if relevant, the current presentation, attempted effort by the family to overcome the difficulties, future fears and the aim of therapy. Parents and other carers are usually the main reporters of their concerns, yet if possible, the child can also be involved in appropriate ways. The aim of the exploration is to reduce any feeling of guilt or responsibility the child may carry for the presenting problem, and therapeutic reframes may be one of the tools the therapist can utilise that will facilitate positive engagement and rapport and reduce the child's or other family members' discomfort.

4. Developing a narrative

Theme development is an important step in NT with children. Gathering the information from both referral problem, attempted solutions, exploration of the child's interests, behaviour during the initial phase of the interview, and the child's engagement with play material, the therapist may offer descriptions of the problem that match the reason for concern, yet phrased in alternative, playful or uncommon ways. For example, for a child with a fear of insects, the therapist may say, 'Oh, these little critters, they are playing tricks with you, giving you the jitters'.

5. Introducing externalisations and personifications

Reframes and re-labels of the problem in the form of externalisations and personifications may be introduced at this stage. These are new descriptions and new labels which encourage multiple or alternative perspectives or emphasise other aspects of the problem (Mattila, 2001). However, when working with young children, the reframing has to be relevant, age-appropriate and meaningful to the child.

In NT with children, externalisations are often personifications, giving the problem a character quality. Externalisations can occur in several ways. The most common ways are externalisations of the problem or the introduction of a helper in personified ways that will assist the child in overcoming the difficulties. The externalisation will help in emphasising the distance between the problem and the child. It is often of benefit if the name of the problem conveys a degree of playfulness, similar to names of cartoon characters, such as Mr Smiley, Mr Grumpy, Mrs Jitters, Scary Crow, or specific names representing the problem, such as 'Pully' for hair pulling or 'Thumby' for sucking thumb. The child is actively encouraged to join the brainstorming exercise to find the right labels for both the problem and later for the helper. Once the concerns are understood and labelled, the next phase of therapy can begin.

Beginning therapists may wish to borrow from established phrases and externalised descriptions, children's books or programs, such as Get Lost Mr Scary (MacGregor & Herger, 2011), Mr Bossy, The Monster in the Closet, Mrs Temper, Sneaky Poo or similar, though we strongly believe that client created and in-session created metaphors tend to be more powerful in shifting presenting problems. Legowski and Brownless (2001) stress the importance of client contribution in the creation of externalisations. However, the young child may require the help of the parent or therapist to find suitable labels. Asking questions such as 'What shall we call it? What would be a good name? What does he look like? Does she have a grumpy face?' may help the child to create a suitable label together in a relaxed and playful atmosphere.

Case Example — Maggie

Five-year-old Maggie was referred by her single mum for longstanding issues with separation anxiety. Maggie's mother, Trish reported that Maggie had always been a clingy child, but her anxiety increased at the age of 3 with the start of preschool. Maggie's parents separated in the first year of Maggie's life. Trish indicated that Maggie had been a surprise pregnancy, and at the time, the child's father had not been ready to take on a parenting role but had since become a committed father, with regular contact every second weekend. The access visits were uneventful, with no separation issues, and the parental relationship was amicable. Trish's aim was to address the separation issues now, as Maggie had been enrolled to start Kindergarten in the following months. The problem of separation was always the same, with Maggie delaying getting ready for preschool on the three preschool mornings but displaying great independence on other days. Repeated anxious questions in the car, such as 'Will you pick me up?' and clinginess with crying in the parking lot of the preschool were common, and Maggie's teacher was needed to assist with the separation. Once Trish drove off to work, Maggie quickly settled into the preschool day. The teacher reported that Maggie had made good friends, and no other developmental concerns were reported. There was some indication that Maggie was a bright child, that she had creative ability and especially enjoyed craft.

In the first session, Maggie readily engaged; she appeared to be a bright child with good language ability for her age. She gave a detailed account of her preschool days, which she confirmed she enjoyed. She named her two best friends and said she liked her teacher. She then reported details of her time with her dad and named her favourite activities at home with her mum, which included crafts and going to the beach. She looked into the craft box and appeared to be excited when seeing the different craft materials available. At this stage, the therapist wondered if some form of craft could assist the therapy process.

We explored the preschool mornings, and Maggie confirmed that separation from her mum was difficult. She gave various reasons, such as 'missing mum', 'worrying about mum', and 'mum might get sick', but could not explain this further. The therapist explored whether 'worrying about mum' was based on a real-life experience, but Trish could not think of any reason except for a mild degree of Post Natal Depression when Maggie was born, and the relationship with the dad deteriorated.

The therapist, looking at small Velcro balls in the craft box, suddenly had an idea. She wondered if these externalised craft materials, the little Velcro balls, could become therapeutic helpers in the form of 'help-needing characters'. After checking for favourite colours, the therapist took out a large and a small Velcro ball and explained that the name of the small ball was 'Clingy'. The therapist explained that Clingy felt nervous and anxious about going to school and needed help. She demonstrated this by making Clingy cling to the bigger ball. She then asked Maggie if she could help Clingy master the task of enjoying his school day. The gender of Clingy was purposefully changed to a male to create more distance between Clingy's and Maggie's problems.

It helps to have a resourceful parent, as in the case of Maggie and her mother. Trish, with enthusiasm, suggested that Maggie could take Clingy to her preschool, so he could get used to 'little' school first and help him to settle in without experiencing fear. She checked with the therapist to make sure that Clingy had permission to leave the clinic and go home with Maggie. We then all created a story together, using the whiteboard, developing a range of different strategies that would assist Clingy in mastering the task of separation and enjoying his preschool day. We cut out paper in the form of book shapes, found small pencils and gave Maggie the task of teaching Clingy to write his name at preschool. We found a small (pretend) backpack for Clingy, and Maggie's mum cut out a small square of tissue paper in case Clingy cried and needed to dry his tears. A follow-up call with the parent indicated that the strategy had worked; Maggie, instead of focusing on her own fear, had focused on helping Clingy attend preschool. Maggie had also shared the story of Clingy with her preschool teacher.

As outlined elsewhere (Stiefel et al., 2017), externalisations can take many forms. External characters can be the problem, with the task for the child and family to gain control over its influence. A well-known example of this approach is Sneaky Poo (Heins & Ritchies, 1985), with Sneaky Poo running and controlling the child's life. The externalisation can also be portrayed as a helper, supporting the child in finding a solution to the presenting problem. In this case, the therapist may suggest a strong hero, a character the child identifies with, to step in and support the child. Finally, the externalisation can represent a character in need of help, as in Maggie's case. Some therapy excerpts present two externalisations, both the problem and the strength that is needed to overcome a problem (White & Morgan, 2006). Michael White stresses the importance of tailor-made interventions (not cookbook approaches), as an intervention that works well for one child may not work for another child (White & Morgan, 2006). We have found the same in our clinical experience.

Case Example — Emma

Emma (aged 4.5 years) was brought to the counselling centre by her mum and dad. The reason for referral was an unsuccessful history with toilet training, with Emma refusing to sit on the toilet, instead insisting on using nappies during the day and night. Compared with Maggie, Emma was hard to engage. She did not respond verbally to questions but eventually played quietly at the kid's table close to her mum, exploring the set of Australian animals available in one of the play boxes. The parents reported that Emma had started toilet training at the age of 2.5 years but reverted back to nappies during a difficult winter season when she experienced a lot of sickness. She attended two days of preschool and would hold on all day and not use the preschool toilet. To avoid accidents, the parents decided to use pull-ups during the day. They were keen to address the issue prior to the start of Kindergarten in 6 months' time.

The parents expressed frustration and said their two-and-a-half-year-old son, who also attended the session, had just mastered toilet training for bladder control (or wee), and they could not understand what was holding Emma back. They had consulted a paediatrician, but no organic cause was established for the problem; instead, counselling was recommended. They had tried stickers and reward charts, but these had not been successful. They had banned the pull-ups for one morning, but this had led to a 4-hour-long tantrum.

The therapist wondered how she could engage Emma. Did Emma have a wish to grow up and leave pull-ups behind? Did she have a favourite story? Did she like to watch certain TV kids' programs, and one of the characters in these could become a helper? Could one of the Australian animals she showed interest in being recruited to assist with the therapy? Could the kangaroo in the kangaroo mother's pouch be somehow used for the development of a story? However, trial attempts by the therapist did not lead to the engagement of Emma. In her desperation, the therapist started to draw the Pull-ups, pretending to have some difficulties with the task and hoping that Emma would join her, which she finally did. The therapist drew happy and unhappy faces on the Pull-ups, depending on their load, with the heavy and wet ones (colouring in blue) expressing unhappiness with their heavy load. Emma produced her own little drawings, and we experimented with different facial expressions and different degrees of heaviness in a playful way. To give the Pull-ups a further impression of 'characters', the therapist drew arms and legs in stick figure format but also added expression. For example, one of the Pull-ups was scratching its head, thinking what she could do to feel less heavy with so much wee water in the Pull-up's body. The Pull-ups also started an interaction with each other, consulting and problem solving, with Emma making her small contributions.

The challenge now was to convince Emma that in order for the Pull-ups to be happier and lighter, the wee had to go elsewhere. The therapist was delighted when Emma suggested the wee should go into the toilet. However, there was no clear plan or solution to the problem as to how this was to be achieved, and the first session ended.

In the second session, the therapist explored with Emma if there were any advantages of not wearing pull-ups, the freedom this would give and allowing them to engage in new activities. Again, a range of drawings was used as these seemed to engage Emma. Pictures of a stick figure of children with and without pull-ups were produced. We talked about the beach, the big water slides in an amusement park, and running under a sprinkler in the backyard, with the stick figures indicating specific facial expressions accordingly. Stick figures with pull-ups had to sit out and look sad and grumpy. Emma finally agreed that she wanted to try one of the activities, going to the beach for a short time without pull-ups and playing in the sand

and surf at one of the quieter beaches. The parents agreed to the strategy and said they would plan at least one visit to the beach prior to the next session.

The case example presented illustrates how the problem (the wee in the pull-ups) is holding Emma back from enjoying new things in her life, especially activities her peers were doing. However, the wee is not directly tackled. Instead, the pull-ups are externalised, and the child is encouraged to explore the restricting effect the wee had on the enjoyment of life for the pull-ups with the blue colour. Emma indeed mastered short times at the beach without pull-ups, and in further sessions, we jointly made a plan for other pull-up-free outings for the family to enjoy.

6. Multi-sensory communication

As stressed, NT with young children requires language adaptation but also enrichment of communication utilising multi-sensory means, including verbal emphasis, pacing, tone of voice and volume, action and demonstrations, physical activities, visual illustrations and at times strong non-verbal expressions or gestures to reinforce important verbal messages. Creative therapist potential is a plus, but we believe that creativity can be learned and practised, both at the verbal (language) and non-verbal level.

7. Developing a plan or strategy to outsmart the problem

The centrepiece of therapy is to develop a plan, a strategy with the child and family to conquer the problem in successful ways. This phase encourages the child, family and therapist to utilise their most powerful and often creative potential. Child input can be helpful but often needs guidance from the therapist to ascertain that the plan is realistic and will likely lead to success. For example, a child may say, 'I will shoot Pully the hair puller with a gun, and it will be gone, 'bang'!' Therapist, carers and child will then develop a more detailed plan for how the shooting Pully could be integrated into a realistic strategy that will stop Pully's behaviour. This may involve a step-by-step plan with good timing of activities at critical times, introduction of new activities and parent input to assist.

8. Maintaining gains

Once therapy reaches a good stage of progress, therapists often warn children that the problem may sneak in again, explore what the likely situations may be and how the child and family can protect or prepare themselves from the intrusion. For a child with school attendance issues, it may be the Monday morning or returning back to school after the holidays, and it is for those times, a backup plan may need to be designed so the child and family can be prepared and address the problem using the preventative measures. The powerful externalised helpers may have a special role to play at this time.

The Evidence Base for NT

Evidence for the effectiveness of NT is gradually developing. Readers are referred to the website of the Dulwich Centre (https://dulwichcentre.com.au), which is attempting to keep an up-to-date account of research in the field. Current research reflects anecdotal evidence, treatment outcome research using a single case study design (Scott et al., 2013), multiple base-line research (Besa, 1994), qualitative research which focuses on client experience (O'Connor et al., 1997) and retrospective analysis of treatment outcome (Silver et al., 1998), to name just a few. There is developing evidence that NT might be the more effective approach in treating childhood encopresis (Silver et al., 1998) compared with standard treatment.

Several researchers express a strong view, proposing that research methods should reflect the principles of NT practice and that research should be a collaborative process (Tootell, 2004). Research that involves the 'subjects', which is relevant to the client group of study, which addresses local needs, and which involves collaboration, action, mobilisation and transformation is favoured compared with classical empirical research designs based on principles of neutrality, objectivity and normative assumptions. Further, it is argued that NT practice is linked with continual evaluation involving the client, using reflective processes during and after treatment, and exploring whether or not the therapy process is relevant and helpful to the client. Denborough (2004) refers to this process as co-research.

We believe further good quality research, quantitative and qualitative, is needed to assess the value of NT. Research questions that need further exploration are: What are the most effective treatment variables in NT? Which client group benefits the most, considering age, social status, culture, race, gender, type of presentation and severity of presentation? In what settings is NT of lesser value compared with other treatment models? If NT wants to survive in the competitive funding climate, cost-effectiveness may also be an issue that requires exploration.

Conclusion

The advantages of the model when working with young children are manifold. NT can be introduced in relaxed and playful ways, using multi-sensory means of communication, including simple drawings, storytelling, acting and dramatisation, appropriate to the developmental level, interests and language abilities of young children. Externalisation techniques in the form of personifications shift the focus from the child as the problem to the third person or character, herewith lifting the burden of fear, guilt or failure that the child may experience as a result of the presenting issues. These forces combined increase the likelihood of child engagement and active participation in therapy.

NT requires both an engaged child and an engaged carer. Older siblings can be great helpers being able to see through the playful strategies employed and contributing with their own unique and creative ideas. They can also offer assistance with the implementation of a specific strategy. However, despite best efforts, NT is not always the model of choice. We have worked with families where child engagement in the form of a narrative approach has not been successful. The reason may be that the therapist cannot capture the child's interest. In some families, parenting capacity may undermine this playful approach, with the parent reverting back to the problem and locating the problems within the child's personality. Current diagnosis-based funding systems can also reinforce the view that the child 'has' a problem that needs to be given a diagnostic label. In this case, alternative approaches may be indicated and more helpful.

The chosen therapy model also needs to be a good fit with the therapist. The model should not only support the therapeutic endeavour but should also fit with the therapist's views about change, the therapist's personality and preferred style of working (Barker & Chang, 2013; Taibbi, 2015). Therapist factors may include a lack of experience working with young children and their carers, struggling with the requirement of developing suitable reframes in the form of externalisations and metaphors, with the therapist feeling overwhelmed with the therapeutic task. As with all therapy training, at least beginner-level NT training and supervision is needed, which includes whole family engagement skills, communication at appropriate levels for both child and parents, experimenting with the development of themes and reframes in the form of externalised language, and training in the application of ideas in the form of tasks for the child and family to carry out.

NT has been criticised for adopting an intrapsychic perspective with a focus on subjective experience and not incorporating a systemic perspective (Phipps & Vorster, 2015). We believe this criticism is unjustified, especially when working therapeutically with young children and their families. First, when working with this young age group, therapy always includes the family system, at least in the form of active parent engagement and contributions. Second, with slightly older preschoolers, the therapist may ask simple systemic questions based on family systems theory, such as 'Who would be most helpful... and what would they do', shifting the focus to the interpersonal dimension. Third, NT has a deep respect for context, both at the level of conceptualisation of problem development and when working on overcoming presenting issues. It is the application of the new story in a social context that is often needed in solidifying the alternative story. Finally, Michael White referring to Vygotsky's theory of development, stresses that learning in early childhood (and in NT) involves social collaboration, which in work with young children refers to the role of skilled caregivers, older peers and siblings, and also therapists. The learning opportunities should be just within reach for the child but also require effort on behalf of the child (White & Morgan, 2006). As with all therapy models, not every model is a good fit for each child, family and therapist. However, if compatibility can be achieved, NT can present a powerful model for helping children overcome developmental problems with a feeling of agency and success. NT will appeal to therapists who enjoy creativity and a degree of freedom in designing therapeutic strategies, but also those who embrace postmodern ideas, are self-reflective and favour an involved and empowering therapy process which gives the child and family maximal opportunity in designing treatment ideas.

Reader's Exercises

Tim, a 5-year-old boy, is referred for therapy. The boy lives with his mother, father and an older sibling, and they all attend the first session. The reason for referral is 'oppositional' behaviours occurring mainly when the mother is in charge of parenting. A paediatrician has given the diagnosis of Oppositional Defiant Disorder, though the child does not display oppositional behaviours in any other setting. The parents report that Tim is 'perfect' when his grandmother looks after him on weekends, and he complies with adult requests. Typical behaviour problems include refusal to change clothes when arriving home from school; ignoring his mother's request to take plate, cup and cutlery to the kitchen sink after breakfast or dinner; leaving his school bag in the hallway; ignoring to take his lunchbox out of his school bag; refusing to come inside the house when playing time finishes; and 'forgetting' to feed the dog despite several reminders. Tim's refusal behaviours always cause significant tension between Tim and his mother with endless arguments. The family reports that Tim loves most types of sports. He is an 'outdoor child', and he is popular with his peers. He is athletic and fit. He engages well with you when you ask about his days at school, his friends and sports activities.

How could you develop an alternative description for 'oppositional behaviour' with Tim and the family? What might be some reframes and externalisations of the problem that could be appealing to Tim? How would you approach this task?

References

Australian Psychological Society. (2018). *Evidence-based psychological interventions in the treatment of mental disorders. A review of the literature.* 4th Edition. APS.

Barker, P. & Chang, J. (2013). *Basic family therapy.* Wiley-Blackwell.

Beaudoin, M. N., Moersch, M., & Evare, B. (2016). The effectiveness of NT with children's social and emotional skill development: An empirical study of 813 problem-solving stories. *Journal of Systemic Therapies, 35*(3), 42–29. https://doi.org/10.1521/jsyt.2016.35.3.42

Besa, D. (1994). Evaluating narrative family therapy using single-system research design. *Research on Social Work Practice, 4*(3), 3009–325. https://doi.org/10.1177//104973159400400303

Botella, L., & Herrero, O. (2000). A relational constructivist approach to NT. *European Journal of Psychotherapy and Health, 3*(3), 407–418. https://doi.org/10.1080/13642530010012048

Brown, J. (1997). Circular questioning: An introductory guide. *Australian and New Zealand Journal of Family Therapy, 18(2),* 109–114. https://doi.org/10.1002/j.1467.8438.1997.tb00276.x

Denborough, D. (2004). NT and research. Compiled by Dulwich Centre Publications. *The International Journal of NT and Community Work, 2,* 29–36. https://dulwichcentre.com.au/publications/dulwich-centre-publications/

Epston, D. (1986). Night watching: An approach to night fears. *Dulwich Centre Review,* 28–39.

Freedman, J., & Combs, G. (1996) *NT: The social construction of preferred realities.* WW Norton Co.

Goldenberg, I., Standon, M., & Goldenberg, H. (2013). *Family Therapy. An Overview (9th Ed).* Cengage Learning.

Heins, T., & Ritchie, K., (1985). *Beating Sneaky Poo.* Dulwich Centre. Retrieved from: www.dulwichcentre.com.au

Hewson, D. (1991). From laboratory to therapy room. Prediction questions for constructing the 'new-old' story. *Dulwich Centre Newsletter, 3,* 5–12.

Legowski, T. & Brownless, K. (2001). Working with metaphor in NT. *Journal of Family Psychotherapy, 12*(1), 19–28. https://doi:10.1200/ J085v12n01_02

MacGregor, C., & Herger, K. (2011). *Get lost, Mr. Scary. An early intervention program for anxious children ages 5 to 7 years. Facilitators Manual.* NSW Department of Education and Training.

Mattila, D. (2001). *'Seeing things in a new light'. Reframing in therapeutic conversation.* Helsinki University Press.

Nicholson, S. (1995). The narrative dance — A practice map for White's therapy. *Australian and New Zealand Journal of Family Therapy, 16*(1), 23–28. https://doi.org/10.1002/j.1467-8438.1995.tb01023.x

O'Connor, T. S. J., Meakes, E., Pickering, M.R., & Schuman, M. (1997). On the right track: Client experience of NT. *Contemporary Family Therapy, 19*(4), 479–495. https://doi10.1023/A:1026126903912

Phipps, W. D., & Vorster, C. (2015). Refiguring family therapy: NT and beyond. *The Family Journal: Counselling and Therapy for Couples and Families, 23*(3), 254–261. https://doi.org./10.1177/1066480715572978

Rasheed, J. M., Rasheed, M. N., & Marley, J. A. (2011). *Family Therapy. Models and Techniques.* Sage.

Scott, N., Hanstock, T. L., & Patterson-Kane, L. (2013). Using NT to Treat Eating Disorders Not Otherwise Specified. *Clinical Case Studies, 12(4),* 307–321. https://doi.org./10/1177/1534650113486184

Silver, E., Williams, A., Worthington, F., & Phillips, N. (1998). Family therapy and soiling: An audit of externalising and other approaches. *The Association of Family Therapy, 20,* 413–422. https://doi.org/10.111/1467.6427.00096

Stacey, K. (1997). From imposition to collaboration: Generating stories of competence. In C. Smith and D. Nylund (Eds.), *Narrative Therapies with Children and Adolescents.* The Guilford Press.

Stiefel, I. Anson, J., & Hinchcliffe, D. (2017). NT with preschoolers. Unfolding the story. *Australian and New Zealand Journal of Family Therapy, 38,* 261–271. https://doi.org.10.1002/anzf.1211

Stiefel, I. (2018). Young children in family therapy. *Advances in Sociology Research, 25,* 151–170. Nova Science Publisher.

Taibbi, R. (2015). *Doing family therapy. Craft and creativity in clinical practice.* The Guilford Press.

Tootell, A. (2004). Decentring research practice. *International Journal of NT and Community Work, 3,* 54–60.

Walters, K. R. (2011). The hungry-for-attention metaphor: Integrating narrative and behavioural therapy for families with attention-seeking children. *Australian and New Zealand Journal of Family Therapy, 32,* 208–219. https://doi.org/10.1375/ anft.32.3.208

White, M. (1989). *Selected Papers.* Dulwich Centre Publications.

White, M. (1991). Deconstruction and therapy. *Dulwich Centre Newsletter,* No.3, 21–40.

White, M. & Morgan, A. (2006). *NT with children and their families*. Dulwich Centre Publications.

Wood, A. (1988). King tiger and the roaring tummies: A novel way of helping young children and their families change. *Journal of Family Therapy, 10*, 49–63. https://doi.org/10.1046/j.1988.00299.x

Chapter 13

Strategic Family Therapy (SFT)

Ingeborg Stiefel and Matthew Brand

Strategic family therapy (SFT) is a brief, pragmatic, problem and outcome-focused family therapy intervention (Rasheed et al., 2011). The first strategic models developed in the late 1950s and 1960s, and many concepts and techniques of the initial models can be found in contemporary applications, such as Solution Focused Therapy, Narrative Therapy and Post Milan Systemic Therapy. One of the model's premises is that problems and symptoms in people cannot be understood and addressed without reference to context, the immediate social context, such as the family, and if relevant, also wider social systems (Madanes, 1991).

SFT conceptualises problems as emerging from problematic interactions between family members. Often the problem itself constitutes the family's attempt to correct or overcome their difficulties. The model's presumption is that families get stuck in stressful interactions because they have not worked out an appropriate alternative strategy to resolve their difficulties. The therapeutic task is for the therapist to gain a clear understanding of the central problem, to observe and explore the problematic family interaction that supports the continuation of the difficulties, and then to develop a therapeutic strategy that will effectively interrupt the problem interaction and as a result weaken or resolve the current symptom (Rasheed et al., 2011). SFT is not interested in the reason why symptoms develop, instead focuses on present concerns as expressed by the family, and the therapeutic task is to integrate the family's stated goal for change into an effective and successful therapy. Intervention strategies attempt to disrupt problematic family interactions that maintain or perpetuate the reported problem. In SFT, the therapist is active, facilitates what happens during the session and is responsible for designing specifically tailored strategies that will effectively address the issue of concern. Interventions can be pragmatic (whatever works to reduce the presenting problem), they tend to be behaviourally oriented, and they do not need to tackle comprehensively all aspects of a problematic family interaction, only those that will facilitate a sufficient shift in the system to resolve the problem (Stanton, 1981). The model places the responsibility for designing strategic interventions with the therapist, and if a strategy is not helpful, it is again the therapist's role to design a new and more effective intervention. Madanes claims that SFT is a suitable model for a wide range of problems for clients of all ages, social and cultural backgrounds (Madanes, 1991). SFT allows the therapist to borrow techniques from other models of therapy and challenges the therapist's own creativity and ingenuity when developing appropriate interventions (Madanes, 1991).

Historical Development

Strategic models of family therapy emerged from several major developments in the therapy field, such as the groundwork on communication established by the proponents of the Communication Model (Watzlawich et al., 1967) and further by the therapeutic approaches and techniques employed by Milton Erickson (Goldenberg et al., 2013; Rasheed et al., 2011; Stanton, 1981; Simon et al., 1985).

Attempts to understand human communication occurred in the 1950s and 1960s by researchers and therapists associated with the Mental Research Institute Group (MRI) in Palo Alto. Members of this group included Gregory Bateson, Don Jackson, John Weakland, Paul Watzlawick, Richard Fish, Arthur Bodin, Carlos Sluzki, Jay Haley and their associates. Watzlawick and colleagues proposed five axioms for effective communication (Watzlawich et al., 1967). These included:

1. All behaviour is some form of communication because one cannot not communicate.

2. Communication has a content aspect and a relational aspect.

3. Communication consists of digital aspects (words) and non-verbal aspects.

4. Communication can be symmetrical or complementary.

5. The meaning of communication depends on punctuation made by the receiver and sender.

Communication theorists studied human communication, verbal and non-verbal, including gestures, intonation, tone of voice, pace, mime and volume. Of interest were both the direct messages contained in exchanges between family members, but also the implied or indirect messages. Bateson and his group explored communication patterns in both normal families and in families where a family member had been diagnosed with schizophrenia. One of the major theories of this time period was the double bind theory. In this theory, problems develop in families where a family member gives two confusing and contradictory (paradoxical) messages, commands or requests to another family member, such as logically inconsistent messages or a contradiction between content and non-verbal expression, which makes it difficult for the receiver to respond. An understanding of problematic family communication patterns became one of the focal points for SFT. The attempt to disrupt and change these was the focus of therapy. Jackson and Fish explored short-term problem-focused, pragmatic approaches to therapy (Rasheed et al., 2011). These stood in sharp contrast to the mainstream models of that time period which were individually focused, lacked a systemic lens, and favoured long-term therapy with the aim of understanding the intra-psychic reasons for symptom development and the 'why'.

Milton Erickson, another prominent therapist associated with the development of SFT, joined the MRI group and brought his unique approaches to therapy, which included hypnotherapeutic techniques, brief, paradoxical instructions and unusual interventions, which also strongly influenced the developing field of SFT (Stanton, 1981). Erickson had a deep respect for idiosyncrasies in people and tolerance for different forms of living (Madanes, 1991). He believed that people had the ability to solve their own problems if they could be encouraged to try out new behaviour. Change could be rapid and the client's resistance could be utilised to bring about change. Erickson's therapy was directive, creative and unconventional at times, and he was a master of paradoxical interventions. Interventions were carefully planned and the therapist took an active role in the therapy process.

The foundational phase was also strongly influenced by cybernetics and systems theory (Goldenberg et al., 2013; Stanton, 1981). Cybernetics focuses on information processing in social (and other) systems and tries to explain how systems maintain a status quo and how they change. Cybernetics pays attention to feedback loops and self-correcting mechanisms that maintain a current status or produce change. Negative feedback (also called deviation minimising feedback) triggers adjustment and correction of deviations that will help the family to return to its previous state of smooth functioning. Positive feedback (deviation amplifying feedback) on the other hand triggers change (Simon et al., 1985). SFT may introduce positive feedback into a family system to unblock a stuck interactional sequence and trigger change.

The growing understanding of family communication and the insight that brief, strategic and innovative techniques can have profound therapeutic effects eventually led to the development of the MRI model of family therapy. Problem-solving and strategic techniques were the landmarks of this model.

Haley, who left the MRI group, worked with Minuchin at the Philadelphia Child Guidance Clinic and later with his wife Cloe Madanes and became the founder of the Family Therapy Institute in Washington DC (Stanton, 1981). The Milan group in Italy, which included Palazzoli, Prata, Boscolo and Cecchin, was also strongly influenced by the MRI group (MacKinnon & James, 1987). They developed their own model of strategic therapy utilising paradoxical interventions, especially for families where a family member had been diagnosed with anorexia or schizophrenia, and in the case of young children, encopresis. Out of the foundation phase three models of SFT emerged: The MRI Brief Therapy Model, the (early) Milan Strategic Model, and the Haley and Madanes Strategic Model of Family Therapy. In this paper we will present theoretical ideas and the main techniques of SFT with consideration of a post-modern application.

Theoretical Concepts

Structural Assumptions

SFT shares similarities with other models of family therapy, particularly with Structural Family Therapy. Structural Family Therapy proposes that families need to have a clear structure, with a parental hierarchy, inter-generational boundaries, clear subsystems and roles in line with the wider cultural expectations of the family. Structural confusion or weakness can be one of the reasons leading to family problems. However, in contrast to Structural Family Therapy, which directly tries to correct structural components of family systems, SFT focuses on ineffective family interaction patterns. Nevertheless, these can sometimes be structural in nature, and as a result, the strategic therapist may attempt to address boundaries and hierarchies and helps to define roles of family members.

Context and Circularity

Strategic family therapy shares the assumptions of circular causality that are found in several other models of family therapy (Nelson et al., 1986). Circular causality addresses the reciprocal processes between family members and assumes that each family member influences every other family member. Problems (symptoms) in a family member or in the system cannot be considered without reference to the whole system. A person's behaviour does not occur in isolation or solely as a result of a linear cause–effect relationships. Instead, family members interact with each other in complex circular patterns. The behaviour of one family member may trigger multiple simultaneous responses in several family members at a given time, and these responses may lead to further responses. Related to the concept of circularity is the term 'Multifinality', which is based on the assumption that any given beginning state can have many possible outcomes. The concept of circularity proposes that one action or event can have multiple, unpredictable effects and complex interaction patterns can develop. The behaviour of person A may lead person B to respond in a supportive way and person C opposing A. As a result, person D may object to person B's response, leading person A to take issue with person D. At this stage, person C may interfere and person D withdraws. SFT assumes that when observed long enough, typical family interaction patterns and sequences can be observed and those relevant to the presenting concern are of special importance. An important therapist task is to understand the problematic circular sequences that maintain the problem before an intervention can be planned.

In the context of early childhood problems, a child may swear at his mother; the mother may firmly state that swearing is not acceptable and will then ask the father to become involved by asking, 'Can you talk to him about not swearing'. But the father may rescue the child by saying, 'Leave him alone, it's not that bad', and the mother and father then fight and the issue does not get resolved but develops into a conflict between the couple. It may shift to another issue, the mother accusing the father of not spending time with his son. The pattern of interaction may become a typical pattern of sequences predicting a certain outcome. The next time the child swears, this sequence repeats itself, and the conflict between the couple may even escalate.

According to SFT theory, families engage in predictable sequences of behaviour that involve different family members in typical ways. One person involved in this process may be viewed as the 'problem'. In the example above, it could be the child swearing, the father minimising swearing and not supporting the mother, the father not spending time with his son or other couple relationship issues. The therapist will observe, form one or several hypotheses and will then intervene in one part of the system that will result in a change to the predicted usual outcome. For example if the mother's reaction to swearing became the focus, she may decide not to respond, or therapy may focus on the father, and he may start to take control over the swearing or support his wife.

Homeostasis, Morphostasis and Morphogenesis

The concept of homeostasis, initially applied to physiology, refers to the ability of biological systems to maintain physiological constancy, a steady state (Simon et al., 1985). The concept was later extended to cybernetics and systems in general (Guttman, 1991). Homeostasis in the family systems context refers to the tendency of the family to maintain a given configuration of relationships among family members that leads to a steady state of functioning that allows the family to function effectively, to adjust and accommodate change when necessary, so the family can fulfil its various functions such as raising children and meeting the physical, social and emotional needs of all family members. The family maintains its current structure and adjusts to new demands with small compensatory mechanisms. This process is also referred to as morphostasis (Simon et al., 1985). Stressful events, changes and developmental life cycle challenges can unbalance the system, and the current structure may be ineffective in dealing with the new demands. A new level of relating and a change in structure may be required, a process referred to as morphogenesis. Problems may develop if the system is structurally rigid, for example when family members try to hold onto a current status quo when structural change is required. Family life evolves with a balance between morphostasis (homeostasis) and morphogenesis, and the family system can remain unchanged for a period of time if the internal and external environment is stable. However, if new demands confront the system, structural changes with new patterns of relationships may be required.

To achieve homeostasis, family members must respond to a given set of rules, which set a range of acceptable and expected behaviour (Guttman, 1991). Rules are relationship agreements that prescribe and limit family members' behaviour over a wide variety of content areas and organise the interaction between the people in the family.

The adjustment to change can be seen in the case of a family where the father loses his job and as a result, the mother increases her working hours. A youth may also start part-time work. These adjustments guarantee that a sufficient income level is established; however, they will also change roles and positions in the family. Once the father finds work again, the family system may undergo a second process of change. The mother may decide that she enjoys her extended working hours, or gets promoted, whereas her husband and older son want her to return to her previous role spending more time at home, carrying out traditional duties. If the family cannot negate this needed change and develop a new homeostasis, symptoms may develop. A young child may develop a symptom, such as separation anxiety or enuresis, as a result of the stress impacting the family and the family's unsuccessful attempt to resolve the issue. The task of the therapist is to conceptualise the symptoms comprehensively from a systemic perspective, which may focus on the conflict over changed roles in the couple's relationship or on the relationship between the young child and his parents to form a hypothesis about the separation anxiety or enuresis.

First-Order and Second-Order Changes

Systemic therapy differentiates between first and second-order change (Davey et al., 2012). First-order change refers to small adjustments and corrections the family may make to achieve the previous steady state of functioning. The family structure remains unchanged (Simon et al., 1985). These changes are often quantitative in nature (e.g., a parent becoming more involved, a family member complaining less). A typical intervention involving first-order change may be the mother increasing descriptive praise when her son talks nicely (e.g., in the example of the child with the swearing problem) without any change in the family structure. The roles of the two parents in addressing the issue remain largely unchanged.

Second-order change refers to qualitative change in the system, change in the body of rules that governs the structure and the internal order of the system (Simon et al., 1985). Second-order change leads to a new pattern of relating, and a new problem-solving ability. In the case of the child swearing, both parents may become equally responsible for child rearing (change in rule), and the mother and father work in a united way, supporting each other (change in rule).

Transitions and Life Cycles

One goal of SFT is to help a family master normal transitions and crises, such as childbirth, a sibling being born, starting school or high school, retirement, losing a job, a family member dying, assisting the family in arriving at a new point of family life (Madanes, 1991). Some families may develop symptoms because the crisis has disrupted the homeostasis severely and they are unable to adjust to the new demands; for example, with the birth of a first baby, where previously the couple subsystem was the primary system, new roles and relationships will need to be negotiated. The 'exclusive' couple subsystem no longer exists, instead, the family consists of a couple, a parenting subsystem and two parent–child relationships. Similarly, a significant transition may constitute the birth of a second child, where the couple and family subsystem now have to adjust to several new subsystems, including the new sibling-to-sibling relationship.

The Double Bind Theory, Paradox and Counterparadox

The double bind theory was conceived by Bateson and colleagues based on research on communication structures in families with a member diagnosed as schizophrenic (Simon et al., 1985). The model assumed that family members create a pathological paradox (a double bind) which makes it difficult for the symptomatic person to act and change. Researchers at the time assumed that this communication pattern was strongly linked to the development of schizophrenia. Following contact with Erickson, Bateson introduced Paradoxical Interventions to Haley and the MRI group, who were influential in studying and popularising the concept. Erickson often produced trance states in clients to resolve problems posed by giving contradictory commands (Goldenberg et al., 2013; Lankton & Lankton, 2013).

In everyday life, people send a multitude of messages. A double bind is created when the first message confuses or contradicts the second message. The second message may be logically inconsistent with the first message or appears difficult to understand as it contains two opposite facts. Classic examples of verbal double bind messages are 'Try harder to be spontaneous', 'The authors who wrote this chapter cannot write at all', or 'I'm telling you, you should not listen to anybody'. Paradoxes may also be expressed with an inconsistency between verbal and non-verbal communication, creating confusion in the receiver as to the intent of the message. Paradoxes can be found in children's riddles and stories, for example:

> They went up to the (post) man. 'Excuse me', said George. 'Could you tell us who lives at the old house down by the stream — you know, the empty house there'. The postman replies that he finds this question rather silly. (Blyton, 1986, page 48).

Earlier writers assumed that some families could be resistant to change, and when common sense approaches failed, a paradoxical intervention was implemented. The Milan team referred to the introduction of a therapeutic double bind as 'counterparadox'. Paradoxical interventions were designed to disrupt the family pattern of relating by using the problem in such a way that it triggers change in the family. The intervention was such that the family could not fail, that it would create a state of confusion or evoke an inquisitive and searching attitude. Deissler (2013) stresses that paradoxical interventions require therapist skill, a very clear definition of the family's problem and a flexible therapist who is able to apply the indirect intervention with artistry (Deissler, 2013). Lankton and Lankton (2013) stress that paradoxical interventions are not tricks, but interventions with sincere intent, with a therapeutic strategy based on valid reasoning specific to the client's situation. Paradoxical interventions impede usual thought associations and stimulate mental search (Lankton & Lankton 2013). It is assumed that these therapy techniques arrest attention, and overload the consciousness, leading to confusion in regard to the roles and behaviours of family members in relation to the symptom. They provide an opportunity to stimulate new experiences, perceptions and pattern of relating. There are various definitions of what constitutes a paradoxical intervention (Deissler, 2013, Watson 2013) and various ways of classifying these (Weeks, 2013). According to Simon et al. (1985) a paradoxical intervention can be a command, a prediction, a request or an instruction given by the therapist, which creates a situation that cannot be resolved by means of logic and which forces the family to develop a new approach to the problem (Simon et al., 1985). An effective intervention will accomplish the opposite of what it is seemingly intended to achieve. Paradoxical interventions produce second order change, change in the rules that govern the family system. Interventions can have rapid and dramatic effects (Weeks, 2013), and lead to a change in the frame, how the problem is being perceived, categorised or valued by the family. From the family's perspective, the instruction given is perceived as not addressing the therapeutic goal in a common sense matter and may appear illogical, counter-intuitive, irrelevant or even strange. The effect of the intervention may be that the family defies the instructions and change occurs. The double bind theory of schizophrenia may not have stood the test of time, however the theory has triggered new developments in the field of therapy (Deissler, 2012).

Triangles

A common assumption of SFT is thinking in threes or triangular relationships (Stanton, 1981). Problems often emerge when two family members form a closed alliance and a third person is excluded. A child's problem may develop as a result of an overly close parent–child relationship that excludes the other parent. For example, the therapist hears that the mother and father are arguing over the child's bedtime, and the child sleeps with the mother in her bed, and the father in another bedroom. The child's bedtime problems may communicate the couple's relationship problems, such as a lack of intimacy or an unsatisfying sexual relationship. The problem to be tackled may not be the child sleeping in her own bed, but the mother and father working together on their couple issue, and as a result, the sleeping problem will resolve. Similar issues may occur in a single-parent family with an over-involved grandparent who tries to compete with the biological parent or undermines her by setting her own rules, for example about junk food intake, and pulls the child into a bind of complying with the grandparent or their parent.

The Therapy Process

Different models of SFT describe different stages of therapy. However, common to all models are the following:

- Introduction to the treatment.

- Addressing and involving all family members initially socially and subsequently in the inquiry about the problem.

- Attempting to achieve a clear definition of each family member's concern, accepting the view of the problem as presented by the family, including an understanding of previous problem-solving attempts.

- Clarifying goals of therapy in observable and measurable ways.

- Understanding the problematic family interaction that maintains the problem from verbal report or from family observation in the interview room and defining it so it can be solved.

- Designing an intervention.

- Assessing change/deciding if a different strategy is needed.

- Termination when the goal has been achieved.

Sequences in Haley's model

Haley, a strategic family therapist, argues that the first session is one of the most important sessions in SFT (Hayley, 1976). Therapy begins with the invitation of relevant family members, those who are involved with the problem. Haley states that this is the quickest way to gain a better understanding of the problem, as it offers a potential observation of family interactions that are maintaining the symptom. Further, the whole family interview prevents the formation of alliances with particular individuals, for example by seeing the mother first, or biased reporting of the problem by getting the perspective of only one family member. Haley recommends inviting everyone living in the same home, but this may also include other people both within or outside of the family, such as a grandmother who provides regular child minding or a teacher in cases where the problems occur at school. Therapy can be offered if only parts of the system are present, but according to this model, this is not the ideal situation.

Once the family attends, Haley (1976) outlines four stages of an initial family interview — the social stage, the problem stage, an interaction phase, and the ending of the interview where the therapist may give a directive, a homework or observation task. He argues that when a family attends the first appointment, they may locate the problem within one family member or within a relationship. Families may not be able to clearly and specifically define their concerns. They may describe their difficulties in vague terms, scapegoating a family member, reasoning in linear ways that this person's behaviour is the reason for their stress, or presenting part of the difficulties without awareness of systemic connections. The therapist starts with the concern reported by the family but maintains an openness that allows him to observe and explore how the reported problem is connected to the system and what possible function it may serve.

Social stage

As the family enter the therapy room, the therapist introduces himself, speaks and acknowledges each family member, regardless of the response from each person. This sends the message that everyone is involved and important. If one person takes over, the therapist intervenes and first encourages each family member to introduce themselves and, in the case of young children, say their name. The therapist is acutely attuned and observes how family members organise themselves, such as in seating arrangements. A young child and parent may sit opposite and not next to each other. Parents may sit together while the child is on the ground, boys sitting together, or a parent accepts the child's chair while the young child occupies a large adult chair. The therapist's astute observations include obvious and subtle interactions between family members. The aim of this stage is to get an emotional temperature of each person and understand their feelings about attending. Hypotheses are made during this stage but are not shared with the family, as further evidence is required. This stage lasts a few minutes.

Problem stage

The therapist then makes a clear shift from the social stage to the therapy stage, where the problem is explored and defined. The family is asked what brought them to the session or what their concerns are, phrased in different ways depending on the family and the age of the children. There is generally one person who is most concerned about the problem. Who the therapist asks first about the problem may send messages to the family about the therapist's own perception of the problem or the therapist's biases. If for example the father is asked first this may imply that he is assumed to be in charge of the household. The therapist accepts the problem description as presented by the family and does not challenge family members.

Therapists should be aware of the hierarchy and respect it where possible, but the therapist may also deliberately talk to someone who is not powerful — for example, encouraging a teenager who is an outsider to the problem or who is being quiet in the session to become involved by stating his view. Haley recommends that the adult who seems the least involved with the problem be asked first, and the person with the most power to be treated with the most respect as they often have the biggest influence over the problem. Haley recommends children are not asked first, as it might appear that the therapist is blaming them for the problem. At other times, the least involved child might be asked first, as this suggests that everyone will be involved, talked and listened to. At other times, the therapist may look at the floor or ceiling and ask, 'Tell me why are you here, what are your worries?'. The person who speaks first may be the spokesperson for the family or is someone who occupies a special position. However, the therapist should not presume that this is always the case; instead observes this, makes hypotheses about the possibilities for this and remains open-minded to further evidence.

It is important that the clinician listens and understands what each person says rather than interpreting, or give advice, or ask how someone feels about the situation. If the person is interrupted, the therapist should take charge and respectfully shift back to the first person talking. Each person will get a turn at talking. The therapist observes speech content and the behaviour of each person, including family interaction and tries to understand who is given responsibility for the problem. Again, the therapist does not verbalise any personal views but uses tracking and paraphrasing statements. Having viewed early video recordings of Haley's interview style during our own in-house training, we were impressed with the calm, respectful and containing way Haley conducted the interview and his inclusiveness of all family members.

When the family describe the problem, they might focus on one person 'Jim (5) is aggressive and he never listens', on a dyad 'Jim and John (husband) always fight' or on three or more people 'Jim does not listen to John or myself (mother), but he will listen to his grandmother'. Often, families will locate the problem in one person, but the therapist widens the view and thinks of the problem in terms of the whole system. When parents say their child has a range of problems, they may also indicate their level of helplessness or frustration or point to other issues in the family that may be linked to the child's difficulties. People or circumstances outside the family may also be relevant, such as issues at childcare centres, problems in the neighbourhoods, or relationships with relatives. The therapist considers the uniqueness of each family, although an experienced therapist will have seen common patterns of family problems. For example, a male child will not listen to his mother, but will listen to his father; or a child's symptom development is connected to a stressful marital separation.

The Interaction Phase

Once everyone has provided their view, the therapist then asks that the family talk to each other about the problem. If family members talk to the therapist, they will be re-directed to talking to each other. The therapist may distance themselves physically to highlight the given task. Haley stresses the importance of this phase and the need to turn them back to each other rather than allowing them to talk to the therapist. If however a family member is excluded or the interaction occurs predominantly between two people, the therapist may ask the family to include a silent family member. Haley encourages the family to move from the past to the present, and he may suggest an action, such as acting out the problem in a role play. For example, a child with a tantrum issue may be asked to have a pretend tantrum, and a child who excessively cries may be asked to pretend to cry.

The therapist observes the process and the sequence of interactions between family members. For example, an adolescent may side with one parent against the other parent or a grandfather may side with a daughter-in-law. Haley described that when there is a symptom in a child, there is often an adult who is overly involved and concerned with the child. In the case of an over-involved grandfather, the therapist may encourage the child to talk to his father or mother and observe if the grandfather allows this.

This phase should lead to an understanding of the core systemic problem and the required change, clarification with the family on what change is desired, and establishment of goals that can be observed. The therapist may explore how each family member would recognise that change has occurred, referring to specific behaviours and interactions or frequency of new behaviour (Haley, 1976).

Ending the interview

The interview ends with setting the next appointment — who will come, who is important to the problem and who is not, or if an additional person is needed in further sessions. A therapist may suggest a directive at this stage, for example an observation or a homework task specific to the presenting issues and family interaction.

Generally, strategic family therapists do not encourage textbook tasks or pre-scriptive interventions, as it is believed that these are not able to respond to the uniqueness of each family (Haley, 1976). The therapist must be creative, flexible, and spontaneous and learn from the experience of what is and what is not effective. The therapist approaches each new family as unique and therefore comes up with a particular procedure or strategy for their problem. This requires that a good assessment take place that takes into account the problem contextually and with detail (e.g., when it occurs, places and people involved and any special conditions and circumstances that might be relevant). For example, a problem may only occur when a particular person is present or when a person acts in a particular way.

SFT focuses on one problem at a given time. This can be linked directly to an immediate goal, or may constitute a step or stage that needs to be achieved first to reach a goal. The family will not necessarily be informed how the particular strategy or plan is thought to address the problem. If the intervention fails, the responsibility lies with the therapist to address the family issues effectively and not blame the family (Haley, 1976).

Hypothesis Formation in SFT

Developing one or several hypotheses about the function of the problem and the interaction patterns that maintain and perpetuate the problem are part of the therapeutic task. Hypotheses are conceptualisations made by the therapist which guide the planning of therapeutic interventions. It is not uncommon that a presenting problem offers a range of possible hypotheses about the systemic characteristics that support the problem. Madanes (1991) describes six dimensions that assist the therapist in an understanding of the symptomatic behaviour and guide the therapist in the formation of hypotheses.

1. **Voluntary versus Involuntary Behaviour**. Strategic family therapists tend to perceive most problems as under the control of the client. Families may present to therapy with a firm belief that the problem is involuntary (e.g., biologically based, a disorder, a temperament characteristic). This view can be challenged with help of a re-definition, or with a directive to deliberately produce the problem in order to control it, but also to prove that the client has control or at least some control over the problem. For a child with compulsive behaviour, the therapist may instruct the child to produce the behaviour fast and repeatedly, then at a very slow speed so to bring it on and manipulate it in a way that they have some control over it.

2. **Helplessness versus Power**. SFT considers where the power lies in relationships. A helpless child with a disability or a psychological problem may have great power over the family life, restricting family members' movement, behaviour or influence. The refusal to eat most foods at home and no food at the preschool is powerful as it produces parental helplessness, anxiety or frustration. The therapist's goal is to redistribute power among family members if needed, and to address states of helplessness linked to the presenting problem.

3. **Metaphorical versus Literal Sequences**. A child's problem may be perceived in literal ways, such as the child struggling with anxiety and refusing to go to preschool. However, problems can also be a metaphor for another issue in the family, representing an issue at another level or in a relationship between other people. With the anxious child, there may be a parent who struggles with separation anxiety herself following a couple's separation, needing the child for comfort and closeness, or the separation anxiety metaphorically represents the power struggle between mother and father prior to the separation, now placed into the relationship with the child. How the problem is hypothesised will determine the therapeutic strategy.

4. **Hierarchy versus Equality**. Strategic therapists consider the family hierarchy and explores who is in charge. Similar to Structural Family Therapy, SFT proposes that caregivers (in most instances) need to be in a position where they can support their child in all

aspects of upbringing and daily care. This hierarchy can be reversed in situations where a carer struggles with a severe physical or psychological condition and the child attempts to care for the parent or in families where the child is 'parentified' (acts more like a parent would) and may even be actively encouraged to step into the role of an adult carer.

5. **Hostility versus Love**. Love can bring out positive qualities (e.g., protectiveness, support, closeness, care, kindness) and negative qualities (e.g., possessiveness, intrusion, anxiousness). A parent may be over-concerned or protective, extremely strict or restricting, or overly permissive and relaxed in their parenting style based on love for the child. Behaviour perceived as hostile may have other roots, such as representing a struggle for independence and individuation in overly close relationships. SFT often utilises positive reframes (connotation) to redefine surface behaviour, addressing the implicit meaning or positive intent.

6. **Personal Gains versus Altruism**. This dimension may also be relevant in early childhood presentations. An overly helpful behaviour (e.g., sharing, pleasing others, helping younger siblings) in a 6-year-old may represent an underlying need for recognition and adult attention in a child with a neglect history. The strategic therapist will consider the underlying wishes and needs that drive behaviour such as seeking personal gains or altruistic acts.

Therapy Techniques

Strategies

To address problems, the therapist sets up behaviourally defined objectives or 'strategies' attempting to change the symptom-maintaining sequence of interactions that support the problem. The strategy may be simple, straightforward or complex, involving one person or several or the whole family (Madanes, 1991). Strategies can involve a wider social network and people outside the family who have influence over the problem, such as preschool teachers or an aunt. If the strategy is not successful, a new strategy is sought. The strategic therapist may also select strategies from a variety of other models of therapy that may help solve the problem. How the problem is approached depends on how the therapist conceptualises the problems hypothetically. For example, for an anxious child, the new 'strategy' might be an exposure hierarchy where the child systematically approaches their fears, and both parents encourage the child to be brave rather than permit avoidance. Alternatively, a therapist may

343

view the anxiety as 'too powerful' in its ability to dictate the family's weekend activities and may prescribe that grandparents look after the child while the family enjoys an 'anxious-free' weekend, thus reducing the power anxiety has. Another therapist may view the child's anxiety as serving the function of distracting from the couple's relationship problems, reducing fighting between each other and instead being united in focusing on the child's anxiety. In this case, the therapist may prescribe for the mother and father to have a 'date night' without the child whenever the child has an anxious-free week.

Directives

Directives are the primary mechanism of change. Haley and Madanes differentiate between two types, direct and indirect directives (Haley, 1973, Madanes, 1991). Direct directives provide clear and overt prescriptions and tasks for the family to complete. They are likely to make sense to the family. For example, a directive might be for the mother and father to be united in their approach to a child, using a solution that was successful in the past. At other times, the directives will fall outside the 'family rules' and may seem absurd. In the case of the child swearing and the father minimising the problem, the father may be asked to put $1 into a jar each time his son swears, and the money collected can only be used for an activity that will involve the couple, not the complete family. Indirect directives often influence change without a clear request for a person to do something. The strategic intent is often hidden or less clear. This leads to a gentle destabilisation of the system, working towards second-order change. For example, the therapist may tell a story about something seemingly unrelated without a clear directive to engage in a particular behaviour. The family however, take something from this story to change.

Paradoxical Interventions

Paradoxical directives are a defining feature of SFT and are often used when problems are difficult to shift. Strategic therapists understand that some family interactions are resistant to change as symptoms have the function of temporarily stabilising the family system. One goal of paradoxical interventions is to have the family rebel against the therapist. A paradoxical directive is a suggestion or request by the therapist for the family to maintain a problematic interaction or behaviour, even advocating or actively encouraging the family to practice it or warning against change. Paradoxical directives appear counter-intuitive and defy common sense and logic in the context of the presenting problem. The therapist may warn that change could make things worse, that the family is not ready for change, or that they should go very slowly with progress as further understanding of the problem is needed.

Paradoxical interventions may work in different ways. In a family that struggles with power issues and constantly claims 'this will not work, we have tried this', the therapist may argue against change, proposing that it could be too dangerous, leading to unexpected outcomes in the family. The family may then try to defy the therapist, proving that she is wrong, and by doing so, inadvertently change their family interaction.

In a family where the husband always attempts to control the therapy process and couple-fighting is a problem, the therapist may give the directive for the couple to argue for 10 minutes every morning when they wake up, making the husband responsible for starting the process. The strategy may circumvent the husband's need for control at two levels, both in the therapeutic relationship with the therapist and in the home with his wife. If he resists the directive, the arguing may also stop. If change occurs, it is important the therapist remains puzzled about the change and does not take credit for it, or may even suggest that the change is probably only temporary.

There are a large range of paradoxical interventions, with different classification systems and descriptions used by different schools of SFT, and some may have a preference for certain paradoxical interventions. The most common ones are:

- **Symptom prescription**: Family members are instructed to voluntarily engage in the specific problem behaviour or interaction they have been trying to change. The therapist may instruct the family to produce the problem on purpose. This instruction is a contradiction (a paradox) in itself. The therapy setting implies that change will take place and that the therapist will facilitate this, yet the therapist recommends an intervention that aims at no change. For a young child with stomach pains, the therapist may direct the child to have a pain after the evening meal and gives the parents the role of exploring characteristics of the pain in detail (where it sits in the body, is it hot or cold, big or small, etc). By prescribing the symptom, the caregiver's involvement may change from helplessness or resentment to active and planned parental control.

- **Ordeal directives**. An ordeal is a directive in which the therapist will instruct the family to complete a difficult task that causes distress to a person equal to or greater than that caused by the symptom (Haley, 1973). Having to endure an ordeal reduces motivation for the behaviour to continue. The client is required to rebel against the ordeal. This does require motivation from the family to follow through and persist with the ordeal. For example, an ordeal might be that when a child does not go to bed on time at

7:00 p.m., he must stay up a whole extra 60 minutes, being allowed only to engage in a boring task.

- **Pretend directive**. Madanes defines a pretend directive as a strategy in which the client pretends that the problem is present and acts accordingly (Mandanes, 1991). By pretending to have the symptom, the client or family members realise they have more control over the symptom than they thought. It also allows family members to observe the pretend behaviour and challenge the interactional components without requiring the therapist. This reduces some of the confrontational elements and buy-in required for paradoxical elements. It is particularly useful for families with young children. The therapist may ask the family in the session to pretend it is 8 a.m. before preschool and the referred child pretends to have a baby tantrum, the rest of the family watching. This simple directive can change the seriousness of the tantrum, with everybody including the child laughing about the performance, and it may also spontaneously trigger alternative responses. Madanes suggest that when a benefit is obtained for the pretend symptom, the real symptom may no longer be needed (Madanes, 1991).

- **Restraining**. When utilising restraining, the therapist strongly discourages change or even questions that change is possible or emphasises negative consequences of change. Tennen et al. (2013) differentiate between implicit, soft and hard restraint. Implicit restraint is a compliance-based intervention that encourages the family to undertake very small steps and to progress extremely slowly in solving their problems. For example with a 6-year-old child who has had a prolonged history of physical complaints following a minor viral illness, leading to lethargy, fatigue and refusal to attend school, a period of 'psychological rehabilitation' is recommended. The therapist observes a close family system, with highly protective and anxious parents who strongly believe in a medical cause for their child's symptoms and, to some extent, still doubt the diagnostic label of a post-viral syndrome. The therapist sensing the sensitivity of the parents, suggested an implicit restraint, a very gentle rehabilitation program with regular bed rest, school attendance of one hour per day only and limited playtime in the afternoon. She stressed how important it is to start rehabilitation in the most careful way after such a prolonged period of illness and that under no circumstance should they exhaust their daughter. Soft restraint refers to a directive given by the therapist that the family should not change, or not change yet, or be guarded,

pointing to the danger of improvement or the negative consequences of change. In the above case, the therapist may say that she
is not certain if psychological rehabilitation should start as yet. It
could make matters worse. Hard restraint is a therapist's opinion
given to the family that they may not be able to change.

- **Exaggeration/Prediction of worsening.** This therapeutic strategy
predicts a negative outlook of the problem in regard to the
frequency or intensity of the problem and may include predicting
relapse or exaggeration of the effect the problem has on the family.
Exaggeration is a strategy that describes the problem in dramatic
terms, and details the position the problem has taken or how it
controls the family. In the case of a child with fears of spiders, this
warning may be given after the first steps towards improvement,
suggesting that the fear may creep in again, unexpectedly and in
sneaky ways.

- **Reframing.** Therapeutic reframes can be used at any stage of
therapy but can especially be effective when delivering a
paradoxical intervention. Reframing involves a re-definition of the
family's struggle, helping the family to consider the issue from a
different angle. Reframes change the family's understanding of the
problem by shifting it to a different frame from which it can be
considered (Mattila, 2001). Reframes change the meaning of the
problem, and they can broaden a restricted view. A young child
with a neglect history may display symptoms of hoarding and
stealing food, which the foster parents may perceive as selfish. A
therapeutic reframe may point out the skill of surviving, which the
child had to learn at a young age, or she may suggest that the
behaviour relates to the early starvation of essential attention symbolically, for which food became a substitute and that it had an
adaptive function in the past. A specific intervention may follow
where the therapist suggests that the child keeps a 'little pantry'
underneath her bed and for the foster parent and child to check
each night that food is left in the pantry. Reframes can involve a
simple rewording, for example, 'she is so stubborn' to 'she clearly
expresses what she wants', or 'he is obsessed' to 'he can hold his
focus for a long time'. Reframes can emphasise positive aspects in a
person's behaviour, and they may involve playing with words.
Positive connotations are sub-types of therapeutic reframes. They
shift the negative meaning of the problem emphasising the positive
value or strength, re-contextualising the problem by emphasising
the advantageous effects the problem has for the family or for

certain family members. For a couple with constant issues of disagreement, the therapist may emphasise that there is still a lot of energy in both of them to ignite their relationship, compared with a couple who have lost interest in each other. For a child with fussy eating, the therapist may point out that the child has worked out that the mother is a great cook who can produce interesting meals like a 5-star Michelin cook in just a few minutes. The mother may respond with humour, suggesting that she will need to lower her cooking skills to the level of the worst fast-food store in the area or even buy frozen pre-cooked meals.

- **Rituals and symbolic tasks.** Rituals are planned and purposeful events that signify or symbolise important past or current occurrences in the family. A family ritual may mark the beginning of a new stage after the family struggles through a challenging time, an unresolved grief that requires closure or a deed helping a family member deal with guilt stemming from their own past behaviour. The ritual or act must be specific, meaningful and relevant for those involved. In a family with unresolved grief in the context of the death of a child and symptom development in the next-born child, the family may decide to visit the cemetery jointly and perform a specific ceremony, such as telling the story about the child or bringing an object that symbolises closure. Symbolic acts represent the problem in condensed and symbolic forms.

- **Repentance and reparations**. Madanes refers to 16 steps for working with sex offenders and their victims that are reportedly therapeutic for both victim and victimising person. This will not be elaborated here, but interested readers can find further information in Madanes (1991).

SFT with Young Children

The rationale for involving preschool-age children in SFT sessions is that family sessions allow the therapist to gain information about important family processes and the interaction between all family members. This observational opportunity acts like a window into the family life and may give special clues as to the problem-maintaining interaction in the system. Further, young children's play themes and their spontaneous verbal and non-verbal responses can offer important information about the family. We have found it fascinating when for example the noise in the corner where the children are playing suddenly quietens down when a parent talks about an important event in their life, such as a significant loss of a relationship. Haley (1976) suggests that for small children it is always good to have toys or puppets in the room so that they can communicate in a developmentally appropriate way. Toys and puppets allow 'action in the room' to observe the pattern of interacting rather than talking *about* action or interactions. Developmentally appropriate questions can also deliver helpful information about the system, such as inquiries about any particular worries a child may have. One should not underestimate the incredible awareness and insight young children can have about their family and the relationships within. A simple question such as 'Why do you think mummy is so angry' or 'Why do you think your big brother is crying' can sometimes reveal highly relevant information but also lead to unexpected, positive interaction between family members, such as hugs, or to humour, which can have a lifting effect when difficult topics are being discussed.

Training in SFT

The question of what are the fundamental skills for family therapy practice has been debated in the literature (Larner et al., 2002; Seaburn et al., 1995). In our experience, becoming a confident family therapist takes time, good training, supervision and regular practice. Before venturing into the field of SFT, therapists should at least have the core skills of engaging families with young children, tracking important process information, and developing strong hypotheses based on systemic theory. Micro skills of asking relevant questions for clarification, utilising circular questions for therapeutic purpose and the art of reframing require practice. We have found that a 'self-exercise', where we utilise SFT skills as applied to one of our own personal issues, to be a powerful training format. However, the scope and range of intervention skills for working in a SFT model is wide and will partially depend on the clinician's preferred way of working and their success with particular strategies in the context of family therapy with pre-schoolers. Initial family therapy training is costly and time intensive. However, once a basic skills level has been achieved, we have experimented with in-house training formats with a low budget, which included analysing training videos of the masters, viewing families behind a screen, role-playing our current 'real' families and practising new skills in this safe space of peer supervision, with a 'start-stop' format, where the group members representing family members can give instant feedback as to the effectiveness of a therapeutic strategy (Stiefel et al., 2013).

The Evidence Base of SFT

Overall there is growing evidence that supports the efficacy of systemic therapy as a stand-alone treatment or as part of multi-model interventions for many clinical presentations of childhood (Asen, 2002; Carr, 2014; Crane & Morgan, 2007; Shaw, 2019). Strategic therapy is one of the models of family therapy where most of the evidence has been developed (Carr, 2014; Stanton, 1981). SFT has been applied to a wide range of problem presentations in children, and early research in the 1960s and 70s offered promising results, including the advantage of the cost effectiveness of SFT (Stanton, 1981). In the 1970s, Haley and his colleagues explored the effects of SFT for complex clinical presentations in young people, including psychosis and schizophrenia, suicidal risk, drug addiction, and anorexia and found that SFT markedly reduced the chance of re-admission to psychiatric hospitals (Haley, 1980). The Milan Team also engaged in research and reported good treatment success with their strategic approach (Rasheed et al., 2011). However, not all studies at the time were well designed according to contemporary research criteria, relied heavily on anecdotal case reports of improvement, lacking random selection of cases and a control group.

We find reference and integration of SFT concepts and techniques in contemporary, evidence-based models, such as Multisystemic Family Therapy (MST) for antisocial behaviours in children and youth (Henggeler et al., 2009). The MST model shows promising results in treating complex psycho-social problems, such as conduct disorder in youth. Brief Strategic Family Therapy (BSFT), an adaptation of SFT, also offer favourable outcomes for a range of problems in children and young people in randomly controlled trials, compared with other treatment approaches (Szapocznik & Williams, 2000). Many current models of family therapy in the treatment of adolescent drug use have their roots in strategic and structural family systems models and have shown to be the most effective treatment approaches for this cohort of children (Rowe, 2012). However, further research is needed, especially in the context of the treatment of problems in pre-schoolers.

Family therapy presents a research challenge. The ultimate goal of therapy is to achieve second order change (Davey et al., 2012). First order change may be evident in the change of frequency of particular problems or symptoms, such as reduced levels of anxiety, sibling fighting, or anger, or increased frequency in positive interaction between parent and child and the measurement of relative change in relation to specific variables lends itself well to common quantitative research designs. Second order change in contrast, consists of qualitative shifts in the family system, with new relationship or communication patterns, changes in family structure, rules, or transactional sequences involving all family members, or in some cases, reframes of relationship needs and finding a new family equilibrium, with multiple and diverse changes in emotions, cognition, behaviours or interactions. Davey et al. (2012) suggest a range of possible research methodologies, including process research, conversation analysis, and non-linear analysis of change.

Further, the uniqueness of each system and potentially also the intervention and the treatment effects in between sessions are research challenges. When discussing how to conduct the first interview, Haley states:

> Any standardised method of therapy, no matter how effective with certain problems, cannot deal successfully with the wide range that is typically offered to a therapist. Flexibility and spontaneity are necessary. (Hayley, 1976, p. 9).

Hence SFT's strength is also its weakness in demonstrated effectiveness when being researched.

Conclusion

Strategic therapy offers a brief and individually tailored therapeutic approach to families that focuses on presenting problems and that captures the family interactions that support the presenting concern. The ultimate goal of SFT is second order change, a change in family rules, structure and interaction, though first order change interventions may be included and even acceptable for some problems. We have found the absence of normative thinking and judgement about families refreshing and helpful in our clinical work.

The early pioneers of the family therapy movement and those associated with early models of SFT have left an enormous legacy in the field of family therapy. Many therapists and researchers that were involved in the development of communication and systems therapy were also key figures in the development of SFT. As a result, we now benefit from their unique thinking, groundbreaking theory development, and their novel treatment approaches to complex human presentations. Due to their legacy, we now have a sound theoretical base and a rich systemic vocabulary that has become the working knowledge of contemporary family therapists. Many concepts developed at the time have become integral parts of family therapy training (Rasheed et al., 2011) and are currently being utilised to understand families who present for treatment. Further, we can see powerful and unique therapy developments emerging which combine systemic, hypnotherapeutic and solutions-focused approaches, such as Gunther Schmidt's hypno-systemic therapy in Germany (Schmidt, 2020), which remind us of the adventurousness and enormous creativity of early strategic family therapists.

Goldenberg et al. (2013) describe SFT as a straightforward intervention. However, we believe the model is complex and requires a high level of therapeutic sophistication and is as much an art as also a technique. The theoretical base is rich and, for beginning therapists, difficult to absorb. We believe at least a rudimentary understanding of theory is needed. In therapy, the therapist needs to explore the most central circular interactive patterns that maintain the problem and interrupt these successfully with a powerful intervention, effective but also acceptable to the family. SFT requires a skilled, well-supervised family therapist. An unskilled or inexperienced therapist may design a paradoxical directive that severely destabilises an already fragile system or intervenes in a blunt or non-convincing way. Stanton recommends that therapists need to have an understanding of essential elements of family sequences, have mastered clinical skills and have developed clinical sensitivity (Stanton, 1981).

Strategic family therapists have been criticised for being manipulative, authoritarian and too directive. However, with the post-modern turn in family therapy, we believe that this criticism no longer applies. Our own experience has shown that SFT techniques can be powerful and have shifted issues dynamically and rapidly. SFT is particularly useful for families where creativity or a fresh approach is needed, for difficult-to-treat problems or where previous interventions have been unsuccessful. Contemporary SFT is a respectful and collaborative process towards well-defined mutual goals and can be integrated with techniques from other models of therapy if indicated (Madanes, 1991).

Reader's Exercises

A mother and her 4-year-old daughter present for treatment. The family has just been through a traumatic separation after the mother found out that the father had a new child from a 2-year-long affair. Family Court matters have been settled, and the child spends every second weekend from Friday morning until Monday morning at her father's house. The mother still carries strong anger and resentment towards the father but tries not to show these feelings in front of her daughter. The child is developing physical symptoms of discomfort on access days and wants to stay at her mother's home. What are possible systemic hypotheses and what type of information would be helpful to obtain before developing an intervention strategy? Based on your most powerful hypothesis, what type of strategic intervention may be appropriate and helpful?

References

Asen, E. (2002). Outcome research in family therapy. *Advances in Psychiatric Treatment, 8*, 230–238. https://doi:10.1192/apt.8.3.230

Blyton, E. (1986). *The adventures of the secret 7*. Chancellor Press.

Carr, A. (2014). The evidence base for family therapy and systemic interventions for child-focused problems. *Journal of Family Therapy, 36*, 107–157. https://doi:10.1111/1467-6427.12032

Crane, D. R., & Morgan, T. B. (2007). *The efficacy and effectiveness of family therapy: A summary and progress report.* Brigham Young University. https://www.researchgate.net/publication/236029438_The_efficacy_and_effectiveness_of_family_therapy

Davey, M. P., Davey, A., Tubbs, C., Savla, J., & Anderson, S. (2012). Second order change and evidence-based practice. *Journal of Family Therapy, 34*, 79–90. https://doi: 10.1111/j.1467-6427.2010.00499.x

Deissler, K. G. (2013). Beyond paradox and counterparadox. In G. R. Weeks (Ed.), *Promoting change through paradoxical therapy,* Revised Edition, (pp 60-98). International Psychotherapy Institute.

Goldenberg, I., Stanton, M., & Goldenberg, H. (2013). *Family therapy: An overview* (9th Ed.) Cengage Learning.

Guttman, H. A. (1991). Systems theory, cybernetics and epistemology. In A. S. Gurman and D. P. Kniskern (Eds.), *Handbook of family therapy*, Vol 2 (pp 41–61). Brunner/Mazel.

Hayley, J. (1976). *Problem solving therapy: New strategies for effective family therapy.* Harper Colophon Books.

Henggeler, S. W., Schoenwald, S.K., Borduin, C.M., Rowland, M.D., & Cunningham, P. B. (2009). *Multisystemic therapy for conduct problems in youth.* The Guilford Press.

Lankton, S. R., & Lankton, C. H. (2013). Ericksonian style of paradoxical treatment. In G. R. Weeks (Ed.), *Promoting change through paradoxical therapy, Revised Edition*, (pp 134–186). International Psychotherapy Institute E-Books.

Larner, G., Lobsinger, A., Arnstein, M., Perlesz, A., McNatty, B., James, K., Brown, J., & Holmes, S. (2002). ANZJFT Symposium: What are the core learnings of family therapy? *Australian and New Zealand Journal of Family Therapy, 23*(3), 128–137. https://doi.org/10.1002/j.1467-8438.2002.tb00502.x

MacKinnon, L. K., & James, K. (1987). The Milan systemic approach. Theory and practice. *Australian and New Zealand Journal of Family Therapy, 8*(2), 89–98. https://doi.org/10.1002/j.1467-8438.1987.tb01209.x

Madanes, C. (1991). Strategic family therapy. In A. S. Gurman & D. P. Kniskern (Eds). *Handbook of family therapy*, (pp 396–416). Brunner/Mazel.

Mattila, D. (2001). *'Seeing things in a new light'. Reframing in therapeutic conversation.* Helsinki University Press: Helsinki ISSN 0358-089X ISBN 952-5017-33-8 ISBN 952-5017-35-4. https://www.researchgate.net/publication/47934289_Seeing_things_in_a_new_light_Reframing_in_therapeutic_conversation

Nelson, T. S., Fleuridas, C., & Rosenthal, D. M. (1986). The evolution of circular questions: Training family therapists. *Journal of Marital and Family Therapy, 12*(2), 113–127. https://doi.org/10.1111/J.1752-0606.1986.TB01629.X

Rasheed, J. M., Rasheed, M. N., & Marley, J. A. (2011) *Family therapy. Models and techniques.* Sage.

Rowe, C. L. (2012). Family therapy for drug abuse: Review and updates 2003–2010. *Journal of Marital and Family Therapy, 38*(1), 59–81. https://doi:10.1111/j.1752-0606.2011.00280.x

Schmidt, G. (2020). *Einfuehrung in die hypnosystemische Therapie und Beratung.* Carl Auer.

Seaburn, D., Landau-Stanton, J., & Horwitz, S. (1995). Core techniques in family therapy. In R. H. Mikesell, D. D. Lusterman, & S. H. McDaniel (Eds). *Integrating family therapy* (pp 5–26). APA. https://doi.org/10.1037/10172-001

Shaw, E. (2019). Evolution of family therapy. *Inpsych. The bulletin of the Australian Psychological Society,* August, 14–20. https://psychology.org.au/for-members/publications/inpsych/2019/august/evolution-of-family-therapy

Simon, F. B., Stierlin, H., & Wynne, L. (1985). *The language of family therapy.* Family Process.

Stanton, M. D. (1981). Strategic approaches to family therapy. In A. S. Gurman & D. P. Kniskern (Eds.), *Handbook of family therapy,* (pp 361–360). Brunner/Mazal.

Stiefel, I., Brand, M. S., Hinchcliffe, D. K., & Innes, W. R. (2013). Developing family therapy skills on a shoe string budget: A peer supervision and training approach. *Australian and New Zealand Journal of Family Therapy, 34*(4), 311–324. https://doi.org/10.1002/anzf.1033

Szapocznik, J., & Williams, R. A. (2000). Brief strategic family therapy: Twenty-five years of interplay among theory, research and practice in adolescent behavior problems and drug abuse. *Clinical Child and Family Psychology Review, 3*(2), 117–134. https://doi.org/10.1023/A:1009512719808

Tennen, H., Eron, J. B., & Rohrbaugh, M. (2013). Paradox in context. In G. P. Weeks, (Ed.), *Promoting change through paradoxical therapy,* Revised Edition, (pp187–215). International Psychotherapy Institute E-Books.

Watson, C. (2013). A Delphi study of paradox in therapy. In G. R. Weeks (Ed.), *Promoting change through paradoxical therapy,* Revised Edition, (pp 2–25). International Psychotherapy Institute E-Books.

Watzlawick, P., Beavin Bavelas, J., & Jackson, D. D. (1967). *Pragmatics of human communication: Study of interactional patterns, pathologies and paradoxes.* Norton & Company.

Weeks, G. P. (2013). *Promoting change through paradoxical therapy.* International Psychotherapy Institute.

Chapter 14

Structural Family Therapy (SRFT)

Ingeborg Stiefel

Structural Family Therapy (SRFT) is a systemic model of family therapy based on clearly defined theoretical assumptions about family functioning and problem development and specified intervention techniques and processes for change (Colapinto, 1991). SRFT is both a body of theory and a group of therapeutic techniques, with a focus on the social and relational context (Vetere, 2001). SRFT tries to understand the structural and organisational characteristics of families, and the main goal of therapy is to conceptualise and then change problematic family structures that lead to problem development. The aim of therapy is to facilitate change in the transactional patterns of interaction between family members (the structure), which if relevant, may also include people or systems outside the family. Hence the therapy process is one of restructuring, which, if successful, will lead to a change in family rules that will allow the family to fulfil their various roles more effectively, leading to growth and potential for conflict resolution (Minuchin, 1974). Therefore, the therapy process is twofold, first trying to understand the unhelpful family structure and later changing relevant components. SRFT utilises spatial concepts to describe problematic systemic patterns and possible solutions, and the process of change is facilitated by action, role play and home-based interventions (Colapinto, 1991). SRFT has a set of core concepts that guide the initial assessment and subsequent assessments of change. SRFT is here-and-now work; however it does consider influences from the past in the current presentation of the problem. The therapist is an active agent in the process of change. SRFT is described as an interventionist model (Minuchin et al., 2006).

SRFT does not embrace a normative model of family functioning. Indeed, it is advised to avoid categorisation of families as normal or deviant (Colapinto, 1991). Although the terms functioning and dysfunctioning are being used to describe families, the description is not an evaluation of the family; instead refers to the question of whether or not the structural patterns characterising the family are serving their function for the family's roles in society. Further, an assessment as to what is functional or dysfunctional is based on the understanding of each family in the social context (Aponte & VanDeusen, 1981). Requirements for survival and growth depend on social class, family tradition, ethnic background and societal expectations which can change over time. What is functional or dysfunctional is also determined by the fit between the family's structural organisation and the requirements of the daily tasks in specific circumstances.

Based on systems ideas of an open living system, constantly developing and adapting to changing environmental demands, SRFT adopts a wide definition of normality. Well-functioning families are not defined by an absence of problems, conflicts or stress but by how well they can deal with these life challenges (Colapinto, 1991). Indeed, Minuchin normalises the experience of families seeking treatment, suggesting that 'feeling mixed up' is an experience common to all human beings (Minuchin, 1974). However, the model claims that all families do need some structure, some hierarchy and some differentiation between subsystems to fulfil its various functions, which include the nurturing and growth of its members. To do this, the family must be able to maintain itself while also coping with change. Connection between family members but also differentiation is required to achieve this goal, though the forms and types of family composition may change and can vary greatly across society, class, different cultures and time.

History and Theoretical Context

The origin of SRFT dates back to the 1960s. At the time, Salvador Minuchin, a psychiatrist and family therapist, and his colleagues were exploring therapeutic approaches for boys displaying delinquent behaviours (conduct issues) at Wiltwyck, a residential setting in New York. The team made the observation that therapeutic gains were not maintained when the boys returned to their families, as the families often experienced multiple problems and had under-organised family structures. This experience called for a search for alternative approaches for the treatment of conduct problems in childhood. The late 1950s and 1960s also saw the emergence of the family therapy movement with an increasing focus on social context and the conceptualisation of conduct issues as a social problem, not just as an individual problem of the child.

SRFT was developed at the Philadelphia Child Guidance Clinic under Minuchin's leadership in the mid-1960s. The clinic attracted other systemic thinkers, including Branlio Montalvo and Jay Hayley, which contributed to the development and refinement of theoretical concepts (Colapinto, 1982). At Philadelphia, the structural model was first tested on psychosomatic presentations in children, including children with diabetes, asthma and later anorexia nervosa. Instead of observing under-organised family patterns, this client group displayed a family structure characterised by enmeshment (poor boundaries), over-protection, poor conflict resolution and rigidity. This observation widened the understanding of structural family components that lead to problem presentations in children.

In the 1970s, the Philadelphia Child Guidance Clinic became a leading family therapy training centre in the USA and this period saw the systematic formulation of the structural model of family therapy. The final stage of development occurred in early 1980 with an expanding application of SRFT to a wide range of child and adult problems, including substance use, school problems, encopresis, delinquency/conduct issues, somatoform presentations and developmental disability (Colapinto, 1982).

The theoretical base of SRFT is General Systems Theory (GST). This theory was developed in the 1940s and 1950s by Ludwig von Bertalanffy, and deriving from biology. In the family therapy movement, both the first and second generations of family therapists were strongly influenced by GST as a model for under-standing processes in families. GST, or sometimes more specifically referring to Family Systems Theory in our context (Steinglass, 1984), views families and other social systems as living open systems with interdependent parts. Families are perceived as whole operational systems in which the parts of the system (family members) form a consistent relationship (Steinglass, 1984). Families are constantly transforming, and to fulfil their various roles, families must create a balance between sufficient stability, maintaining a present state (referred to as homeostasis, constancy, or morphostasis), yet also accommodating to change requirements when called upon (morphogenesis). The homeostatic patterns can function well, helping the family to fulfil its roles and functions, or they can be non-helpful, trapping the family in a problematic or outdated cycle of interaction which leads to stagnation or conflict. Change and adaptation are especially needed when the family moves from one developmental stage to the next, and the current pattern of functioning becomes outmoded. Examples of transitional stages are the birth of the first child or subsequent siblings, children progressing developmentally to a new developmental phase, such as from infancy to toddlerhood, or from the primary school years to the high school years and eventually leaving home. Each stage requires a different organisation within the family system. Challenges for the parental subsystem may be changes in employment or unemployment, studying, downsizing, retirement, separating or looking after an older family member. With each stage, a new set of family rules is needed, and the family needs to achieve a new equilibrium that will assist in the day-by-day tasks of family life. Families may fail to accommodate new developmental demands by not adopting a new structure, changing boundaries, or developing new rules, instead holding onto an outmoded homeostatic pattern of relating.

GST postulates that a system is larger than the sum of its parts. Each member of the system affects each other in a circular way. Circularity refers to the mutual determination of behaviour within families, two-way sequences of interaction, which are part of the complex interwoven net of family transactions. Each event (such as an interaction between people) is simultaneously a precedent and an antecedent behaviour to the other. Families are rule-governed systems with a number of subsystems (James & MacKinnon, 1986). Families as open systems influence other systems, and they are also influenced by other systems. Rules are also imposed by external systems, by society in general and by culture, for example, in regard to school attendance, behavioural expectations in public, work-related behaviour and engagement in society. Internal pressure impacting families may come from developmental changes in family members or from changes in subsystems, or they may come from outer influences, such as COVID, war or other stressful life events impacting the family. While maintaining continuity, families must also be able to adapt to new demands and develop new patterns of interaction and a different structure. The new family structure must be such that the emerging needs can be met and a new equilibrium in family function is established. Further, families must facilitate both individuation and differentiation of family members, but also connection with each other (Minuchin, 1974). Complementary interaction between parents or between parents and children allows families to run smoothly. The different roles merge, with each supporting and appreciating the input of the other.

What is SRFT?

There are a number of main concepts involved in SRFT. Firstly, the main focus of SRFT is on the **structure** of the family, which refers to the organisational characteristics of the family system at a given time, which includes family subsystems, overt and covert family rules, which regulate the observable behavioural exchanges between the people in the family (Vetere, 2001). Families have a large repertoire of dominant structures on which most of the family's operations are based (Aponte & VanDeusen, 1981). Families develop transactional patterns, repeated interactions and ways of relating that regulate family members' behaviour based on the family's rules. The family structure must be in accordance with the various roles and functions of the overall family, the subsystems and the roles and positions of individual family members in the family.

Secondly, each family has a set of **rules** which regulate the interaction between family members. Family rules are a central concept in SRFT. Rules define who participates with whom, when, in what kind of situation, who does what, when and where, and who is excluded from the participation. The rules differ for each subsystem, such as for the parents or main carers, the children/siblings, grandparents or other relevant extended relatives. Rules can become complex in blended families, especially if they are not well defined, and the role of each parent in addressing nurturing and disciplinary needs of the children can become confusing. Society, the family's culture in the broader sense, also imposes family rules (Colapinto, 1982). Families have a repertoire of rules that enable the family to carry out recurrent operations on a daily basis. Yet a family may fail to establish a new set of rules, unable to achieve a new equilibrium when change is required, for example, when an adolescent demands more freedom. Their relational pattern becomes stagnated and ineffective with rigid adherence to current rules. This prevents the growth and healthy adaption of the family as they move through common family life cycles. For example, an immigrant family from a traditional cultural background may struggle with the adaptation to a Western culture which allows expressiveness and relative freedom for their offspring.

Thirdly, **boundaries** define subsystems in the family, determine the function of the subsystem and the membership in subsystems, the participation of family members in certain tasks or situations and their level of authority and control. Boundaries stipulate as to who is included in what ways and who is not. Boundaries facilitate differentiation within the family and define roles for members of the system. In SRFT's understanding, the parenting couple should have a distinct boundary in relation to the parenting tasks, and the children should not intrude on the parental issues. SRFT has a hierarchical understanding, where the parenting subsystem is usually at the highest level of the family system. Nevertheless, other adults or even older children can be invited into the subsystem as long as their roles are clearly defined. If boundaries are diffuse, members from other subsystems may interfere inappropriately. Children may oppose the role of the parent; grandparents may undermine a parent or try to control interaction in the family, overstepping their roles.

At the other end of the continuum, boundaries can be too rigid, with strong divisions resulting in a rigid and inflexible structure and possible disengagement between family members, as can be found in distant families. Well-functioning families have clear boundaries which regulate their interaction with each other and with systems outside the family, such as grandparents, aunts and uncles, neighbours, social and educational institutions, ex-partners or biological parents in the case of fostering or adoption.

Fourthly, family members belong to several **subsystems**. Subsystems are defined by their boundary and their function. The mother, if the father is present, belongs to the parenting (couple) subsystem, the mother–daughter and mother–son subsystem, and if the maternal grandmother lives at home, to the mother–maternal grandmother subsystem. Common subsystems are the parenting figures, the children, and subsystems according to gender, interest or roles in the family. Subsystems must be allowed a degree of freedom from interference from other subsystems. The teenage daughter, for example, needs to learn the skill of negotiating relationships with her peers, a teenage brother or sister if present. Subsystem boundaries should be clear but not rigid so that the subsystem can carry out its tasks, yet there should also be sufficient contact between the subsystem and other family members. The parent subsystem may include other parenting figures, such as a grandparent, as long as the lines of responsibility and authority are clear. Families with diffuse boundaries between subsystems often struggle and lack the resources to adapt to new developmental tasks or life challenges.

Fifthly, families may display **enmeshment or disengagement** in their interactions. Families characterised by poor and diffuse boundaries, with an extreme sense of closeness between family members or a strong sense of loyalty to the family are classified as enmeshed families. Extreme degrees of enmeshment hinder the process of individuation and separation of the children, and the differentiation of roles and functions becomes unclear. Enmeshment may occur at an inter-generational level, between a child and an adult, or in a couple's relationship. Enmeshment leads to conflict avoidance for the sake of closeness. Signs of enmeshment in family therapy sessions with young children may include an exaggerated expression of concern, a high level of protectiveness described and observed, speaking for a child, pressure for the child to comply with adult views, restriction in individual expression, or an over-reliance on the family as a source of support, with the exclusion of external sources of support.

Disengaged families, on the other hand, can have strong and rigid boundaries between members; they can be overly structured and tightly organised with a rigid pattern of interaction, which affects the communication between people. Signs of disengagement in sessions with young children may be a parent not attending or appearing disengaged in the session (looking bored, yawning), emotional distance between parent and child, parallel play instead of mutual play or reciprocity, lack of nurturing and guidance or dismissive comments when a child is hurt. The family gives the impression that family members have little to do with each other. However, families may show characteristics of both enmeshment and disengagement at times. Nevertheless, they maintain effective family functioning.

Sixthly, **alignment** refers to the joining and supporting of family members in carrying out an operation in the family. Family members join each other to carry out tasks, such as parents supporting each other and agreeing to each other's parenting attempts or older siblings carrying out age-appropriate chores as a team. A related concept is an alliance, when family members share a common interest that is not shared by other family members, such as father and son enjoying a game of sport or mother and daughter painting their nails.

Seventhly, the term **stable coalitions** refers to a family interaction pattern in which family members join against other people or subsystems in the family, as in the case of two teenage children protesting and opposing a single parent's rule. Trans-generational coalitions may develop, such as a father and the paternal grandmother forming a coalition against the mother or a foster carer involving systems outside the family, such as a child protection worker or staff at the child's school aligning against the biological parent. Transgenerational coalitions subvert natural hierarchies in the family. A 'Detouring Coalition' is a stable form of coalition in which the stress between two people (such as the parents) is diffused by attacking or blaming others for their stress. For instance, teenagers' behaviours are being used as a reason for parental stress, yet the main source of conflict may lie in the parenting dyad, yet this issue cannot be acknowledged.

Eighthly, **triangulation** is a coalition in which a child (or other family member) is drawn into a conflict between two people in the family. There is a potential risk for triangulation after a non-amicable divorce between parents, where each parent may try to draw the child into the adult conflict, creating a stressful conflict of loyalty for the child. Both parents may involve the child in their conflict by revealing inappropriate or incorrect information about the other parent to the child with the aim of drawing the child into a coalition at the exclusion of the other parent. A mother may state to her 6-year-old child that the father is having extra-marital affairs, and as a result, the child should have no further contact with him. The father may say to the child that the mother is a 'nutcase' and does not know how to take care of the child, and that it would be better if the child would stay with him full-time.

Ninthly, **power and hierarchy** are important in family systems. Power relates to the relative influence family members have on the outcome of their actions or interaction (Aponte & VanDeusen, 1981). Power issues may be indicated by an interaction between a parent and a five-year-old child in relation to the child's response to discipline, such as picking up toys or eating dinner. The child may oppose parental authority, and the parent finally gives in. The parent lacks functional (executive) power, unable to fulfil the role of a guiding parent. Hierarchy refers to the level of decision-making and influence people in subsystems have over others. SRFT claims that for families to function well, there must be a power hierarchy in which the parents (main carers), teenage children and younger children have different levels of authority. Loss of power may also occur in a close-knit family in which the child is hindered from venturing out and engaging in age-appropriate social activities or tasks due to an illness, disability or high enmeshment with a parent. The family hierarchy does not need to reflect a traditional family but can include others, perhaps a teenage daughter who minds the younger children or a grandparent who also looks after the children.

Finally, **problems** in SRFT's understanding are based on a non-functioning family structure. However, they may also be triggered by other life events. Problems can develop when the family is unable to cope effectively with developmental demands or external events due to a lack of capacity to modify its pattern of transaction or due to fear of change. Presenting problems are the initial reason for referral, but the underlying structure will become the focus for the therapist. While the parents may report that their child disobeys their rules in regard to teeth cleaning, getting ready for school or eating dinner, the structural family therapist will try to understand the systemic pattern, the interactional network of behaviours between those involved that support the problem (Colapinto, 1982). The central question is: What is the structure that supports the occurrence and maintenance of the problem? What are the characteristics of boundaries, rules, subsystems, roles, positions of power and alignments relevant to the problem? SRFT is interested in the sequential pattern around the problem situation and in the possible function, the problem may have for the family or for certain family members.

The Process of SRFT

Phase 1: Treatment Alliance (Joining), Assessment and Hypothesis Formation

From the information at intake, the therapist may have formed a working hypothesis as to the structural issues a family are facing. However, the assessment of the family begins with the first family interview, which usually involves the complete family, the family members who are living together. The therapist's task in the beginning phase is to form a solid therapeutic relationship, to understand the current structure relating to the reported problem, particularly the recurrent transactional patterns that organise the family, and to explore the family's strength.

The therapist will explore the reason for referral, but also any relevant contextual issues, such as current stress that might be impacting the family, as well as trying to understand the developmental stage in the family's life cycle. The therapist listens to the content of the conversation while at the same time observing a vast amount of process information, including non-verbal cues, tone of voice, gestures, interaction sequences, seating arrangements, involvement of family members or changes in emotional climate during conversation.

In the beginning phase, the therapist and family must come to some agreement as to the nature of the problem and the goals for change, though these do not need to be well defined. The therapist must join the family for two reasons. First, to form a treatment alliance, and second, to understand the family system from 'within' the newly developing family-therapist system. While experiencing the family 'from within', the therapist must maintain the ability to take an outsider position as an observer to understand the family dynamics at a conceptual level and later for effective intervention in the restructuring phase of therapy. Throughout therapy, from beginning to end, joining with the family but also facilitating change through challenging interventions remains a delicate balance of which the therapist must remain aware. Overly joining the family will not facilitate a shift in relationship patterns, whereas excessive probing or re-directing may jeopardise the treatment alliance with the family as the family may feel unsupported or threatened.

In the assessment phase, the therapist tries to define the problem jointly with the family, even though the family may present the issue as an individual problem of a family member, not as a relationship problem. The aim of therapy is explored, which may, even in the early phase, involve a reframe by the therapist, locating the problem in a relational context and understanding how the different family members participate in maintaining an unhelpful transactional pattern, including the relative influence they have over change. The larger context is always included, such as an exploration of other systems or people contributing to the problem or the effect the family's problem may have on others.

The assessment gives a map of the family and may reveal unhelpful alliances or coalitions, isolation of family members, poor or rigid boundaries between subsystems or communication breakdown due to a high level of distance between family members. Yet the therapist's eye is also on the strength of the family, individual family members' resources, underutilised or underdeveloped skills, or external family supports. Based on the information obtained, structural family therapists may subsequently work with different subsystems, excluding specific family members or including external family members if relevant to the presenting problem.

Minuchin describes the assessment as a four-step process: Decentralising the problem or the symptom bearer; exploring the pattern that maintains the problem; exploring what key family members bring from the past that still influences the present (e.g., in restricted views of self and others); and re-defining the problem and opening up options for change (Minuchin et al., 2006).

Phase 2: Restructuring

The second part of therapy is a process of restructuring. Interventions focus on unhelpful transactional patterns through therapist probing, advancing, directing, re-directing, experimenting or even withdrawing. Subgoals may include establishing clearer or new boundaries, softening inflexible boundaries, or defining new roles. During this phase, the therapist may disassemble a structural pattern, construct a new pattern, or encourage the family to utilise one that is underdeveloped but still occurring in the family. In early SRFT, the structural hypothesis (how the presenting problem is linked to the family structure) was usually not shared with the family. During the process of therapy, structural hypotheses are then tested out via active here-and-now interventions, experiments and actions.

Therapeutic change is achieved when a sufficient structural adjustment has been made and the problem or problematic interaction starts to change. Interventions may aim at changing the relative position between family members to more distance or less distance, clarifying and supporting hierarchies, addressing unhelpful coalitions against other family members, disrupting triangulation, introducing new rules to the family system, extending roles, or allowing more flexibility in communication between people or subsystems. Therapy is completed when the referral problem is resolved; however, in some cases, higher-order changes may also be the result of therapy. In some families, other issues emerge, which can be addressed with ongoing therapy.

Joining and restructuring are artificial distinctions, as all therapeutic tasks are in constant flow between observation, probing, joining, and restructuring (Minuchin, 1974), alternating between being in the formed therapist-family system and looking inside from an outsider position. Structural goals determine the therapist's intervention. However, Aponte and VanDeusen (1981) point out that experienced therapists may not always work at a planned and conscious level. Instead, some of their interventions occur at unconscious levels. Restructuring interventions create movement towards the intended goal, and they challenge the current structure of the family (Minuchin, 1974).

SRFT requires an active therapist, not a quiet, passive listener, though active listening is part of the therapist's role. The therapist will explore, clarify, invite comments from others, suggest an information exchange between people, move people within the room, engage one person and exclude others, and encourage a family member to become involved or request others to hold off with their input. The therapist's task can be taxing, as a constant assessment of the therapist's input is needed as to the effect it has on the family system. Colapinto (1982) describes the role as similar to a stage director. Minuchin perceives the therapist to be a primary instrument of change (Minuchin et al., 2006).

Who is involved in therapy depends on who is involved in sharing and maintaining the problem. However, therapy may also include people from other ecosystems if seen as being relevant for therapeutic change. SRFT does not stipulate a standard length of sessions, session numbers, space in-between sessions or location for sessions to be held. Earlier experience at the Child Guidance Clinic in Philadelphia suggests therapy session average to be between 6–10 sessions, with sessions to be held once per week. However, some families require longer treatment periods, for example those with more enmeshed family structures (Aponte & VanDeusen, 1981).

SRFT Techniques

SRFT is a balance between joining with the family, interchanged with challenging and unbalancing a family. There are a number of techniques that can be employed in either task, and therapists will often move in and out of these multiple times in a session. Some of these techniques are summarised below.

Joining

Joining is a multi-faceted task consisting of experiential, cognitive and evaluative components, and it is a process between therapist and family that will lead to the formation of a new therapeutic system of family and therapist. Minuchin (1974) stresses that the therapist must join the family from within to understand the family structure, not only from an outsider observing position. Joining has emotional components, such as experiencing the pain of a family member or the tension between two people. Joining requires that the therapist has a genuine interest and is personally involved and affected by the family (Colapinto, 1982). The therapist shows respect for the current rules of the system and tries to understand these. Yet, the therapist must at the same time maintain the observing, understanding and conceptualising capacity. Staying aware as to what is happening is equally important, without being swallowed up by the rules or behaviour of the system, trying to please or accommodate excessively to the family's needs or wishes. Joining requires rapid multi-sensory processing with a cognitive component, with the aim of engaging all, which includes relating to family members of different ages, gender, culture or intellectual levels. The therapist accepts the family style as initially presented in the session and blends with the family. Joining creates a new therapeutic system from which the therapist can introduce more challenging interventions. Joining is a two-sided process, and the family must also accept the therapist. Joining techniques are usually not intervention focused, but they can trigger therapeutic change. Minuchin (1974) states that the process of joining in family therapy is not well described and may be occurring partially outside the therapist's awareness. However, joining can also be a deliberate attempt by the therapist. Joining includes the following therapeutic techniques:

- **Accommodation** refers to the therapist's adjustments and adaptation to the family system. The therapist may display sensitivity to family members, takes their perspective without judgement and adjusts to the emotional tone, pace and atmosphere in the room. The therapist joins by respecting the rules of the family system.

- **Search for Strength:** Strength can be observed in individual family members, in dyads or in the complete family with therapist comments on intention, beliefs, observed behaviour or interaction. Family strength may refer to family processes that are already working well between some family members or have worked well in the past. They may also include aspects of family functioning already occurring yet outside the family's awareness. These may be pointed out by the therapist; the family may be invited to comment, or the therapist may just notice strength without sharing the information.

- **Maintenance** is a therapeutic technique that honours the current transactional pattern of interaction, the family structure, without challenging it. The therapist expresses acceptance and respectful curiosity and may actively make confirmation statements of an observed interaction, supporting an existing structure or a family subsystem. It may even include accepting the family's language relating to the problem in pathological terms, referring to the index person, supporting family strength or emphasising important roles family members have.

- **Tracking** relates to both tracking content and process, with the first focusing on the verbal account of family members' contributions. Tracking content elicits more specific information about an issue. The therapist may ask family members to expand, give details or recall an example. The therapist's responses may also include paraphrasing and summarising without challenging the family. Confirming statements can be made, which assist the family to trust that the therapist understands and values their contributions. The tracking of the process is a complex multi-sensory task in which the therapist needs to pay attention to the multitude of non-verbal information, both between family members and between family and therapist. It is a therapeutic task that beginning therapists often find challenging as the aim is not only to notice relevant processes but also to decide which interaction has the most relevance or should be responded to at a given time.

- **Reframing**: Therapeutic reframes are relabels and aim to achieve a cognitive shift in the perception of a family problem. They may focus specifically on complementary behaviour between family members or attempt to re-direct from a negative individual description to a positive systemic one. For example, if husband and wife blame each other for 'controlling' and 'nagging' behaviour, the therapist may attempt to point out that it is their current way to resolve an issue over housework, although they both agree and wish that they could do it in a different way. Positive reframes encourage participation and reduce anxiety in family members as a result of being blamed for the family's problem.

- **Mimesis** is a therapist's behaviour that often occurs spontaneously and outside the therapist's awareness; however, it can also be a deliberate attempt to join with the family or with a particular family member. Mimesis includes matching or mirroring a person's non-verbal behaviour (postures and gestures), tone of voice, pace of conversation, or copying a person's movement. The therapist's speech volume may change when talking to a young anxious child, or the therapist's level of excitement may increase observing an active young child. The therapist leaning over when another family member does, or crossing legs, or in the 1970s therapy session excerpts, lighting a cigarette when another family member does. These can all potentially be signs of matching with a family member.

Challenging and Unbalancing

Challenging and unbalancing are restructuring interventions aimed at disturbing the family's accustomed way of interacting and creating a disequilibrium. Restructuring techniques can be stressful, and the therapist must be aware of the family member's threshold for such confrontational intervention. Further, the family must sense that the therapist's strategy is to the benefit of all. At this phase of therapy, the therapist may be active and directive, for example, blocking a family member's contributions, temporarily joining a coalition or forming an alliance with a particular family member, changing a seating arrangement, de-emphasising or increasing the intensity of a problem. Challenging should not be felt as an attack on a family member or the family but as a challenge.

Enactment

Enactment is the hallmark of SRFT. While spontaneous enactment of transactional patterns occurs in many family therapy sessions, enactment is the planned actualisation of a particular transactional pattern under the control of the therapist. Enactment is a purposeful creation of a family scenario that may initially assist in the assessment of the family but, most importantly, becomes an opportunity for in-session action and change. Hence, it is used for both assessment and restructuring purposes. Some families give long verbal recalls describing their problems, presenting their sometimes rigidly held view as to the nature of the problem with limited information that might be helpful for therapy planning. When therapists ask the family to enact a conflict situation, both the family and therapist have a chance to experience and observe the transactional pattern. Who interrupts, complies, tries to help, confirms, withdraws, or opposes may be part of a typical interactional pattern, offering opportunities for probing, testing and change. The therapist will then ask the family to interact again but in different ways to their usual pattern (Minuchin et al., 2006).

During enactment, the therapist becomes actively involved in directing, suggesting and encouraging different ways the family relate to each other, as well as interrupting a person or supporting a specific family member, to escalate the process of change. The therapist can slow an interaction, intensify it, suggest an alternative or an experiment, or highlight a particular sequence that points to the strength of a family member. A further advantage of enactment is that it pulls the therapist out of a central position and encourages interaction between family members. Enactment helps to actualise the problematic transactional pattern around the reported problem, leading to a better understanding of interactional components. Enactment may include a suggestion by the therapist to the family to talk to each other to re-play an interaction. However, the direction may have a strategic intent, for example, to include a family member whose position is outside the family. Therapists must be clear about the goal of their input and the planned intervention, helping the family to experience the alternative pattern.

> **Example**: A therapist may ask a family of mother, father and a 4-year-old female child to enact a bedtime situation. The child has a very close relationship with the mother and, according to the family, is showing a lot of separation anxiety. The mother may stay with the child until the child falls asleep, which is exhausting for the family. The father feels the mother 'pampers the child too much' and states that he is doing a better job when the mother is away at times. The therapist may ask the family to enact the different scenarios in the session. First, the mother 'puts the child to bed' while the father stays on the outer, then the father puts the child to bed without the mother's input, and then a combined approach (discussed first

between the parents), in which they agree on the approach to take before it is enacted. The therapist's underlying hypothesis was that the parents were not aligned in their parenting, and the therapist was hoping that the third enactment would bring them together.

The therapist may intensify an interaction, asking family members to repeat a sequence, or increase the level of challenge. Enactment and the altered behaviour between family members offer the chance that the family's perception regarding the problem changes or that the enactment in itself offers a different solution.

Homework

In-session enactment may be insufficient for substantial change to occur. Homework tasks can be based on the changed interaction between family members following the restructuring in the session. In the above family, the therapist may ask the family to continue with option three for one week and note the success of this strategy.

Punctuating

The therapist may highlight a specific transactional segment, pointing out its significance, hoping to achieve a shift in family members' perspectives by becoming more aware of its relevance. The therapist selects an interaction in accordance with the therapeutic goal, and highlights it verbally or in the form of a more active intervention.

Boundary Making

This technique refers to the participation of family members or the timing of their involvement in an interaction, such as who should be involved, when and in what ways and who should stay outside. Structural family therapists may actively block a family member from responding, move people's position in the room, encourage experimenting with different positions or change their own position.

Example: In a family session where the youngest child always takes a big chair and forces the parent to sit in the preschool-age chair, the therapist may ask the mother to swap chairs with the child for 5 minutes or play with the toys while the child cannot play for 5 minutes.

Unbalancing and Crisis Induction

Unbalancing and Crisis Induction are higher-risk techniques involving strategies that may put the treatment alliance at risk. Here the therapist may enter a coalition between people, support a peripheral family member or side with a person in a couple relationship. Crisis induction may involve bringing problem situations into the session, such as a mealtime with a family where the child is diagnosed with an eating disorder.

The Evidence Base of SRFT

SRFT has a small but longstanding history of empirical support (Lebow & Gurman, 1995). The gradual development of SRFT in the 1970s saw a strong research interest in the model (Colapinto, 1982; Minuchin et al., 2006), though research quality reflects this time period. Minuchin and colleagues explored the effectiveness of SRFT in the form of many case studies, though small in sample size and not controlled for with a comparison intervention. They explored treatment outcomes for children and adolescents with unstable diabetes (n = 20), with 88% of cases showing total recovery, young people with eating disorders (anorexia) (n = 53), with 86% of the clinical population obtaining normal eating patterns, and children with severe asthma (n = 17) with 82% of cases showing full recovery. Aponte and VanDeusen (1981) also report on the early period of research, which included controlled studies for heroin addiction, therapy process studies and research on the effects of training.

More recent qualitative research on parental experience of SRFT suggests that SRFT may be especially beneficial for families struggling to establish a clear parental hierarchy and effective executive function (Weaver et al., 2019). Further, the authors argue that SRFT offers the advantage of addressing the psychological issues of more than one member within a family system, which may be especially relevant for situations where access to mental health services is limited, such as in rural or remote communities. Clossey and colleagues explored the effectiveness of a modified model of SRFT, Ecosystemic Structural Family Therapy, which integrates strength-based components and trauma-informed thinking with traditional structural family therapy concepts. Their pilot study suggests that Ecosystemic SRFT improves both family functioning and child functioning in children with very severe psychological issues and risk of out-of-home placement by disrupting core negative interactional patterns in these families (Clossey et al., 2018). Process research which explores client change within the session and specific therapist variables of SRFT, found that two variables correlated highly with change: focusing on core problems and intensity of therapist interventions. A greater change was obtained for more experienced therapists (Miles, 2005).

As with most systemic models, SRFT lacks a research base with high-quality qualitative and quantitative studies exploring the effectiveness and efficacy of this model compared with other treatment modalities. Early research suggests that the model's focus on the structure has value for both over and highly under-organised families. However, contemporary research is needed to explore the value of SRFT more fully. Minuchin, though agreeing with the need for good research into the efficacy of family therapy, makes an important point regarding family therapy research. In an attempt to establish its role by utilising clinical trial methods, family therapy has compromised some of its core values and assumptions. Focusing on specific mental disorders or diagnoses as the target of intervention reinforces the belief that mental illness is a real, objective disease, and it loses its relational perspective. Further, manualised techniques and procedures, which have been a strong focus in research, often do not consider the therapist as a fundamental instrument for change (Minuchin et al., 2006). The author is hoping that family therapy research in the future will develop a research method that preserves some of the field's foundational insights and perspectives.

Discussion

SFRT is an evolving and diverse model of family therapy, which can be applied in an integrative way when working with families (Minuchin et al., 2006). SRFT's theoretical concepts and its systemic vocabulary have made a profound impact on the development of systemic family therapy in general. The language used by SRFT has stood the test of time in that it has become a common language for clinicians working with children or families by describing significant family characteristics or processes, though not necessarily referring specifically to SRFT as the underlying model for these concepts. The structural description of families gives a condensed, spatial image of central family characteristics, like a snapshot observation of the family. Most family therapy training courses introduce SRFT as part of their learning, at least at a theoretical level, as the model offers useful concepts to beginning but also to experienced family therapists.

SRFT has been applied to a wide range of child and adolescent problems. SRFT blends well with other approaches available in the treatment of young children and families, including those based on social learning theory and behaviour modification (Aponte & VanDeusen, 1981). As occurs with other treatment modalities, such as CBT (Kazantzis, 2021), contemporary SRFT is often applied in an integrated way. McLendon and colleagues combine traditional SRFT with group work and strength-based models (McLendon et al., 2005). Structural models are especially popular in North America as they offer a way of conceptualising issues families bring from a problem formulation point of view but also offer resolutions for the presenting issues (Reiter, 2016). Important concepts of SRFT have been adapted and integrated into many forms of systemic therapy. We see an important place for SRFT in the treatment of children and families where low organisation and ineffective hierarchical structure are the main characteristics, leading to ineffective parental leadership and serious childhood presentations, including neglect, such as educational and medical neglect. We can find strong components of SRFT in evidence-based programs such as Multisystemic Therapy for Antisocial Behavior in Children and Adolescents (MST) and the related program MST CAN (Child Abuse and Neglect; Henggeler et al., 2009).

The joining task of the therapist reminds us that any form of therapy is both an application of theoretical concepts and techniques and also a powerful human experience embedded in the newly formed family-therapist system. Critique of early models of systemic therapy, which includes SRFT, was that therapists took an outside perspective and manipulated the family. This critique does not appreciate the essential component of joining so clearly outlined in SRFT.

The involved and, at times, direct style of the therapist during the session is taxing, as a high level of complex processing is needed and a high frequency of active therapist behaviour. SRFT may increase therapist burnout. SRFT has been criticised for its heavy reliance on in-session observation, both of spontaneous family interaction and those induced by the therapist. These observations may not give a complete picture of family functioning as would occur in the family's natural environments, leading to incorrect or incomplete hypotheses about family structure (James & McKinnon, 1986).

James and McKinnon (1986) argue that the model is easy to teach. We take this assumption with caution. While the theoretical aspects are very clearly outlined in this model, the therapy process is often complex in many situations, and the multi-focal lens which the therapist needs to maintain is not an easy undertaking. Specific systemic training and but also good supervision are required for therapists to master the skill of effective SRFT (Minuchin et al., 2006).

Family therapists influenced by postmodernism, social constructivism and critical theory (see Narrative Therapy in this book for more details) have questioned the assumption that the problem is maintained by the systemic structure and have suggested that one could equally argue that the problem controls the system (James & McKinnon, 1986). SRFT has also been critiqued for its normative assumptions in assessing families and that it does not take into account the multitude of possible ways family may function. We believe this critique is based on a misunderstanding of the model. SRFT explicitly warns against normalising families; it heavily takes into consideration the family's context and idiosyncratic structure. Aponte and VanDeusen (1981) stress that the assessment as to what is functional or dysfunctional is based on an under-standing of the family in its social context, which will be different based on social class, culture, social environment, ethnicity and race. This context creates different requirements for survival and growth. Though Structural Family Therapists historically referred to functional or dysfunctional, the judgement is based on the fit of the family system's structural organisation to the requirements in specific circumstances. For a family identifying as Aboriginal or Torres Strait Islander in Australia, the involvement of a larger network of kinship support, biologically related or not, may be part of a systemic structure that functions well in the case of a young mother with a new baby who is not living with her biological family. Further, the family therapist may assess a family structure as functional or otherwise, but it is ultimately the family's achievement of their goals and their judgement whether or not a new structure helps in achieving daily tasks as a family.

Early models of family therapy theoretically based on GST, such as SRFT, have been critiqued by those who have adopted a postmodern stance and a social constructivist position. Critique has focused on respectfulness, sensitivity to culture, gender roles, power, social imbalance or the role of the therapist as an expert, with a concern that the structural family therapist may even inadvertently reinforce negative societal structure by not addressing them directly, such as addressing issues of power in relationships (Vetere, 2001). SRFT is a child of its time. While the model makes strong reference to the family's immediate context, such as families living in poverty, SRFT has not taken an active position questioning societal structures and issues of dis-empowerment outside the family or in the family's immediate context. Critique has come especially from feminist writers encouraging therapists to take a more active political position in addressing these issues (Mills & Sprenkle, 1995).

The family therapy movement experienced a significant paradigm shift in the mid-1980s. SRFT belongs to the early historical phase of therapy, which saw a shift from the individual focus to the family system, with an underlying theory of GST, Cybernetics, and in the case of SRFT, also Structuralism. The second phase embraced Postmodern ideas, including Social Constructivism and Post-structuralism. Although the link between SRFT and Structuralism has only been made in some earlier writings (Aponte & VanDeusen, 1981), assumptions and concepts of Structuralism are clearly visible in SRFT. Structuralism developed in the early 2000s century. Structuralism is a theory of both culture and methodology and postulates that human culture must be understood by its relationship to broader systems. Structuralism proposes that there is an inherent structure in systems such as individuals, families, or groups (Dickerson, 2010). The model tries to uncover the structures that underlie all things human, the way we think, feel, judge and believe. The phenomena of human lives can be understood through their interrelations; these relations constitute a structure. In the late 40s, Structuralism was applied to psychology by Piaget (2001) and later to systemic therapy with the development of SRFT.

Opponents of Structuralism have argued that structures and related concepts are creations made by the therapist; they are not 'real' and given (James & McKinnon, 1986). In our view, SRFT appears to be one of the models that has been judged unfairly. Simon (1995), in considering the therapeutic technique of enactment as a defining element of SRFT, argues that SRFT is a model which is grounded in assumptions of competence and uniqueness. Competence relates to the belief that families are stuck in non-useful relational patterns and, with the help of intervention, can release unused resources and potential, and every family does this in their unique and idiosyncratic ways (Simon, 1995).

Nevertheless, the language used in the early literature of SRFT is outdated and in need of rephrasing as therapy in the 2020s has become more sensitive to the power of language and its potential impact in therapy as both a source of strength or negative control. Language translation needs to maintain what the original concepts were trying to describe, and simple rephrasing such as 'what is the family's structure that currently supports the family in achieving its goals' could simply be a translation for a 'functional family'.

Conclusion

SRFT is a systemic model that has left a strong legacy in the field of family therapy with its powerful concepts and systemic vocabulary. The model has been widely applied to a range of childhood problems, addressing externalising and internalising problems in children, family stress, medical conditions, and substance use. The application of SRFT has changed over the past 20 years, as Postmodern ideas have infiltrated the complete field of therapy to a more collaborative, strength-based undertaking, with greater sensitivity to the language used. SRFT has become part of an integrative way of utilising and blending concepts and techniques from different models (Minuchin et al., 2006). Vatere (2001) believes SRFT is a practical, consumer-friendly, problem- and present-focused model appealing to many families with time-limited intervention. We believe SRFT is a suitable model for working with families of young children, especially for those families where structural components appear to be major contributing factors in symptom development in the child.

Case Study — The Wolpe Family

The Wolpe family were referred by a child protection service to a treatment team. The family consisted of Tacquira (26) and her two younger children, Tahmara (6) and Bry (5). There was limited contact with the children's father, who had moved interstate. The Child Protection Agency was concerned about the children's poor school attendance record. The older child, Tahmara, had missed half of the school year, and the younger child, Bry, was about to start Kindergarten. He had also missed many days at preschool. Tacquira and her children identify as Aboriginal. Tacquira's concern was that she could not get her children ready for school, mostly due to their disobedience and disregard for her rules. Tacquira's received some support from her sister (age 18) and her mother, who lived in the neighbourhood. However, the relationship between Tacquira and her mother was not close. Tacquira reported that her mother was always critical of her parenting, and Tacquira did not like her mother's new boyfriend, describing him as 'creepy'.

The first session was a family session with the mother and the two children in the office. The children were noisy and started pulling toys out of various toy boxes, and soon the floor was covered randomly with different toys. Tahmara discovered the textas and started to draw on the wall, which Tacquira then attempted to prevent by shouting 'stop it' five times until her daughter eventually responded. Tacquira commented, 'She is only stopping it because you are here; at home, she would simply ignore me'. Next, Bry took a texta, and Tahmara snatched the texta off her son, which led to Bry crying loudly. The therapist already felt exhausted and wondered what Tacquira was feeling at the time of the session but also at home when these behaviours occurred frequently.

The therapists explored the mother's understanding of the problem. She responded by saying that her children simply did not listen to her, especially Tahmara, and Bry always copied his older sister's behaviour. There were moments of warmth between Tacquira and her children. Bry approaches her; Tacquira smiles at him when he shows her a toy. On another occasion, when reporting about Tahmara's schooling issues, Tacquira gently strokes Tahmara's head. Tacquira said she had tried everything, a parenting program with rewards and consequences, time out, star charts, and rewards for attending school, but nothing had worked or only for a very short time. The school had not been overly helpful, just reminding Tacquira that it was her legal responsibility to bring the children to school.

The therapist thought she could do two things in the session: First ask the family to perform a task for observation, similar to an enactment, where Tacquira asks the children to put away all the toys back into the boxes. Secondly, the therapist thought it would be helpful to understand the family's evening and morning routines to get a better understanding of the presenting problem.

The observation of the 'packing away toys' task was interesting. Tacquira gave repeated commands, asking the children to pack up toys, which both children initially ignored. She then pulled out a box and illustrated the task. Bry placed 3 toys into the box with prompting but then started playing with a new toy. Tacquira appeared to become frustrated, raising her voice. Bry looked scared. She said to Tahmara, 'If you don't help, you will not get an ice cream when we leave'. When Tahmara again did not respond, Tacquira quickly gathered up all toys, put them out of reach, and told the children that they would now miss out on ice cream and an outing to the park. Tahmara now started crying and complaining that it wasn't fair. Tacquira turned to the therapist and said, 'It is like this all the time'.

The therapist's thoughts at this stage were: There is no clear and effective parental hierarchy in the family, and establishing this would be one of the main tasks. The boundaries between the mother and the children are not clearly defined, and Tacquira is not functioning effectively in her role as a parent. There are issues of power that also need to be addressed. Tahmara was acting as a pseudo parent in the family, bossing both her mother and younger brother at times.

The therapist then explored the evening routine. While Tacquira had a good routine for dinner (at 5:30 pm) and a shower afterwards, the bedtime routine lacked a clear structure. From Tacquira's description, it appeared that her commands were equally ineffective, as had been observed during the packing-away tasks in the session. Tahmara would simply ignore Tacquira, grab her phone, play games, or play with her toys. Bry would not stay in bed, come out and rest on the lounge until falling asleep. When Tacquira tried to carry him back to bed, he would wake up and scream. Tahmara would try to outsmart her mother's attempts to get her to bed by hiding underneath her mother's bed, using the bed as a trampoline, locking herself into the bathroom, or even on one occasion, opening the back door and hiding in the backyard at night. Tacquira admitted that she had resorted to smacking Tahmara, and this had, on occasion, worked.

The morning routine was also fairly stressful. Tacquira would wake her children at 7 am, but Tahmara would not get up. She probably was tired, as bedtime was late, between 9 and 11 pm, but Tacquira saw Tahmara's behaviour also as a refusal, as on some days (e.g., outings), Tahmara was ready and dressed by 7:30 am.

The therapist then suggested working on 'mum being the boss', and 'mum being in charge', and she brainstormed with the children's advantages and disadvantages of having mum being the boss. The advantages of this role included getting their nice favourite meal, being taken to the park, helping them get dressed, going on play dates, having a warm bath in the evening, getting birthday presents and having nice toys at home. The therapist tried to get very specific details about the children's likes. She then asked them what would happen if Mum was not the boss, and she would just sit there and do nothing. With some prompting, the children were able to list a range of disadvantages, such as nobody would take them home, they had to walk by themselves, there would be no dinner or bedtime story, they would have to dress themselves, do their hair, and they would not see other children.

The therapist thought a session with Tacquira alone would be helpful to introduce the concept of 'mum in charge', explore Tacquira's understanding of effective rules, routines, consistency, and any successes she may have had with a clear parenting structure, introduce the idea of a parental hierarchy, the benefit and then deciding with Tacquira on a plan of action. Tacquira felt 'practising being in charge' would be best at a time when she did not feel tired or extremely stressed, which were always the times before school and bedtime routines. The therapist and mother both felt 'cleaning away toys in the afternoon before dinner' would be the best time to practice being in charge. The time was ideal for a second reason. Instead of employing complicated start charts and reward systems, Tacquira said she could simply say, 'When you have cleaned up these toys (marking a section for each child with a chalk line on the carpet), you can have dinner'. She made sure that she would serve the children's favourite meal for the first 3 nights. The therapist and mother role-played in the session how to give brief, effective commands and what Tacquira would do if the children did not respond. The therapist role-played an angry and demanding child to help the mother experiment with different skills. Tacquira said it would be best if, in this situation, she would only call the children once, wait and, if they would not respond, place the meal in the fridge until her children had completed their task. She would then start eating her dinner. When the children would later ask for their dinner, she would simply state, 'You know what you have to do first'. Tacquira expected that the firmness would be hard for her, but she could see how a clear plan was initially needed until her children understood that 'mum was in charge'.

The first night was stressful, as Tahmara refused to clean up toys but demanded dinner. Tacquira struggled not to give in, scream or hit her daughter. However, she understood from the session that she needed to maintain 'the hierarchy' and give Tahmara the message that she was now the boss. The bedtime was very late, and after a lot of arguments initiated by Tahmara, Tahmara finally cleaned up most of her toys but was very tired when she had her dinner. The second night went smoother; both children cleaned up most of the toys and enjoyed their dinner.

The following session was a family session, and the therapist explained to the children that she had heard that wonderful things had been happening at their home, asking the children if they could play with the toys and then show her how they had done the toy clean up at home. This task went well and Tacquira gave clear instructions and praised the children but also showed how pleased she felt with herself as a mum, achieving this step successfully. She said, 'I now understand why I need to be on top of the hierarchy'.

Therapy progressed over the next 10 sessions, tackling the bedtime routine and then the morning routine, with an increase in Tacquira's confidence in being in charge, with good rules and instructions and a calmer maternal tone of voice. The family achieved a clearer structure, and the children started attending two consecutive weeks of school and daycare. One further session was booked when Bry started Kindergarten to ascertain that the new structure and rules were still working effectively for the family following this new transition.

Reader's Exercises

The Smyth family consists of a single mother (Kassy), her boyfriend (Mario), who sometimes stays with the family, and Kassy's two children, Trixy (6) and Mel (4). There is limited contact with the children's biological father. Kassy reports that Trixy refuses to eat her meals. She has always been a fussy eater, but to Kassy's annoyance, she eats everything provided if she spends time with her grandparents. The mother describes the following. At 5:30 pm, she calls her children to come and have dinner. Trixy usually ignores her mother, or if she sees what has been served, demands different food. In the past, Kassy had been providing different meals for Trixy, but she stopped this extra work after Trixy also started to refuse the different meals provided. Mario has no patience for Trixy's behaviour and feels Kassy needs to be firmer. He comes from a large Italian family and says that as children they would not have questioned or opposed any meal their mother had cooked for them. He thinks a good smack is needed. There are other situations when Kassy's and Mario's parenting styles are not aligned. For example, when the family goes shopping, Trixy always demands a toy, and Mario wants to stop this behaviour. The couple often argue about the children, and Mario has threatened in the past to move out if Kassy does not toughen up with her children. The evenings are also stressful. Mario wants to watch the news after dinner, but Trixy and Kassy are still arguing over dinner, with Kassy eventually giving in to Trixy by providing junk food after a lengthy debate.

- How do you conceptualise this current family problem from a structural perspective?

- What type of assessment could be helpful?

- What structural interventions may be helpful based on your hypothesis?

- If you were able to help the family to succeed with a good mealtime routine, what 'higher-order' changes may develop as a result?

References

Aponte, H. J., & VanDeusen, J. M. (1981). Structural Family Therapy. In A. S. Gurman & D. P. Kiniskern, (Eds.). *Handbook of Family Therapy* (pp. 310–360). Brunner/Mazel.

Clossey, L., Simms, S., Hu, C., Hartzell, J., Duah, P., & Daniels, L. (2018). A pilot evaluation of the rapid response program: A home-based family therapy. *Community Mental Health Journal, 54*(3), 302–311. https://doi.org/10.1007/s10597-018-0231-2

Colapinto, J. (1982). Structural Family Therapy. In: A. M. Horne & M. M. Ohlsen (Eds.) *Family, counselling and therapy*. F. E. Peacock: Illinois. Retrieved from https://www.colapinto.com

Colapinto, J. (1991). Structural Family Therapy. In A. S. Gurman & D. P. Kniskern (Eds.). *Handbook of Family Therapy* (pp.1209–1273). Brunner/Mazel.

Dickerson, V. (2010). Positioning oneself within an epistemology: Refining our thinking about integrative approaches. *Family Process, 49*(3), 349–68. https://doi.org/10.1111/j.1545-5300.2010.01327.x

Henggeler, S. W., Schoenwald, S. K., Borduin, C. M., Rowland, M. D., & Cunningham, P. B. (2009). *Multisystemic Therapy for antisocial behavior in children and adolescents* (2nd Edition). The Guilford Press.

James, K. & MacKinnon, L. K. (1986). Theory and practice of Structural Family Therapy: Illustration and critique. *Australian and New Zealand Journal of Family Therapy, 7*(4), 223–233. https://doi.org/10.1002/j.1467-8438.1986.tb01184.x

Kazantzis, N. (2021). The evolution of CBT. Introducing a family of cognitive behavioural therapies. *InPsych. The Bulletin of the Australian Psychological Society, April/May, 43*(2), 31–35.

Lebow, J. L., & Gurman, A. S. (1995). Research assessing couple and family therapy. *Annual Review of Psychology, 46*, 27–57. https://doi.org/10.1146/annurev.ps.46.020195.000331

McLendon, D., McLendon, T., & Petr, G. D. (2005). Family-directed Structural Therapy. *Journal of Marital and Family Therapy, 31*(4), 327–329. https://doi.org/10.111/J.1752-0606.2005.tb01574x

Miles, D. L. (2005). *The influence of therapist interventions in structural family therapy: A process study*. Virginia Consortium for Professional Psychology (Old Dominion University). ProQuest Dissertations Publishing, 2005. 3191363.

Mills, S. D., & Sprenkle, D. H. (1995). Family therapy in the postmodern era. *Family Relations, 44*(4), 368. https://doi.org/10.2307/584992

Minuchin, S. (1974). *Families and Family Therapy*. Harvard University Press.

Minuchin, S., Wai-Yung, L., & Simon, G.M. (2006). *Mastering Family Therapy. Journeys of growth and transformation.* Wiley.

Piaget, J. (2001). *The psychology of intelligence,* (1st ed 1947). Routledge.

Reiter, M. D. (2016). A quick guide to case conceptualisation. *Journal of Systemic Therapies, 35*(2), 25–37. https://doi.org/10.1521/jsyst.2016.35.2.25

Simon, G. M. (1995). A revisionist rendering of structural family therapy. *Journal of Marital and Family Therapy.* Hoboken, *21*(1), 17–26. https://doi.org/10.1111/j.1752-0606.1995.tb00135.x

Steinglass, P. (1984). Family Systems Theory and therapy: A clinical application of general systems theory. *Psychiatric Annals, 14*(8), 582–586. https://doi.org/10.3928/0048-5713-19840801-09

Vetere, A. (2001). Structural Family Therapy. *Child Psychology & Psychiatry Review,* 6(3), 133–139. https://doi.org/10.1111/1475-3588.00336

Weaver, A., Greeno, C. G., Fusco, R., Zimmerman, T., & Anderson, C. M. (2019). 'Not just one, It's both of us': Low-income mothers' perceptions of structural family therapy delivered in a semi-rural community mental health centre. *Community Mental Health Journal, 55*(7), 1152–1164. https://doi.org//10.1007/s10597-019-00444-2

Psychodynamic Therapy (PDT)

Ingeborg Stiefel

Psychodynamic therapy (PDT) for children and their families originates from the psychoanalytic theory and therapy of Sigmund Freud (Lee, 2009). Contemporary models and applications of psychodynamic therapy are based on a wide range of theories and therapy practices, and currently, there is no unified model of psychodynamic child and family therapy (Lipner et al., 2017). We use PDT as an umbrella term, referring to insight-oriented therapies based on diverse psychoanalytic and psychodynamic theories, attachment theory, family systems theory, neurobiology and theories of child development. Despite the wide range of therapeutic models and applications, all psychodynamic therapies share the assumption that surface behaviour, such as relationship conflicts, challenging behaviour and emotions, are influenced by unconscious dynamics that occur both within each person and often within relationships between family members or others (Stiefel et al., 1998). As such, PDT is both an intrapsychic therapy and an interpersonal model. It is the intricate dynamic that develops both within a person and within relationships that occurs at both conscious and unconscious levels that become the specific focus of PDT and is the hallmark of the psychodynamic model, which differentiates PDT from other approaches to therapy with young children.

One of the model's assumptions is that early childhood experiences with significant others exert a powerful influence on one's current behaviour. PDT helps family members to understand unhelpful current relationship patterns, conflicts and psychological symptoms by linking them with past experiences and by exploring unconscious psychological coping mechanisms occurring within a person and played out within relationships, dynamics that maintain and support psychological symptoms and relationship stress. The relationship between therapist and client is central insofar as a safe and trusting relationship needs to be developed before the client can explore and process challenging experiences or gain insight into defensive symptom-maintaining behaviour and interactions. The transference relationship serves as a tool to understand processes between therapist and client, and the therapist's role is that of a translator, interpreting observations that help the client make sense of relationship patterns. Further, the therapist will help the family to recognise defence mechanisms the child or caregiver may be using and gently bring these dynamics to the family's attention. While the symptom presentation of the young child leads to the referral for therapy, the child or any part of the family system can become the focus of the intervention (Herman, 2005). The therapy length and format can vary depending on client characteristics, the therapist's training and preferred model of working and may include the child, the child in the presence of the parents, parallel work with child and caregiver, parent or couple intervention, or a whole family systems approach. While research into the treatment effects of psychodynamic therapy for adults is growing and promising, outcome studies exploring the treatment benefits of psychodynamic therapy with young children and their families are sparse. This chapter presents a contextual approach to psychodynamic child and family therapy appropriate for symptom presentation in young children, where the child is treated in the context of the parent or family.

Historical Development of PDT

Guntrip (1977) states that psychoanalytical theory has been in a continuous state of development. Ermann (2009) describes three stages of psychoanalytic development, the first beginning with Freud, the second period starting in the post second world war years and the third stage beginning in the mid-1970s.

The First Stage

Freud's theory of personality started to develop in the late 19th Century and evolved over time. The theory is intrinsically complex and has often been trivialised and misunderstood. Kernberg (Kernberg & Stierlin, 2006) defines Freud's work as a theory of personality and motivation, a method to explore unconscious forces which are perceived as important aspects of personality and as a treatment method. In the context of this chapter, four main concepts of Freud's theory will be highlighted.

Freud proposed a structure of the individual personality consisting of the id, ego and superego (Zhang, 2020). He conceptualised the id as based on biological drives, seeking fulfilment of human needs. The ego is seen as the structural component of the psyche, following the reality principle and providing direction, whereas the superego represents the conscience and moral aspects of personality (Zhang, 2020). The role of the ego is also to negotiate between id impulses and superego demands (Lee, 2009).

Defence mechanisms develop if the ego is threatened by perceived danger. The most common defence mechanism is repression. Repression assures that unacceptable unconscious material (thoughts, feelings, internal conflicts) does not enter the conscious mind (Zhang, 2020).

An example from therapy is provided below:

> A mother reported in the first family interview that she could not recall any early memories of herself in the relationship with her mother prior to starting school. Her mother was a single parent and always worked. During therapy which focused on her over-indulgence of her daughter, an image occurred in which she looked up to her mother, but her mother's focus was elsewhere. The memory evoked intense feelings of sadness. The memory of this brief episode, which triggered a range of strong feelings, was repressed from consciousness.

There are various concepts and dimensions of the unconscious. Freud focused on unconscious processes in which previous conscious material becomes repressed due to internal anxiety. However, he also had a broader awareness that there are other unconscious parts of personality that have never been repressed (De Sousa, 2011).

Freud proposed five stages of psychological development. During the first oral phase (from birth to 12–18 months of age), the infant's mouth is seen as the erogenic zone, giving pleasure and satisfaction, initially expressed in contact with the mother. During the anal phase (18 months to 3 years), the anus and bodily functions of controlling bladder and bowel movement become the focus; the third stage, the phallic phase (age 3–6 years), focuses on the genital area, the latent stage between the age of 6–12 years is a relatively dormant state, followed by the genital stage which starts with puberty and reaches into adulthood, moving the focus from the self to adult sexual relationships as the focus of pleasure (Mcleod, 2019). The pleasure-seeking energetic forces are linked to the id and are embedded in Freud's drive theory.

The cornerstones of Freud's theory, which still hold relevance for contemporary psychodynamic therapy, are the assumptions of unconscious intrapsychic processes and defence mechanisms occurring in daily life. However, according to Kernberg, Freud was also aware of the powerful effects of early experiences on personality development, though his focus remained primarily on intrapsychic processes, such as the defence mechanisms (Kernberg & Stierlin, 2006). Freud's focus included children, for example, in the treatment of Little Hans, a child with a horse phobia treated via his father in the early 20th Century, and he developed a theory of child development. Many scholars influenced the field of early psychoanalytic theory, including Carl Jung, Alfred Adler and Harry

Stack Sullivan (Messer, 2015). The early stage of psychoanalytic therapy also saw the emergence of psychoanalytic child therapy with early approaches developed by Melanie Klein and Anna Freud and the observation by Hermine von Hug-Hellmuth that unresolved parent conflicts can play an important role in the creation and maintenance of child pathology (Lee, 2009).

The Second Stage

The second phase in the development of psychoanalytic theory and treatment occurred in England and the USA due to the complete banning of psychoanalysis by the Nazi regime, leading prominent psychoanalytic therapists to exit Germany (Leuzinger-Bohleber & Plaenkers, 2019). New developments in psychoanalysis occurred approximately between 1940–1975 and include Anna Freud's outline of child analysis in the 1960s (Lee, 2009), the development of Self Psychology in the USA with the prominent figure of Heinz Kohut and the development of Object Relations Theory in England by Melanie Klein, Donald Winnicott, Ronald Fairbairn, Harry Guntrip and others (Messer, 2015; Stiefel et al., 1998). With this, psychoanalytic theory started to move from a primarily intrapsychic theory to an interpersonal therapy (Ermann, 2009).

The Third Stage

With the development of attachment theory, object relations theory, the concept of intersubjectivity, advances in neuroscience, research in the field of memory, infant–parent research and the consolidation of systems theory, the psychoanalytic theory went through a third stage, roughly from the middle of the 1970s onward (Ermann, 2009). This third stage sees an integration of diverse theories and clearly transfers psychodynamic therapy to the field of interpersonal science. The relationship needs of people became a strong focus combined with a better understanding of the effects of early relationship experiences on lifelong developmental outcomes. Psychodynamic models of family therapy and attachment-based models started to blossom during this time period (Byng-Hall, 1995; Scharff & Scharff, 1987; Slipp, 1988). Therapists at the time tried to understand how the child's early experiences with significant carers are absorbed, organised in the internal world and played out in relationships with others (Stiefel et al., 1998). Lipner et al. (2017) refer to the third stage as the relational movement of psychoanalysis, which is also influenced by postmodern ideas, including the feminist movement.

Theoretical Concepts of Contemporary PDT

The Unconscious

The dynamic unconscious is a central concept of psychodynamic theory. Freud (1915) defined the unconscious as a repository for emotions without any sense of time, place or logic (Stiefel et al., 1998). The unconscious can speak through symbols, imagination, art, jokes and errors (such as Freudian slips) in everyday language. Healy et al. (1931) perceived the unconscious as aspects of mental life that were either never conscious or previously conscious but repressed from awareness. In contemporary cognitive psychology, the unconscious has been variously conceptualised as implicit memory or non-declarative knowledge (LeDoux, 1994).

Drive Theory

The concept of drives underwent considerable changes in psychodynamic theory as it developed over time (Demir, 2013). In Freud's early writings, drives are seen as libidinal energy forces, biologically informed but placed within the psyche (Mills, 2004). These forces seek satisfaction aimed at one's own body or at external objects. Object relations theory stresses the object-seeking nature of libidinal energy (Demir, 2013). Depending on psychoanalytic theory, internal and external processes regulate the expression of the energetic forces. In Freud's theory, societal norms restrict the expression, and he placed the role of negotiation between personal needs, urges, desires and societal requirements in the ego, whereas object relations theory, such as Winnicott's, also stresses the important role of the caregiver in containing the expression of excessive energy in the child (Demir, 2013).

Defense Mechanisms

Defence mechanisms can be defined as automatic psychological strategies, occurring mostly at an unconscious level with the purpose of protecting the person against danger, anxiety, internal or external stress and conflict (Berlin, 2011; Tallandini & Cander, 2010). Defence mechanisms can have both adaptive and maladaptive roles. The research by Tallandini and Cander (2010) suggests that the use of defence mechanisms changes with age, with younger children using displacement, idealisation, and regression more often, whereas older children and those with higher verbal IQ show more frequent use of rationalisation. Overall, boys shower higher rates of externalising, whereas in girls, more internalising defences occur (Tallandini & Cander, 2010). Repressed material can still influence behaviour, feelings and thought and can surface in symptoms, dreams or Freudian slips (Berlin, 2011). The number of defence mechanisms cited in the literature varies, and currently, there is no common taxonomy (Liebert & Liebert, 1998; Tallandini & Cander, 2010). There are numerous defence mechanisms, but common ego defence mechanisms in the context of psychoanalytic therapy involving children and parents/caregivers include:

- **Repression**: The blocking of stressful experiences or difficult thoughts from entering consciousness. Repression can be defined as a generic defence mechanism, as repression is involved in all specific sub-types. For example, a child who never gets selected into sports teams may unintentionally forget to wear their sports uniform on a sports day.

- **Denial:** Refusal to acknowledge facts or authentic feelings. A 5-year-old child involved in a fight might insist that they did not hit another child. A child may deny feelings of vulnerability, stating that they were not afraid in an obviously stressful situation. A child may deny that their parent has died but want to believe they are 'Just away on holiday'.

- **Displacement**: Transferring feelings that originated in a stressful situation onto someone else. For example, a child living with their grandmother states that the grandmother is hitting her. In the conjoint session with the mother, who has lost custody of her child, the mother reveals that she used to hit her child. The displacement protects the child from realising that her mother was abusive towards them. Another example is a child getting bullied at school but is afraid to retaliate. The child comes home and bullies their younger sibling.

- **Regression:** Behaviours that are immature considering a person's age and developmental level. An example may be excessive help-seeking behaviour, regression to immature speech and having toileting accidents despite being previously toilet trained when a sibling is born as a way of dealing with feelings of jealousy of the attention given to the new baby.

- **Reaction Formation**: Expressing the opposite of the person's feelings, feelings that are unacceptable to the self. For example, a child who previously had a close relationship with his father, who is in jail, may state they 'Never even wanted a dad'.

- **Rationalisation:** Finding a logical explanation for an event that caused strong feelings. A boy who did not get selected into a debating team (and cannot acknowledge the feeling of hurt) may say that he would not have enjoyed being part of the team as it was a team of boys and girls and he prefers 'all-boy' teams.

- **Sublimation:** Channelling unacceptable feelings or conflicts into a productive outlet. A young child with social skills deficits experiencing rejection by peers may channel all their energy into becoming a competitive online chess player.

- **Idealisation**: Recognising the positive aspects of a person or situation in an unbalanced way which is common in grief responses. For example, a child stating that their life would be perfect and all problems would disappear if their mother and father were back together again, despite significant and repeated domestic violence episodes. If there is limited contact with the father (e.g., supervised access with the father four times a year), the child may claim that their father was the greatest dad, stating examples of involvement that have no reality base.

- **Acting Out:** Engaging in extreme or unusual behaviour as an expression of feelings or thoughts that cannot be acknowledged directly. For example, a child might get upset and hit their mother in response to their grief over their father's death.

- **Splitting:** Polarisation, black and white thinking, often involving idealisation and devaluing of another person. A parent may compliment the therapist excessively, saying she is the greatest therapist on earth. However, after a difficult session, the client may state that the therapist is utterly useless.

- **Projection:** Projecting attributes, negative or positive, into another person. A girl may unconsciously project her own aggressive feelings into others, claiming that her peers are bullying and pushing her.

Projective Identification

This is an important concept in psychodynamic therapy and involves an unconscious two-person process occurring between people who have an ongoing relationship. Projective identification can be defined as a reciprocal process occurring between family members (or others) where one person, the projector, unconsciously attributes aspects of themselves to another family member (Stiefel et al., 1998). The recipient can be the child. In this process, the recipient is then induced into feeling and behaving according to the projected aspect, identifying with it. Projective identification involves disavowal of an unwanted part of self and a blurring of boundaries between the two people. When negative aspects are projected into another person, the projector may overly focus on the child's negative behaviour, or criticise the child, whereas the child may oppose the parent's behaviour and a negative cycle between carer and child develops. An example may be a parent who unconsciously projects a negative part of self into their child, then becomes highly sensitive to any expressed negative child behaviour and responds with increased criticism or punitive parenting behaviour. A parent who experienced a neglectful upbringing may project the deprived part into their child and responds with over-indulgence or over-protection in their parenting (Herman, 2005).

Mental Representations

Mental representations start to develop early in life and are based on repeated experiences with important caregivers. Mental representations are affective and cognitive schemas of self, others and relationship patterns; they have conscious and unconscious aspects and undergo change and development. Mental representations can be perceived as templates of how one sees oneself and others, and they provide the basis for social interaction (Blatt et al., 1997). There is increasing evidence that there are neural underpinnings to these templates (LeDoux, 1994). The term object or internal object often occurs in earlier writing (e.g., Melanie Klein) and can be understood as mental representations, resulting from introjection and internalisation of relationship experiences with significant people early in life, and also include self-representations, which combined form the complex network of object relations.

Attachment

Attachment is critical for the survival of the young child, and disruption in the bond between child and primary caregiver has disastrous effects on the child's development. Secure attachment increases the stress-coping ability and sense of self (Lee, 2009). The quality of the attachment relationship between caregiver and child has important relevance in the context of paediatric psychodynamic therapy. Object Relations theory emphasises the lifelong need for connection and good-enough relationships. Good-enough in the context of child development refers to a constellation of relationship qualities, including the caregiver's awareness of the physiological and psychological needs of the child and attending to these with some level of consistency and predictability. The parent is present and responds to the child's needs with sensitivity, warmth and empathy, is physically and emotionally available, mirrors the child's affect, talks about the child's feelings and soothes when the child becomes distressed (Stiefel et al., 1998). Good enough parenting does not mean that these processes occur all of the time, but they do occur to some degree to provide 'good enough' care for healthy development.

The Treatment Process

Assessment

How the therapist approaches the assessment will depend on the therapist's training, preferred way of working and reason for referral. However, contemporary psychodynamic child therapy considers the child in context. The context can be defined as the child's immediate environment, usually the child's family, but the assessment process will also take into consideration the quality of the parent–child relationship, and significant experiences of all family members, which may be relevant in the symptom presentation of the child, and an exploration as to how these experiences have been processed. Most psychodynamic approaches would explore the developmental history of the child in detail, the parent's own experiences during pregnancy, birth and during the post-natal period, the parent's recall of their own growing up years in their families of origin, the quality of current relationships with relevant others such as the extended family members, current and in the past, the quality of the couple relationship, and if separation has occurred, the relationship with ex-partners and their new network of relationships. In the case of adoption or fostering relevant information may be obtained from child protection agencies. Exploring qualitative experience, not facts, is important, with questions such as 'What stands out from your experience as a child?', 'What are your earliest memories?', 'How would you have described your mother and father, using three words when you were a child?', 'How did you and your partner meet?', 'How did you both respond when you first found out you were pregnant?', 'What was your first thought when you saw your baby?' and 'Who in your extended family do you feel close to and is providing support?'.

These questions explore if stressful events occurred in the child's and parent's life and how these have been processed. They assess the quality of past and current relationships, mental representations and working models as relevant to the roles of different family members. This aspect of the assessment can be referred to as the collection of important content information. Some therapists prefer to meet the whole family for the initial assessment, while others proceed with separate assessments, often with the parents attending first, to allow for sensitive information to be discussed, followed by a session with parent and child or with the child only, depending on the age and level of maturity of the child.

In regard to the assessment of young children, there are a wide range of assessment techniques suitable for this young age range. The therapy room should offer toys that allow manipulation and creation by the child, such as a doll's house with furniture and small dolls representing three generations of people of different ethnicity, domestic animals, paper and pencils, and some wild animals such as tigers, a children's tea set, blocks, soldiers, cars, a medical kit and emergency vehicles. Most children spontaneously engage in play or will do so after being encouraged by the therapist. Observation of free play may give important assessment information about the child's preoccupations, themes in play or in drawings and unconscious processes. The interpretation of play is part of the psychodynamic model.

If the child separates from the parent without undue distress, the therapist can utilise specific projective techniques (questions and drawings) to explore the child's inner world of feelings, thoughts and fantasies and also the child's recall of experiences. Common projective drawings include:

- Draw a dream.
- Draw your family.
- Draw a picture of yourself.
- Draw a house.
- Draw anything.
- Draw yourself as a fruit tree.

Projective questions include:

- The Three Magic Wishes.
- If you could change one thing in your life what would it be?
- If you ended up on a deserted island but could only take one person, who would you take with you?
- If you could take three people in a rocket ship, who would you take?

The assessment of the child's creation or response leaves room for interpretation; however, the child's play and verbal responses usually also follow some sense of logic. For example, in the family drawing, does the child only use a black pencil with body shapes shaded and the figures squeezed into the corner, representing self and mother, or even say they cannot draw their family? Is the picture colourful with a bright sky and the sun in the left corner? Does the child say they would take their baby brother to the desert island or their neighbour, or are people from the immediate family selected, naming reasons such as 'I would take dad, he knows how to fish, so we would have something to eat'; or 'I would take mum she would look after me'. Does the house have five windows representing the five family members with one person waving, a garden and picket fence added, and their dog smiling, or does the house represent a vague shelter with one single grey door? A child's magic wish may be for 1000 lollies, all the chocolates in the world and a mountain of ice cream that never melts, or it may be for the cat they recently lost due to illness to be back in the family, or better friends, no school, or dad coming back home after a difficult separation. However, the clinician can also utilise standardised tools for assessing children's drawings, such as Fury et al.'s (1997) ratings of children's representations of attachment relationships in family drawings. Therapists, even in this early stage, may comment on the child's answers or drawings with therapeutic intent, asking for qualifications or even offering gentle interpretations. However, this will depend on the child's presentation and the issues involved. The process aspect of the assessment, however, is also highly relevant. PDT encourages an openness on the part of the therapist to all channels of communication, initially without censorship. Micro behaviours can include minute gestures, subtle changes in posture, tone of voice or facial expressions displayed by the client. There may be a small pause when the therapist asks a certain question, a brief freezing in facial expression, or a child looking at their mother in response to an utterance or looking at the ground. Repeated small mannerisms may be noticeable to the astute observer but may not reach immediate conscious awareness in the therapist. However, this 'unprocessed' experience gradually takes form and is then processed with self-reflective questions during the session or in subsequent supervision with peers, such as 'What is this telling me?' and 'What did I notice?'.

Empathy, Containment and Holding

Empathy is the basis of all therapeutic endeavour, and Bromfield (2003) lists empathy as an important therapy variable in psychodynamic child therapy. For the therapeutic work to progress, clients may get in touch with painful memories, feelings of failure as a parent, or they may be becoming increasingly aware of unhelpful relationship patterns in which they play a part. These need to be processed, and in PDT, this includes gaining an understanding of the defence mechanisms involved, which may have been adaptive at times of distress in the past. For therapeutic work involving the resolution of internal conflicts and relationship stress, the therapeutic relationship needs to feel safe. Herman (2005) stresses that work with parents requires an empathic therapist, who respectfully acknowledges family members' feelings, listens to unconscious themes and uses confrontation judiciously and with sensitivity.

> **Example**: A parent may say that their child did not enjoy last week's session, being critical of the therapist. Statements like these need to be explored with sensitivity in a calm, non-defensive, attentive and non-judgemental way. The therapist may explore the statement with questions such as 'Can you help me understand what it might have been that was unpleasant for your child, related to my behaviour or the content of the session?'. Self-reflection is also warranted to exclude specific therapist behaviours as contributing factors. The aim of this exploration is to understand the child's (or the mother's) experience but also to strengthen the therapeutic bond with openness on the part of the therapist.

Therapeutic holding is a related term. Bromfield (2003) describes therapeutic holding in child therapy as a process in which the therapist absorbs the distress or excitement that children cannot carry themselves. Confirmation of the child's experience with empathic listening and shared enjoyment is also indicated when positive changes occur. Winnicott's concept of the therapist as a container is helpful in this context (Demir, 2013). Demir explains that for the 'true self' to emerge, the client needs to be contained, held, and nurtured through a 'good-enough' therapeutic relationship. A contained therapist–client relationship that feels safe and in which empathy is expressed will allow family members to gently confront defence mechanisms stemming from their own experience of growing up and being played out in their interaction within the family or within the therapist–client relationship.

Play

The assessment of the child's play is an important tool when working with young children, as young children often do not have the verbal or cognitive capacity to recall important experiences or assess their psychological states. Melanie Klein perceived child's play as an equivalent to Free Association (Blomfield, 2003), a technique used by S. Freud in which the client was encouraged to report anything that comes to mind in an uncensored way. In the play, a range of feelings can be expressed, including feelings of abandonment, longing, rage, joy and envy. Play is also the vehicle for interpretations and offers access to unconscious processes (Bromfield, 2003). Play allows the child to place conflicts within themselves or with other people into the symbolic form of constructive play, action or interaction with the therapist (Bromfield, 2003). Play in PDT is client-led and non-directive, in which the child freely engages with the play materials, with the therapist following and sometimes joining the child in play. Play is inherently therapeutic, helping the child to work through themes and issues repeatedly if needed. The therapist's interpretations of play have to be well-timed so the child can tolerate them, integrating the new information without causing undue distress or defensive behaviour (Lee, 2009).

The following brief excerpt is from the second assessment session with a young child and her grandmother, which illustrates the symbolic representation of the child's experience expressed in the play.

> Miriam was a 4-year-old girl referred to therapy by her maternal grandmother, who had recently taken full-time care of her granddaughter. Both parents had severe drug addiction with failed rehabilitation, which led to the neglect of Miriam and the removal of Miriam from her parents' care. The grandmother's main concerns were what she described as 'unusual' states, where Miriam would stare into space. Miriam also displayed separation anxiety at night, talking about 'burglars and robbers' who may break into the house. The paediatrician had excluded a medical reason for the presentation. Miriam and her grandmother were seen jointly. At the start of the second session, Miriam went to the doll house and played very noisily with the dolls. One of the dolls representing a child was noisily running up and down the stairs, looking out of the window, and talking to herself, saying

'hello', 'shut the door' when pretending to shut the front door, and 'go to the toilet' when pretending to go to the toilet, and overall giving a fairly hyperactive impression. The girl doll was alone in the house. Miriam then took an adult female doll out of the box, and her movement stopped for perhaps five seconds, but it was marked, as it was in such contrast to the noise. Miriam then placed the adult doll back in the box quietly, disregarded the doll house and asked her grandmother for something to eat.

The therapist's thoughts were that the play may have represented Miriam's actual experience when in the care with her parents, the restless and typical activity in the house when her parents were physically and psychologically not present but influenced by substances in a disorganised way and the emptiness when actually seeing her mother who could not hold Miriam psychologically in her mind due to the severe drug addiction. The pausing possibly represents the moment where hope for connection emerges but is disappointed again, and the doll is disregarded.

Transference and Countertransference

The processing of the transference/countertransference response is an important tool in psychodynamic therapy. Countertransference has been conceptualised in various ways since Freud introduced the concept, and the concept is still evolving (Cartwright, 2017). In the context of this paper, we refer to countertransference as an unconscious reaction in the therapist as a result of the client's transference of unconscious aspects of self onto the therapist. The therapist's training and supervision help the therapist become more aware of processes in self when reflecting on sessions, trying to make sense of their observation and personal (including somatic) responses to family members. An example of transference and countertransference is below.

A therapist saw a mother (Shannon) with her two boys, John (age 6) and Peter (age 4), for the first time. The 6-year-old had been referred for anger issues. In the first session, the two boys engaged quietly in play at the children's table. During the session, the therapist experienced a feeling of dislike for the mother. The mother was articulate, well-groomed, and an attractive lady, and at first, the therapist could not make sense of the countertransference experience. The husband did not attend the interview; Shannon said he worked in the mines and was currently in Western Australia. The therapist sought group supervision and shared her experience of the session. The group explored the therapist's feelings, asking her to give details of the session and allowing for reflection. Two images appeared strongly in the therapist's recall. First, she reported that the mother appeared to act differently with her two boys. The therapist noticed this at the beginning of the interview, and she recalled feeling annoyed. With the younger child, the mother expressed warmth and gentleness, whereas there was a subtle expression of harshness, expressed non-verbally, when she interacted with her older son. The therapist's second recall from the session was that the mother appeared to pause for brief moments when she was asked to describe her relationship with her own mother, and her answers appeared to be very brief and factual. There was good trust in the supervision group, and the therapist also explored if the apparent dislike related to anything past or present occurring in the therapist's life. However, the therapist could not think of any specific reason. The group concluded that understanding the mother's history further might give more information about the apparent feeling of dislike. However, all members of the group felt that the therapist should explore this area with great sensitivity.

When exploring Shannon's personal history further, the following emerged. Shannon reported that she was the older child of two in her family of origin. Shannon said she always felt her mother did not like her. She herself was a bright child, and her mother often stressed that bright children did not fit well into their Irish working-class family culture. When her first child was born, Shannon finally cut contact with her mother, as her mother remained critical and non-supportive of Shannon. Shannon recalled severe post-natal depression following the birth of her first child. She saw a female therapist for two sessions, who reminded her of her mother, with a cold and critical attitude towards Shannon, which she found extremely stressful. However, her husband supported her during this difficult time and took care of their firstborn son. Shannon said things changed when she was pregnant with her second son. By then, she had gained employment in a high-powered position and earned money and status, and this had a significant effect on her self-esteem. Her employer valued her work, allowed her time to bond with the second child, and, when her son was 9 months old, returned to work on a part-time basis. She said she was still feeling confident and appreciated in her work.

The therapist wondered whether the initial dislike of Shannon was related to Shannon's mother's negativity, possibly projected into the therapist, who then experienced Shannon in negative terms. It was interesting to note that the therapist's dislike of Shannon changed over the following session to one of compassion and empathy. This change often occurs in therapy when the transference/countertransference dynamic is understood.

Forming a Psychodynamic-Systemic Hypothesis

Therapists form hypotheses about their clients, consciously and intentionally, or unconsciously, trying to make sense of the information presented and the specific responses of the therapist to the clients. The psychodynamic working hypothesis will be tested out, and important elements will be shared with the family in gentle and respectful ways with probing, interpretations and sometimes gentle confrontations.

> **Example**: The therapist's formulation was that Shannon's internal representation of the mother–child relationship was compromised by Shannon's perception of a rejecting and critical mother, most likely based on repeated experiences early in Shannon's life. The mental representation of the mother–child relationship was activated when the first child was born, leaving Shannon without a solid internal working model, which would have guided her intuitively into her role as a competent and confident mother. Instead, motherhood became a struggle with a renewed experience of loss of the supportive mother Shannon never had, complicated by her reaction to depression and lack of enjoyment in being a mother to her first son. Guilt, despair, fatigue and helplessness were strong feelings Shannon experienced at the time. Painful negative relationship aspects and repressed anger were transferred both into her older child and initially also into the therapist as these were dominant relationship schema.

Interpretation

Therapeutic interpretations are translations, helping the client make sense of unconscious processes that occur within the person and within relationships. In PDT, this may include the interpretation of unconscious processes occurring in the client–therapist relationship. Interpretations are the testing out of a working hypothesis with the client. Safe interpretations, in our experience, are those that 'Follow the Affect'. With empathic reflection, for example, in the case of Shannon, the therapist may try to capture Shannon's experience, but also the wished-for relationship qualities, the longing for relationship needs that were most likely repressed in anger and distancing. In cases of clients like Shannon, powerful interpretations also involve the mother's positive intention towards her child; the attachment needs of both, which was hindered by events in the mother's own life. Reaching the 'unconscious dreams', the hoped-for relationships, both past and present, and allowing for painful affect to be understood are often turning points in PDT with children and families. The therapist must assess if the client is ready to hear the interpretation, whether the timing is right, or when to hold off. The aim of therapy is to help the client to understand and process stressful memories and related defences, and the interpretation should loosen the need to suppress memories, feelings and thoughts and not increase the defensive struggle.

An interpretation may be worded in the following: 'It must have felt like you could not reach your child. Your mother was not there for you when you really needed her, and then you felt you could not be there for your son when he needed you, and your husband had to try to hold it all together in his own manly way as 'best as he could'.

When affect is expressed, the therapist will stay with this and, if the children are present, may translate the sad feelings to them. 'John, your mum is really sad. When you were born, your mum's mum (your grandmother) did not help her to look after you. You also became very sad because you needed your mother like all babies do. Daddy helped a lot, but he was also away at work a lot'. (John nods). 'Mum, you, John and Peter — you are here to make it better. I think Mum has told us how much she loves you both, but sometimes you (John) and Mum cannot get close, and that makes her very upset'. When the interpretation is correct, a child will often show agreement.

The therapist may now link the unfulfilled relationship needs with the referral problem in such a way that nobody feels blamed or made responsible for the presenting problem. 'I am wondering whether the expressed anger in John is related? Perhaps everybody in the family sometimes gets angry. Mum gets angry with her own mum, and you (to the boys) get angry with your mum or dad, perhaps John, a little more?'.

The following step of therapy may involve the therapist's observation of the different treatment of the boys to see if the mother and older child agree with the observation. The therapist felt that the family were ready to explore this next step. A safe way to proceed may be to put the observation into question form, in case the observation is felt to be too confrontational, especially for the mother, or to use phrases such as 'Does it sometimes seem as if …'.

In psychodynamic therapy, change sometimes occurs following a powerful interpretation. At other times, techniques from other models can be added. In the above case, the therapist's observation was explored. John agreed that he felt his mother would often favour his younger brother, and the therapist tried to link this with the mother's experience in her family of origin in which the younger sister received the positive maternal attention. This fairly bright mother responded well to the concept of representation of relationship experiences, and we jointly explored how maternal attention could shift to a more equal distribution. John was helpful in that he was very specific about what he enjoyed most doing with his mother, which was his mother watching him play soccer for a whole game.

Treatment Length and Outcome of PDT

PDT, in general can be open-ended and long-term with high session frequency of several sessions per week or relatively brief, time-limited and more focused with one weekly session (Messer, 2015). Messer (2015) defines time-limited

PDT as therapy with no more than 25 sessions and up to 40 sessions for clients with personality disorder. In the context of childhood presentations, the length of therapy can vary considerably. However, the assessment tends to be more involved compared with many other models of therapy, and this will add to the overall length of therapy. The goal of PDT is to resolve conflict, overcome interpersonal problems and repair aspects of self (Messer, 2015). For young children, the aim of PDT is to resolve developmental arrest, restructure repressed memories, fantasies and wishes, and reorganise defence mechanisms (Lee, 2009). Depending on the model used, the therapy process will assist family members in acknowledging and working through stressful life experiences, understanding projective processes occurring within the family, and eventually experiencing symptom relief.

Evidence Base

Compared with adult psychodynamic therapy, which is starting to show good treatment gains, research into the treatment effectiveness of psychodynamic and psychoanalytic therapy with children is limited (Midgley & Kennedy, 2011). In Midgley and Kennedy's (2011) extensive exploration, there were only 9 studies that reached level 1 research criteria, with many other studies lacking a control group or a large enough sample size. However, clinical case studies, which are a popular form of research in the field of psychodynamic therapy, were not included in their search. Midgley and Kennedy (2011) report a prospective study by Kronmueller and colleagues which suggests that long-term psychodynamic treatment has a strong treatment effect of 1.41, with indicators of improved attachment and family functioning. Fonagy's and Target's (1996) retrospective study of a large cohort of children treated at the Anna Freud Centre reports an interesting finding. Overall, younger children and those receiving intensive forms of treatment showed great improvement, and children with emotional disorders overall did better compared with children presenting with disruptive behaviour disorder. However, children with disruptive disorder also improved with higher intensity and length of treatment. Children with severe clinical presentation did not respond well to weekly treatment. However, 80% showed reliable improvement when intensive forms of psychodynamic therapy such as 4–5 sessions in a week were offered.

A long-term follow-up study by Schachter and Target (2009) reported by Midgley and Kennedy (2011) revealed that adults who had received therapy as children were functioning well on a wide range of measures. Psychoanalytic treatment for children who have experienced abuse, neglect and trauma has also been explored. Trowell et al. (2002) assessed the treatment effects for girls with a history of sexual abuse and demonstrated a treatment effect size of 0.64. Muratori et al. (2003) explored the long-term effects of short-term psychodynamic treatment for emotional disorders and found a possible sleeper effect, showing ongoing improvement after treatment ceases with further gains 2 years following treatment. Midgley and Kennedy (2011) concluded that the small number of studies indicates that psychodynamic therapy with children is effective and appears to be equally effective compared with other forms of treatment. There is strong evidence for psychodynamic treatment to be an effective form of treatment for depression in children and young people. Treatment change occurs slower but is more sustained and continues to improve after treatment. Children with emotional disorders and younger children overall benefit more. Children with externalising disorder are harder to engage and have a higher dropout rate, but if they stay in treatment, they also benefit from psychodynamic therapy. Psychodynamic treatment may be an indication for more severe childhood presentations, including trauma and abuse. Seeing children in isolation (without parent involvement) may hamper treatment effects (Midgley & Kennedy, 2011). Wiegand-Grefe et al. (2016), in their exploration, conclude that short-term psychodynamic therapy is effective for children presenting with anxiety, depression and externalising disorders, showing long-term effects. However, they point out that family dynamics also determine success rates.

Exploring the effects of long-term psychodynamic therapy is a research challenge as a waitlist control group presents an unethical research design (Midgley & Kennedy, 2011; Wiegand-Grefe et al., 2016). Research into the effectiveness of psychodynamic therapy has been conducted mostly in naturalistic clinical settings. This fact is both a weakness and a strength. While comparability and generalisation of results are compromised, naturalistic research represents the real world of many clinical settings, with mixed and often complex clinical presentations of clients. Advances in technology in the field of neuroscience confirm S. Freud's assumption that much of mental life, including thoughts, feelings and motivation, occur at an unconscious level (Berlin, 2011). Empirical studies are beginning to elucidate the neural basis of classical psychoanalytic concepts, leading to a revival, refinement and enhancement of key psychodynamic concepts (Berlin, 2011). According to Berlin (2011), emotions can be processed without conscious awareness, and it is likely that phylogenetically older, subcortical processes are involved in unconscious processes.

Training in PDT with Children and their Families

Strupp et al. (1988), referring to training in psychodynamic therapy in general, suggest that training should include three components: didactic coursework on theory and technique, supervised clinical practice, and personal psychoanalytic therapy. The training focus also needs to consider two dyads, the client–therapist and the therapist–supervisor dyad, each with their developing transference and countertransference relationship. Further, training should foster the therapist's empathic understanding as an important component of therapeutic work. Training in psychodynamic child psychotherapy in similar ways includes theory, personal psychoanalytic therapy and supervision, and in this context, clinical work with a child, adolescent and a parent. In addition, many courses in psychoanalytic child therapy request that trainees complete an infant observation. Course participants need to have completed degrees in psychology, social work, nursing or related disciplines.

Training options in Australia include the pathway of training in psychoanalytic adult therapy first, which involves a minimum of 5 years part-time study, with subsequent child training. Alternatively, training in child psychoanalysis is offered by the Child Psychoanalytic Psychotherapy Association in Australia (CPPAA), involving a minimum of 3 years of study. The curriculum is extensive in both theory and practice. In contrast to the Australian landscape, some training options in the UK are funded by the NHS for British citizens. The Tavistock Portman course offers clinical supervision in a range of psychodynamic approaches (such as short-term and long-term, brief and family work) but also adds a research component. For therapists wishing to work specifically with families, training and supervision options may also include a family systemic training pathway with the development of generic family therapy skills combined with specific psychodynamic family therapy techniques.

Conclusion

There is no other model of therapy that assists the therapist in processing the relationship between client/s and therapist at different levels; the therapist's conscious and unconscious experience. This processing tool for understanding the transference/countertransference relationship is of enormous relevance for any therapist regardless of therapeutic orientation and should, at least in rudimentary forms, be part of any therapy training and supervision course. The unconscious indicates to the sensitive therapist that something is occurring that needs attention and processing; it reaches the therapist's awareness with images, feelings, thoughts or impulses and can subsequently be processed in a self-reflective way with questions such as 'What is happening here?', 'This feels very uncomfortable', 'Something has changed', 'What is the client telling me?', 'Something doesn't feel right, it is different?', 'I can't make sense of it' and can also evoke positive feelings, such as of being touched emotionally by the client. The analysis of the transference and countertransference is especially helpful when working with complex clients where, according to psychodynamic theory, ego integration is fragile, the client's interpersonal boundaries are weak, and conflicts are played out in the therapist–client relationship.

It is of interest to note that several fathers and mothers of powerful therapeutic models of therapy (e.g., therapists of the Milan systemic school, Aaron Beck, Salvador Minuchin) were trained first in psychoanalysis and in implicit ways, aspects of the richness of psychoanalytic thinking, theory and practice still filter through in subtle ways in their new approaches. We also see an integration of psychodynamic theory and therapy practices in contemporary evidence-based treatments, such as Child Parent Psychotherapy.

The aim of psychodynamic therapy is symptom relief, reduction in states of anxiety, anger or depression, resolution of feelings of grief, overcoming trauma or reducing relationship distress. However, Bromfield (2003) stresses that psychodynamic therapy goes beyond these symptoms and involves an integration of various aspects of the personality, which results in a stronger sense of self, increased resilience and adaptability, which enhances the future adjustment to life events. PDT can be costly and time-consuming, especially in Australia, where shorter-term funding models prevail. However, if the complete family attends treatment, psychodynamic family work can also be highly effective and cost-saving, and we now know that family therapy overall is an effective form of treatment for many child presentations (Carr, 2014). PDT not only addresses the presenting symptoms of the child referred but also addresses family relationship stress and fosters internal changes within other family members, depending on the issues, leading to improvements in the whole family's functioning. Hopefully, future research will explore the specific child conditions for which PDT is specifically indicated and superior to other available treatment models.

Case Vignette

Juliette and Franco attended the first assessment session jointly with their 5-year-old daughter Marcia. Reasons for referring were Marcia's extreme separation anxiety during the day and at night. However, preschool integration was of particular concern. Over the past 6-months, preschool days were stressful as Marcia would cry and cling, especially when her mother dropped her off on preschool days. However, once Juliette left the preschool, Marcia would usually settle into the daily routine, though she tended to be shy and lacked self-esteem. Taking the family history, the parents reported that separation anxiety had been an issue from birth. Marcia had been a very unsettled baby, and they attended a specialist sleep and settling service when the baby was 4 months old to help with settling. The small family were fairly isolated, Juliette's mother died, and she had infrequent contact with her father, and Franco's parents lived overseas, though there were regular phone contacts. The parent's own history revealed that Franco came from a large Spanish family, and he and his brother immigrated to Australia when they were young. He settled in Australia when he met Juliette. Juliette, on the other hand, reported that her mother died 6 years ago, and she had sporadic contact with her father, who lived in the country. At this point in time, the therapist noted a change, which was hard for her to describe with words, a change in the 'climate' of the room. Marcia, who had engaged in play with the dollhouse, seemed to slow in her movement, and the 'atmosphere' appeared to become heavy. The therapist gently asked Juliette, 'What happened to your mum?'. At this point, Juliette broke down and cried and said that her mother had taken her own life after a long struggle with depression. The therapist allowed space for the emotions, and Marcia started moving in her chair, feeling uncomfortable. At this stage, the therapist said to Marcia, 'Your mum is very sad', and again allowed space to respect Juliette's sadness about the loss of her mother. Marcia spontaneously voiced, 'Mum is sad; she lost her lunchbox'. At this moment, Juliette and Franco both laughed (they later explained to the therapist that this morning, Marcia had been very upset as she had left her favourite lunchbox at the preschool). Juliette then reached out to her daughter, drew her closer and said, 'Yes, I am also so sad, like you, when you could not find your favourite lunchbox'. This lifted the 'temperature' in the room, and the therapist gently explored the meaning of the lunchbox and, subsequently Juliette's loss of her mother. Juliette reported that she had felt very close to her mother, but the family lived in constant fear that her mother's depression could worsen and therapeutic options were running out. From time to time, the therapist tried to help Marcia to make sense of her mother's experience, with language appropriate to a 5-year-old, such as 'Your mum still misses her mum so much, she had to go to heaven so early'. The focus then shifted to Marcia's separation anxiety, with the therapist wondering whether Marcia's separation anxiety could be linked in some way to Juliette's loss, with both mother and child wanting to make sure that both felt safe and would not lose each other.

Reader's Exercises

The following exercise is suitable for group supervision but can also invite reflection for those not in supervision.

1. If you are currently working therapeutically, try to reflect on one of your clients that occupies your thoughts more compared with other clients. Describe your very first impression when you met this

client. Describe it as if you were producing a film the group partic-ipants were watching. Now describe your thoughts, feelings, images, urges, and sensations associated with the client. You may even apply free association, using words or images that come to your mind in a fairly uncensored form. Now process with questions such as 'What is this image, sensation, or thought telling me?'. If you are in group supervision, you can also invite your peers to reflect, allowing thoughts, emotions and images to come up.

2. Think about your childhood or events in your current life. If you have never been in therapy, reflect on which aspects of your current or past life experience are 'fragile and sensitive' and may possibly be triggered by certain responses from a client in the future. What could be warning signs indicating to you that these sensitivities have been triggered?

3. What type of responses do you tend to notice first when important moments are occurring in therapy, e.g., bodily sensations, general or specific feelings, visual images, words, a heightened awareness of the tone of voice in clients, smells, or gestures you observe in the client?

4. Imagine you are seeing a parent with a 3-year-old child. The reasons for referral are anxiety issues. In session three, you observe the child's play with a baby doll, dummy and bottle. The play appears normal, but you suddenly get unpleasant goosebumps and a feeling of darkness. What would you do with this experience, and what could it possibly mean?

References

Berlin, H. A. (2011). The neural basis of the dynamic unconscious. *Neuropsychoanalyst, 13*(1), 5–31. http://dx.doi.org/10.1080/15294145.2011.10773654

Blatt, S., Auerbach, J. S., & Levy, K. N. (1997) Mental representations in personality development, psychopathology, and the therapeutic process. *Review of General Psychology, 1*(4), 351–374. https://doi.1037/1089-2680.1.4.351

Bromfield, R. N. (2003). Psychoanalytic play therapy. In C. E. Schaefer (Ed.), *Foundations of Play Therapy,* (pp 1–13). Wiley.

Byng-Hall, J. (1995). Creating a secure family base: Some implications of Attachment Theory for Family Therapy. *Family Process, 34,* 45–58. https://doi.org/10.1111/j.1545-5300.1995.00045.x

Carr, A. (2014). The evidence base for family therapy and systemic interventions for child-focused problems. *Journal of Family Therapy*, *36*, 107–157. http://doi: 10.1111/1467-6427.12032

Cartwright, C. (2017). Countertransference. In: Zeigler-Hill, V., & Shackelford, T. (Eds.) *Encyclopedia of Personality and Individual Differences*. Springer. https://doi.org/10.1007/978-3-319-28099-8_888-1

Demir, A. M. (2013). *The Drive: A comparative analysis of Freudian, Object Relations and Lacanian Theory* https://www.academia.edu/en/2428306/The_Drive_A_Comparative_Analysis_of_Freudian_Object_Relations_and_Lacanian_Theory

De Sousa A., (2011), Freudian theory and consciousness: A conceptual analysis. In A. R. Singh & S. A. Singh (Eds.). *Brain, Mind and Consciousness: An International, Interdisciplinary Perspective*, MSM, *9*(1), 210–217. https://doi.org/ 10.4103%2F0973-1229.77437

Erman, M. (2009). *Psychoanalyse heute — Entwicklung und aktueller Bestand*. Vorlesung im Rahmen der Lindauer Psychotherapiewochen 'Dem Fremden begegnen, Der Gewalt begegnen'. https://shop.auditorium-netzwerk.de/archiv/fachbereiche/lindauer-p.sychotherapiewochen/2009-dem-fremden-begegnen-der-gewalt-begegnen-/?l=list

Fonagy, P., & Target, M. (1996). Predictors of outcome in child psychoanalysis: a retrospective study of 793 cases at the Anna Freud Centre. *Journal of the American Psychoanalytic Association*, *44*(1), 27–77. https://doi10.1177/000306519604400104

Fury, G., Carlson, E. A., & Sroufe, L. A. (1997). Children's representations of attachment relationships in family drawings. *Child Development*, *68*(6), 1154–64. https://doi.org/10.1111/j.1467-8624.1997.tb01991.x

Freud, S. (1915). The Unconscious. In J. Strachey (Ed. & Trans.). On metapsychology: The theory of psychoanalysis. *The Pelican Freud Library*, *11*, (pp161–221). Penguin.

Guntrip, H. (1977). *Personality structure and human interaction*. Hogarth Press.

Healy, W., Bronner, A. F., & Bowers, A. M. (1931). The structure and meaning of psychoanalysis as related to personality and behaviour. *Nature, 127*, 268. https://doi.org/10.1038/127268c0

Herman, J. (2005). Psychoanalytic insight-oriented parent counselling based on concepts of projective identification and reparative repetition. An object relations perspective. *Journal of Infant, Child, and Adolescent Psychotherapy*, *4*(4), 442–256 https://doi10.1080/15289160409348517

Kernberg, O. & Stierlin, H. (Moderator) (2006). *Psychonalyse fuer Nicht-Psychoanalytiker. Original-Vorträge*, Symposium Heidelberg, 26–28 Oktober

2006. https://zentralbuchhandlung.de/itm/psychoanalyse-fuer-nicht-psychoan-alytiker-887d-sfb-video-8867.html

Lee, A. C. (2009). Psychoanalytic play therapy. In K. J. O'Connor & L. D. Braverman (Eds). *Play therapy theory and practice: Comparing theories and techniques* (pp. 25–81). Wiley.

LeDoux, J. E. (1994). Emotion, memory and the brain. *Scientific American, 270*, 50–57. https://doi.org/10.1038/scientificamerican0694-50

Leuzinger-Bohleber, M., & Plaenkers, T. (2019). The struggle for a psychoanalytic research institute: The evolution of Frankfurt's Sigmund Freud Institute. *International Journal of Psychoanalysis, 100*(5), 962–987. https://doi.org/10.1080/00207578.2019.1576528

Liebert, R. M., & Liebert, L. L. (1998). *Liebert & Spiegler's Personality: Strategies and Issues (8th Ed.).* Brooks/Cole Publishing Company.

Lipner, L. M., Mendelsohn, R., & Muran, J. C. (2017). Psychoanalysis. In A. Wenzel (Ed.), *The Sage Encyclopedia of Abnormal and Clinical Psychology.* Sage.

McLeod, S. A. (2019). *Psychosexual stages.* Simply Psychology. https://www.simplypsy-chology.org/psychosexual.html

Messer, S. B. (2015).The psychoanalytic psychotherapies: Long-term and short-term. In R. L. Cautin & S. O. Lilienfeld (Eds.). *The Encyclopedia of clinical psychology*, (pp 1–10). Wiley.

Midgley, N. & Kennedy, E. (2011). Psychodynamic psychotherapy for children and adolescents: A critical review of the evidence base. *Journal of Child Psychotherapy, 37*(3), 1–37. https://doi.org/10.1080/0075417X.2011.614738

Mills, J. (2004). *Clarification on Trieb: Freud's theory of motivation was reinstated.* Psychoanalytic Psychology. https://doi10.1037/0736-9735.21.4.673

Muratori, F., Picchi, L., Bruni, G., Patarnello, M., & Romagnoli, G. (2003). A two-year follow-up of psychodynamic psychotherapy for internalising disorders in children. *Journal of the American Academy of Child and Adolescent Psychiatry, 42*(3), 331–9. https://doi.org/10.1097/00004583-200303000-00014

Scharff, D. E., & Scharff, J. S. (1987). *Object relations family therapy.* Aronson.

Slipp, S. (1988). *The technique and practice of Object Relations Family Therapy.* Aronson.

Smyrnios, K. X. & Kirby, R. J. (1993). Long-term comparison of brief versus unlimited psychodynamic treatments with children and their parents. *Journal of Consulting and Clinical Psychology, 61*(6), 1020–7. https://doi.org/10.1037//0022-006x.61.6.1020

Stiefel, I., Harris, P., & Rohan, J. A. (1998). Object relations family therapy: Articulating the inchoate. *Australian and New Zealand Journal of Family*

Therapy, 19(2), 55–62. https://doi.org/10.1002/j.1467-8438.1998.tb00314.x

Strupp, H. H., Butler, S. F., & Rosser, C. L. (1988). Training in psychodynamic therapy. *Journal of Consulting and Clinical Psychology, 56*(5), 689–695. https://doi:10.1037//0022-006x.56.5.689.

Tallandini, M. A., & Cander, C. (2010). Defence mechanisms development in typical children. *Psychotherapy Research, 20*(5), 535–545. https://doi.org/10.1080/10503307.2010.493536

Trowell, J., Kolvin, I., Weeramanthri, T., Sadowski, H., Berelowitz, M., Glasser, D., & Leitch, I. (2002). Psychotherapy for sexually abused girls: Psychopathological outcome findings and patterns of change. *British Journal of Psychiatry, 180*, 234–47. https://doi.org/10.1192/BJP.180.3.234

Wiegand-Grefe, S., Weitkamp, K., Lauenroth, K., Baumeister-Duru, A., Hofmann, H., Timmermann, H., Wulf, A., & Romer, G. (2016). Langfristige Wirksamkeit psycho-analytischer Therapien von Kindern und Jugendlichen. *Psychotherapeut, 61*, 491–498. https://doi.10.1007/s00278-016-0150-z

Zhang, S. (2020). Psychoanalysis: The influence of Freud's theory in personality psychology. *Advances in Social Science, Education and Humanities Research, 433*, 229–232. https://doi10.2991/assehr.k.200425.051

www.ingramcontent.com/pod-product-compliance
Lightning Source LLC
Chambersburg PA
CBHW080242030426
42334CB00023BA/2675